FORWARD

FORWARD

LISA MAAS

ARSENAL PULP PRESS
VANCOUVER

FORWARD
Copyright © 2018 by Lisa Maas

ARSENAL PULP PRESS
Suite 202 – 211 East Georgia St.
Vancouver, BC V6A 1Z6
Canada
arsenalpulp.com

The publisher gratefully acknowledges the support of the Canada Council for the Arts and the British Columbia Arts Council for its publishing program, and the Government of Canada, and the Government of British Columbia (through the Book Publishing Tax Credit Program), for its publishing activities.

BRITISH COLUMBIA | BRITISH COLUMBIA ARTS COUNCIL An agency of the Province of British Columbia | Canada Council for the Arts Conseil des arts du Canada | Canadä

This is a work of fiction. Any resemblance of characters to persons either living or deceased is purely coincidental.

Design by Oliver McPartlin
Printed and bound in Canada

Library and Archives Canada Cataloguing in Publication:
Maas, Lisa, author, illustrator
        Forward / Lisa Maas.

Issued in print and electronic formats.
ISBN 978-1-55152-722-2 (softcover).—ISBN 978-1-55152-723-9 (PDF)—ISBN 978-1-55152-724-6 (HTML)

        1. Graphic novels. I. Title.

PN6733.M28F67 2018   741.5'971   C2017-907222-6
                                               C2017-907223-4

For Lisa

ACKNOWLEDGEMENTS

To my friend and editor Genevieve Grant: I am incredibly thankful and indebted to you. Your thoughtful insights always pushed me to dig deeper and do better. Your willingness to work with me on the project made this book possible.

Ruth Lytle, you were my first friend and my first fanboy. Thank you for your enthusiasm and your amazing attention to detail.

Thanks as well to Gareth Gaudin of Legends Comics and Books for your encouragement and for generously sharing your knowledge.

To all the wonderful and special souls that I have the privilege to know: I feel incredibly lucky to have you in my life. Whether I get to see you once a year or every day, I am so grateful for your love and support, your humour and positivity, your patience and kind-heartedness.

And of course to my parents and sister: They say you can't choose the family you were born into, but if that were the case, I would have chosen you anyway! Thank you for your unconditional love and support.

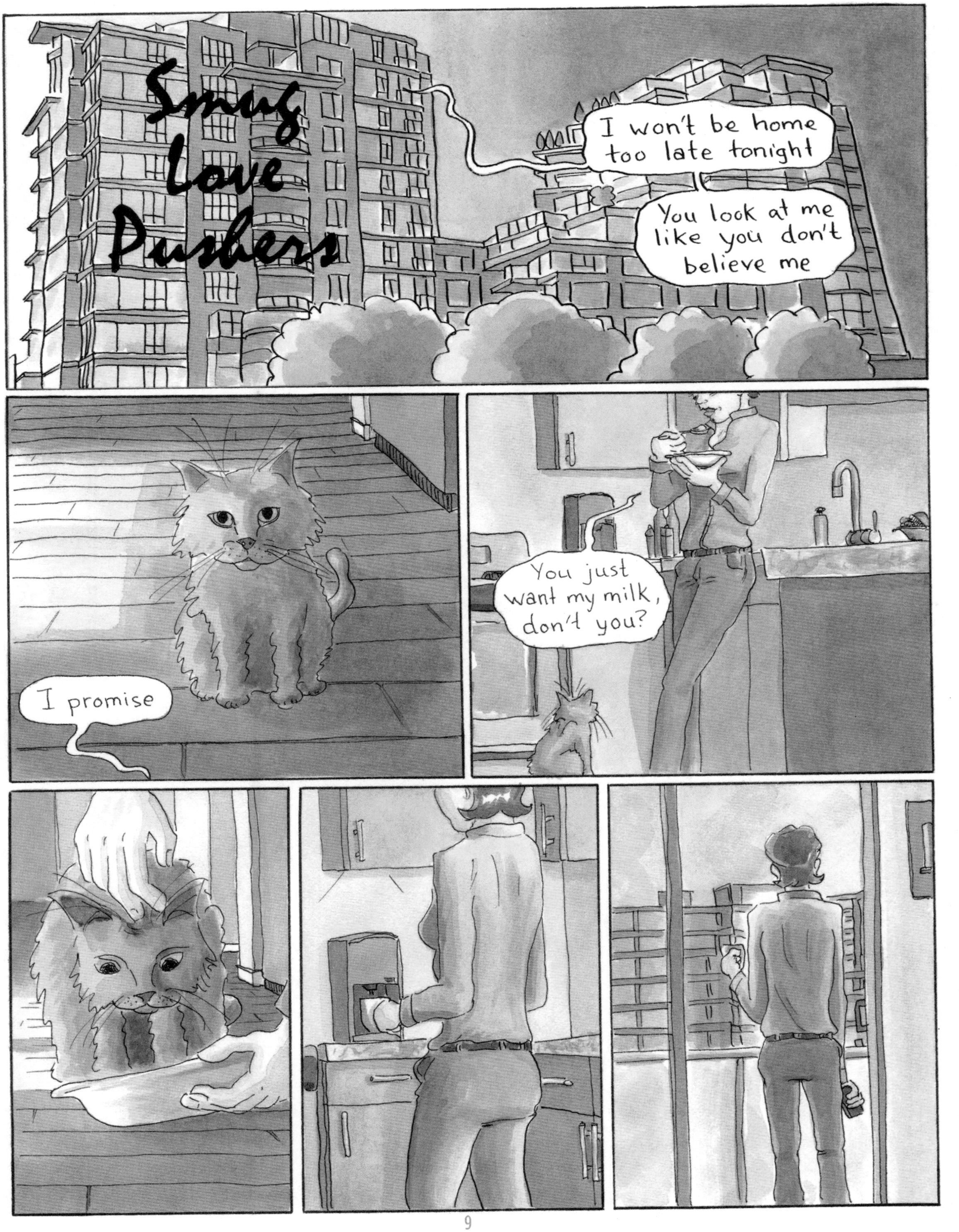
Smug Love Pushers
I won't be home too late tonight
You look at me like you don't believe me
I promise
You just want my milk, don't you?

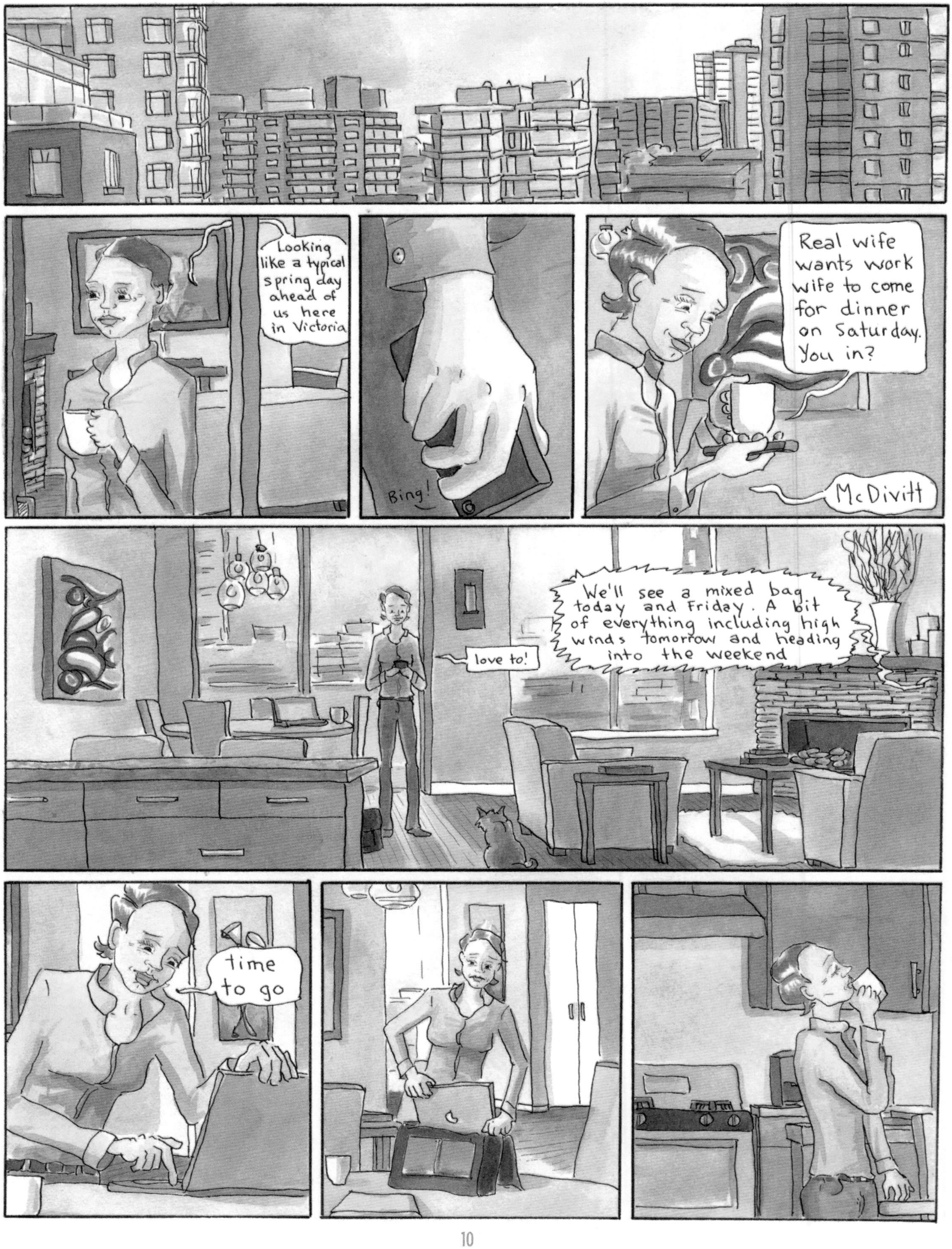
Looking like a typical spring day ahead of us here in Victoria
Bing!
Real wife wants work wife to come for dinner on Saturday. You in?
McDivitt
We'll see a mixed bag today and Friday. A bit of everything including high winds tomorrow and heading into the weekend
love to!
time to go

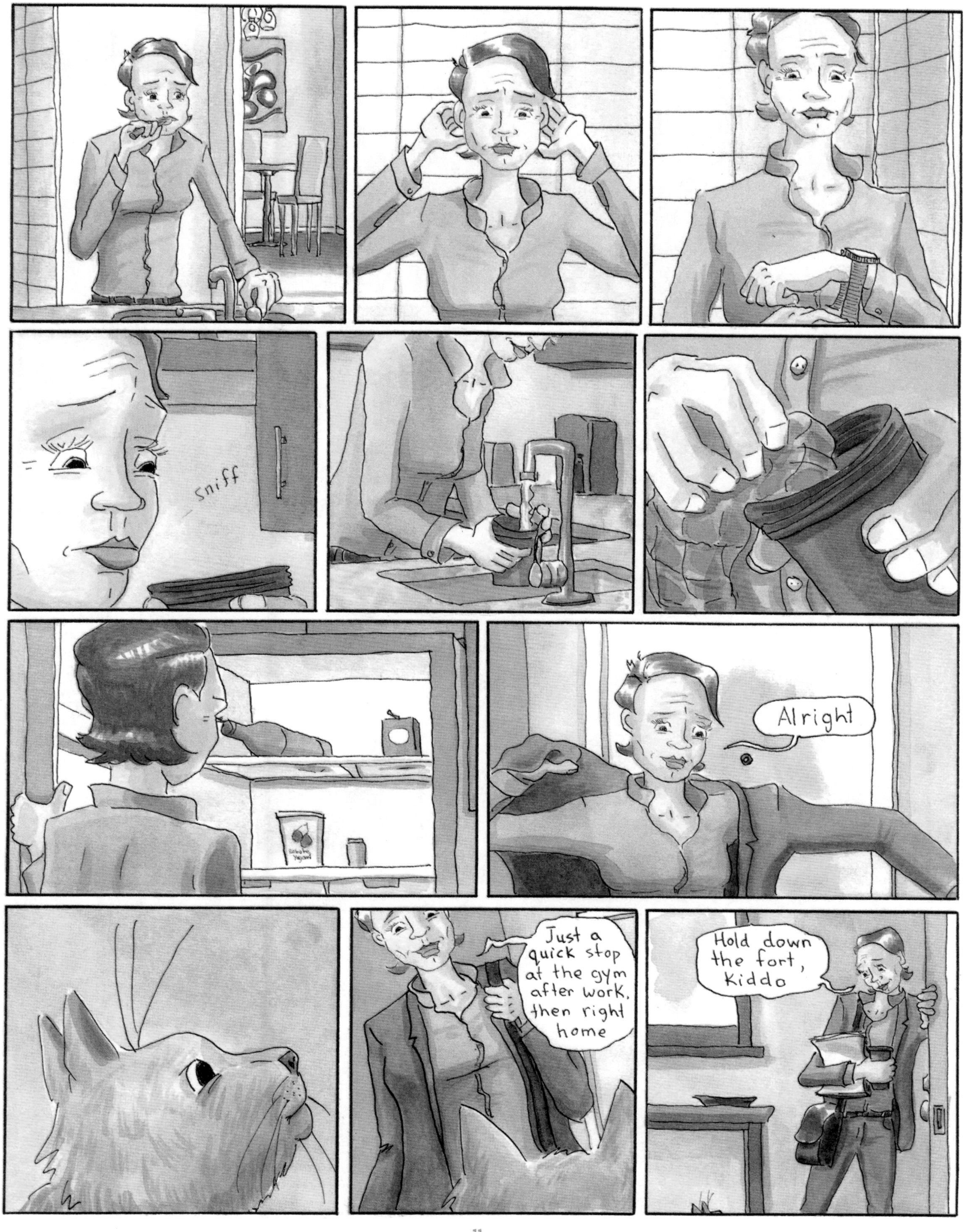
Sniff
Alright
Just a quick stop at the gym after work, then right home
Hold down the fort, kiddo

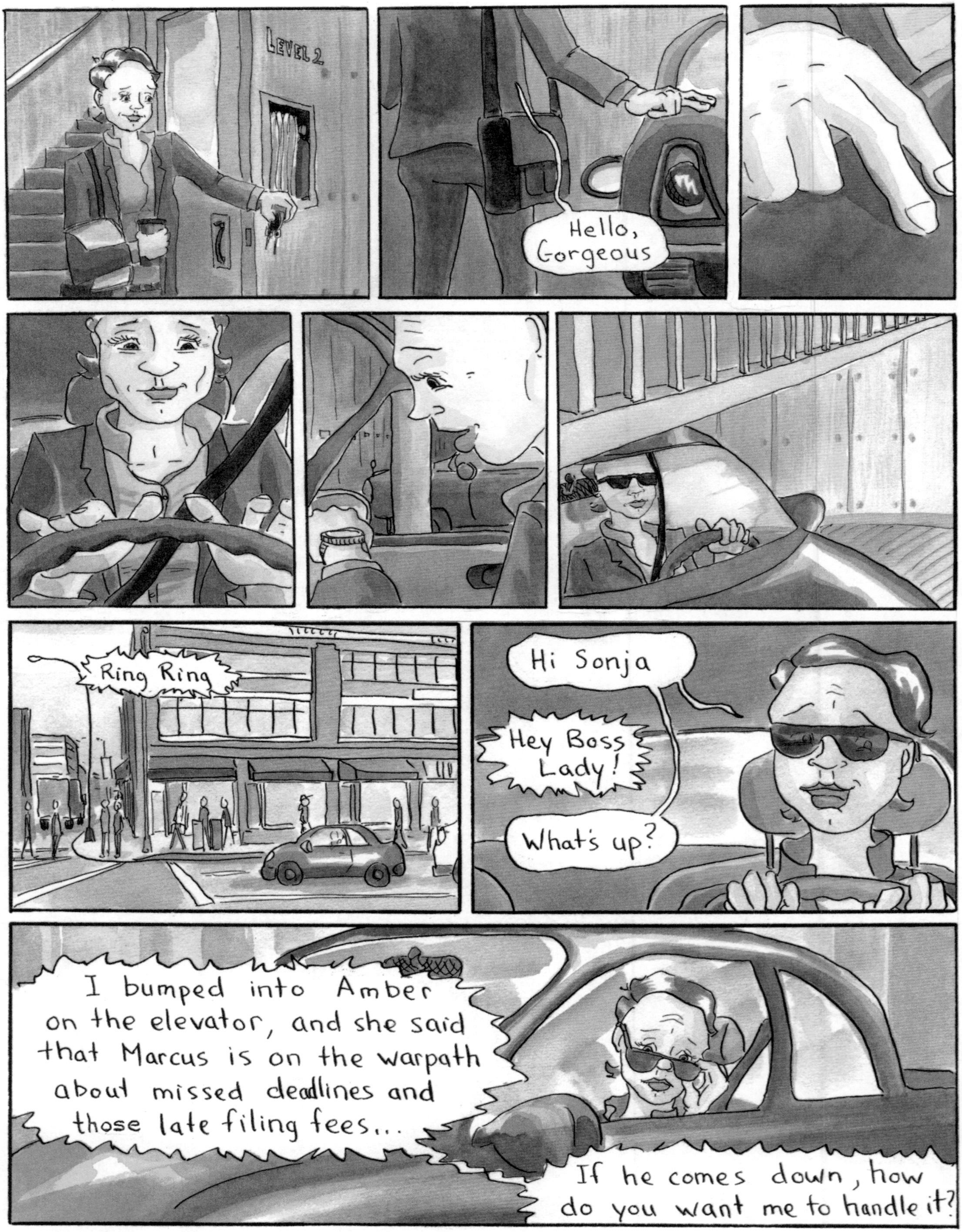

LEVEL 2
Hello, Gorgeous
Ring Ring
Hi Sonja
Hey Boss Lady!
What's up?
I bumped into Amber on the elevator, and she said that Marcus is on the warpath about missed deadlines and those late filing fees...
If he comes down, how do you want me to handle it?

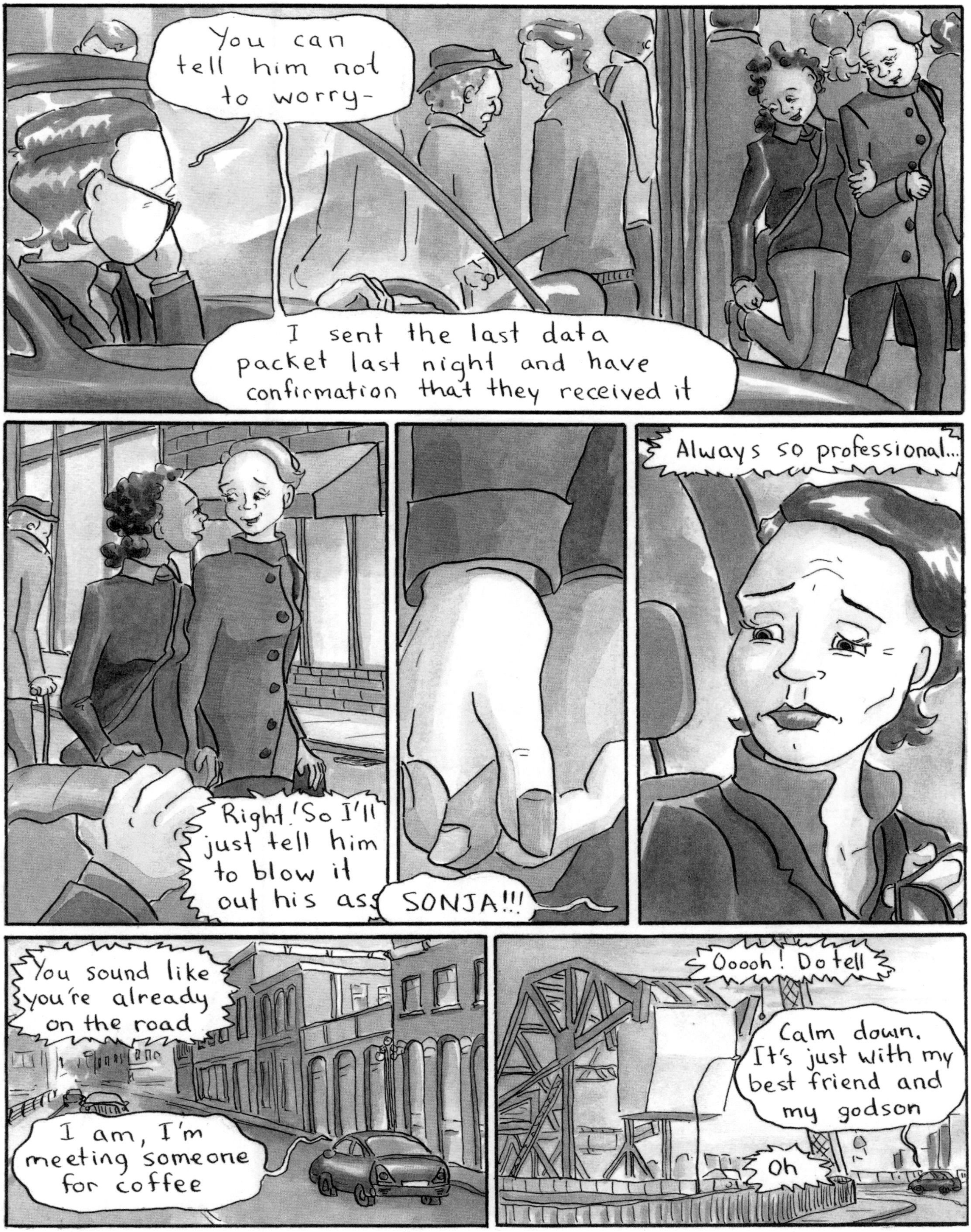
You can tell him not to worry-
I sent the last data packet last night and have confirmation that they received it
Right! So I'll just tell him to blow it out his ass
SONJA!!!
Always so professional...
You sound like you're already on the road
I am, I'm meeting someone for coffee
Ooooh! Do tell
Calm down. It's just with my best friend and my godson
Oh

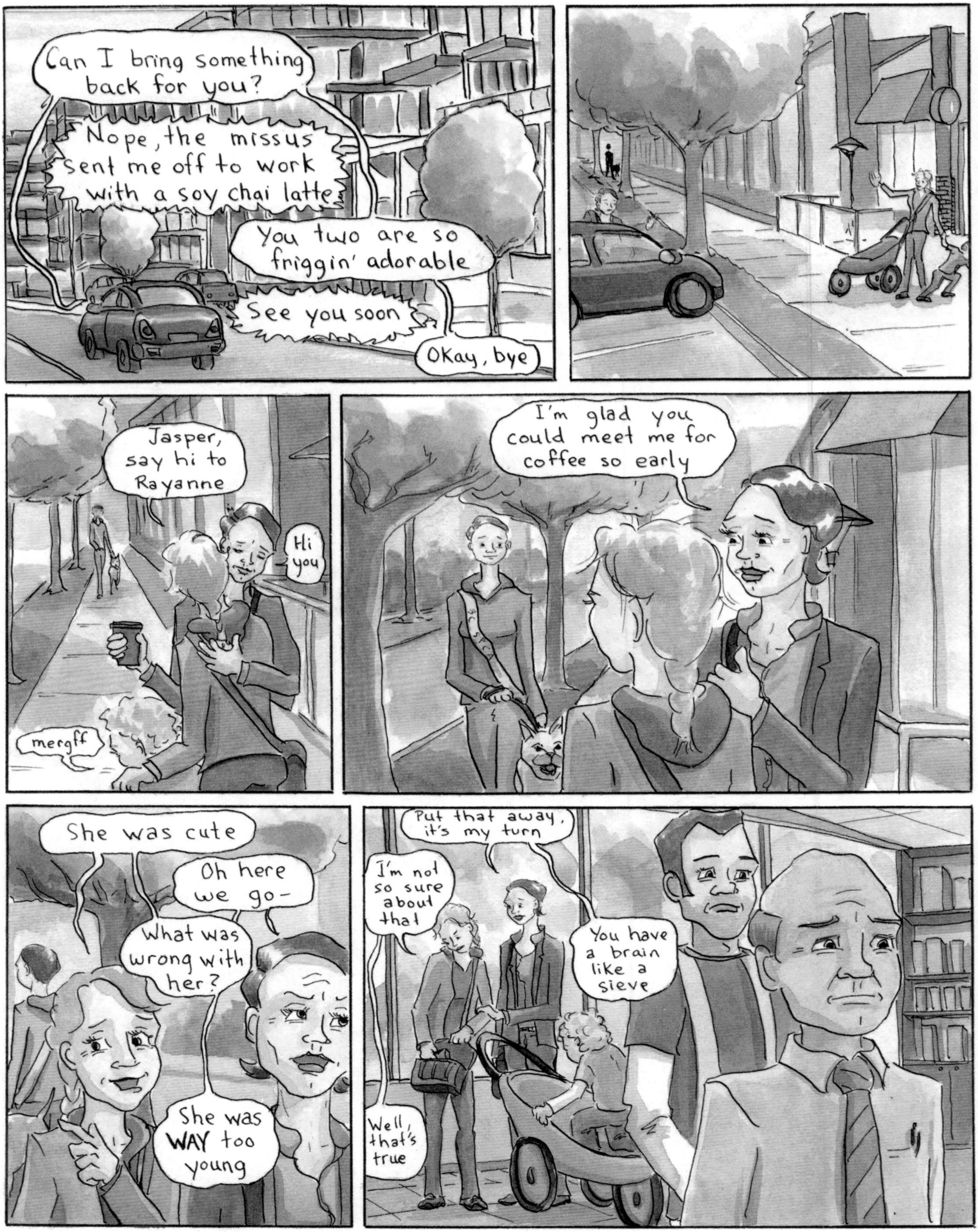
Can I bring something back for you?
Nope, the missus sent me off to work with a soy chai latte
You two are so friggin' adorable
See you soon
Okay, bye
Jasper, say hi to Rayanne
Hi you
mergff
I'm glad you could meet me for coffee so early
She was cute
Oh here we go-
What was wrong with her?
She was WAY too young
Put that away, it's my turn
I'm not so sure about that
You have a brain like a sieve
Well, that's true

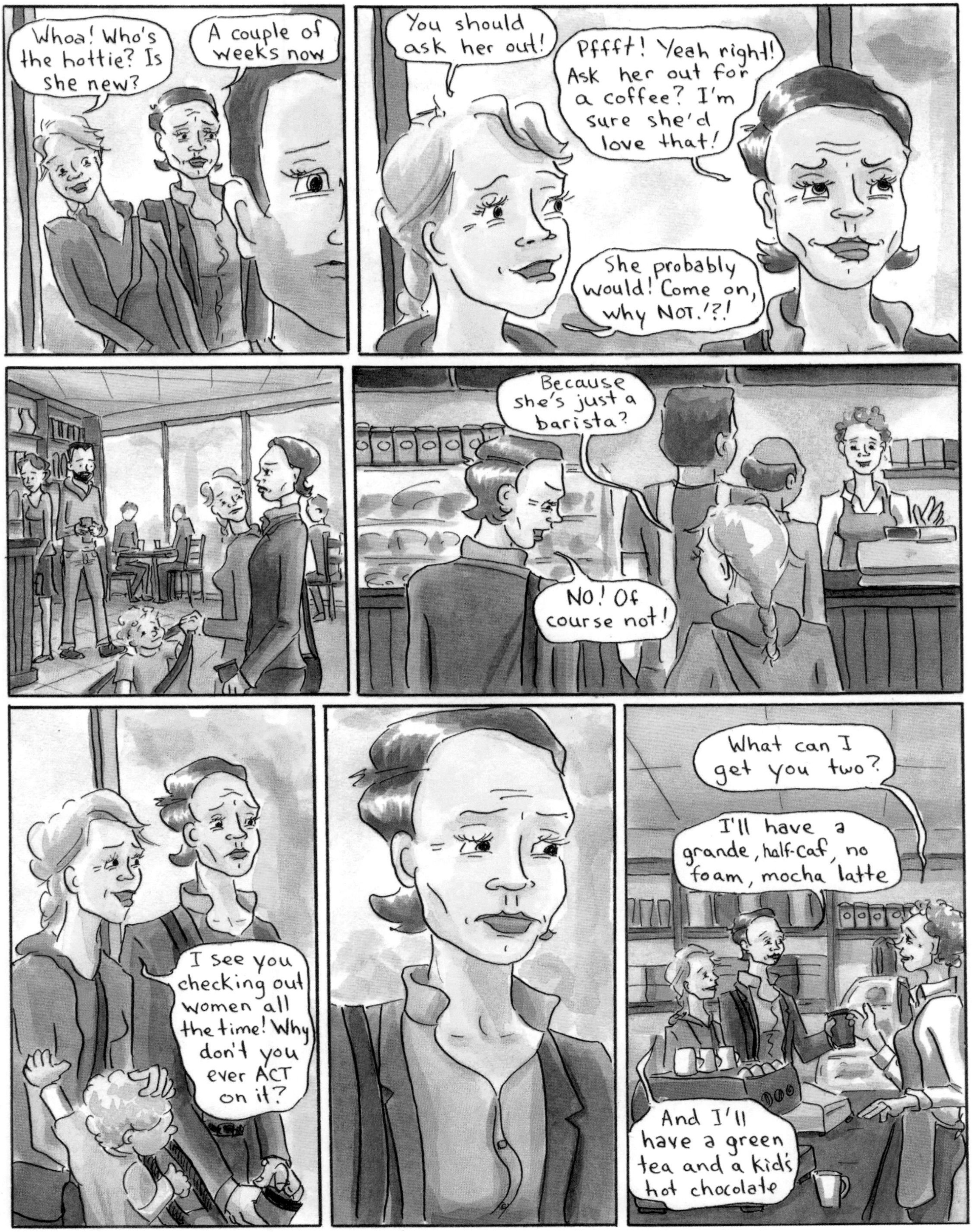
Whoa! Who's the hottie? Is she new?
A couple of weeks now
You should ask her out!
Pffft! Yeah right! Ask her out for a coffee? I'm sure she'd love that!
She probably would! Come on, why NOT.!?!
Because she's just a barista?
NO! Of course not!
I see you checking out women all the time! Why don't you ever ACT on it?
What can I get you two?
I'll have a grande, half-caf, no foam, mocha latte
And I'll have a green tea and a kid's hot chocolate

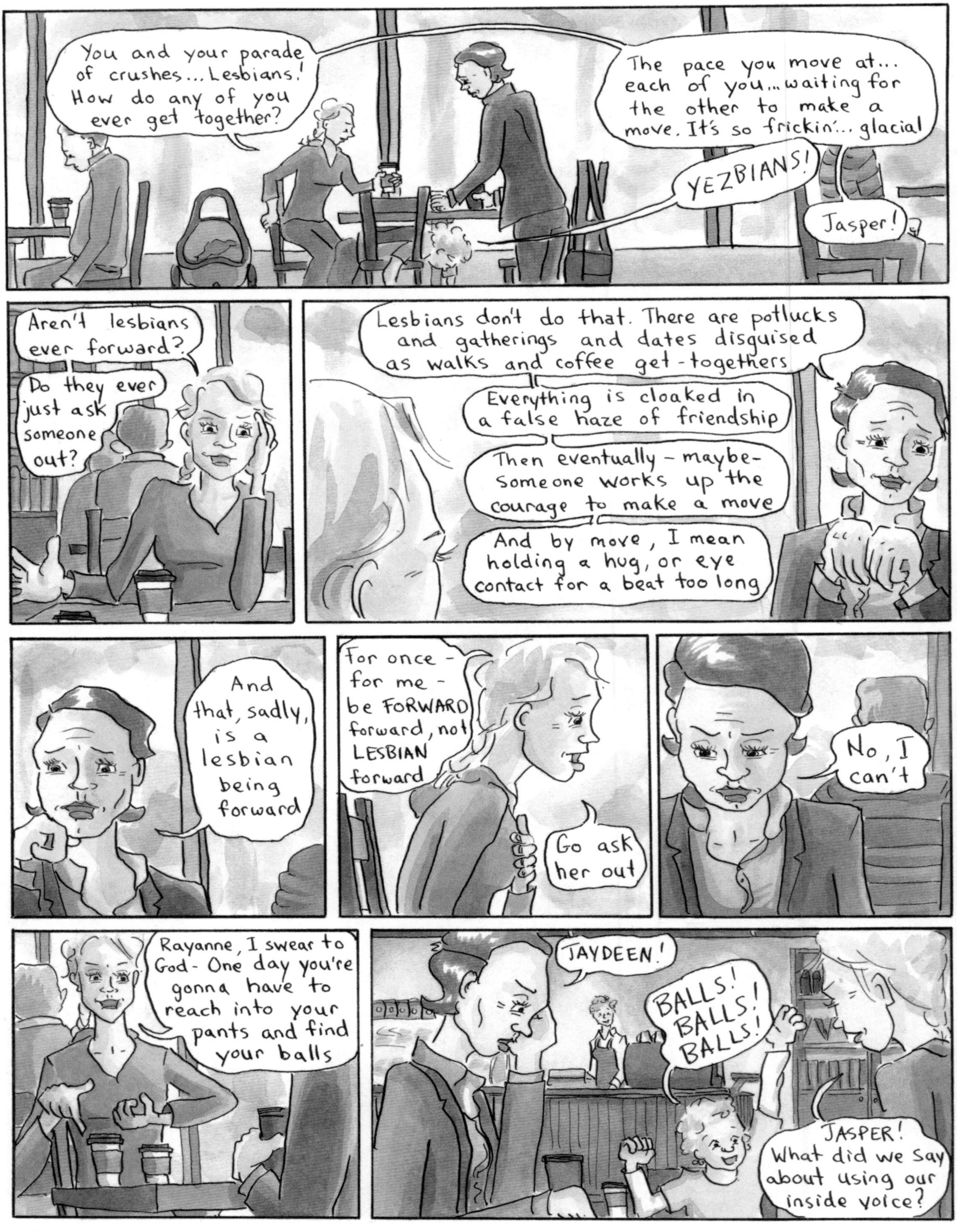
You and your parade of crushes... Lesbians! How do any of you ever get together?
The pace you move at... each of you... waiting for the other to make a move. It's so frickin'... glacial
YEZBIANS!
Jasper!
Aren't lesbians ever forward?
Do they ever just ask someone out?
Lesbians don't do that. There are potlucks and gatherings and dates disguised as walks and coffee get-togethers
Everything is cloaked in a false haze of friendship
Then eventually - maybe - someone works up the courage to make a move
And by move, I mean holding a hug, or eye contact for a beat too long
And that, sadly, is a lesbian being forward
For once - for me - be FORWARD forward, not LESBIAN forward
Go ask her out
No, I can't
Rayanne, I swear to God - One day you're gonna have to reach into your pants and find your balls
JAYDEEN!
BALLS! BALLS! BALLS!
JASPER! What did we say about using our inside voice?

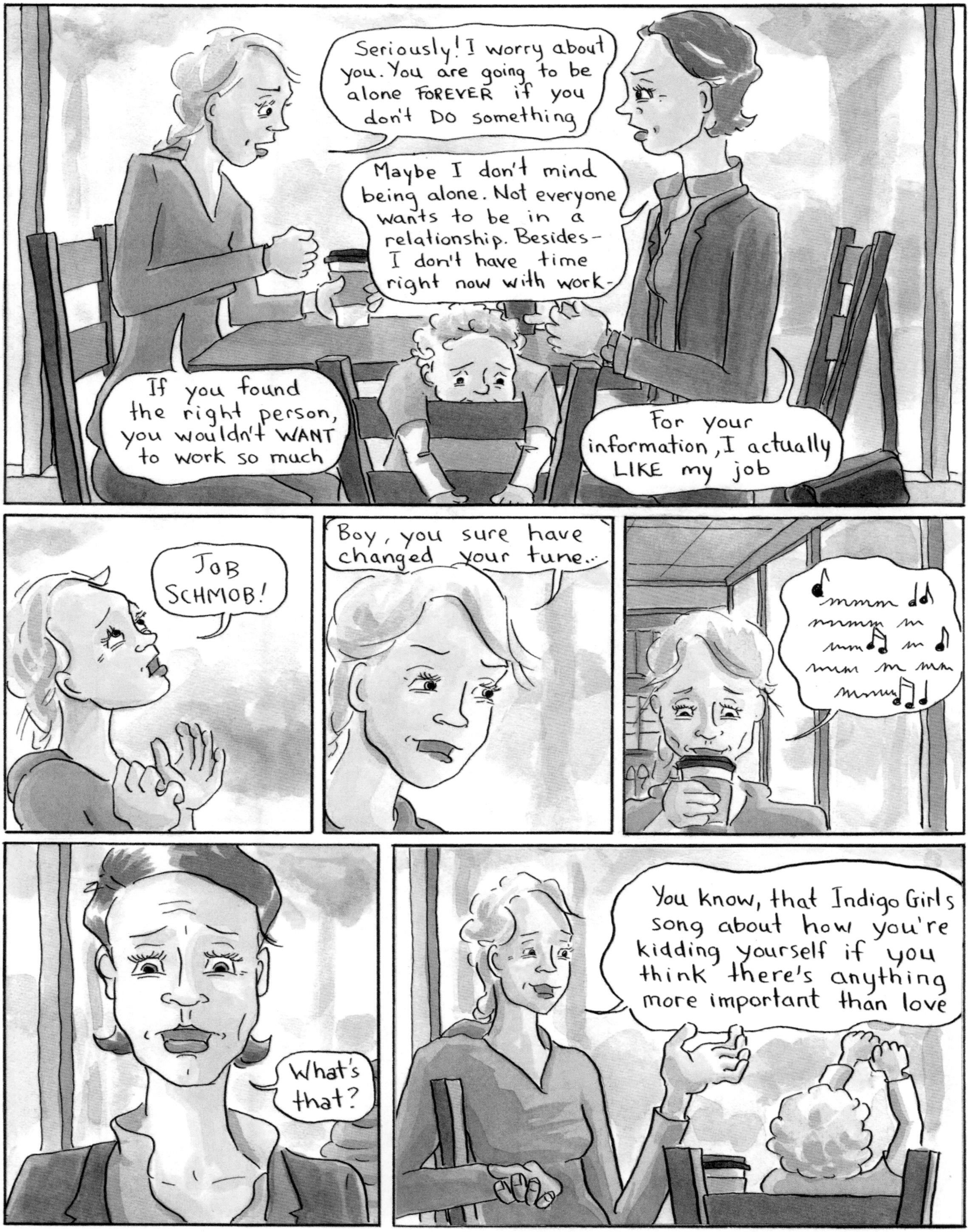
Seriously! I worry about you. You are going to be alone FOREVER if you don't DO something
Maybe I don't mind being alone. Not everyone wants to be in a relationship. Besides- I don't have time right now with work-
If you found the right person, you wouldn't WANT to work so much
For your information, I actually LIKE my job
JOB SCHMOB!
Boy, you sure have changed your tune...
mmm mmmm m mm m m mm m mm mmmm
What's that?
You know, that Indigo Girls song about how you're kidding yourself if you think there's anything more important than love

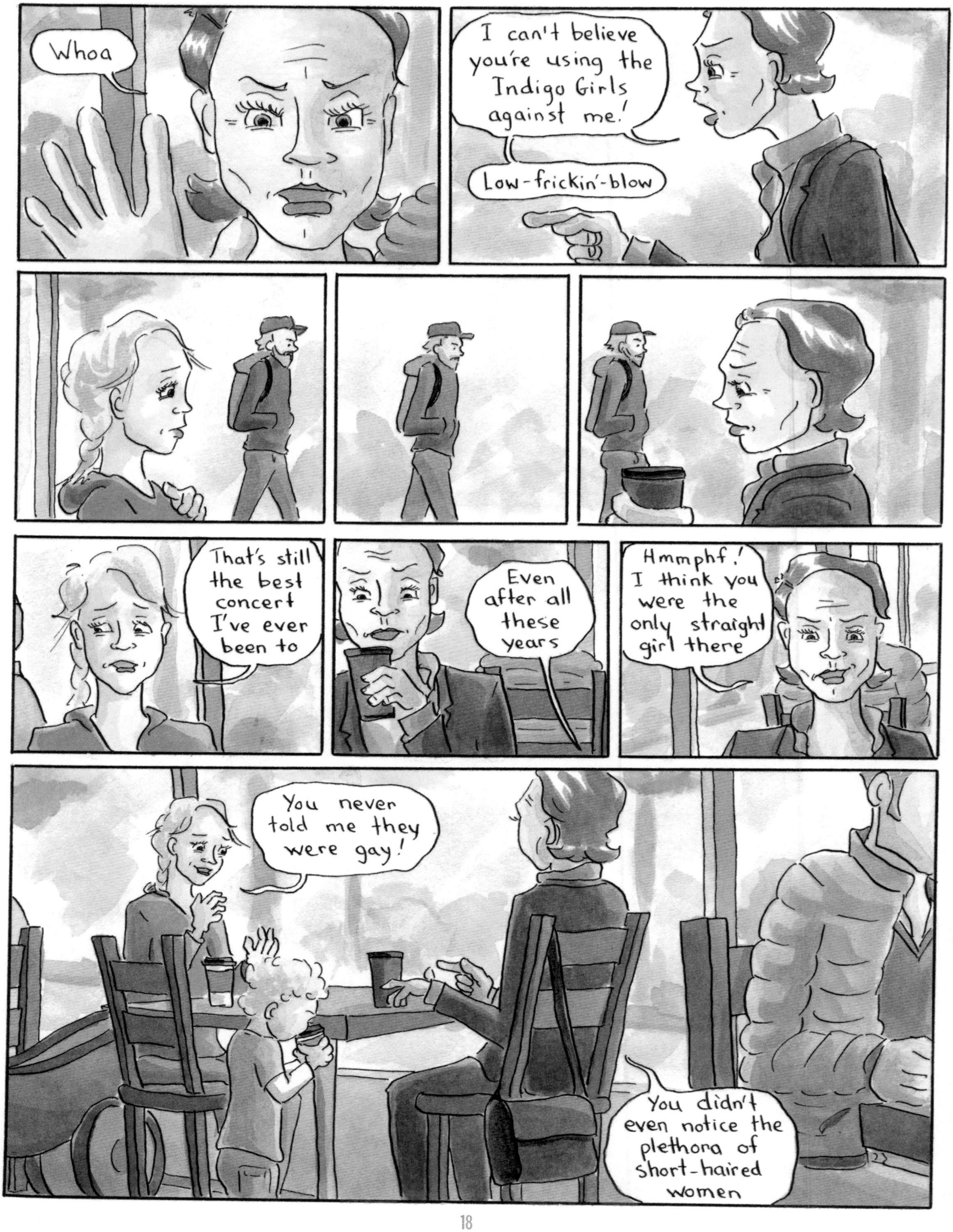
Whoa
I can't believe you're using the Indigo Girls against me!
Low-frickin'-blow
That's still the best concert I've ever been to
Even after all these years
Hmmphf! I think you were the only straight girl there
You never told me they were gay!
You didn't even notice the plethora of short-haired women

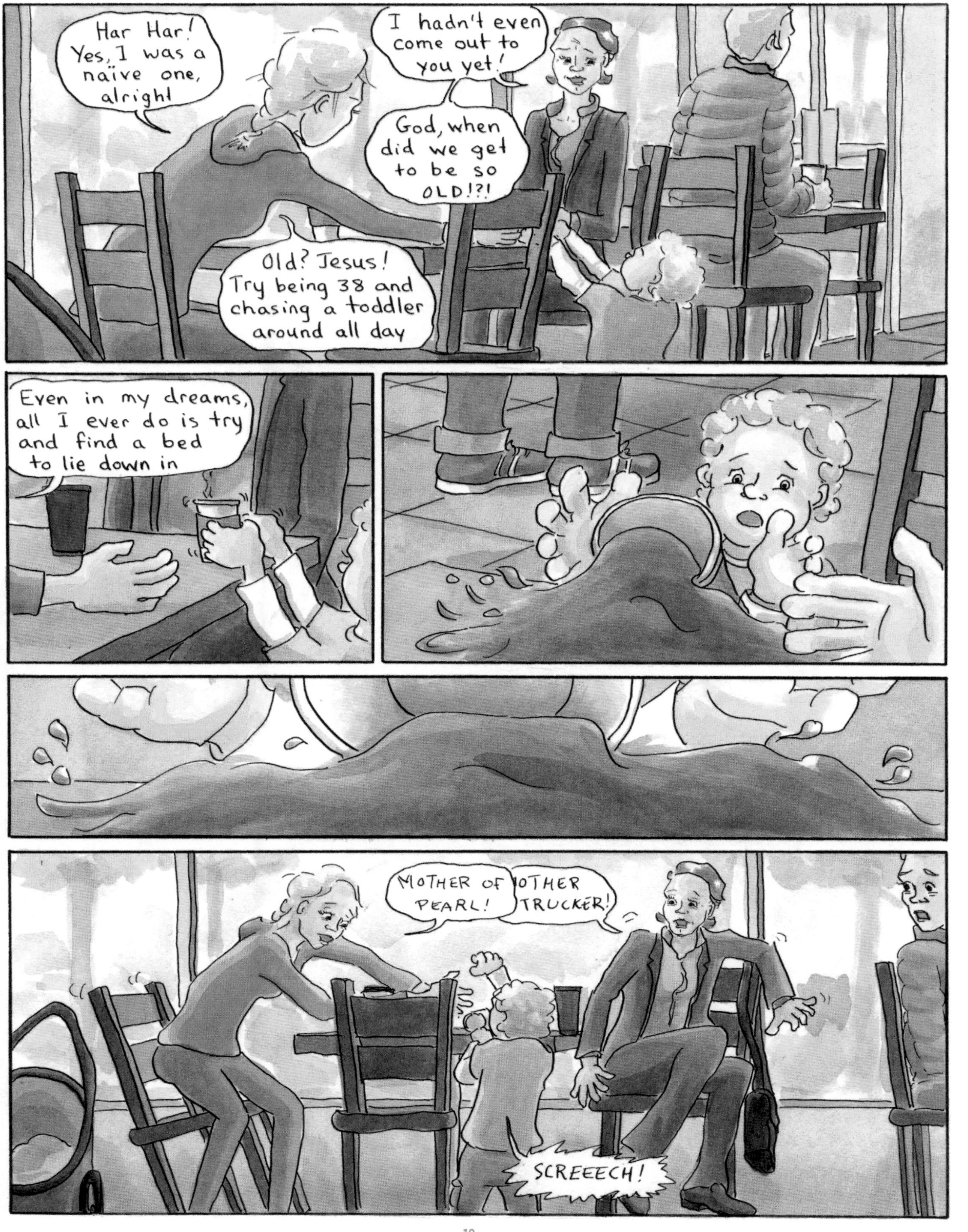
Har Har! Yes, I was a naïve one, alright
I hadn't even come out to you yet!
God, when did we get to be so OLD!?!
Old? Jesus! Try being 38 and chasing a toddler around all day
Even in my dreams, all I ever do is try and find a bed to lie down in
MOTHER OF PEARL!
MOTHER TRUCKER!
SCREEECH!

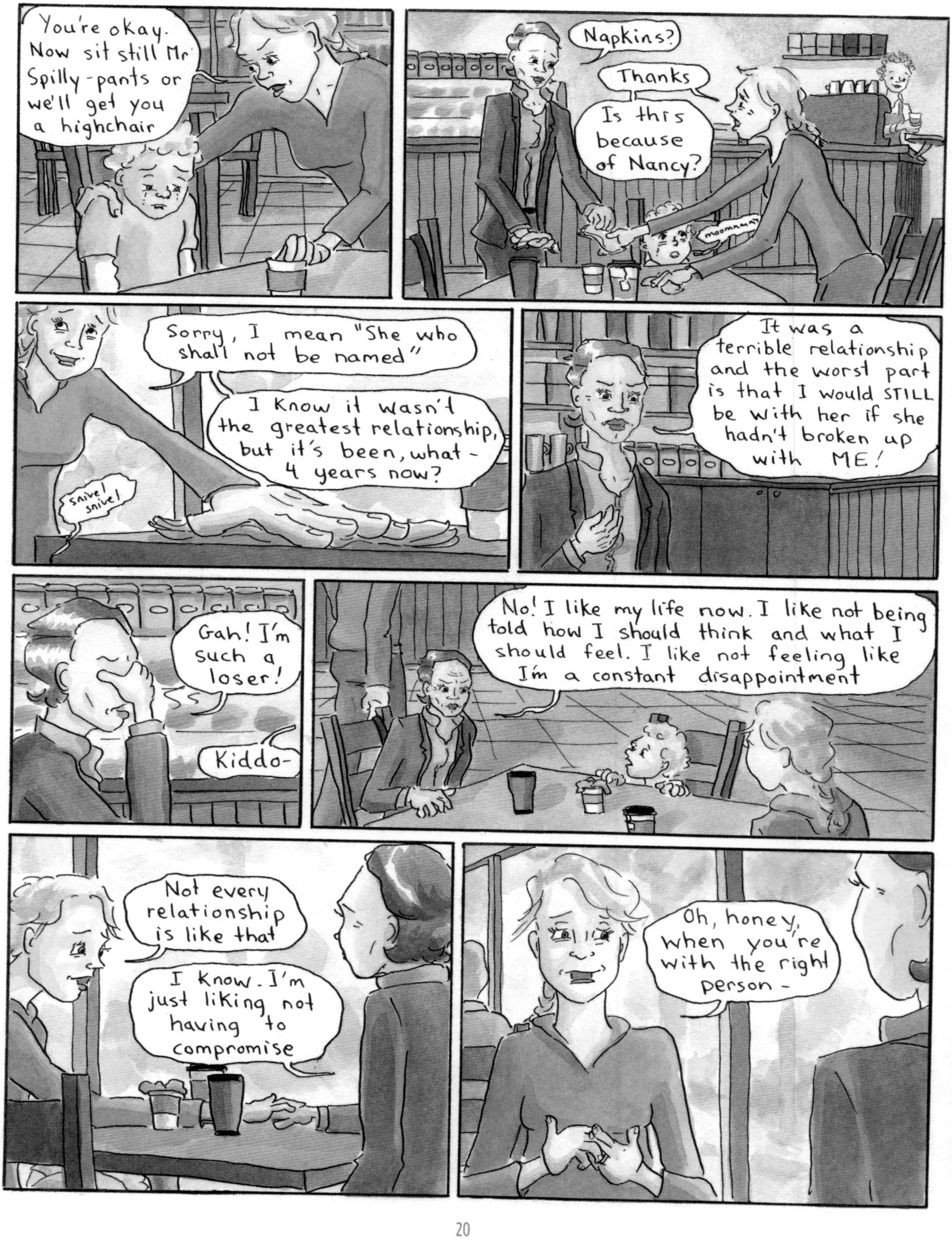
You're okay. Now sit still Mr Spilly-pants or we'll get you a highchair
Napkins?
Thanks
Is this because of Nancy?
moommmmy
Sorry, I mean "She who shall not be named"
I know it wasn't the greatest relationship, but it's been, what - 4 years now?
snivel snivel
It was a terrible relationship and the worst part is that I would STILL be with her if she hadn't broken up with ME!
Gah! I'm such a loser!
Kiddo-
No! I like my life now. I like not being told how I should think and what I should feel. I like not feeling like I'm a constant disappointment
Not every relationship is like that
I know. I'm just liking not having to compromise
Oh, honey, when you're with the right person -

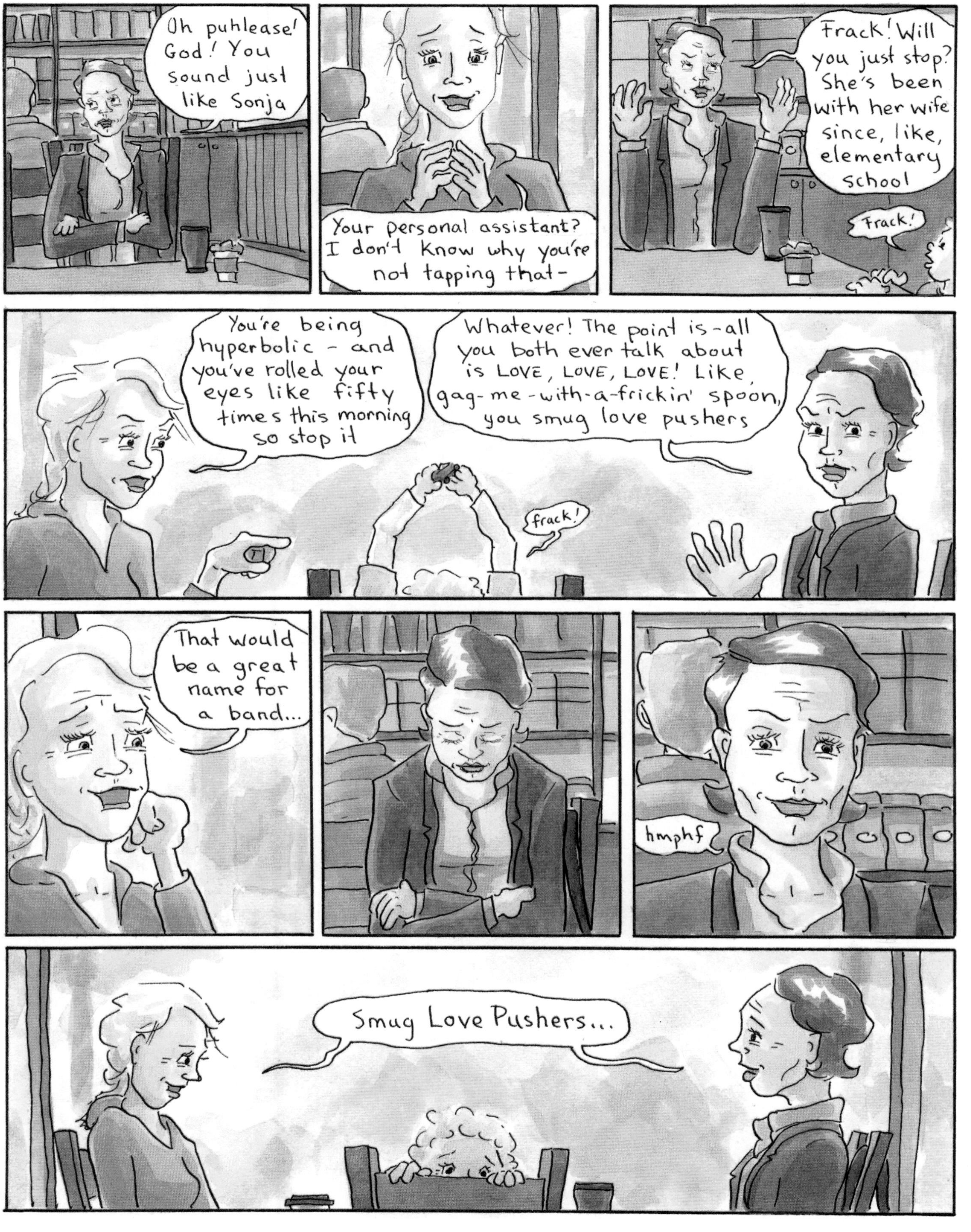
Oh puhlease! God! You sound just like Sonja
Your personal assistant? I don't know why you're not tapping that-
Frack! Will you just stop? She's been with her wife since, like, elementary school
Frack!
You're being hyperbolic - and you've rolled your eyes like fifty times this morning so stop it
Whatever! The point is - all you both ever talk about is LOVE, LOVE, LOVE! Like, gag-me-with-a-frickin' spoon, you smug love pushers
frack!
That would be a great name for a band...
hmphf
Smug Love Pushers...

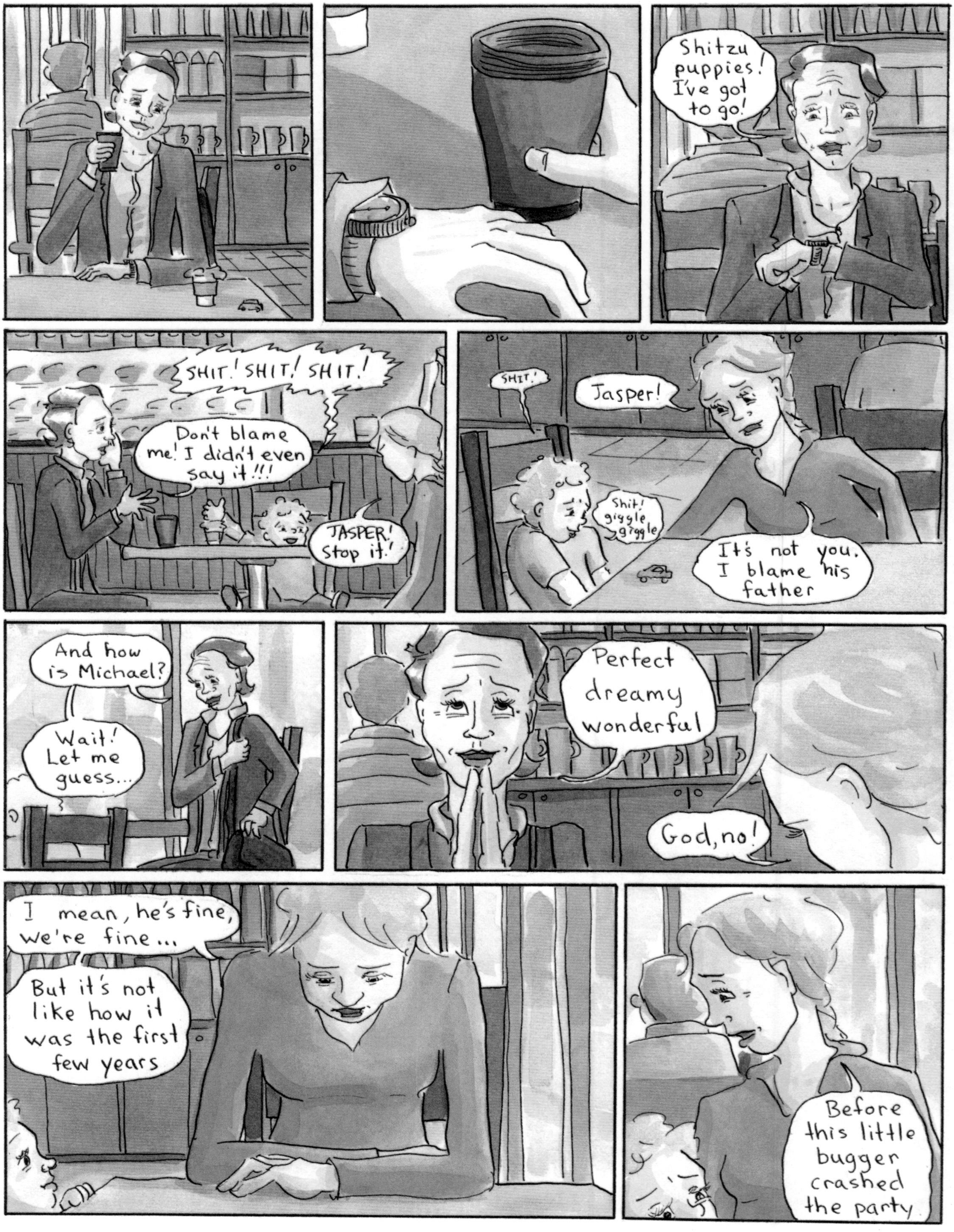

Shitzu puppies! I've got to go!
SHIT! SHIT! SHIT!
Don't blame me! I didn't even say it!!!
JASPER! Stop it!
SHIT!
Jasper!
Shit! giggle giggle
It's not you. I blame his father
And how is Michael?
Wait! Let me guess...
Perfect dreamy wonderful
God, no!
I mean, he's fine, we're fine...
But it's not like how it was the first few years
Before this little bugger crashed the party

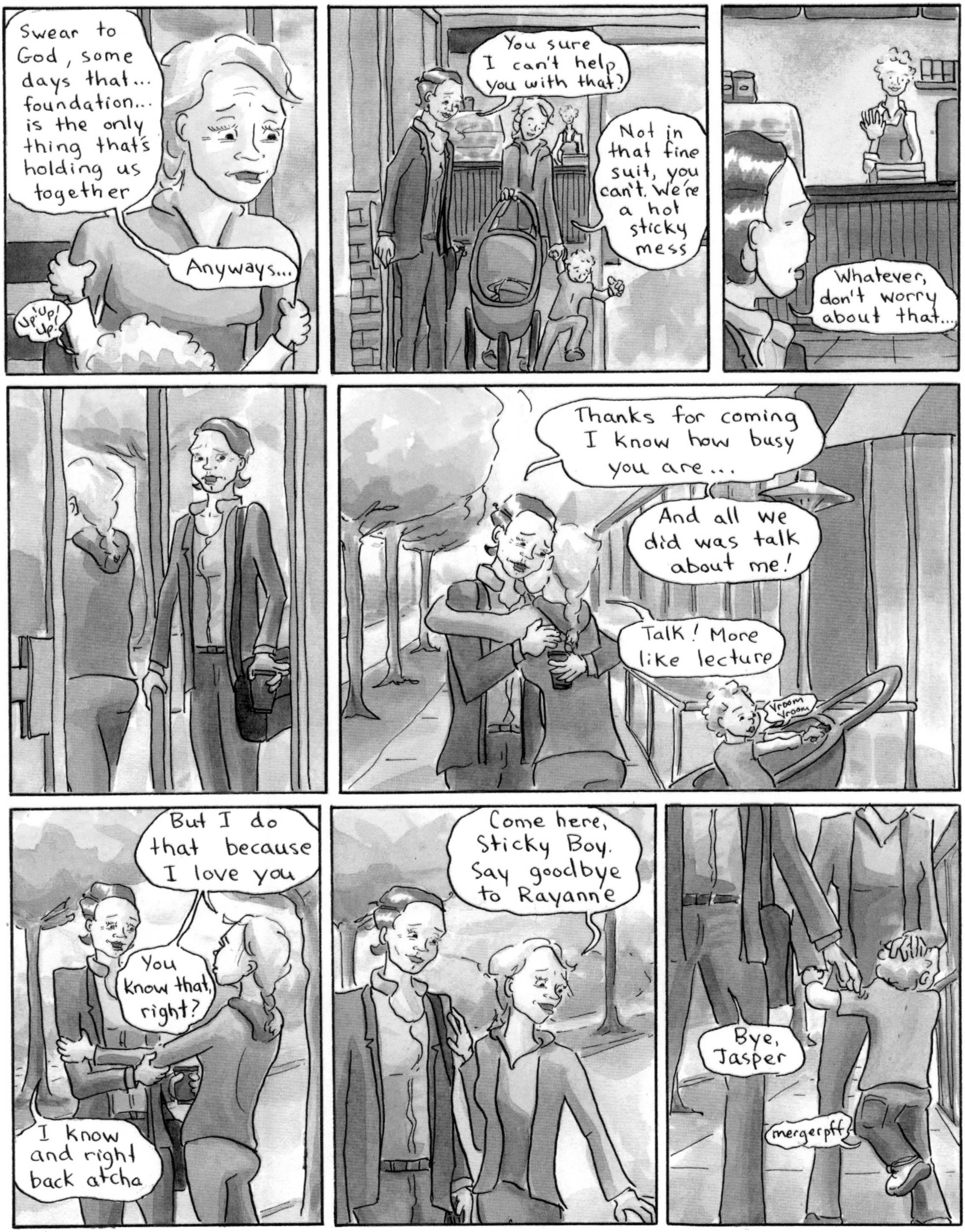
Swear to God, some days that... foundation... is the only thing that's holding us together
Anyways...
Up! Up! Up!
You sure I can't help you with that?
Not in that fine suit, you can't. We're a hot sticky mess
Whatever, don't worry about that...
Thanks for coming I know how busy you are...
And all we did was talk about me!
Talk! More like lecture
Vroom Vroom
But I do that because I love you
You know that, right?
I know and right back atcha
Come here, Sticky Boy. Say goodbye to Rayanne
Bye, Jasper
mergerpff

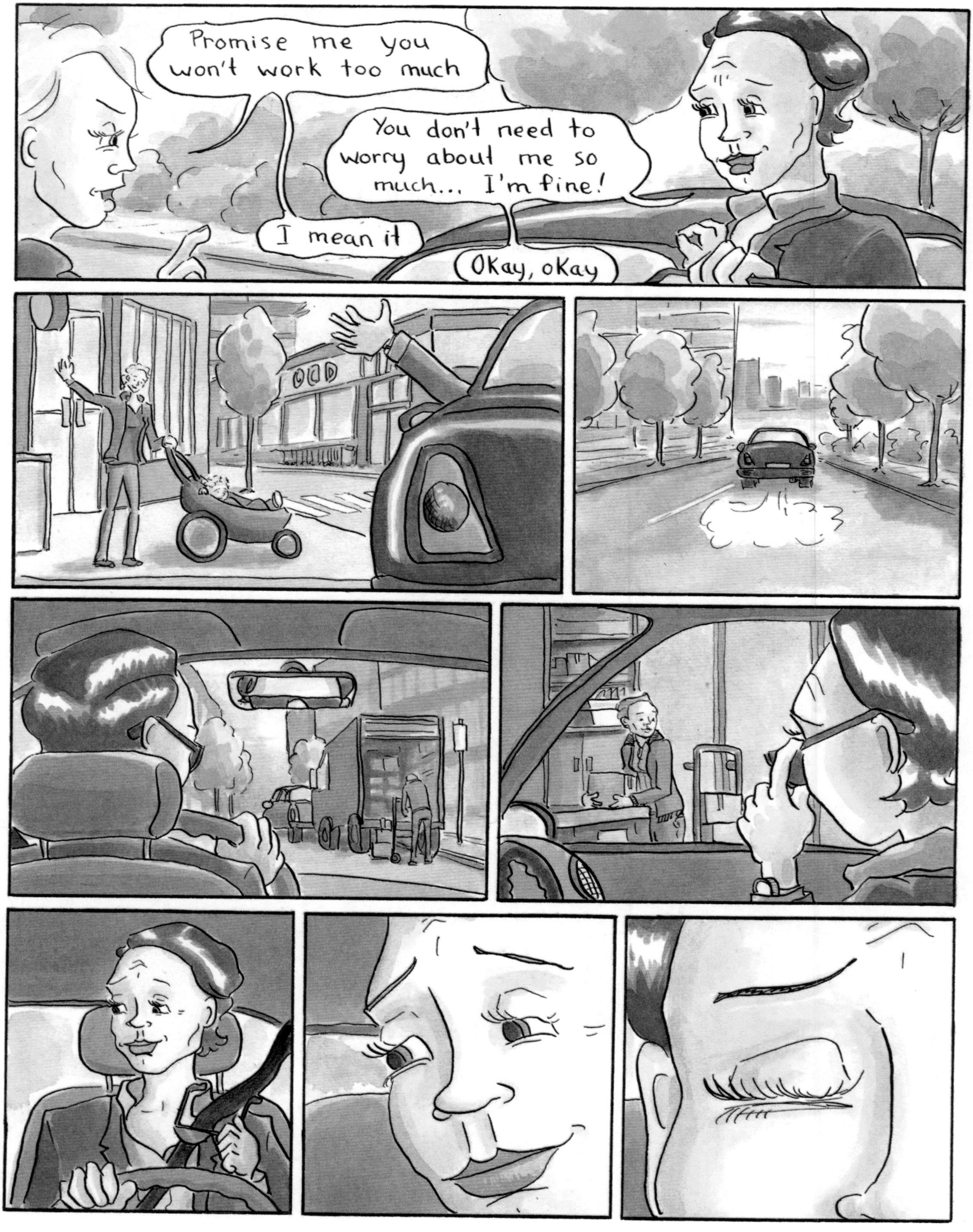
Promise me you won't work too much
You don't need to worry about me so much... I'm fine!
I mean it
Okay, okay

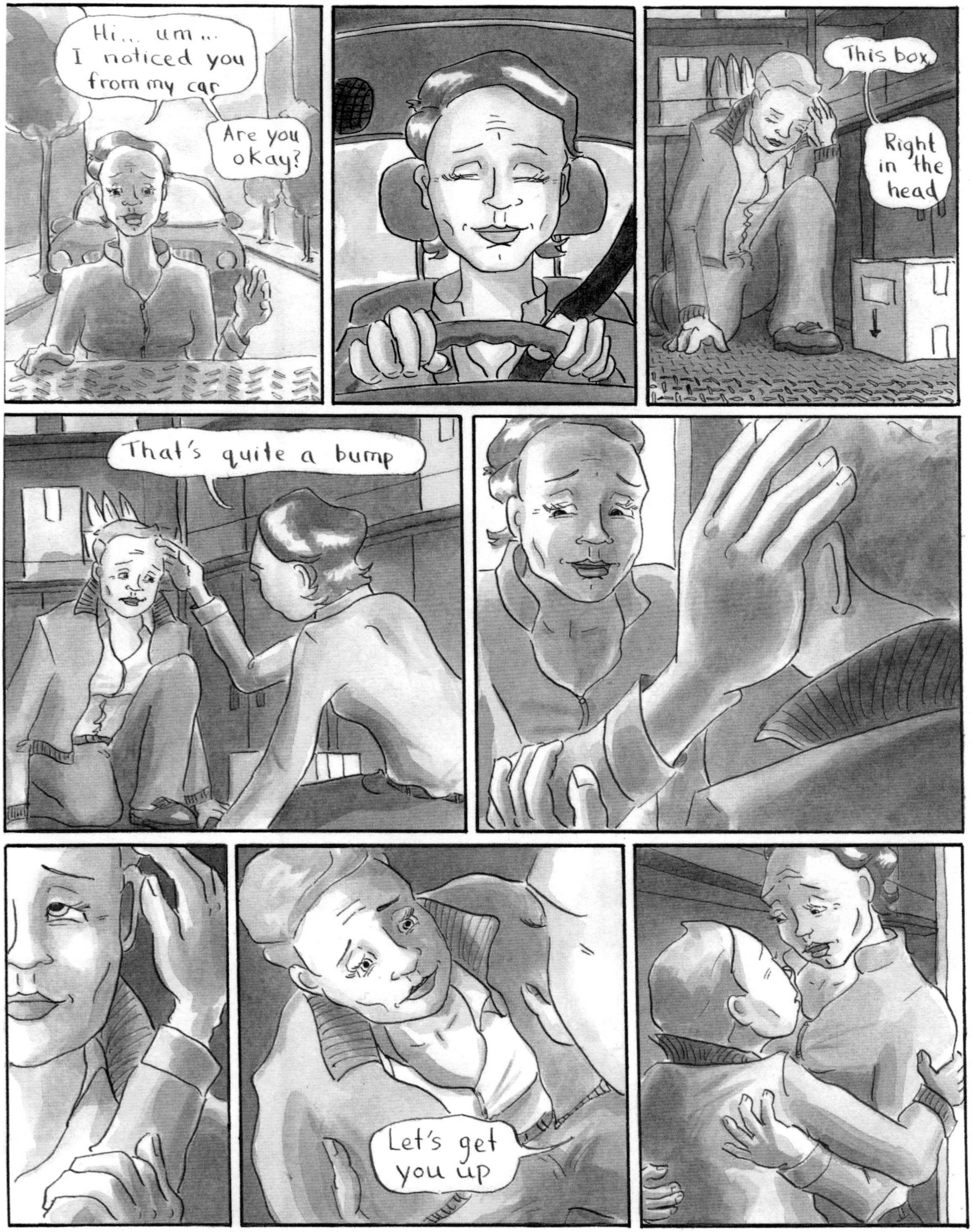
Hi... um...
I noticed you
from my car
Are you
okay?
This box,
Right
in the
head
That's quite a bump
Let's get
you up

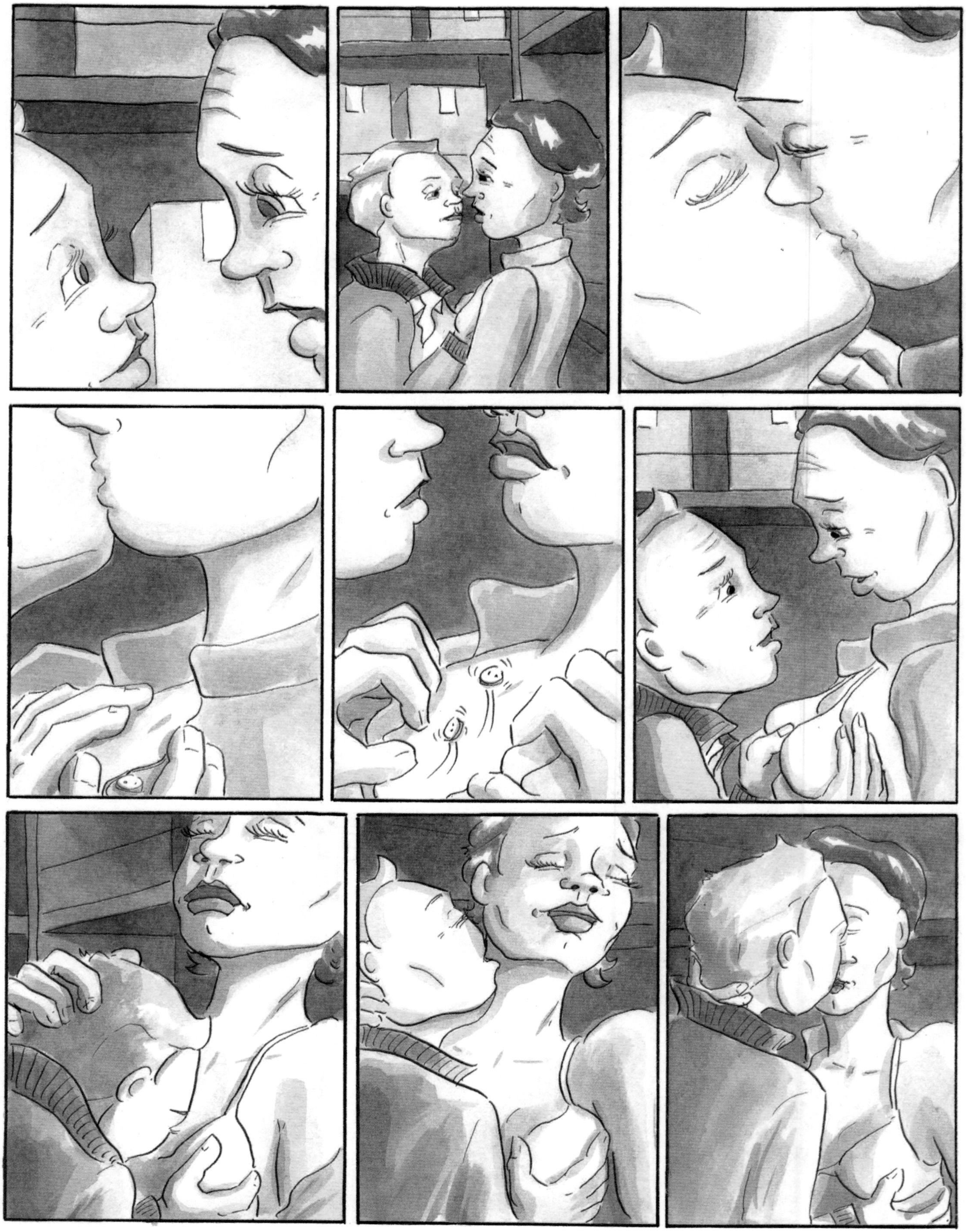

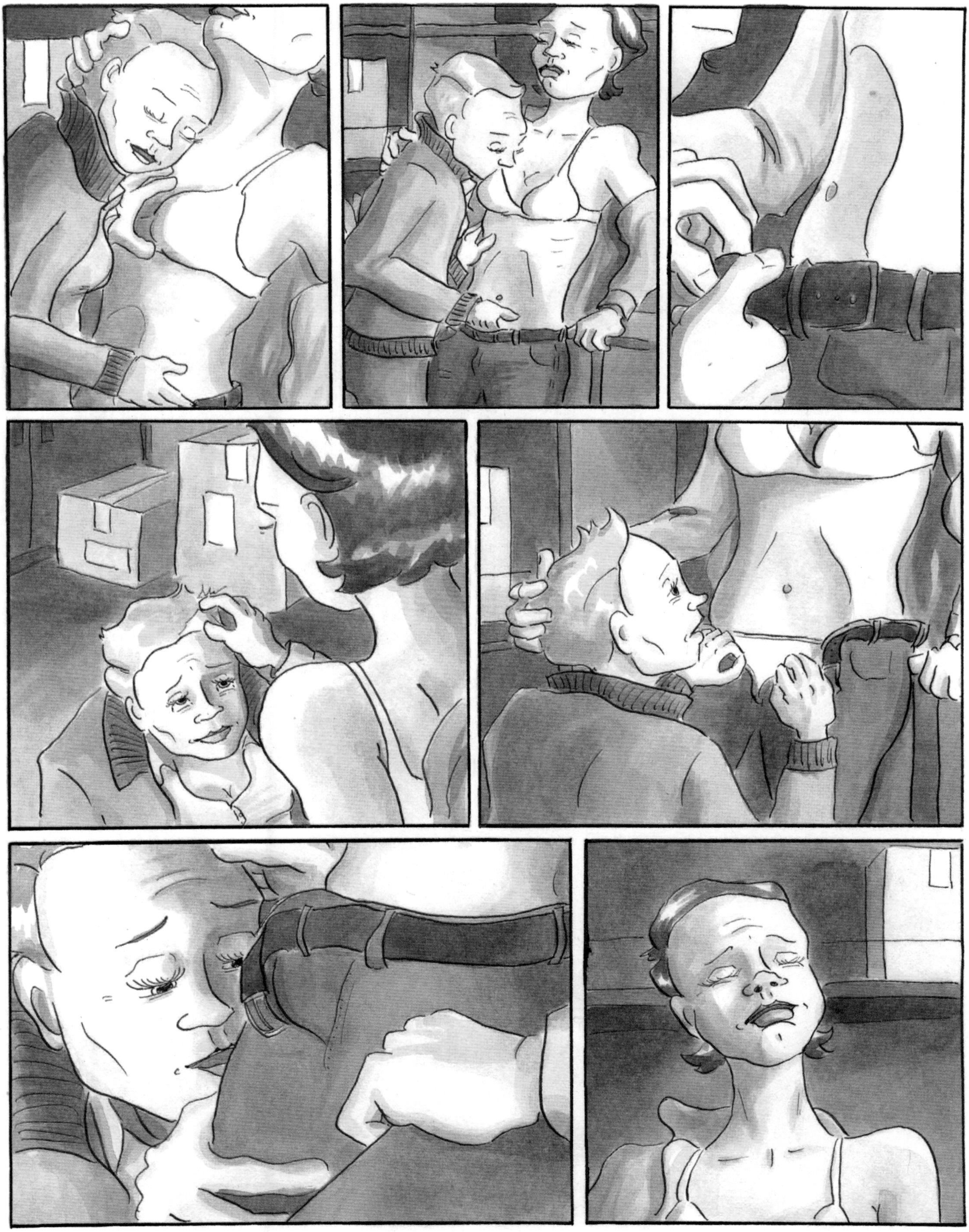

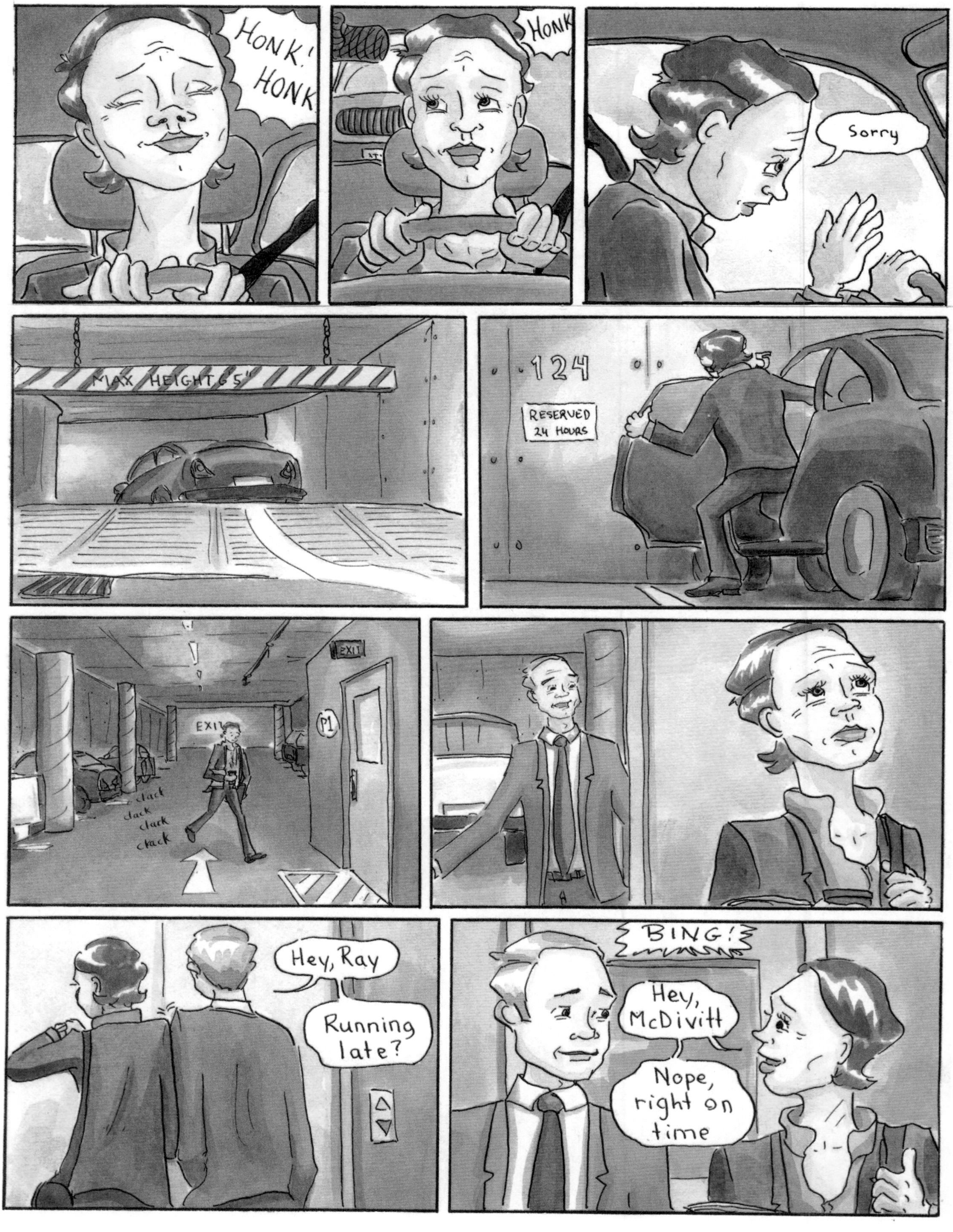
HONK! HONK
HONK
Sorry
MAX HEIGHT 6'5"
124
RESERVED 24 HOURS
EXIT
EXIT
P1
clack clack clack clack
Hey, Ray
Running late?
BING!
Hey, McDivitt
Nope, right on time

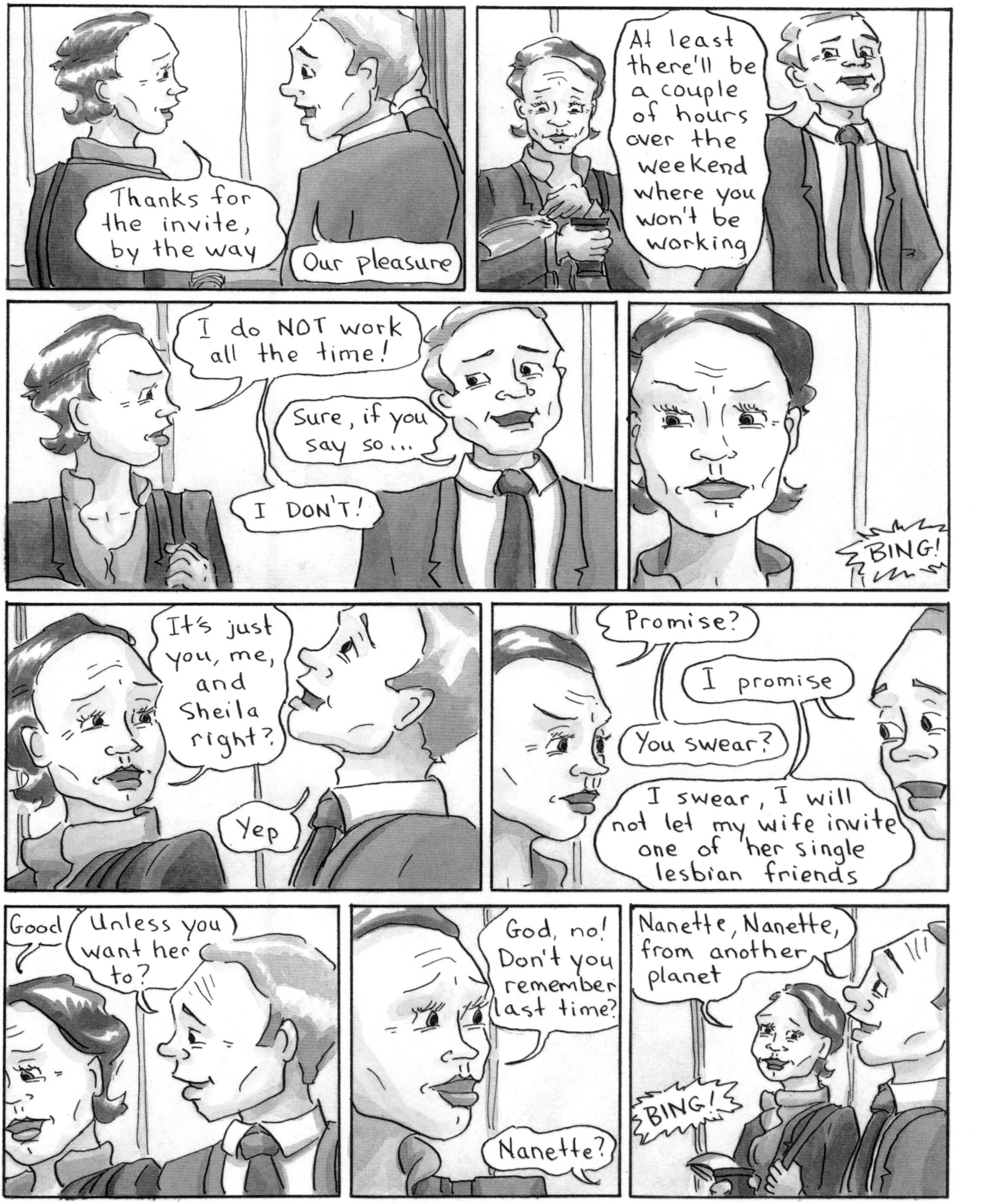
Thanks for the invite, by the way
Our pleasure
At least there'll be a couple of hours over the weekend where you won't be working
I do NOT work all the time!
Sure, if you say so...
I DON'T!
BING!
It's just you, me, and Sheila right?
Yep
Promise?
I promise
You swear?
I swear, I will not let my wife invite one of her single lesbian friends
Good
Unless you want her to?
God, no! Don't you remember last time?
Nanette?
Nanette, Nanette, from another planet
BING!

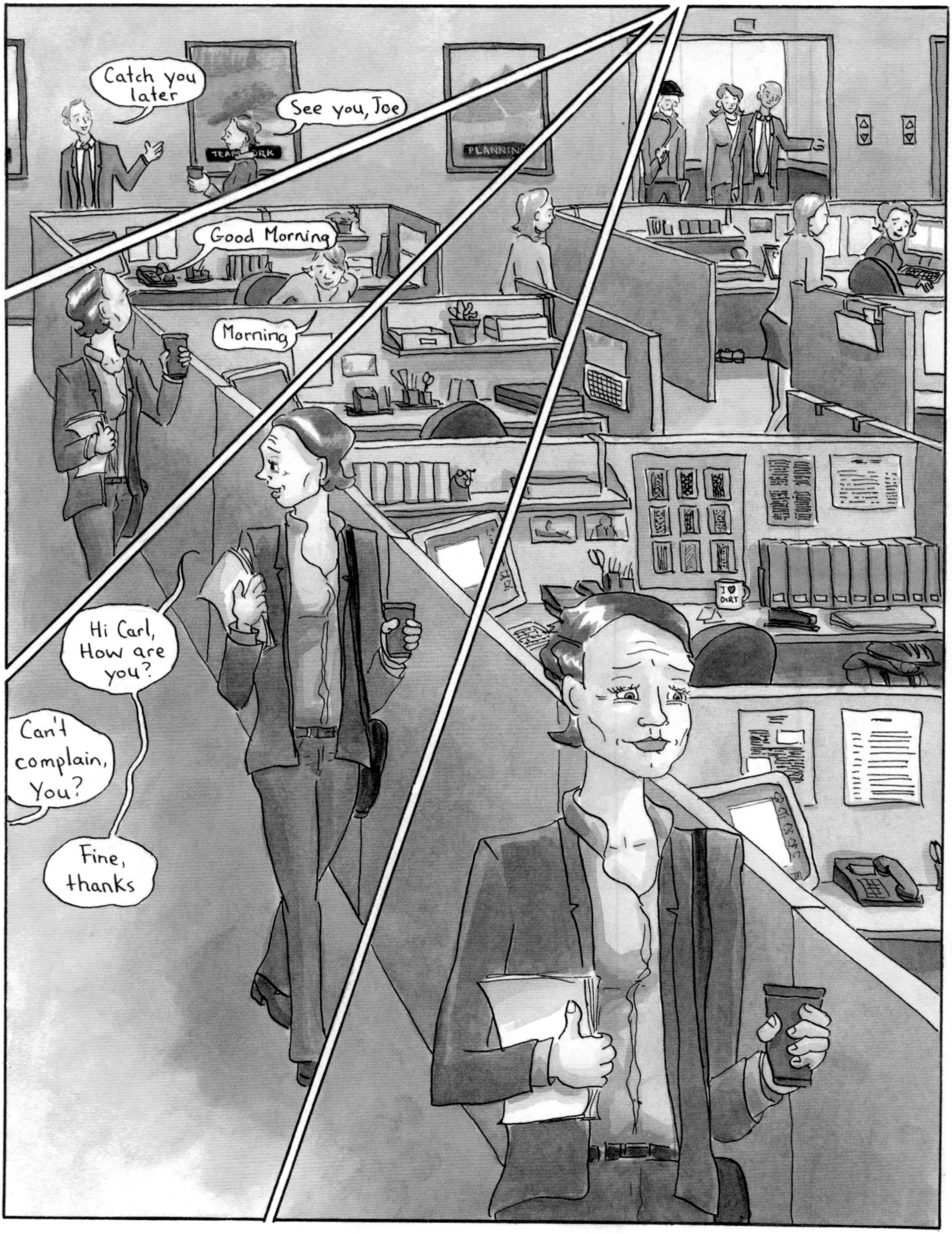
Catch you later
See you, Joe
TEAMWORK
PLANNING
Good Morning
Morning
I ♥ DIRT
Hi Carl, How are you?
Can't complain, You?
Fine, thanks

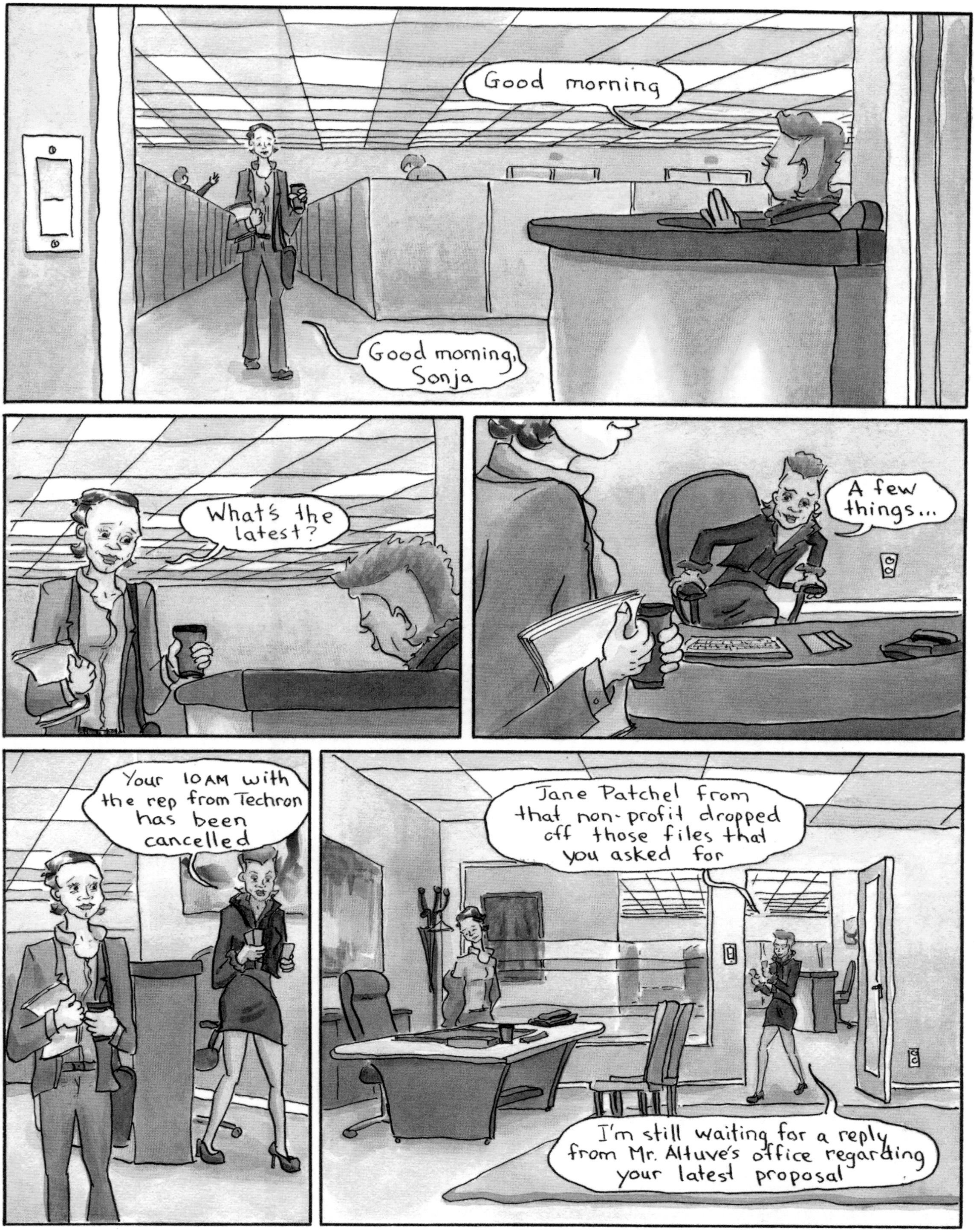
Good morning
Good morning, Sonja
What's the latest?
A few things...
Your 10AM with the rep from Techron has been cancelled
Jane Patchel from that non-profit dropped off those files that you asked for
I'm still waiting for a reply from Mr. Altuve's office regarding your latest proposal

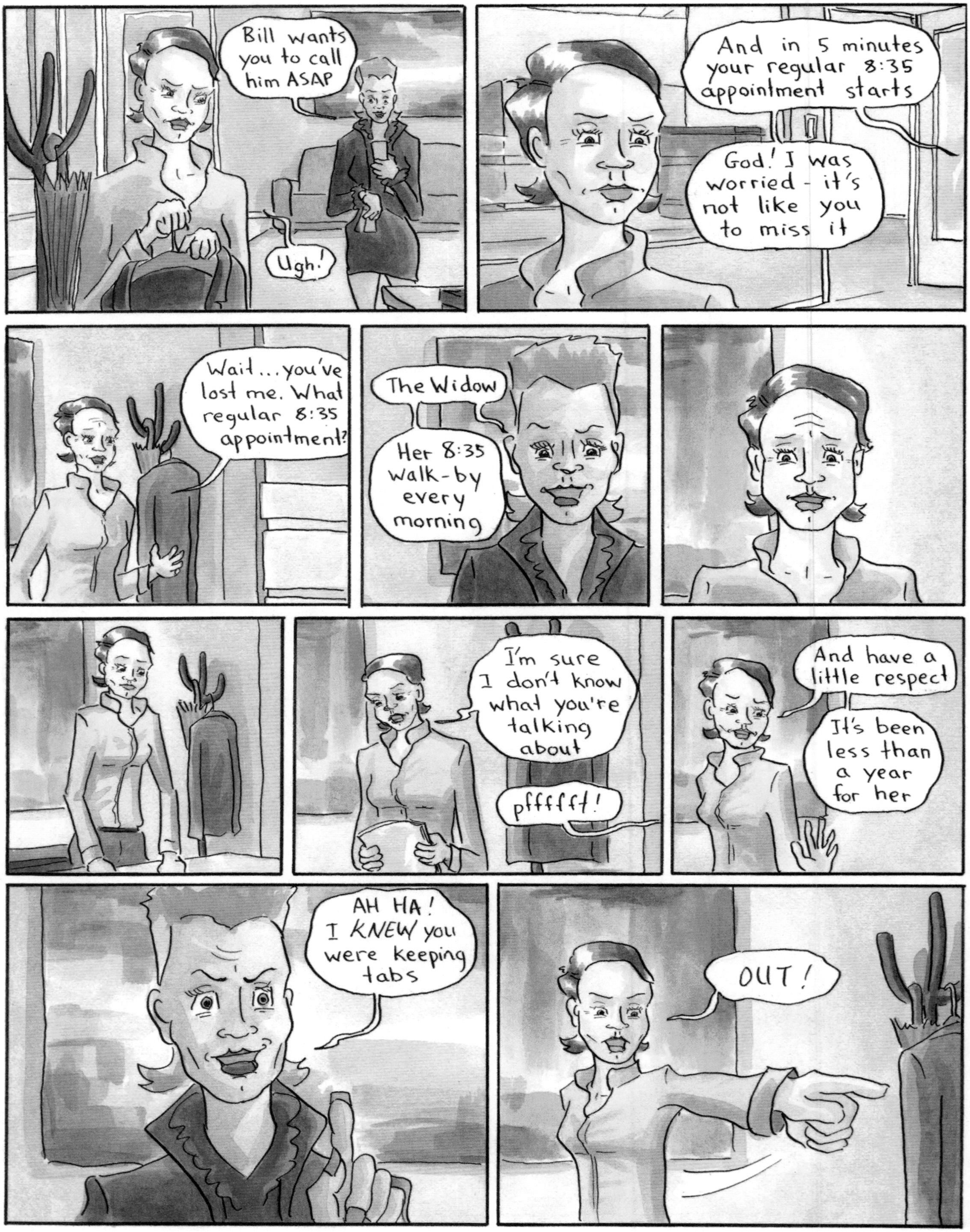
Bill wants you to call him ASAP
Ugh!
And in 5 minutes your regular 8:35 appointment starts
God! I was worried - it's not like you to miss it
Wait... you've lost me. What regular 8:35 appointment?
The Widow
Her 8:35 walk-by every morning
I'm sure I don't know what you're talking about
pffffft!
And have a little respect
It's been less than a year for her
AH HA! I KNEW you were keeping tabs
OUT!

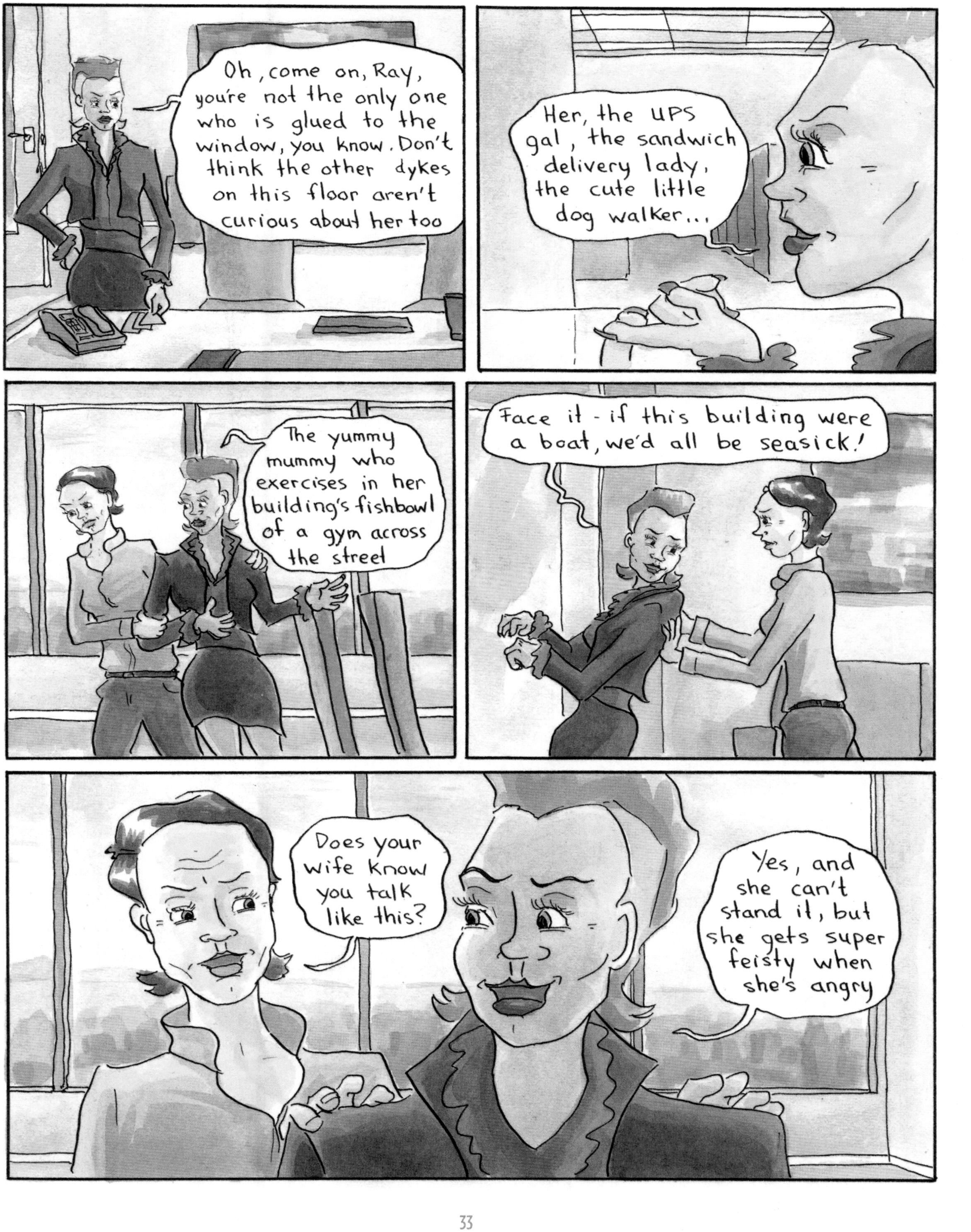
Oh, come on, Ray, you're not the only one who is glued to the window, you know. Don't think the other dykes on this floor aren't curious about her too
Her, the UPS gal, the sandwich delivery lady, the cute little dog walker...
The yummy mummy who exercises in her building's fishbowl of a gym across the street
Face it - if this building were a boat, we'd all be seasick!
Does your wife know you talk like this?
Yes, and she can't stand it, but she gets super feisty when she's angry

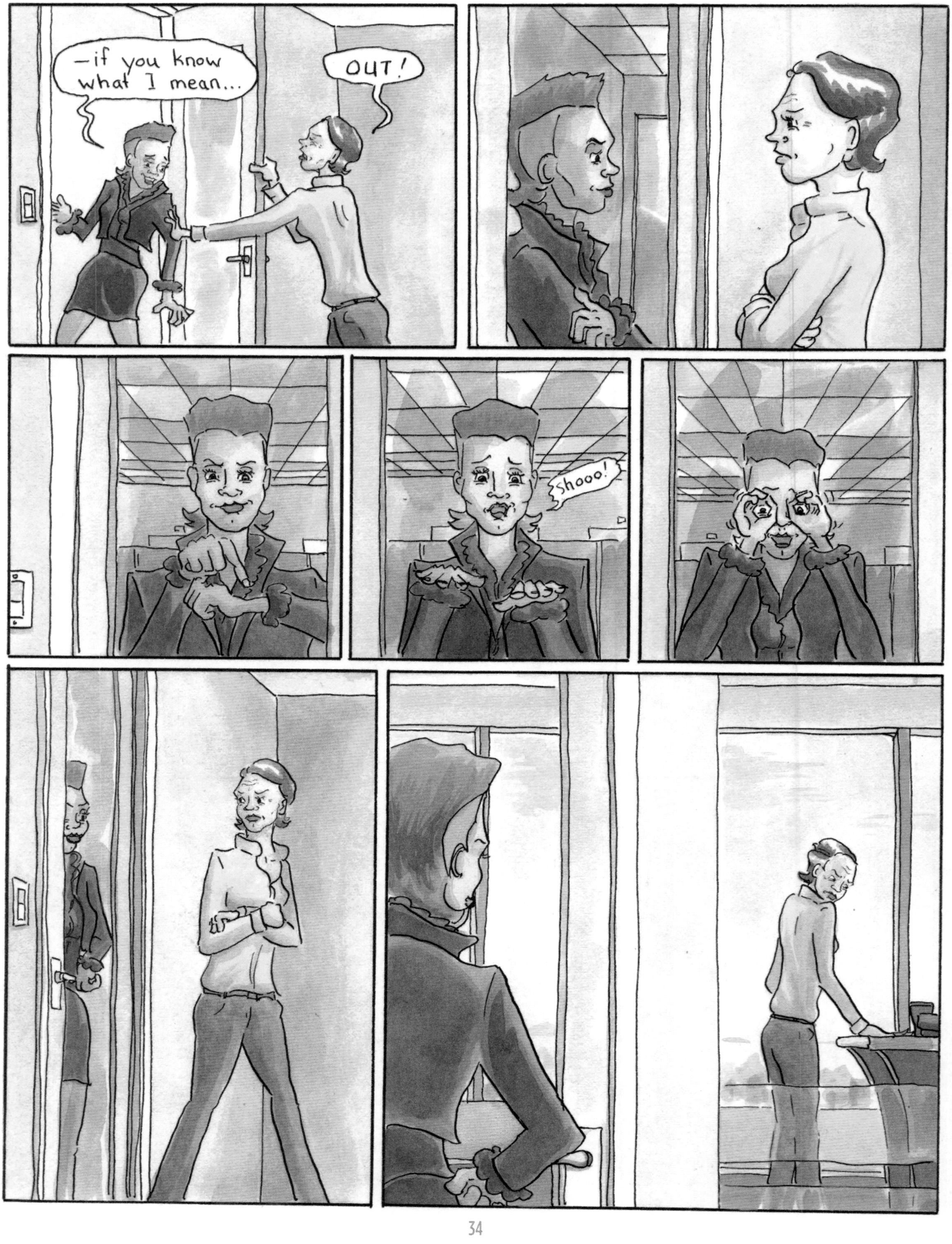

—if you know what I mean...
OUT!
Shooo!

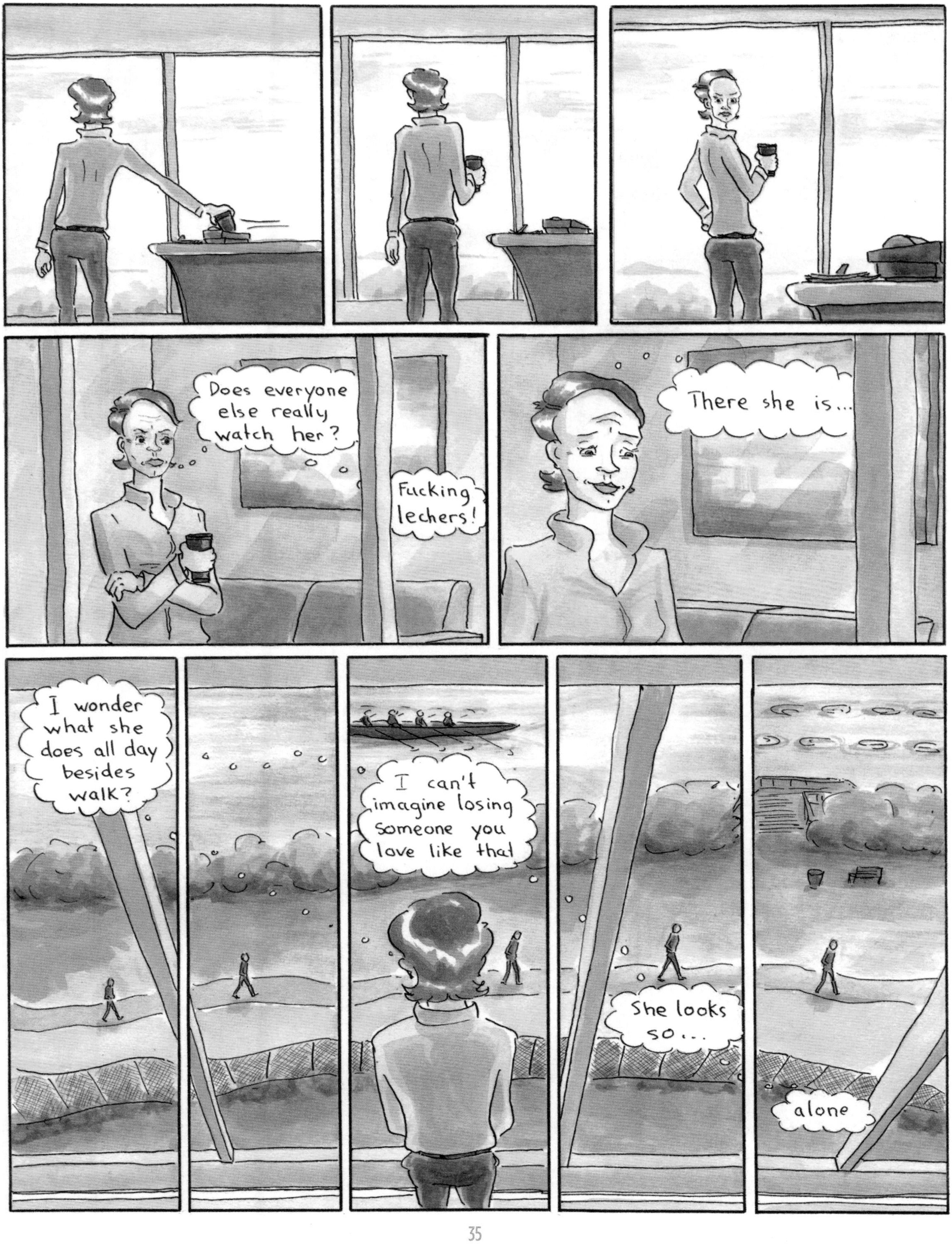
Does everyone else really watch her?
Fucking lechers!
There she is...
I wonder what she does all day besides walk?
I can't imagine losing someone you love like that
She looks so...
alone

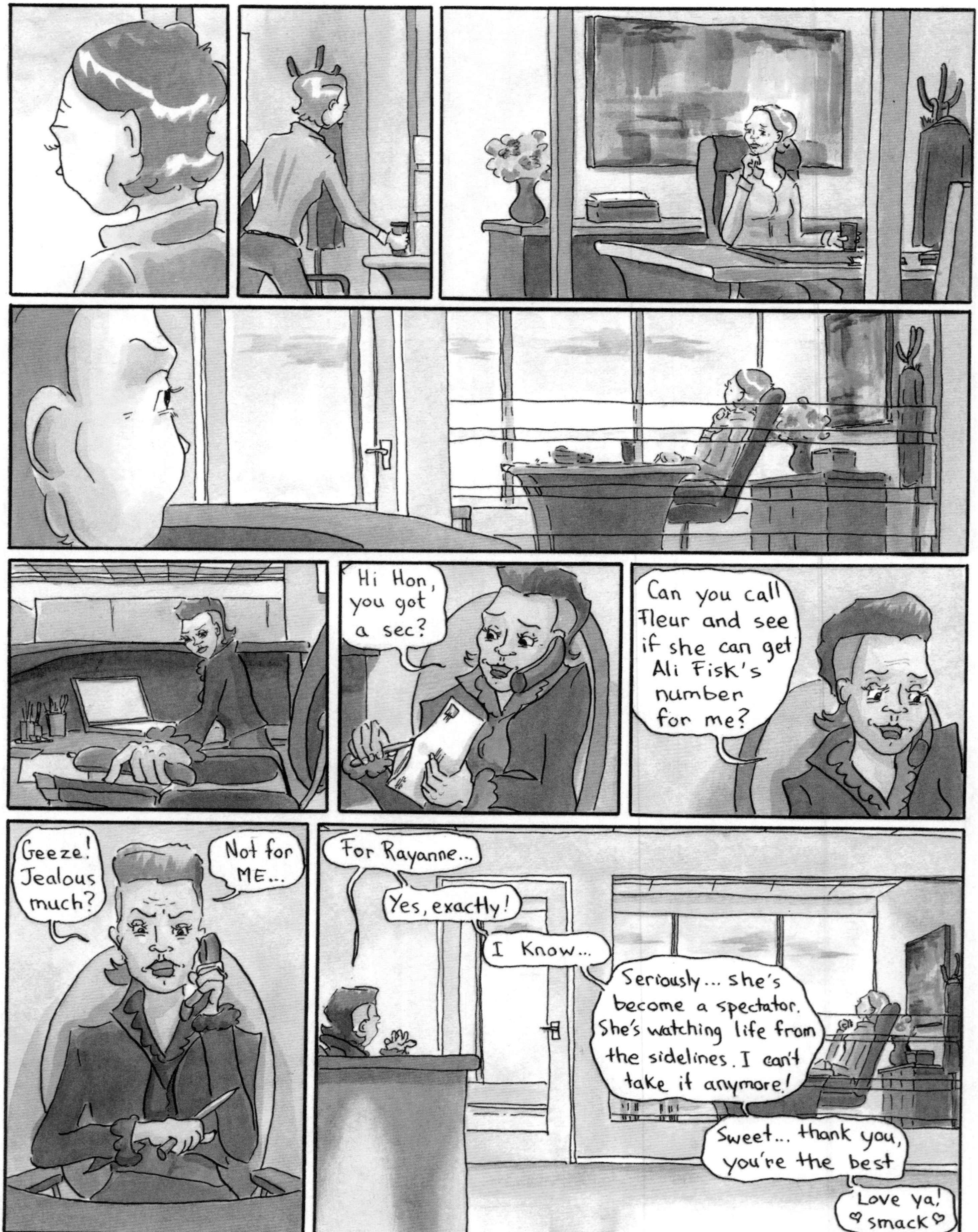
Hi Hon, you got a sec?
Can you call Fleur and see if she can get Ali Fisk's number for me?
Geeze! Jealous much?
Not for ME...
For Rayanne...
Yes, exactly!
I Know...
Seriously... she's become a spectator. She's watching life from the sidelines. I can't take it anymore!
Sweet... thank you, you're the best
Love ya! smack

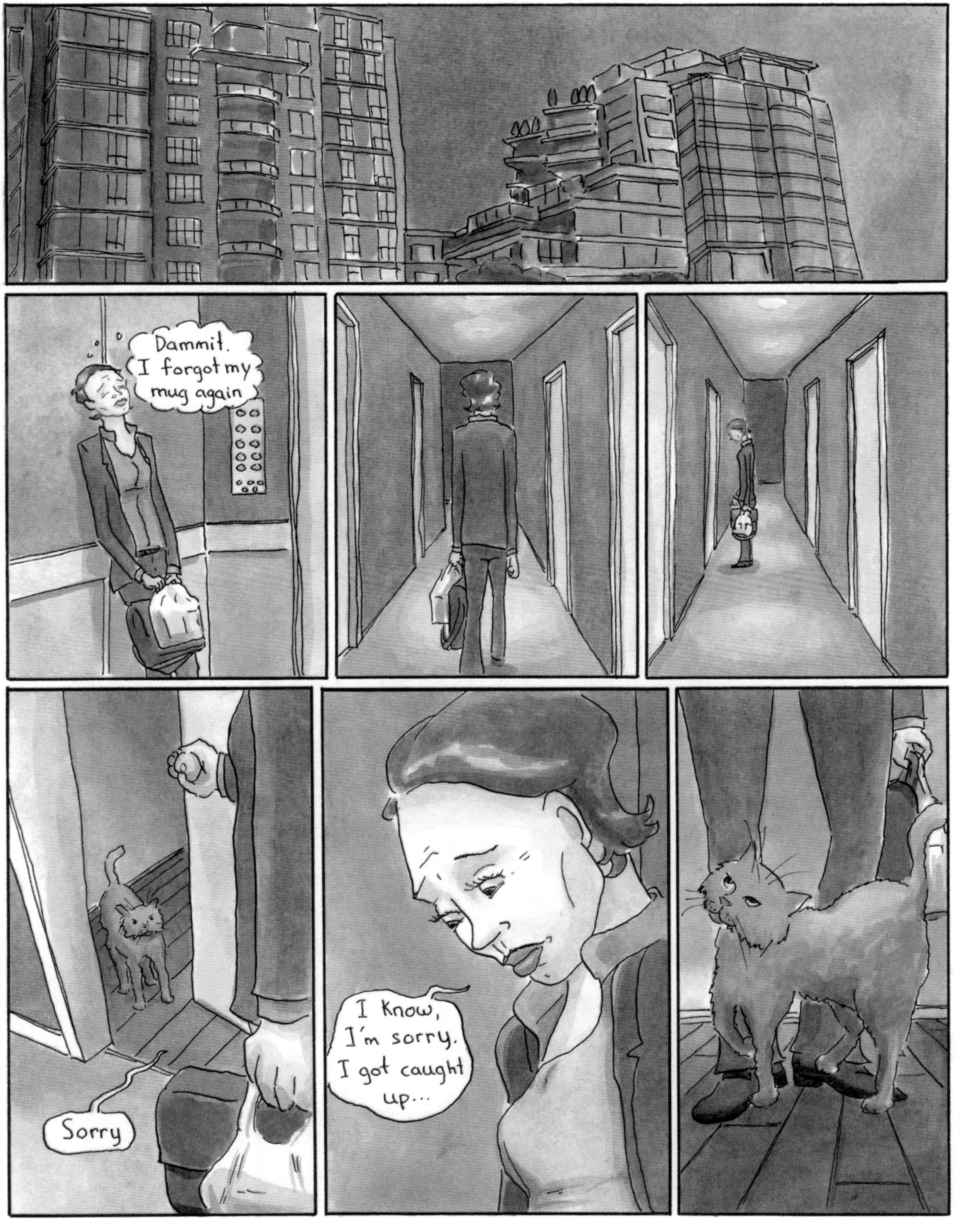
Dammit. I forgot my mug again
Sorry
I know, I'm sorry. I got caught up...

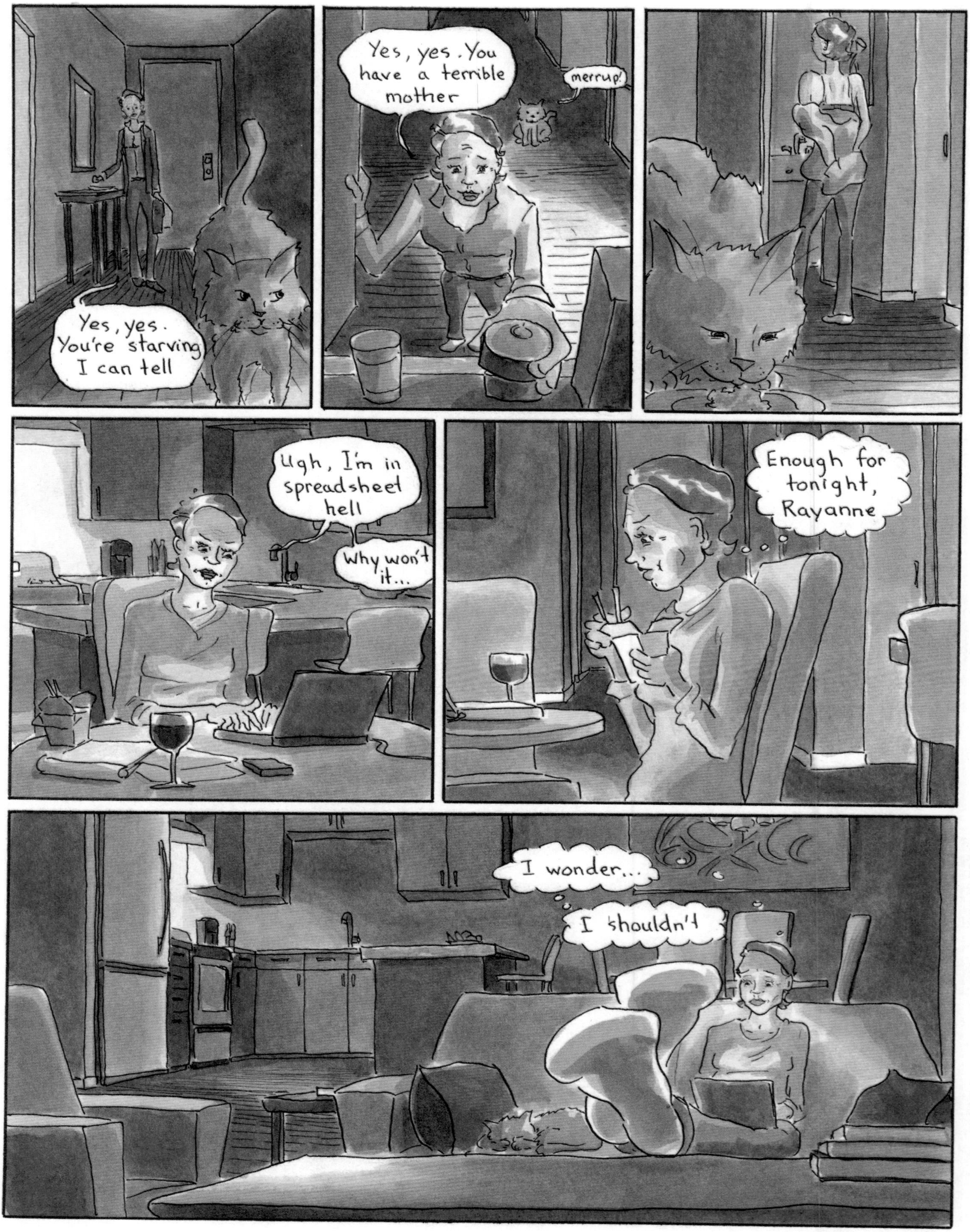
Yes, yes. You're starving I can tell
Yes, yes. You have a terrible mother
merrup!
Ugh, I'm in spreadsheet hell
Why won't it...
Enough for tonight, Rayanne
I wonder...
I shouldn't

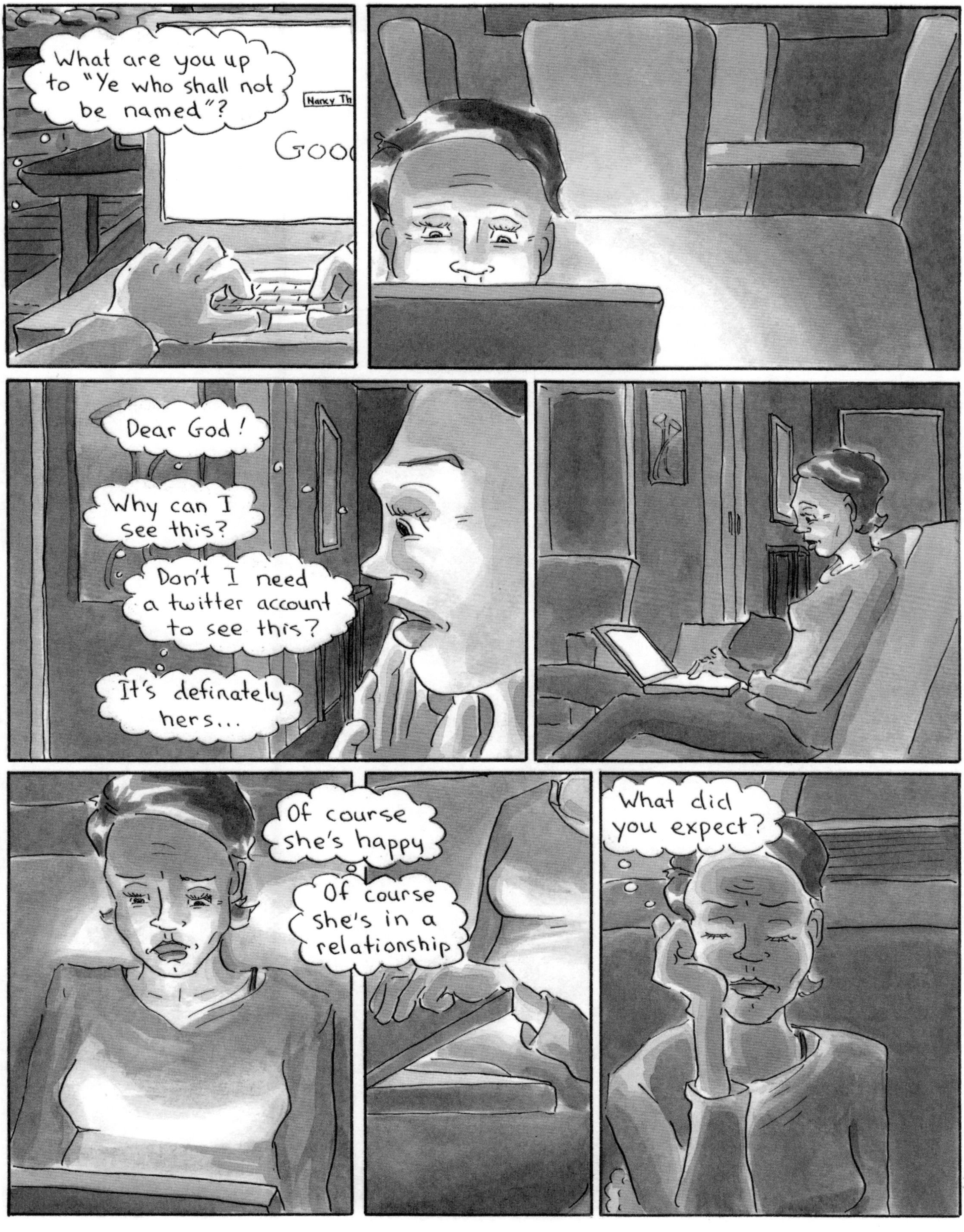
What are you up to "Ye who shall not be named"?
Nancy Th
Goo
Dear God!
Why can I see this?
Don't I need a twitter account to see this?
It's definately hers...
Of course she's happy
Of course she's in a relationship
What did you expect?

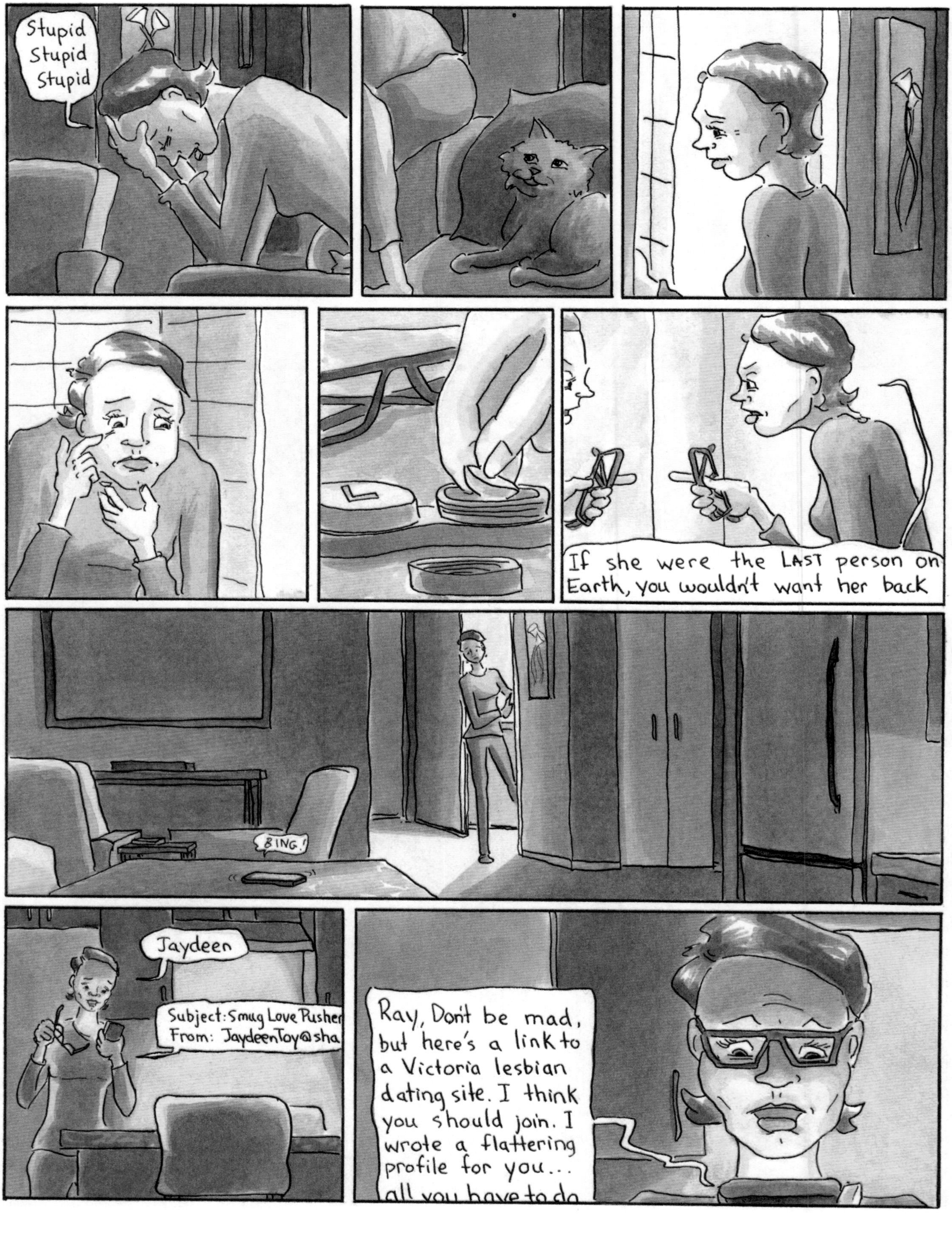
Stupid Stupid Stupid
If she were the LAST person on Earth, you wouldn't want her back
BING!
Jaydeen
Subject: Smug Love Pusher
From: JaydeenToy@sha
Ray, Don't be mad, but here's a link to a Victoria lesbian dating site. I think you should join. I wrote a flattering profile for you... all you have to do

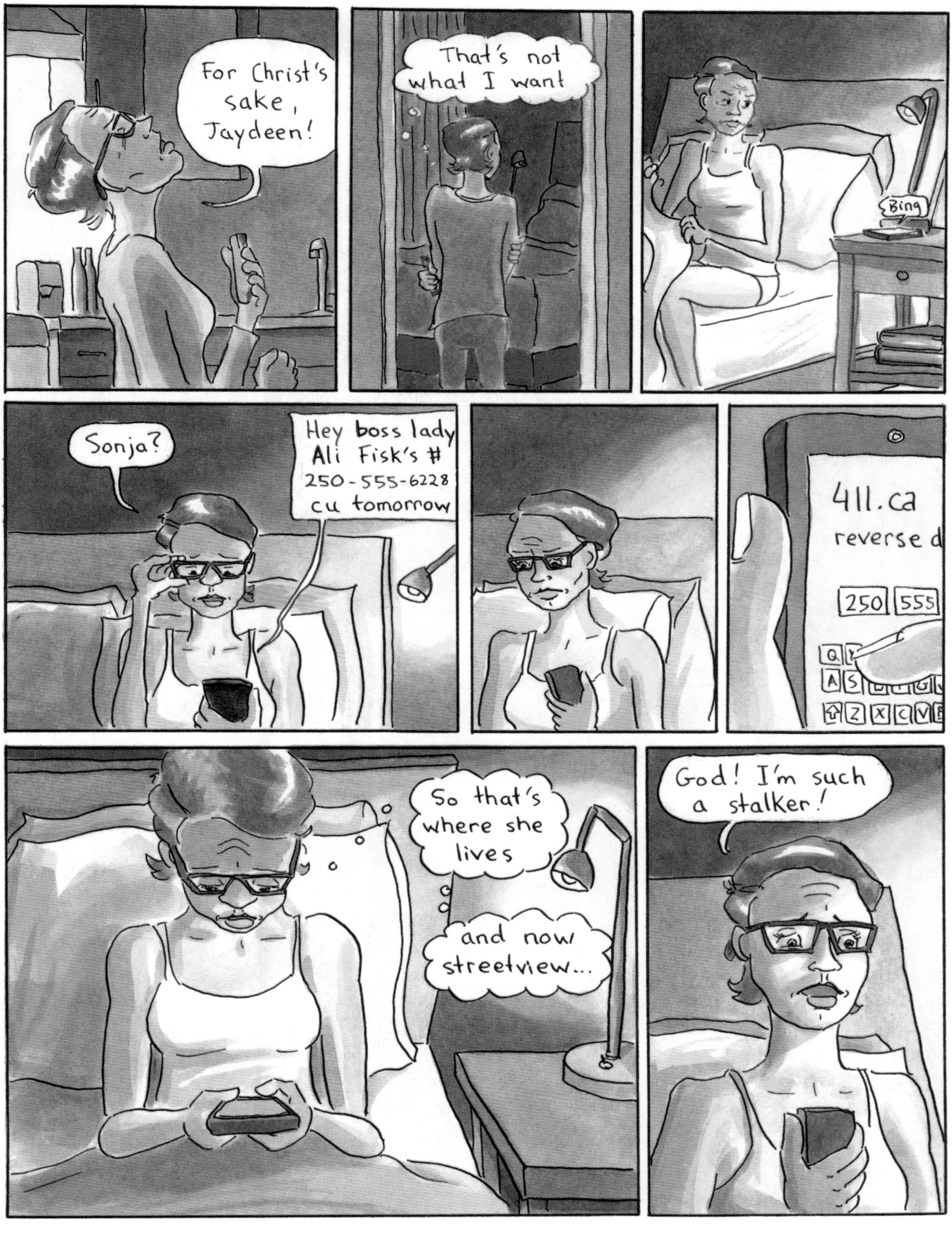
For Christ's sake, Jaydeen!
That's not what I want
Bing
Sonja?
Hey boss lady
Ali Fisk's #
250-555-6228
cu tomorrow
411.ca
reverse d
250 555
So that's where she lives
and now streetview...
God! I'm such a stalker!

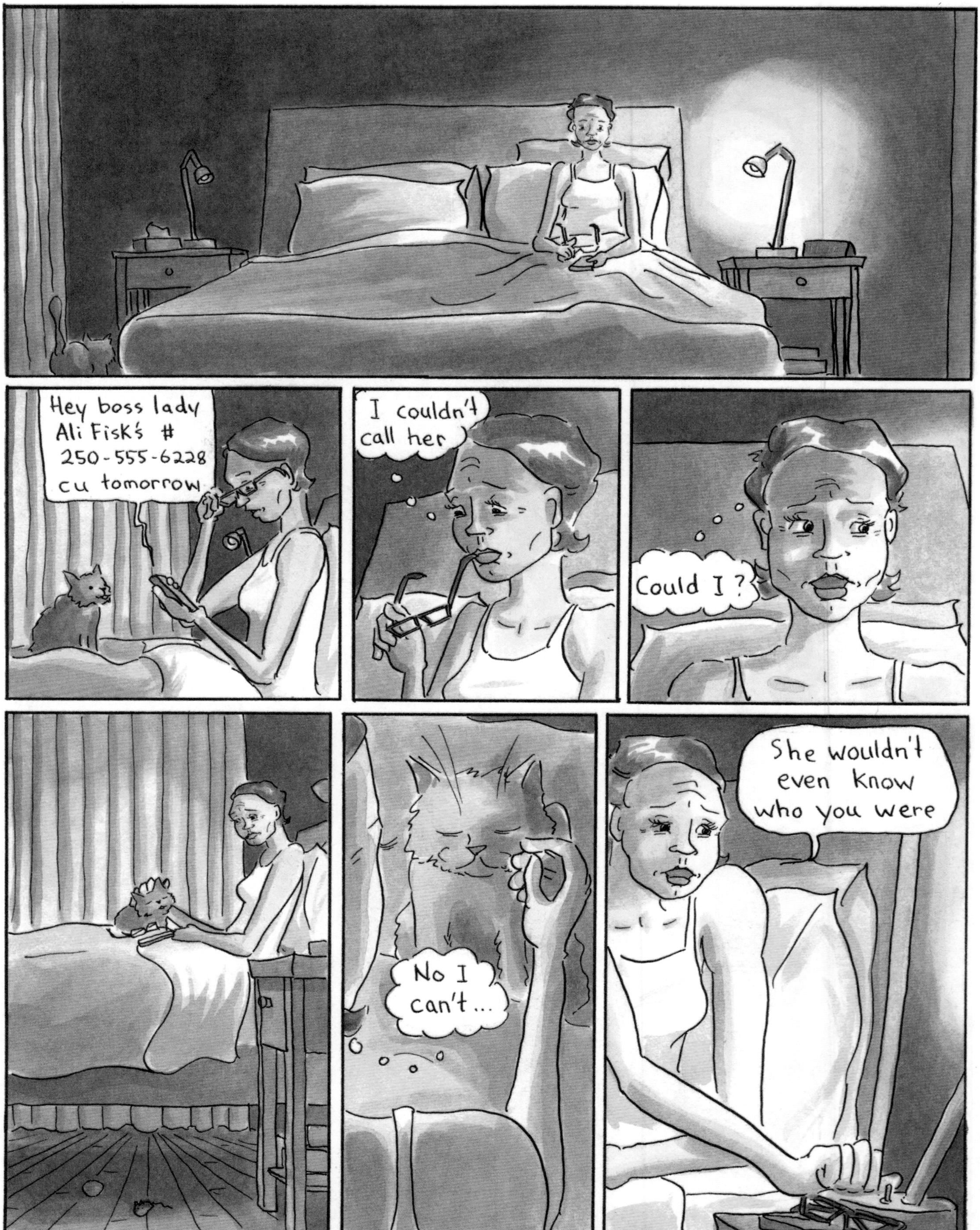
Hey boss lady
Ali Fisk's #
250-555-6228
cu tomorrow
I couldn't call her
Could I ?
No I can't...
She wouldn't even know who you were

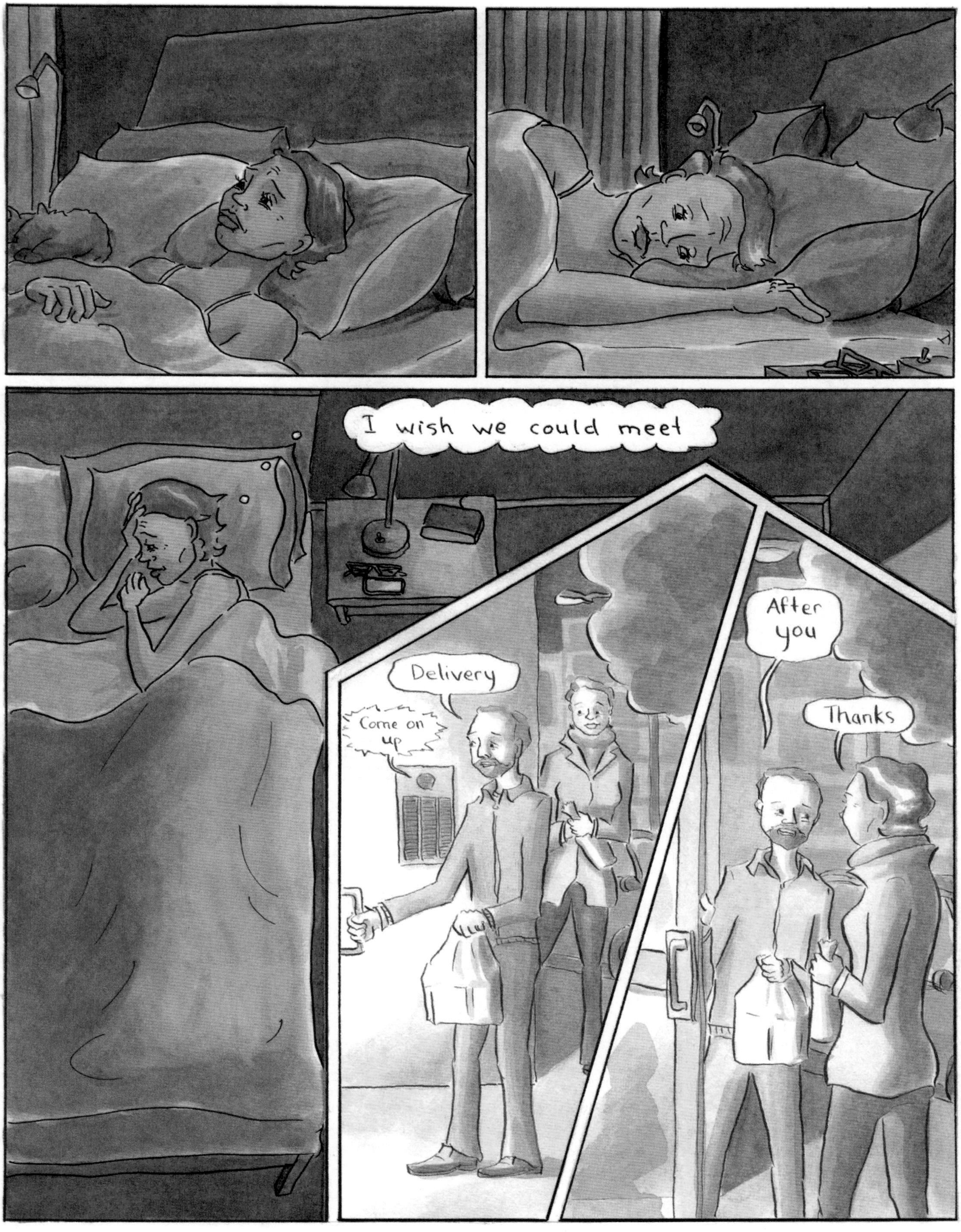
I wish we could meet
Delivery
Come on up
After you
Thanks

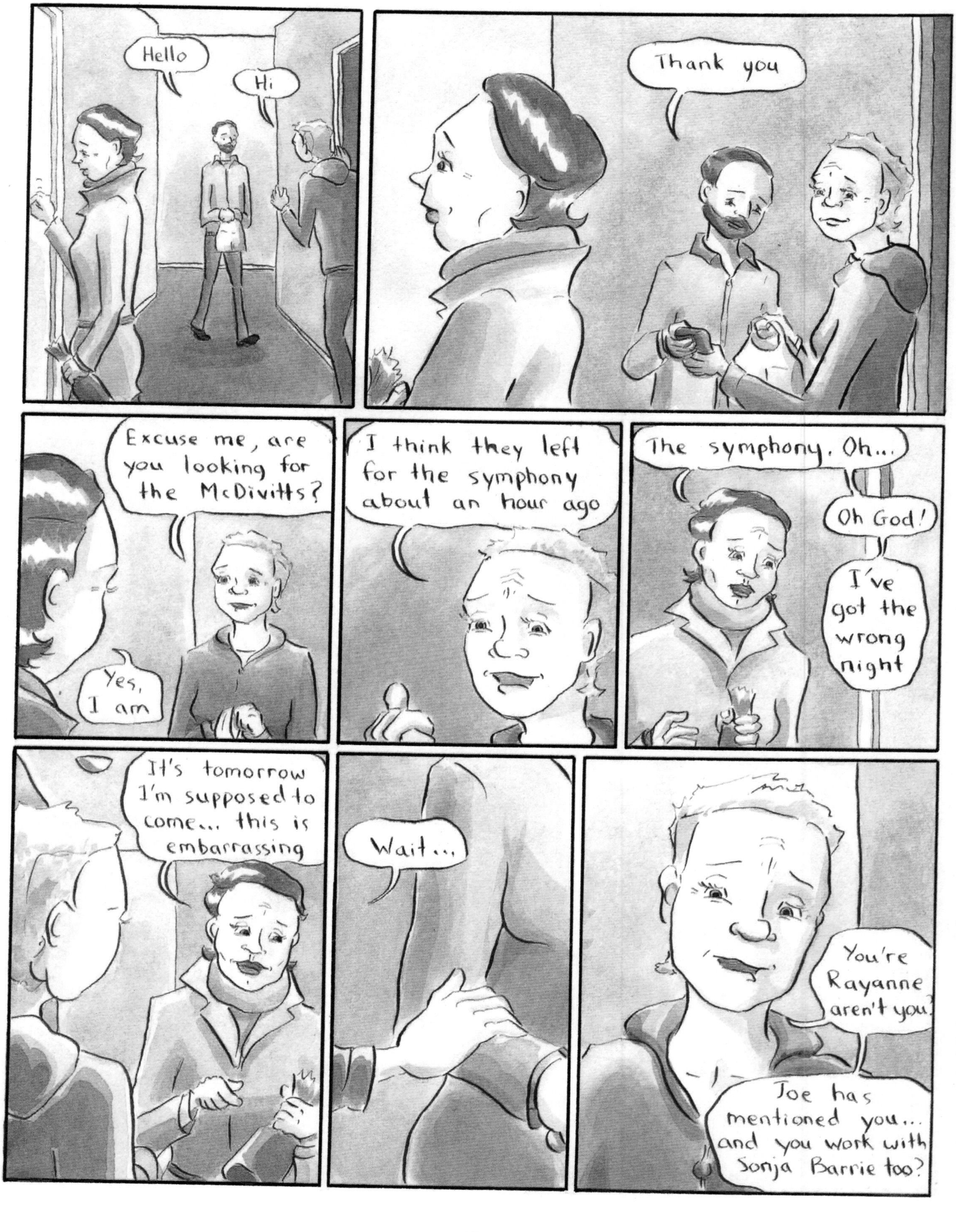
Hello
Hi
Thank you
Excuse me, are you looking for the McDivitts?
Yes, I am
I think they left for the symphony about an hour ago
The symphony. Oh...
Oh God!
I've got the wrong night
It's tomorrow I'm supposed to come... this is embarrassing
Wait...
You're Rayanne aren't you?
Joe has mentioned you... and you work with Sonja Barrie too?

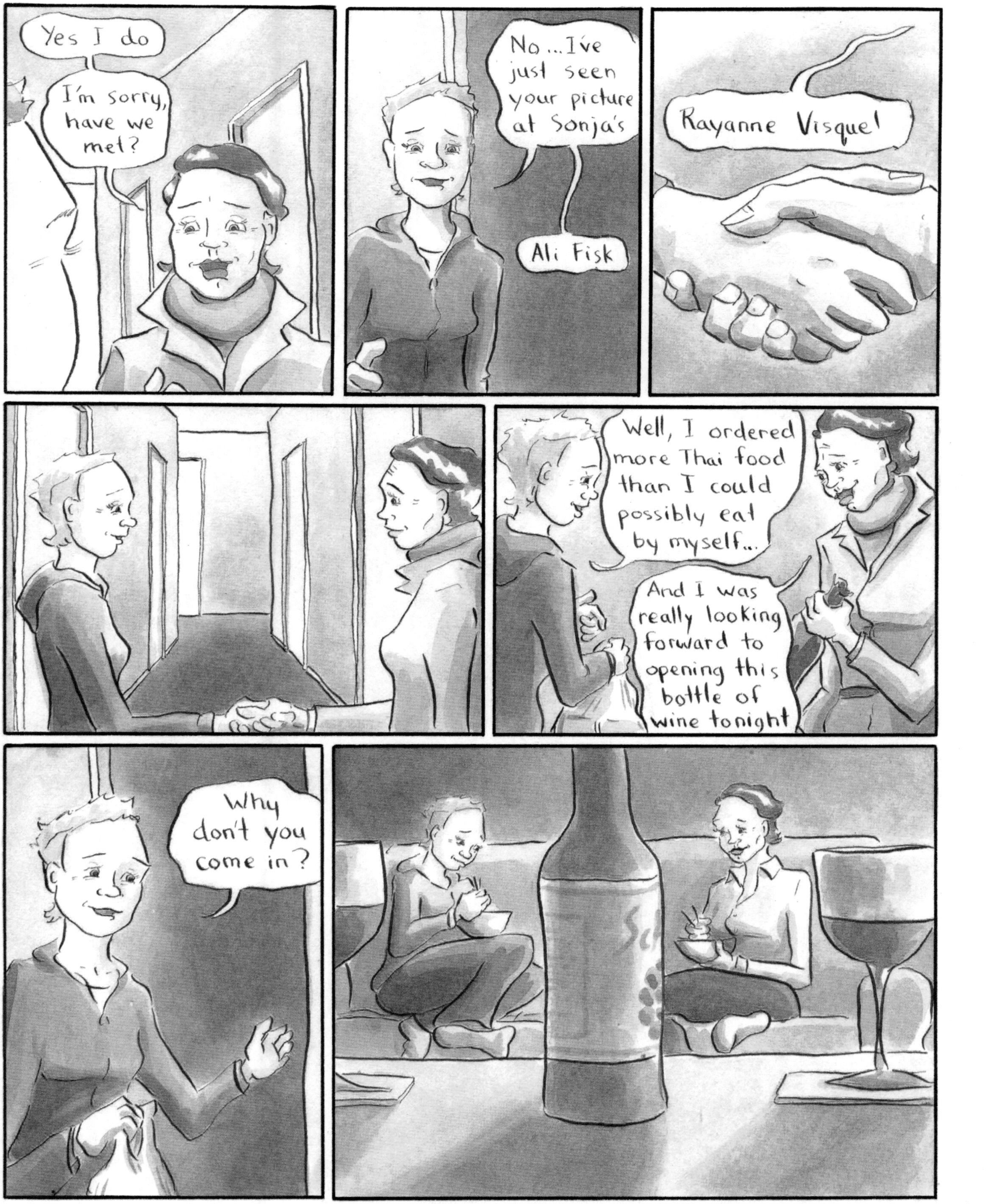
Yes I do
I'm sorry, have we met?
No... I've just seen your picture at Sonja's
Ali Fisk
Rayanne Visque!
Well, I ordered more Thai food than I could possibly eat by myself...
And I was really looking forward to opening this bottle of wine tonight
Why don't you come in?

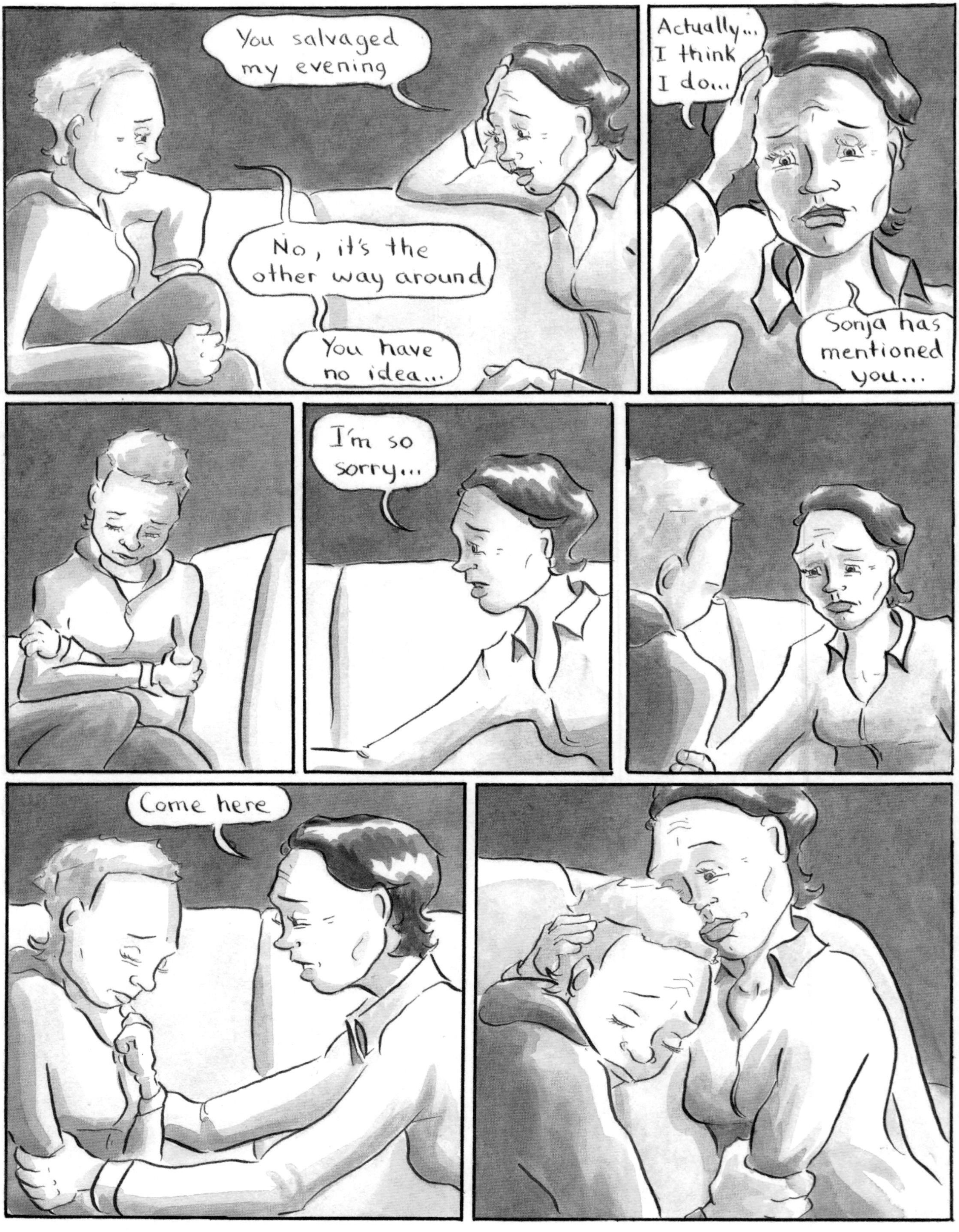
You salvaged my evening
No, it's the other way around
You have no idea...
Actually... I think I do...
Sonja has mentioned you...
I'm so sorry...
Come here

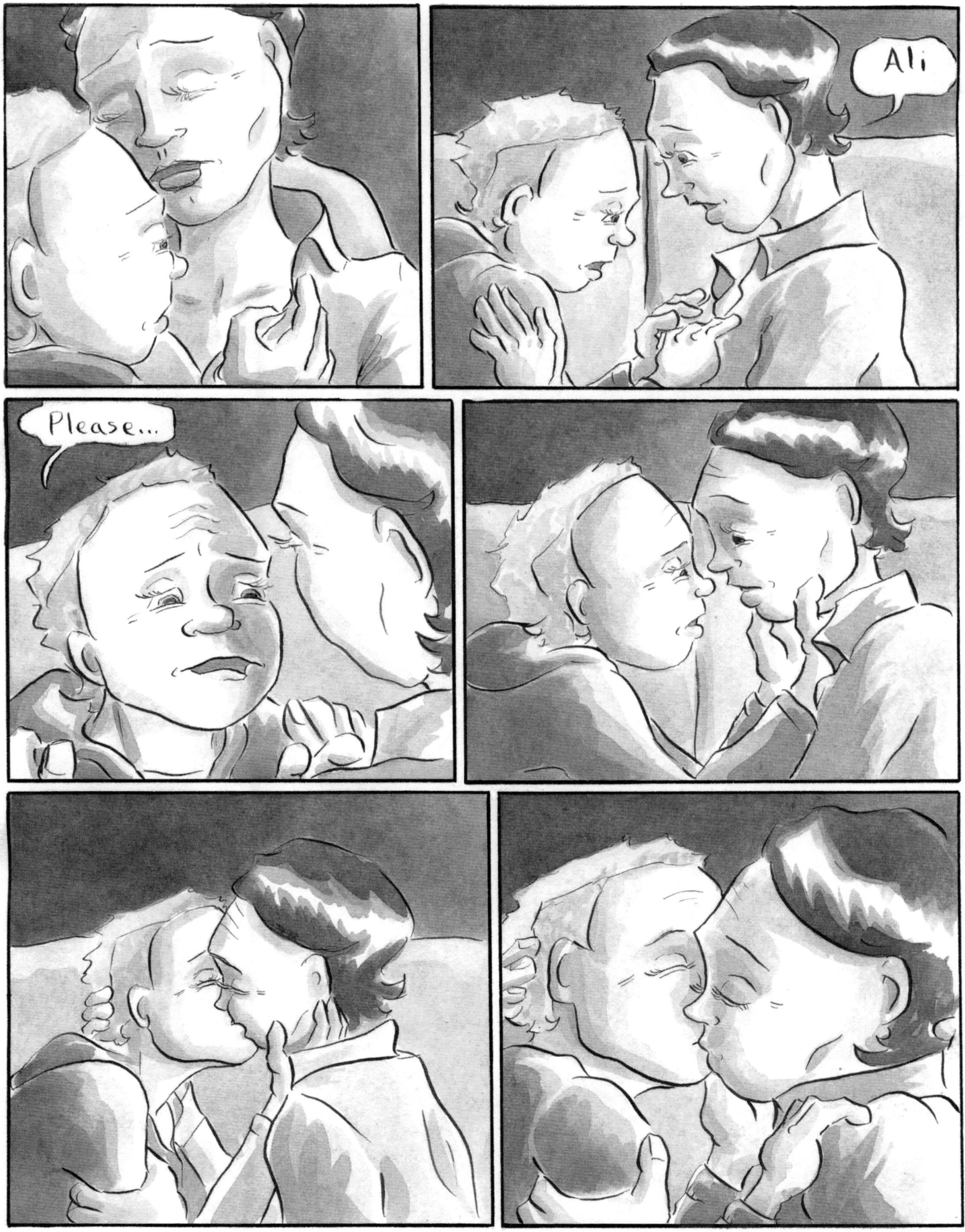
Ali
Please...

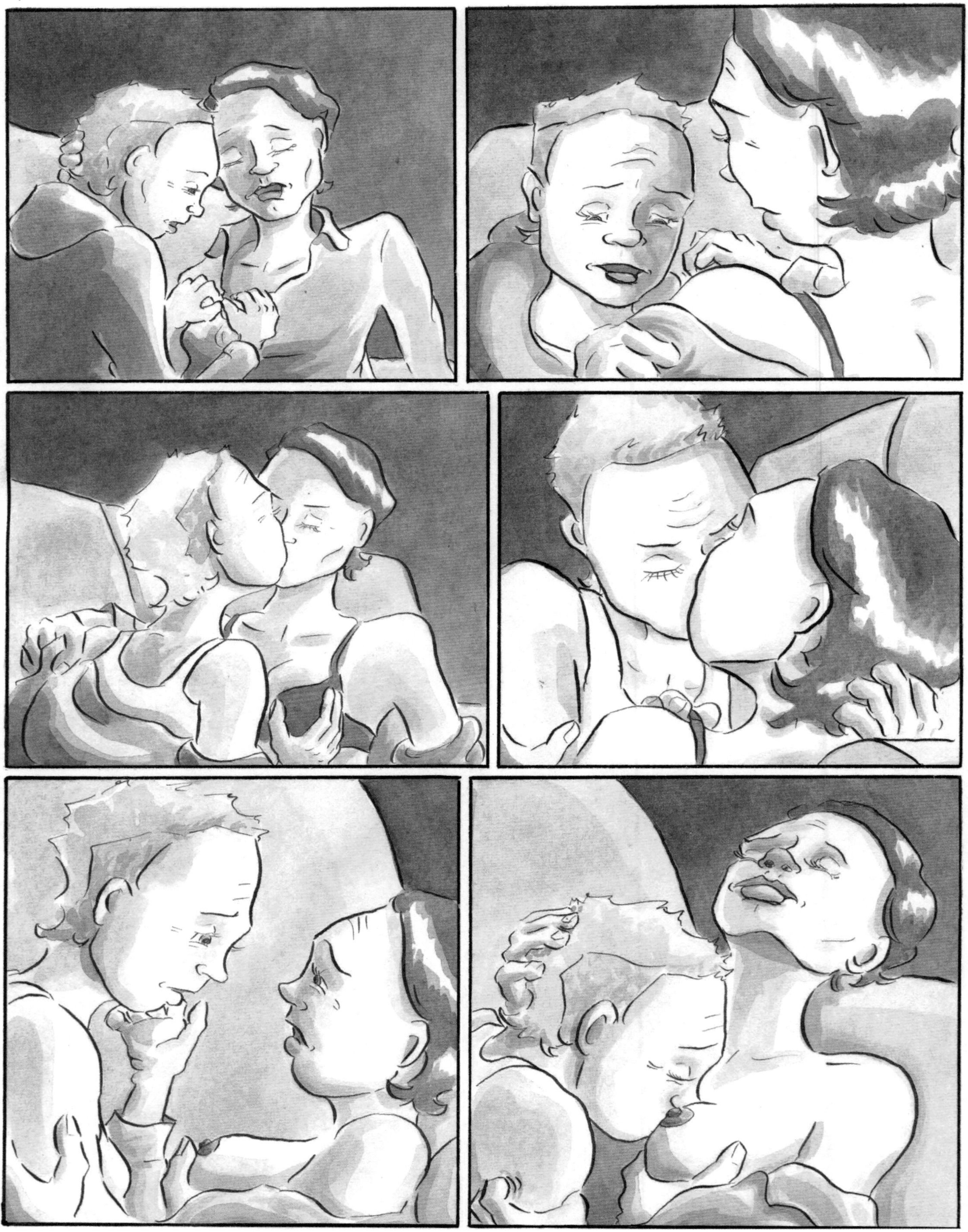

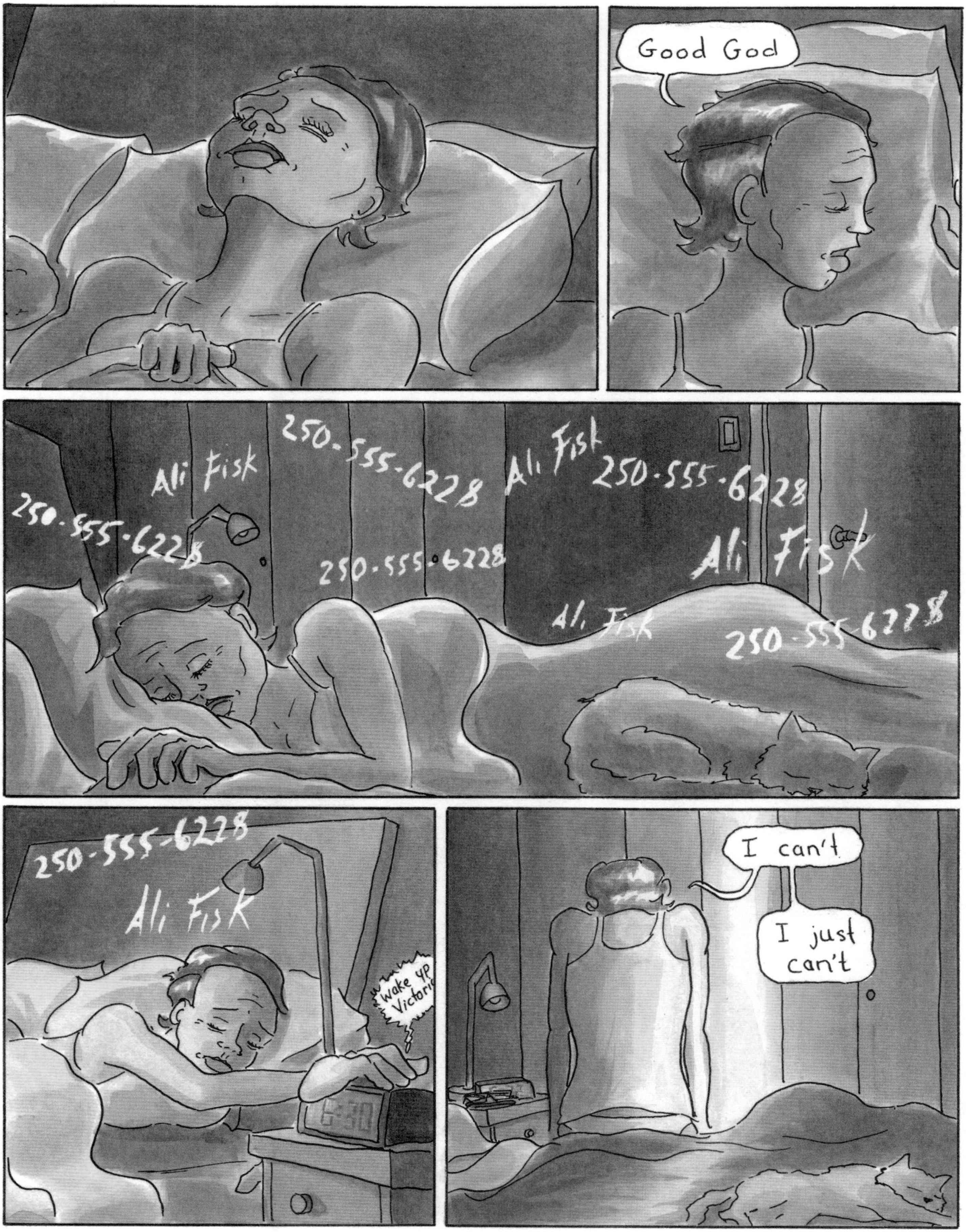
Good God
250-555-6228
Ali Fisk
250-555-6228
Ali Fisk
250-555-6228
250-555-6228
250-555-6228
Ali Fisk
Ali Fisk
250-555-6228
250-555-6228
Ali Fisk
Wake up Victori
I can't
I just can't

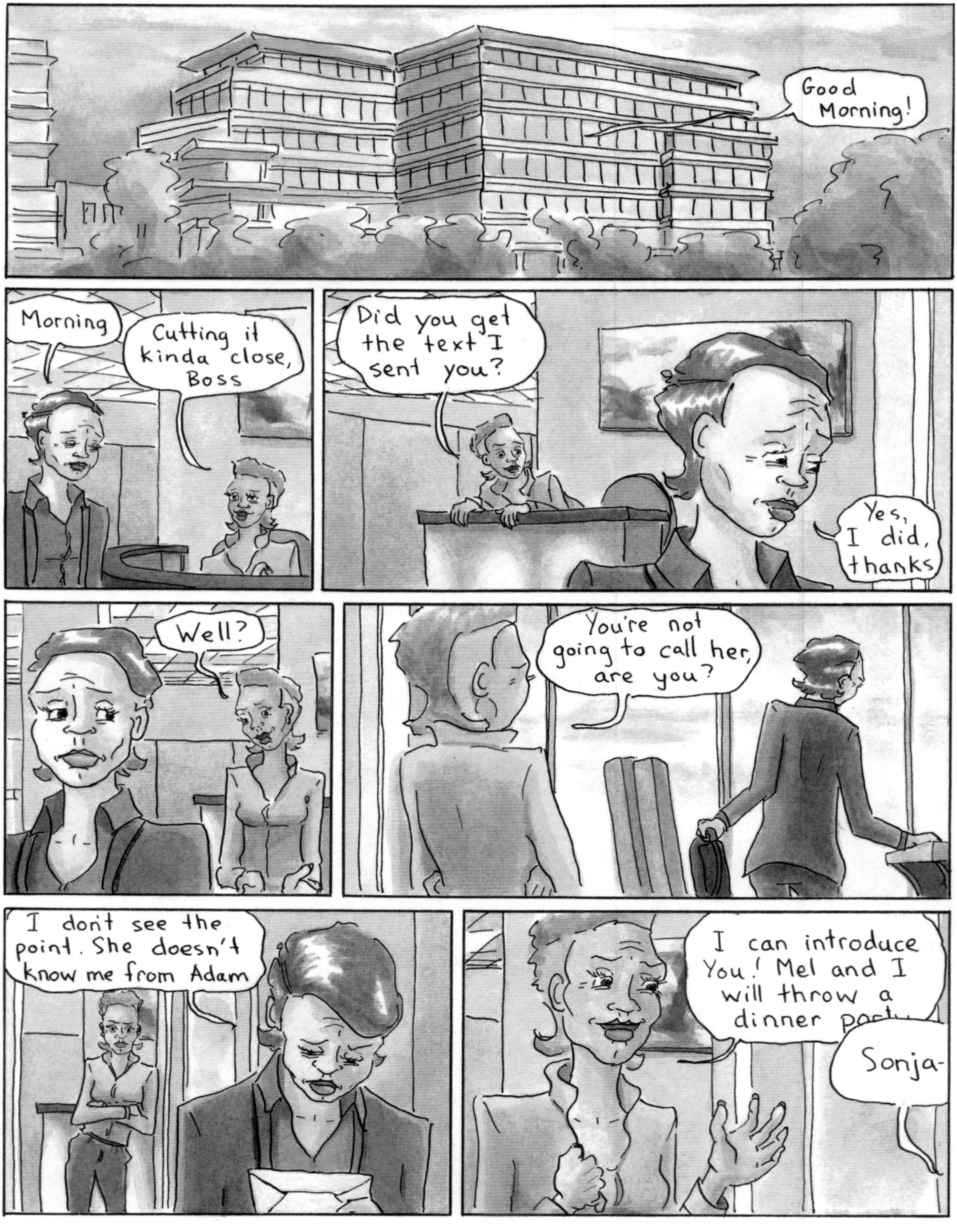
Good Morning!
Morning
Cutting it kinda close, Boss
Did you get the text I sent you?
Yes, I did, thanks
Well?
You're not going to call her, are you?
I don't see the point. She doesn't know me from Adam
I can introduce You! Mel and I will throw a dinner
Sonja-

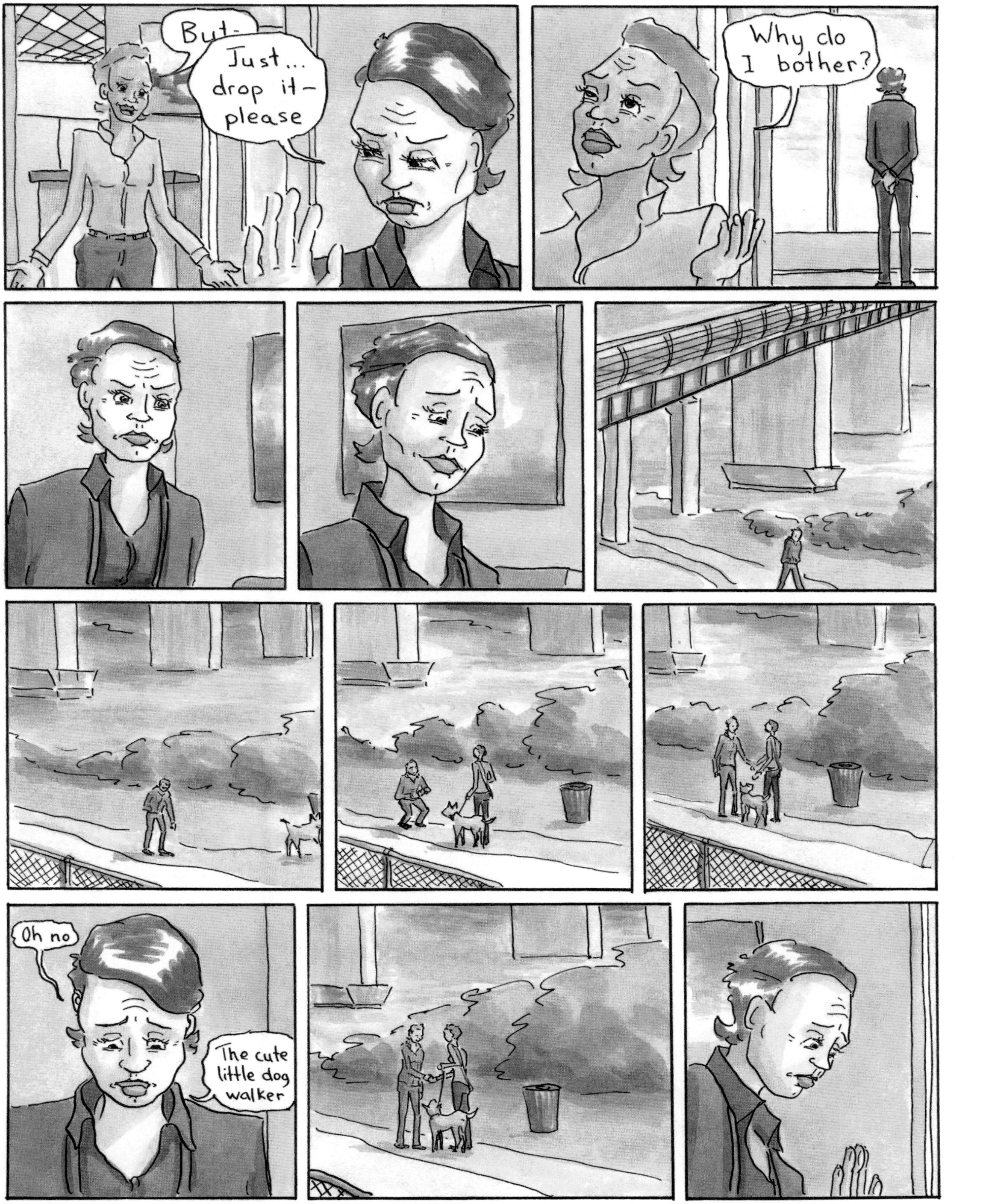
But-
Just...
drop it-
please
Why do
I bother?
Oh no
The cute
little dog
walker

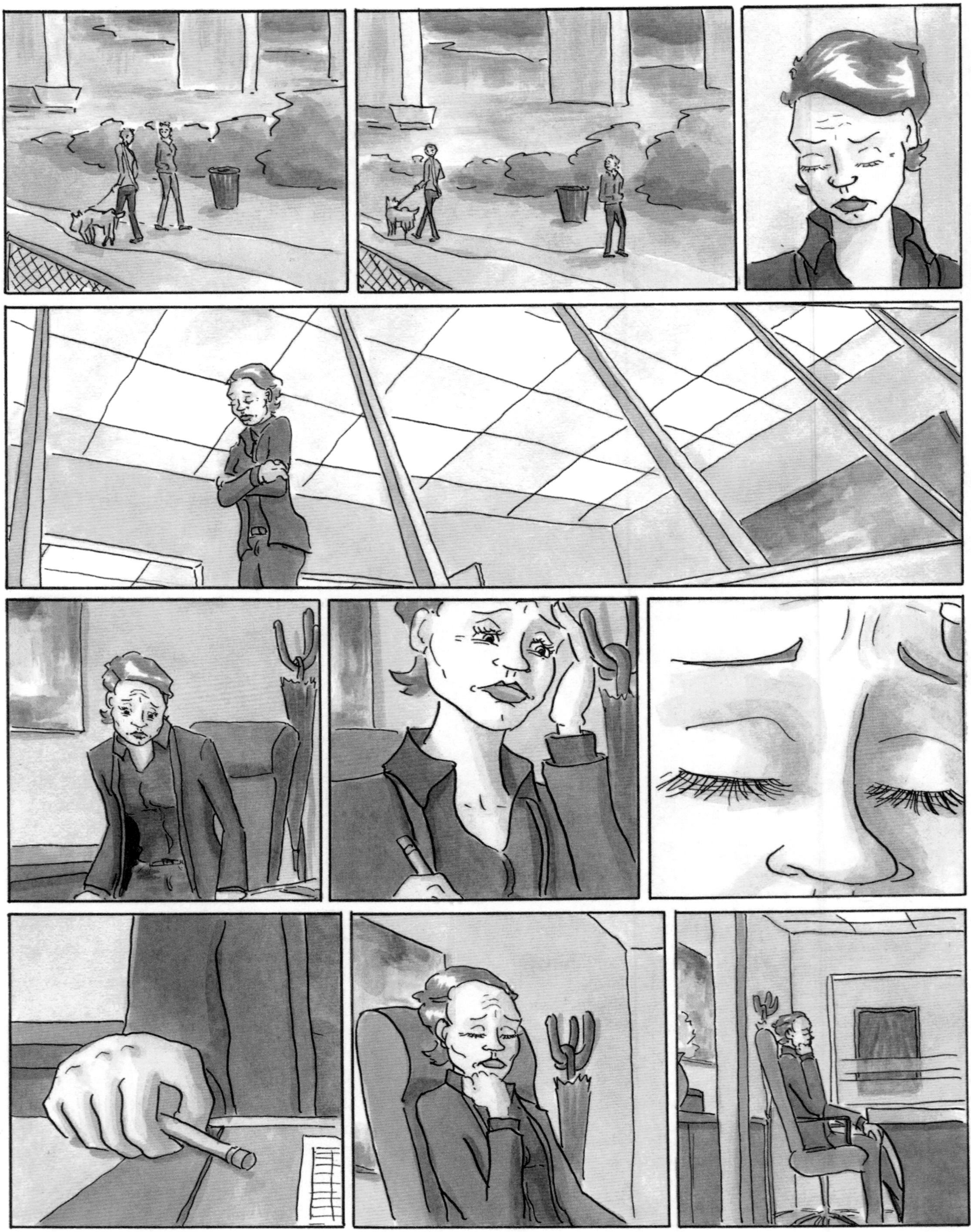

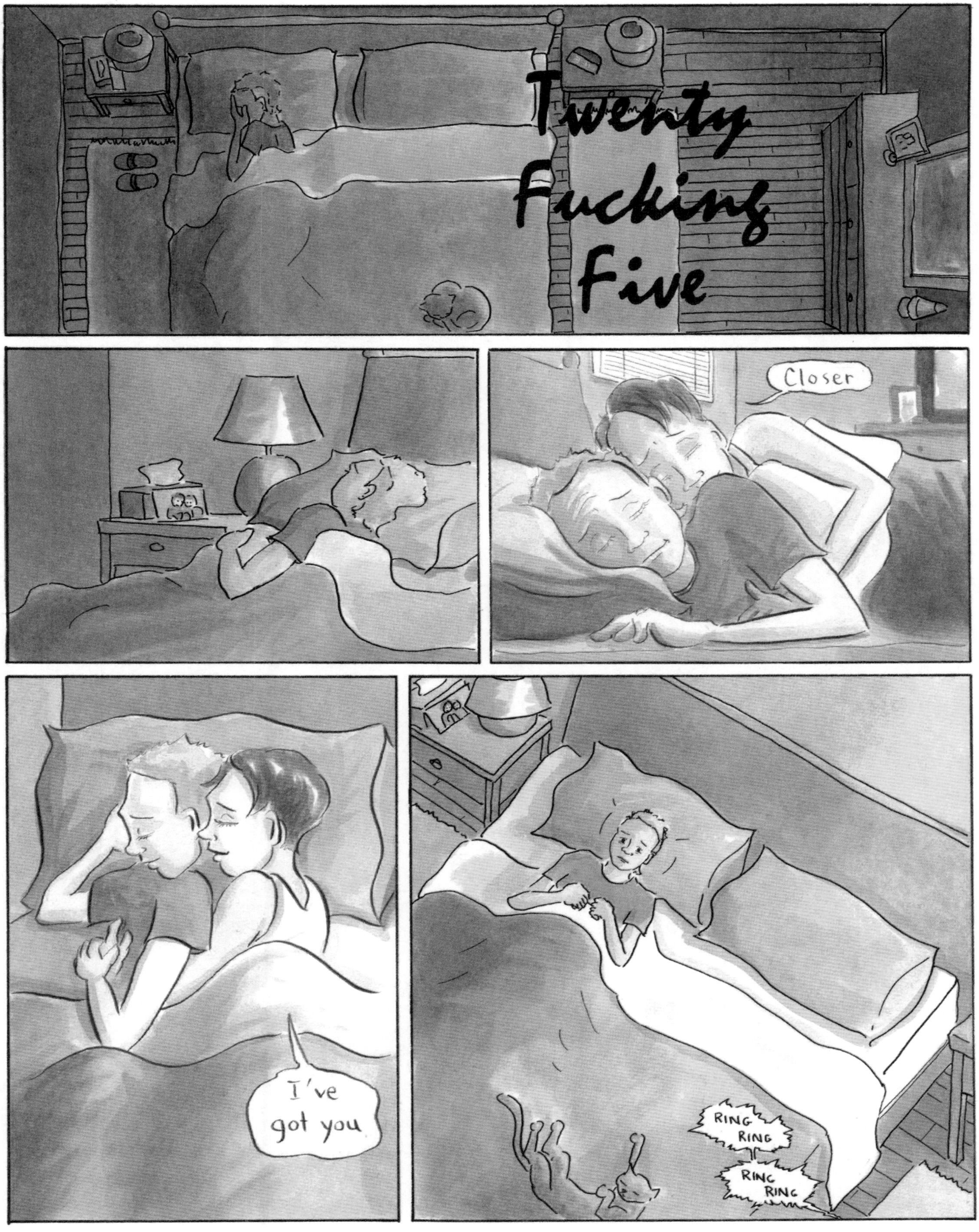

Twenty Fucking Five
Closer
I've got you
RING RING
RING RING

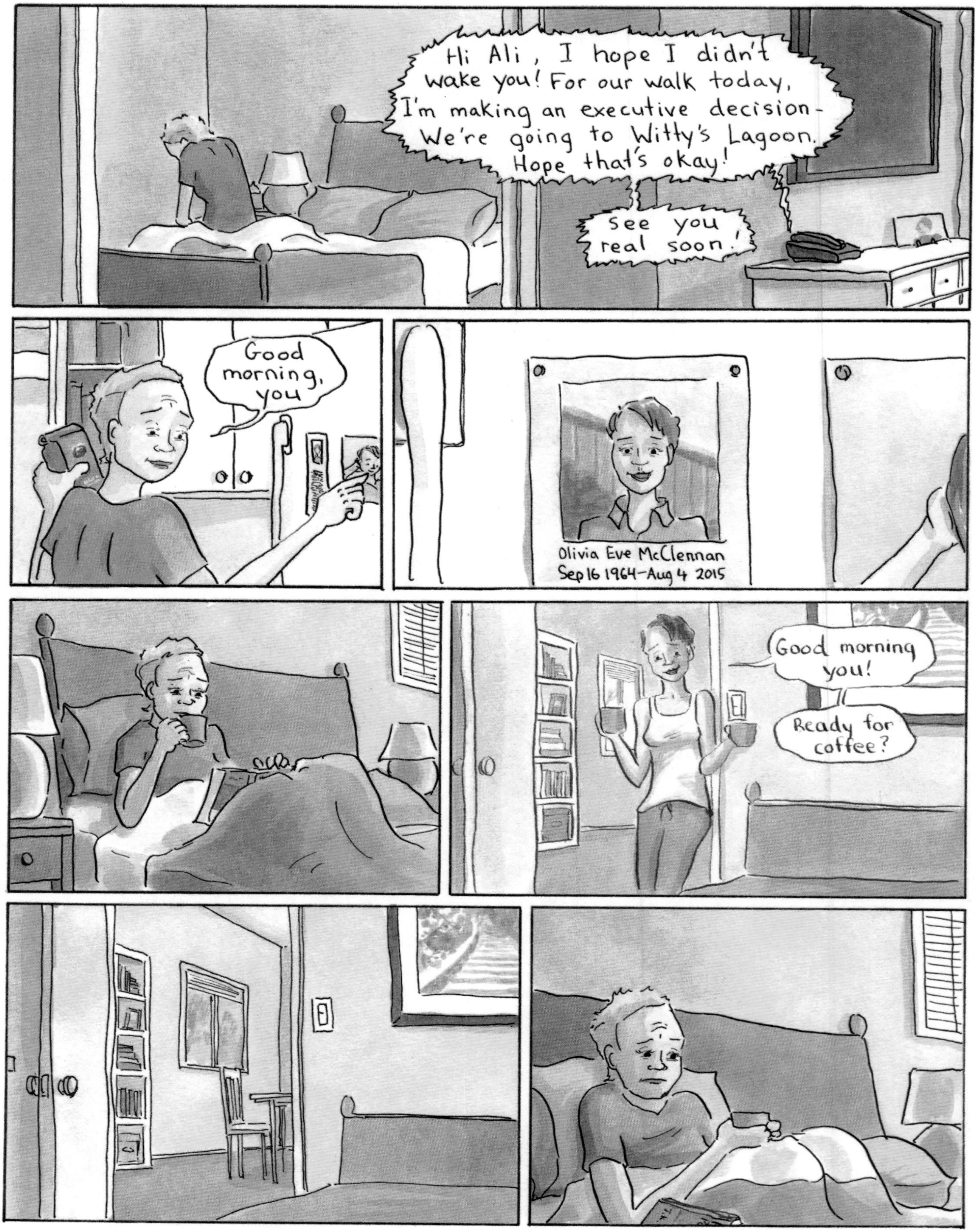
Hi Ali, I hope I didn't wake you! For our walk today, I'm making an executive decision- We're going to Witty's Lagoon. Hope that's okay!
See you real soon!
Good morning, you
Olivia Eve McClennan
Sep 16 1964–Aug 4 2015
Good morning you!
Ready for coffee?

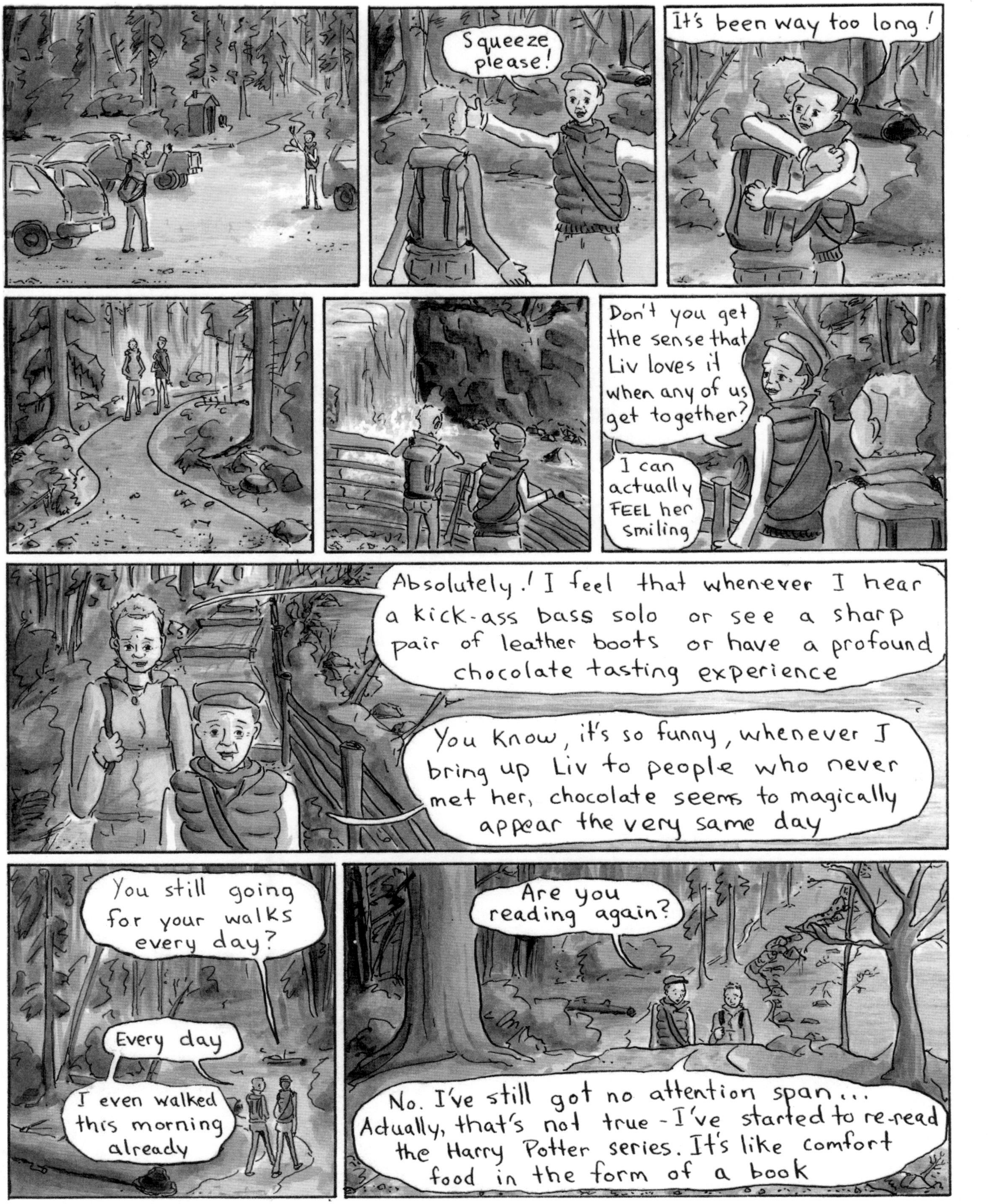
Squeeze please!
It's been way too long!
Don't you get the sense that Liv loves it when any of us get together?
I can actually FEEL her smiling
Absolutely! I feel that whenever I hear a kick-ass bass solo or see a sharp pair of leather boots or have a profound chocolate tasting experience
You know, it's so funny, whenever I bring up Liv to people who never met her, chocolate seems to magically appear the very same day
You still going for your walks every day?
Every day
I even walked this morning already
Are you reading again?
No. I've still got no attention span... Actually, that's not true - I've started to re-read the Harry Potter series. It's like comfort food in the form of a book

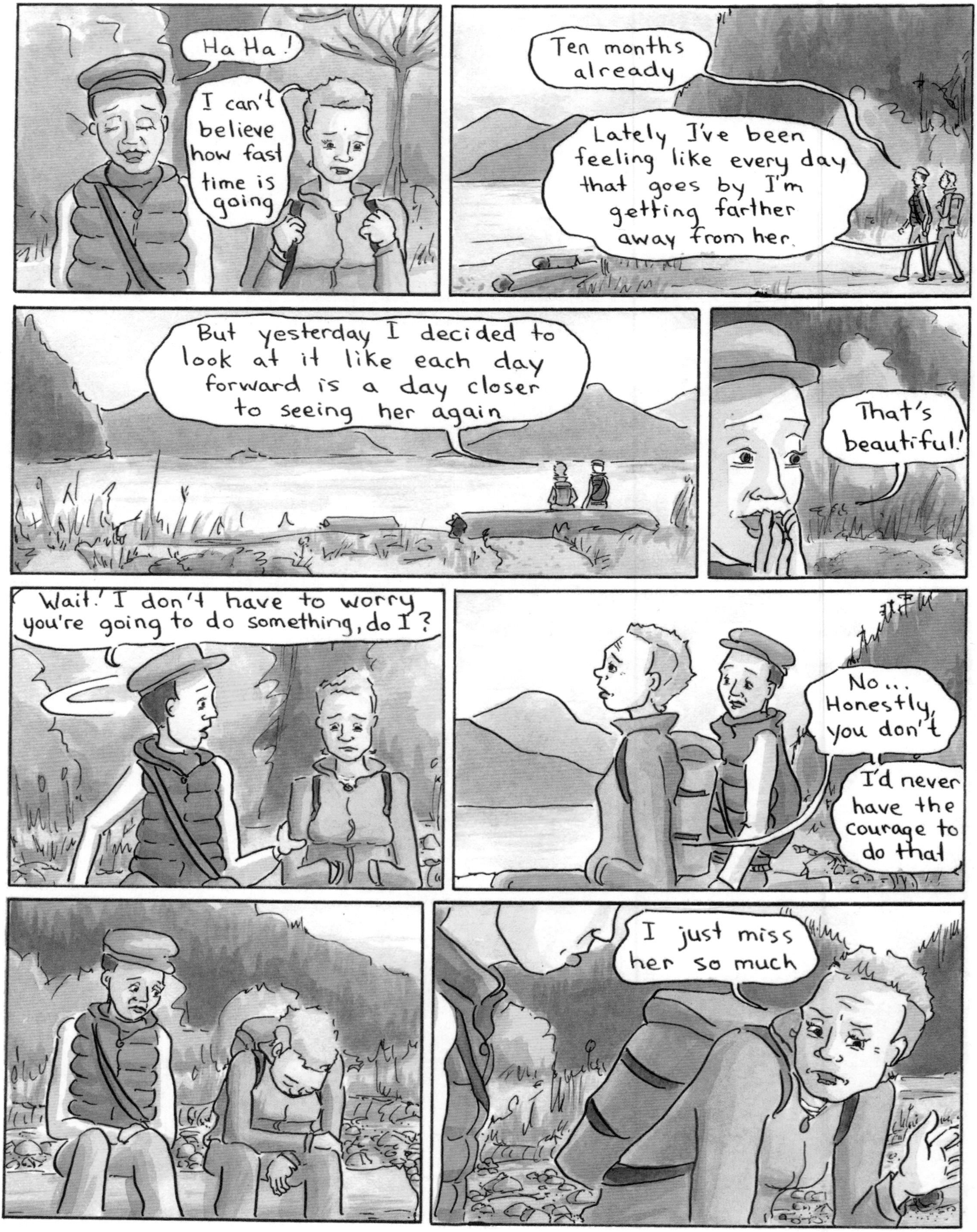
Ha Ha!
I can't believe how fast time is going
Ten months already
Lately I've been feeling like every day that goes by I'm getting farther away from her.
But yesterday I decided to look at it like each day forward is a day closer to seeing her again
That's beautiful!
Wait! I don't have to worry you're going to do something, do I?
No... Honestly, you don't
I'd never have the courage to do that
I just miss her so much

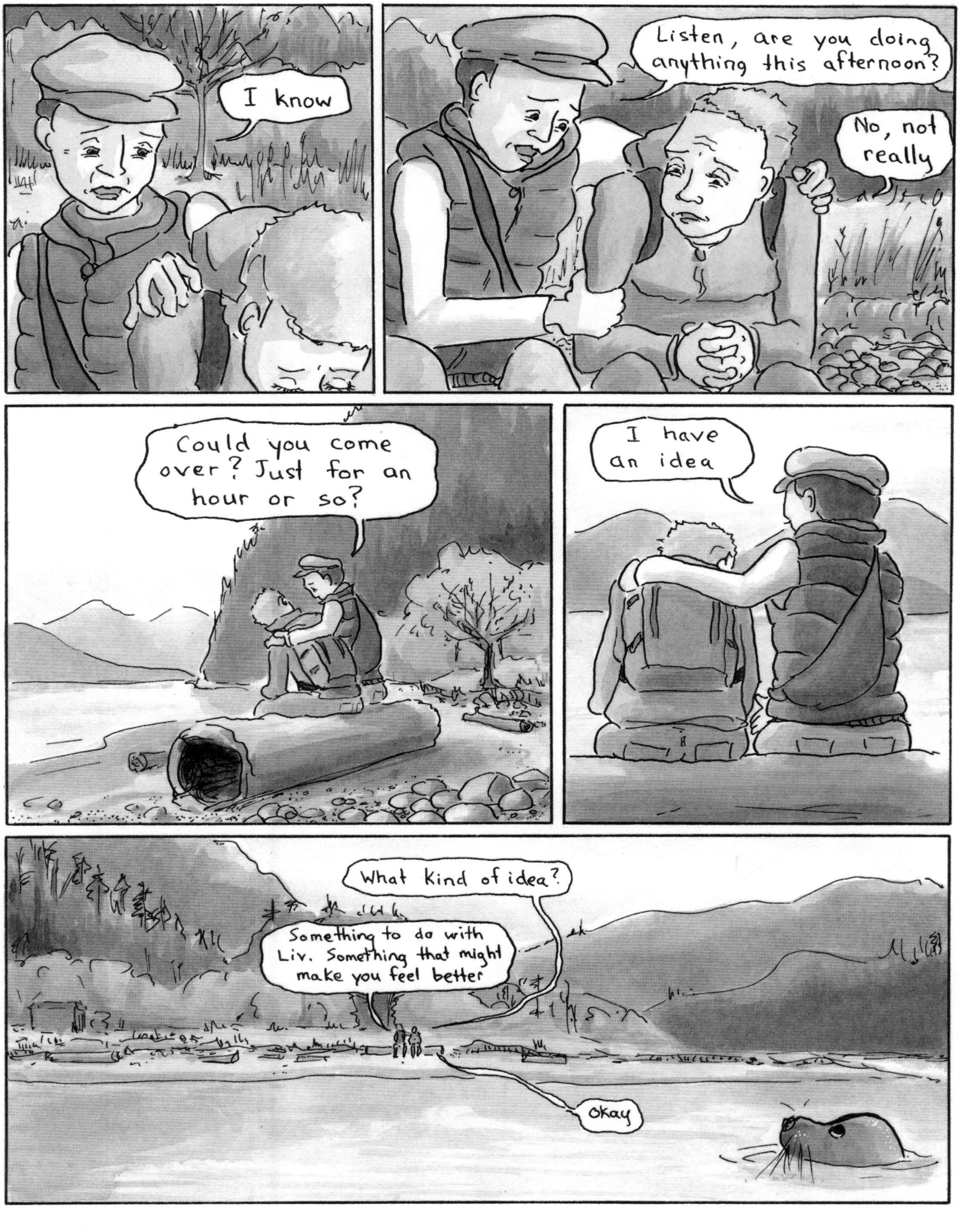
I know
Listen, are you doing anything this afternoon?
No, not really
Could you come over? Just for an hour or so?
I have an idea
What kind of idea?
Something to do with Liv. Something that might make you feel better
Okay

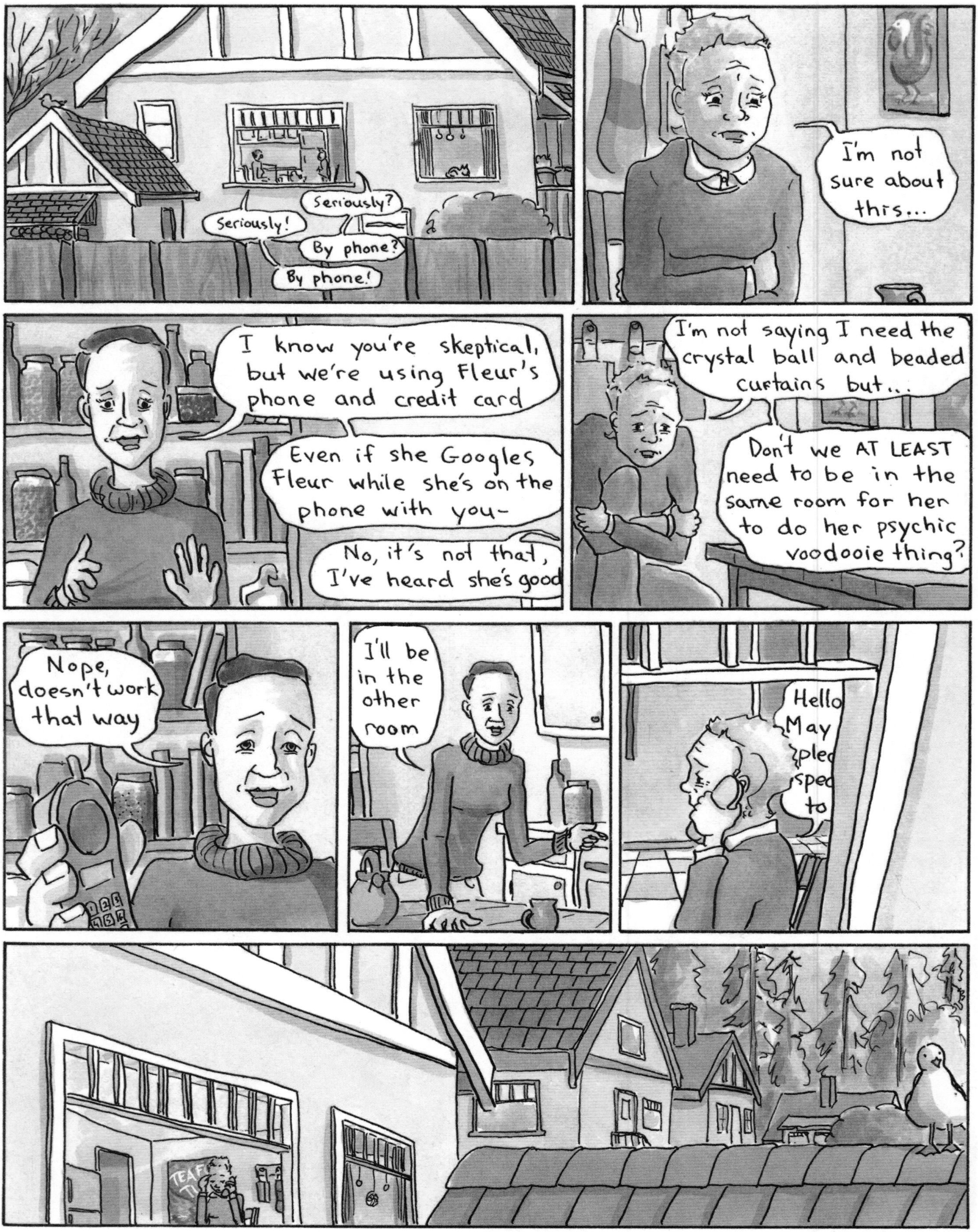
Seriously!
Seriously?
By phone!
By phone?
I'm not sure about this...
I know you're skeptical, but we're using Fleur's phone and credit card
Even if she Googles Fleur while she's on the phone with you-
No, it's not that, I've heard she's good
I'm not saying I need the crystal ball and beaded curtains but...
Don't we AT LEAST need to be in the same room for her to do her psychic voodooie thing?
Nope, doesn't work that way
I'll be in the other room
Hello May ple spe to

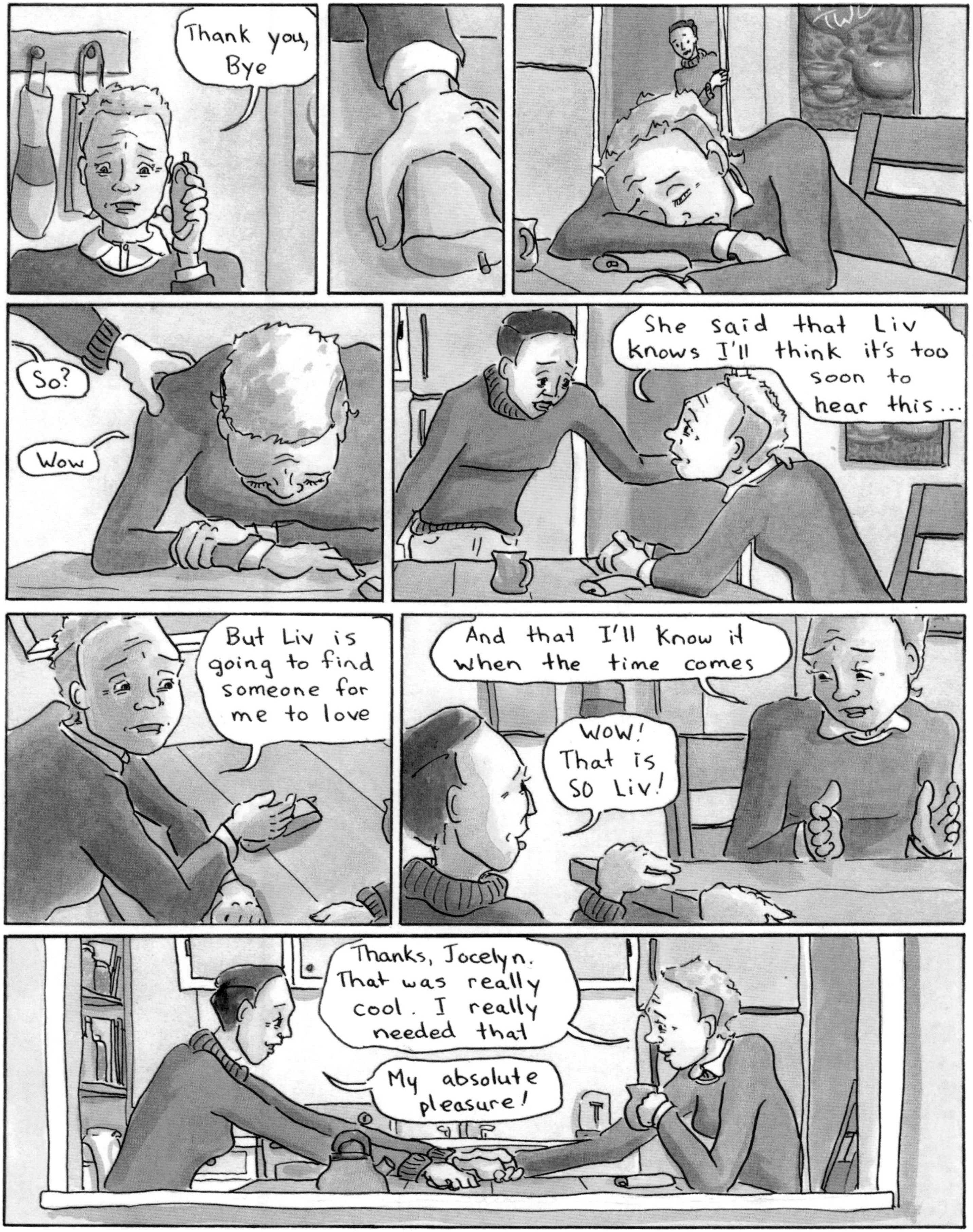
Thank you, Bye
So?
Wow
She said that Liv knows I'll think it's too soon to hear this...
But Liv is going to find someone for me to love
And that I'll know it when the time comes
WOW! That is SO Liv!
Thanks, Jocelyn. That was really cool. I really needed that
My absolute pleasure!

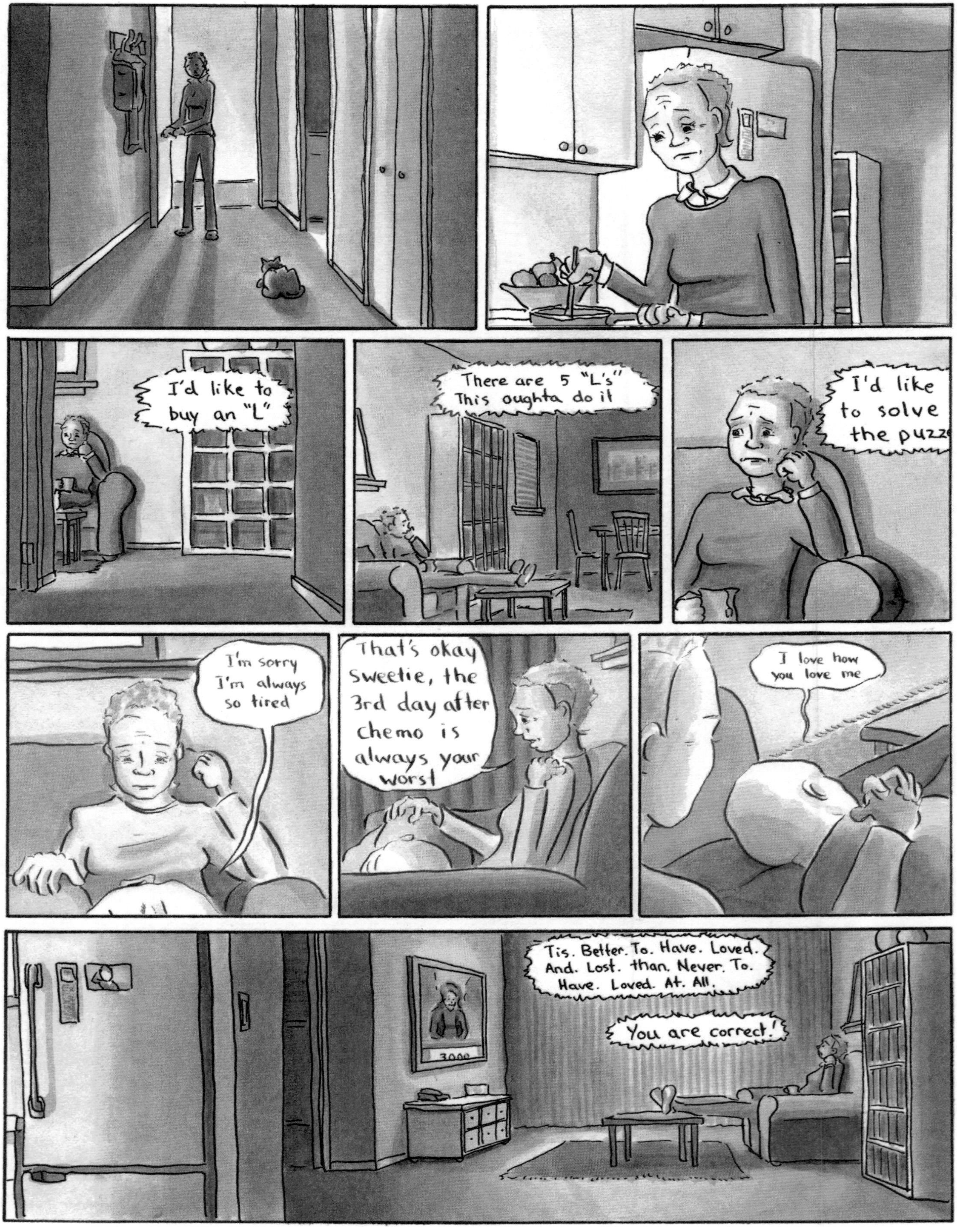

I'd like to buy an "L"
There are 5 "L's" This oughta do it
I'd like to solve the puzz
I'm sorry I'm always so tired
That's okay sweetie, the 3rd day after chemo is always your worst
I love how you love me
Tis. Better. To. Have. Loved. And. Lost. than. Never. To. Have. Loved. At. All.
You are correct!
3000

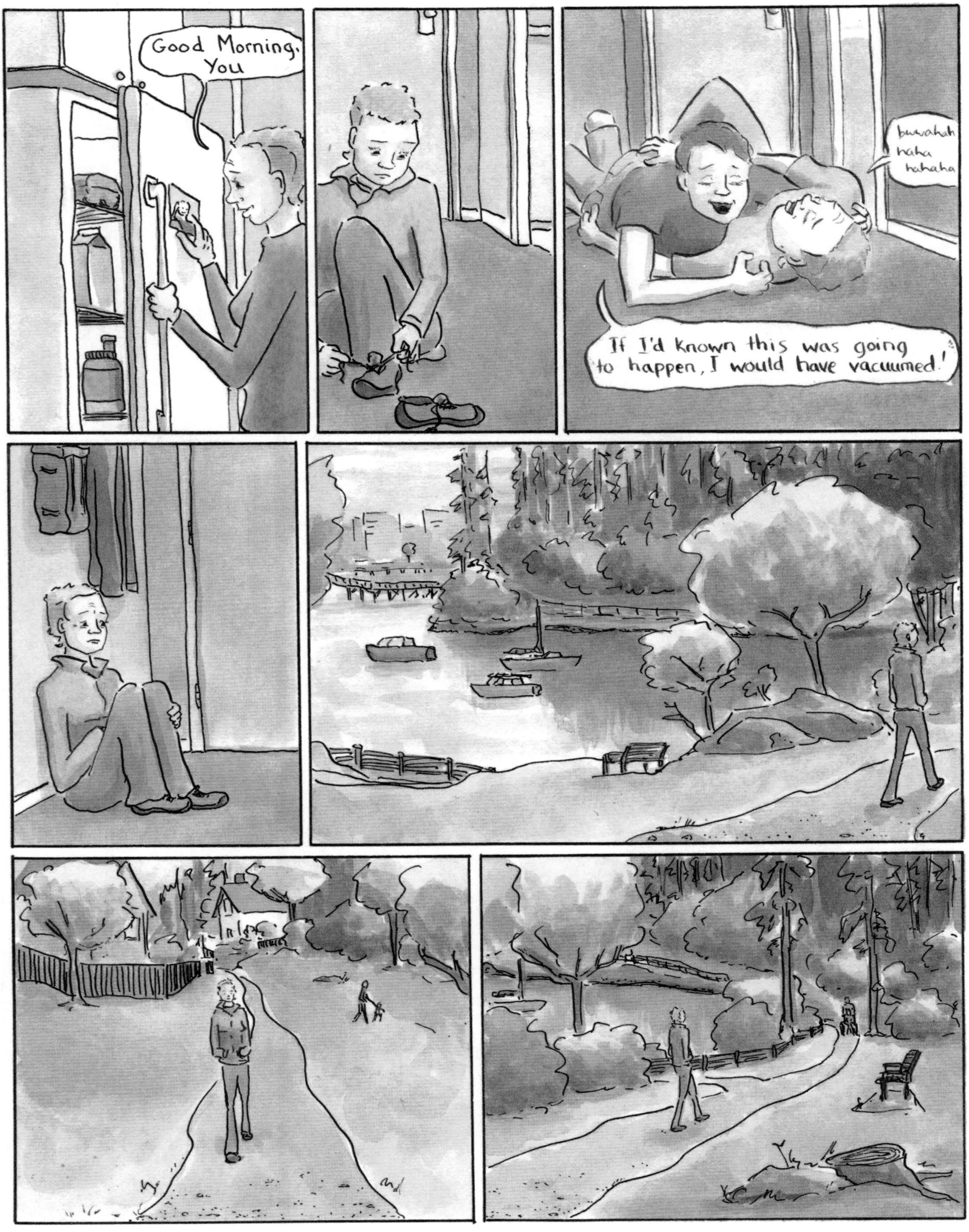
Good Morning, You
buwahah haha hahaha
If I'd known this was going to happen, I would have vacuumed!

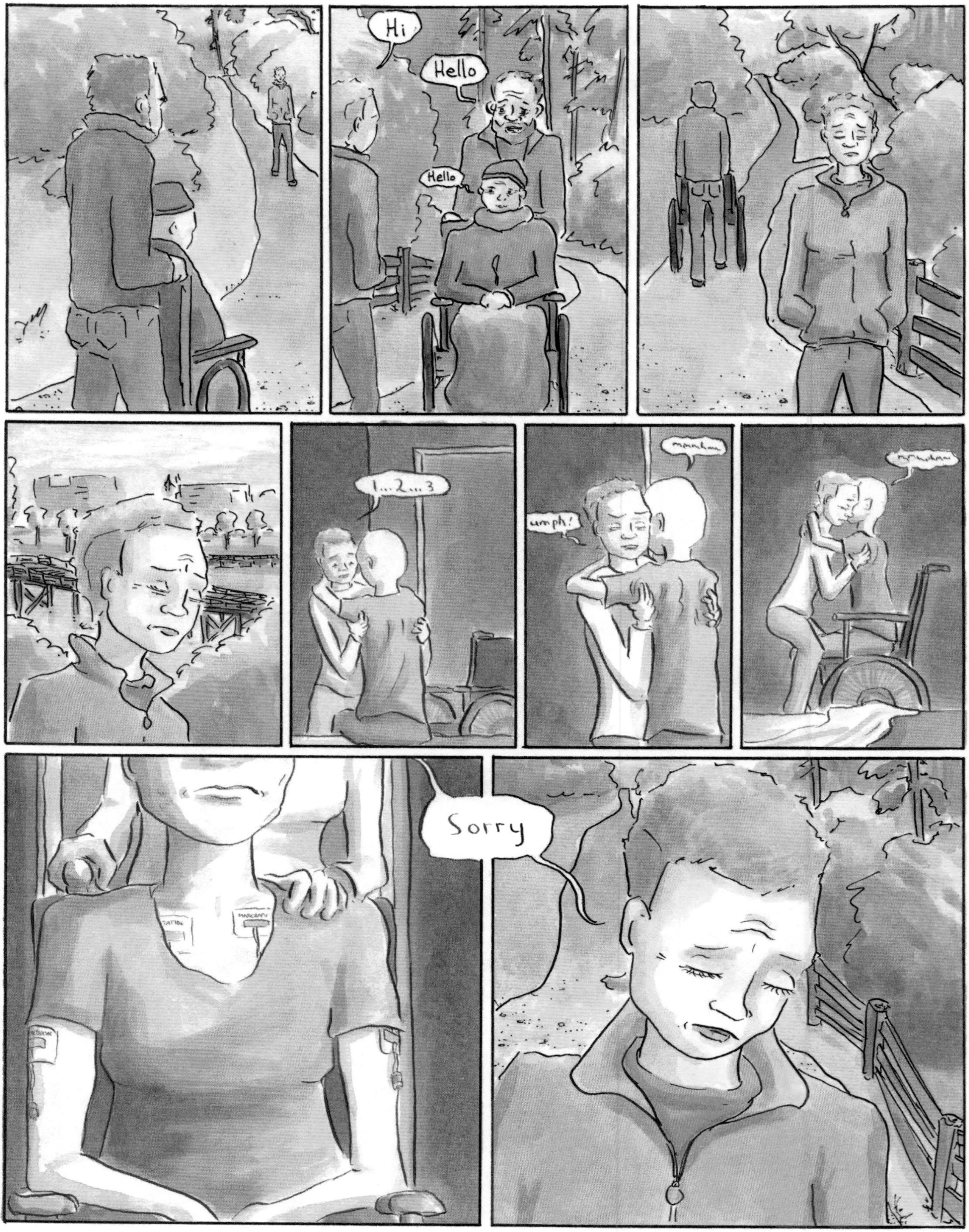
Hi
Hello
Hello
1...2...3
mmmhmm
umph!
mmmhmm
Sorry

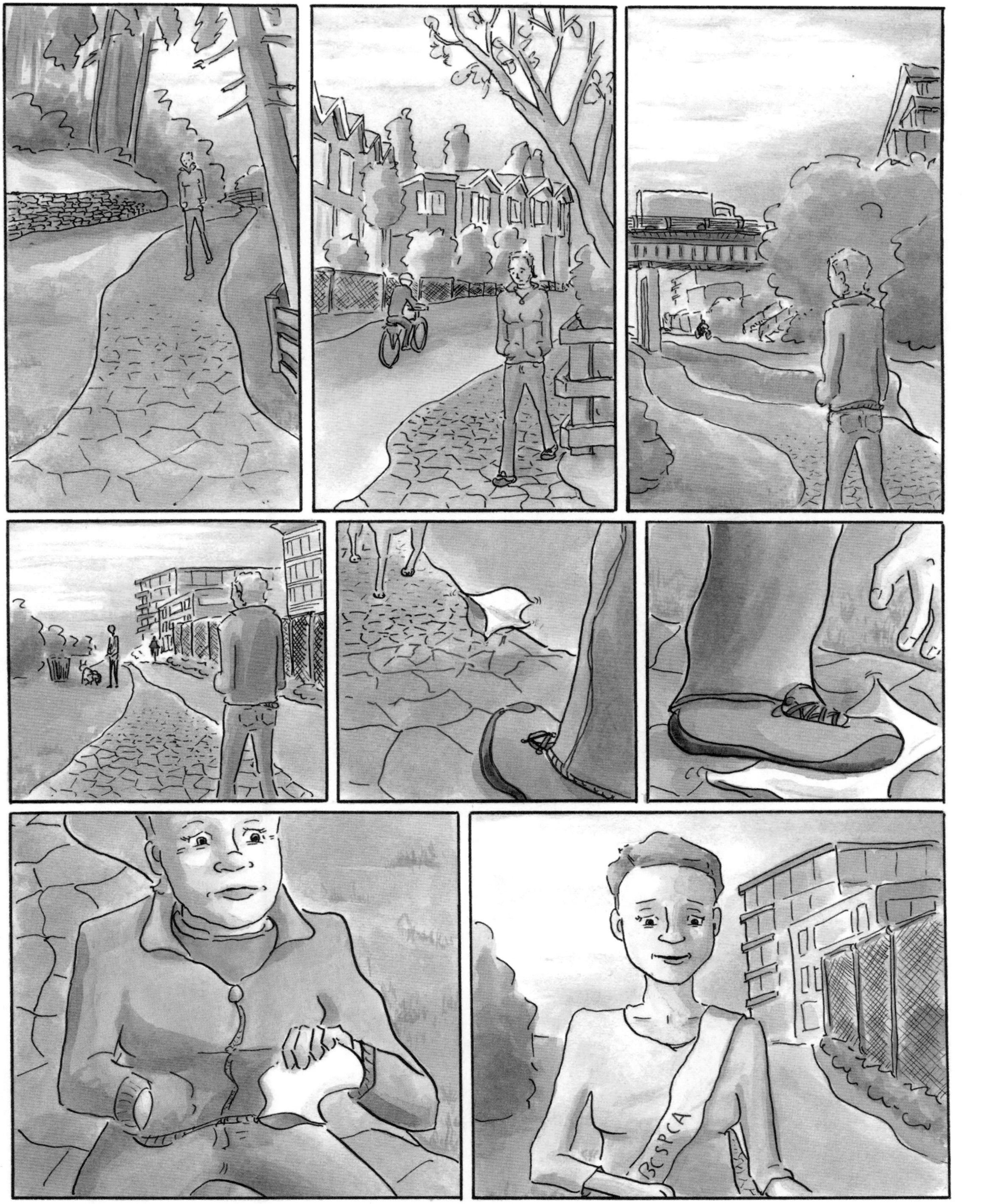
BCSPCA

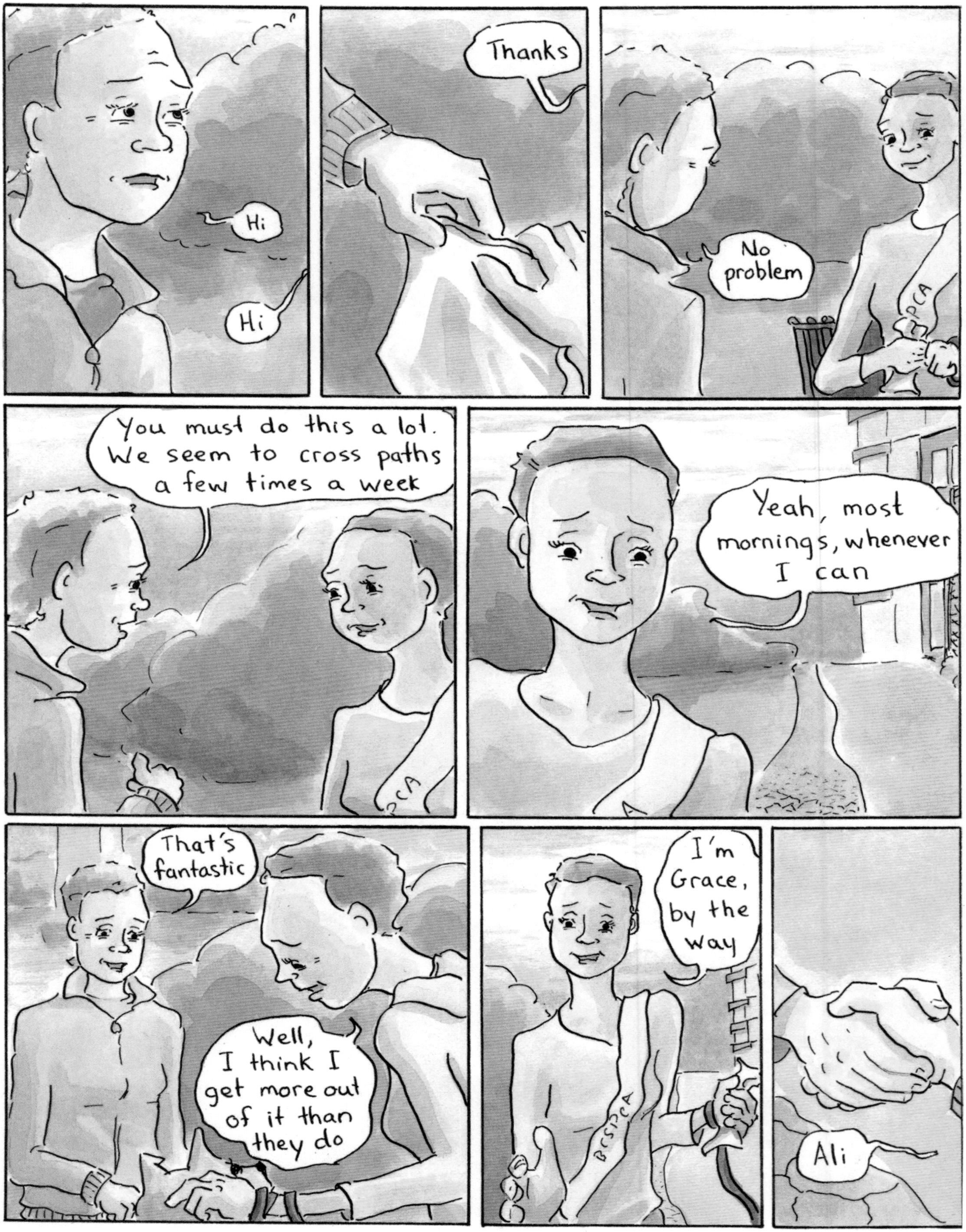
Hi
Hi
Thanks
No problem
You must do this a lot. We seem to cross paths a few times a week
Yeah, most mornings, whenever I can
That's fantastic
Well, I think I get more out of it than they do
I'm Grace, by the way
Ali

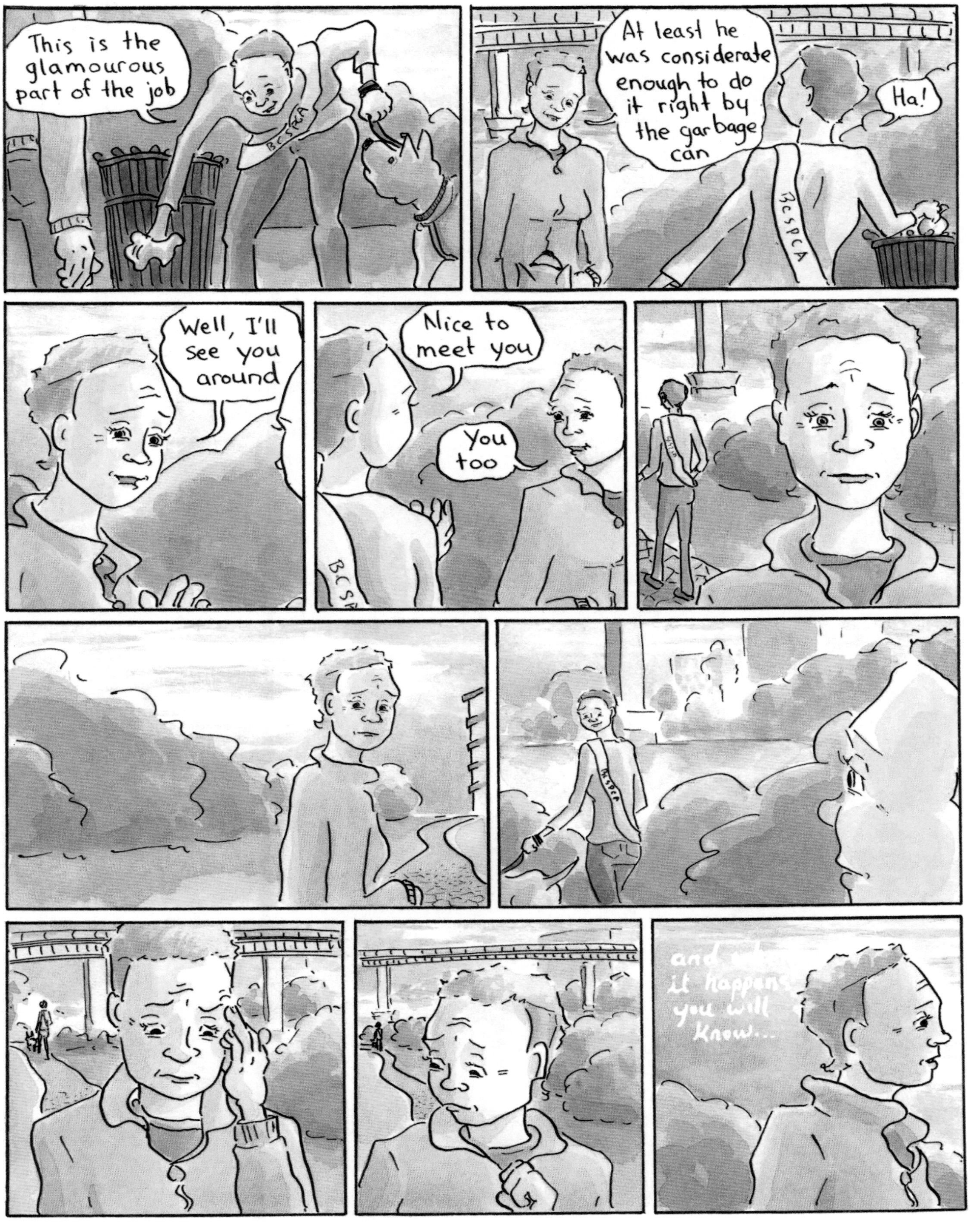
This is the glamourous part of the job
BCSPCA
At least he was considerate enough to do it right by the garbage can
Ha!
BCSPCA
Well, I'll see you around
Nice to meet you
You too
BCSPCA
and
it happens
you will
know...

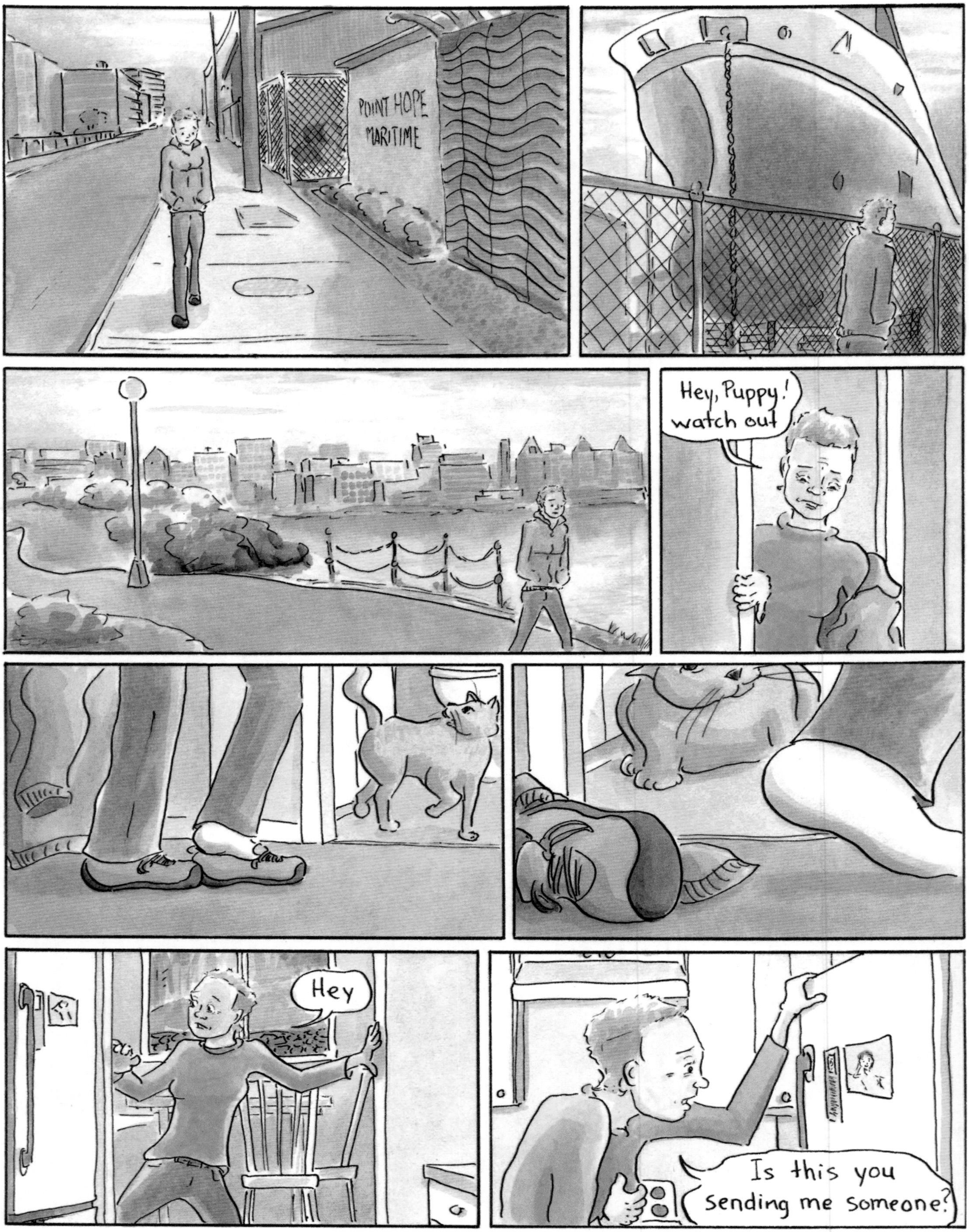
POINT HOPE MARITIME
Hey, Puppy! watch out
Hey
Is this you sending me someone?

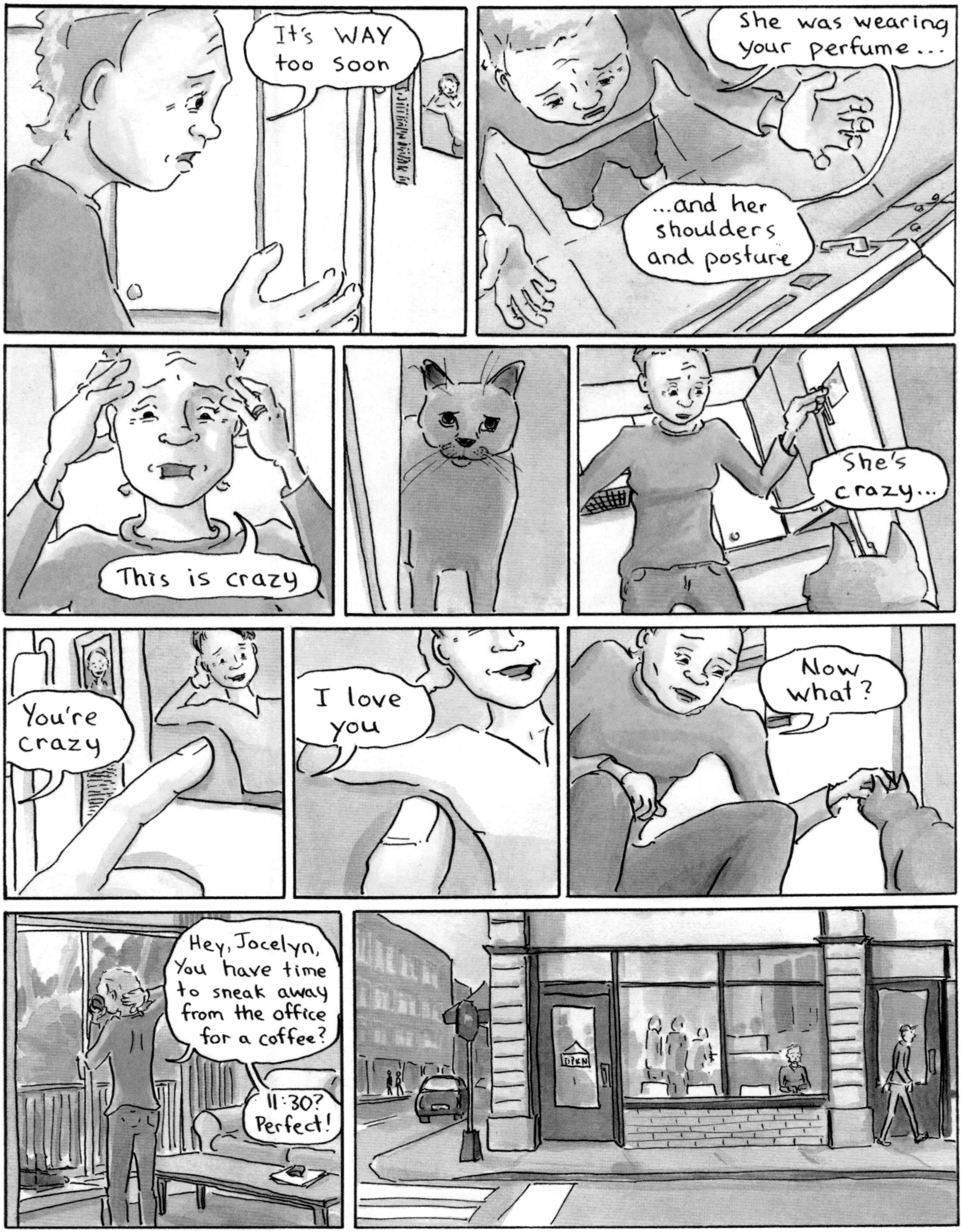
It's WAY too soon
She was wearing your perfume...
...and her shoulders and posture
This is crazy
She's crazy...
You're crazy
I love you
Now what?
Hey, Jocelyn, You have time to sneak away from the office for a coffee?
11:30? Perfect!
OPEN

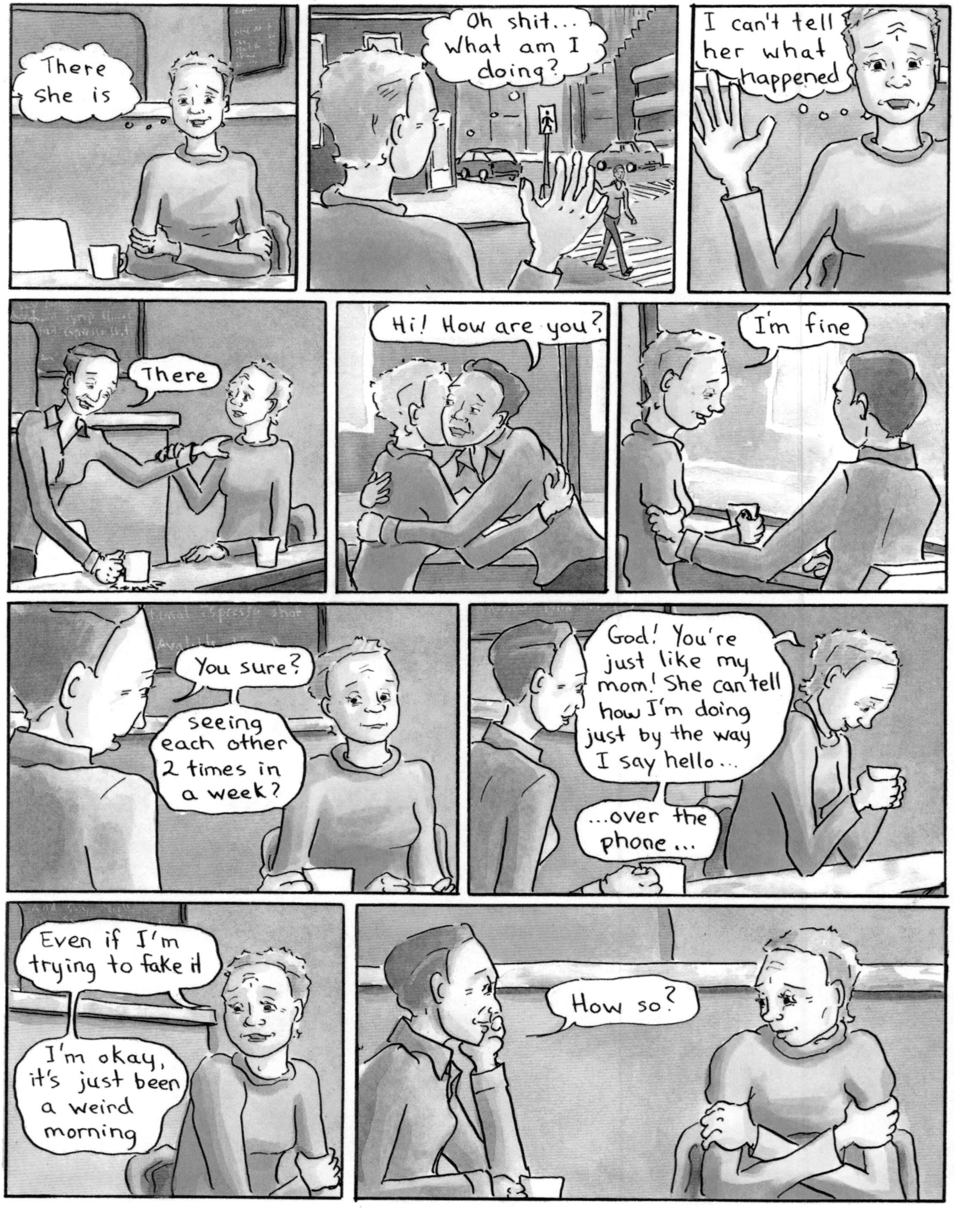
There she is
Oh shit... What am I doing?
I can't tell her what happened
There
Hi! How are you?
I'm fine
You sure?
seeing each other 2 times in a week?
God! You're just like my mom! She can tell how I'm doing just by the way I say hello...
...over the phone...
Even if I'm trying to fake it
I'm okay, it's just been a weird morning
How so?

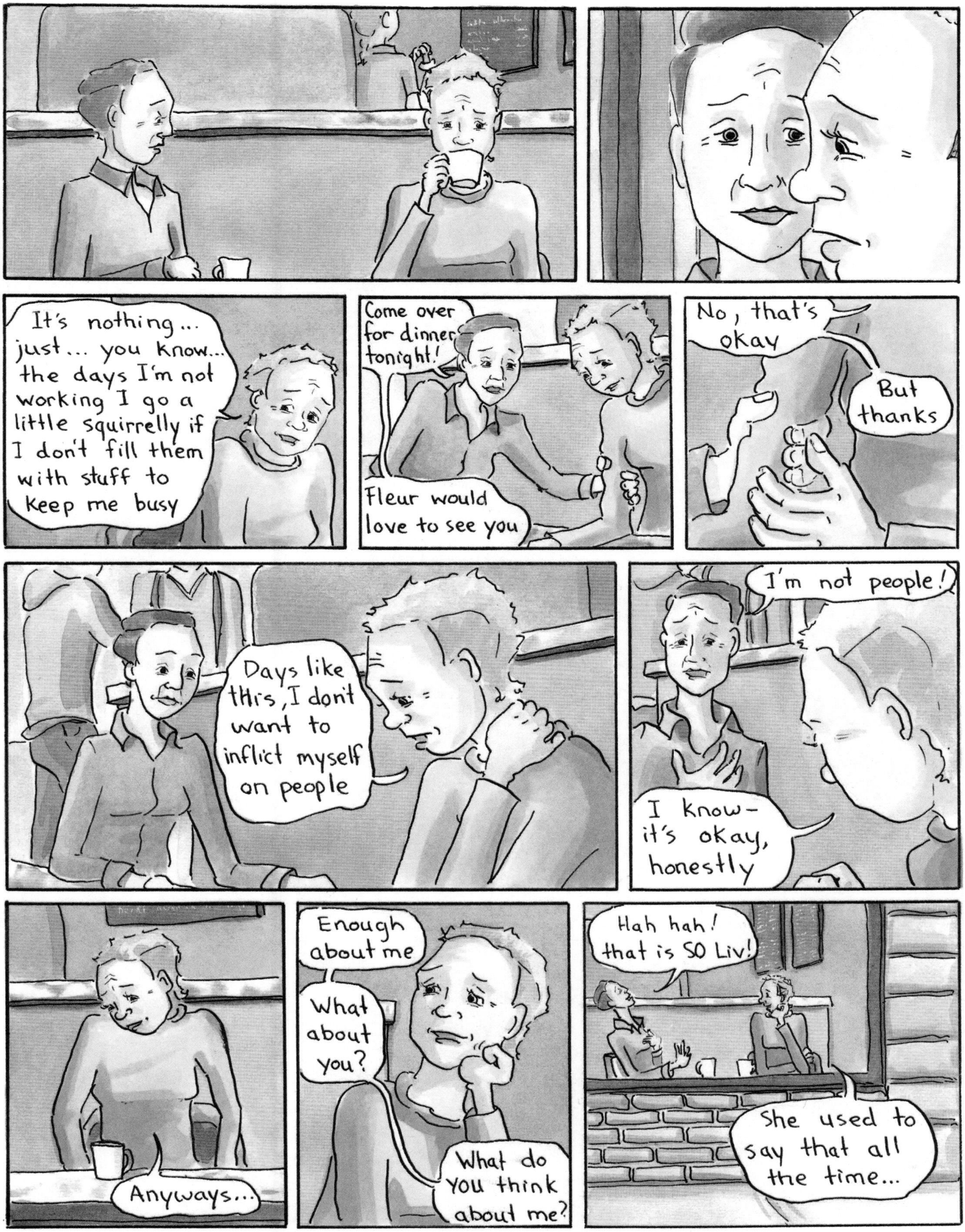
It's nothing... just... you know... the days I'm not working I go a little squirrelly if I don't fill them with stuff to keep me busy
Come over for dinner tonight!
Fleur would love to see you
No, that's okay
But thanks
Days like this, I don't want to inflict myself on people
I'm not people!
I know- it's okay, honestly
Anyways...
Enough about me
What about you?
What do you think about me?
Hah hah! that is SO Liv!
She used to say that all the time...

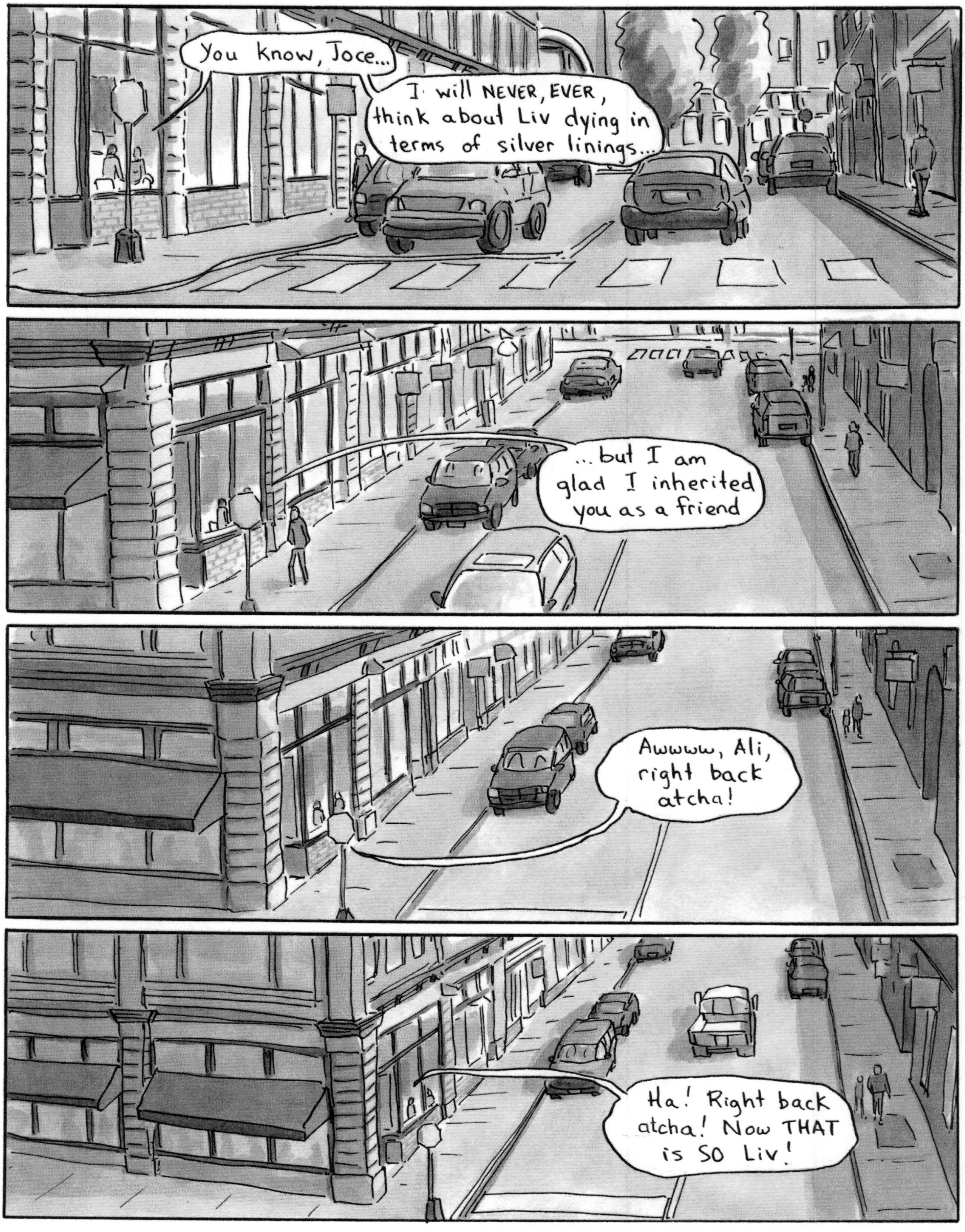
You know, Joce...
I will NEVER, EVER, think about Liv dying in terms of silver linings...
...but I am glad I inherited you as a friend
Awwww, Ali, right back atcha!
Ha! Right back atcha! Now THAT is SO Liv!

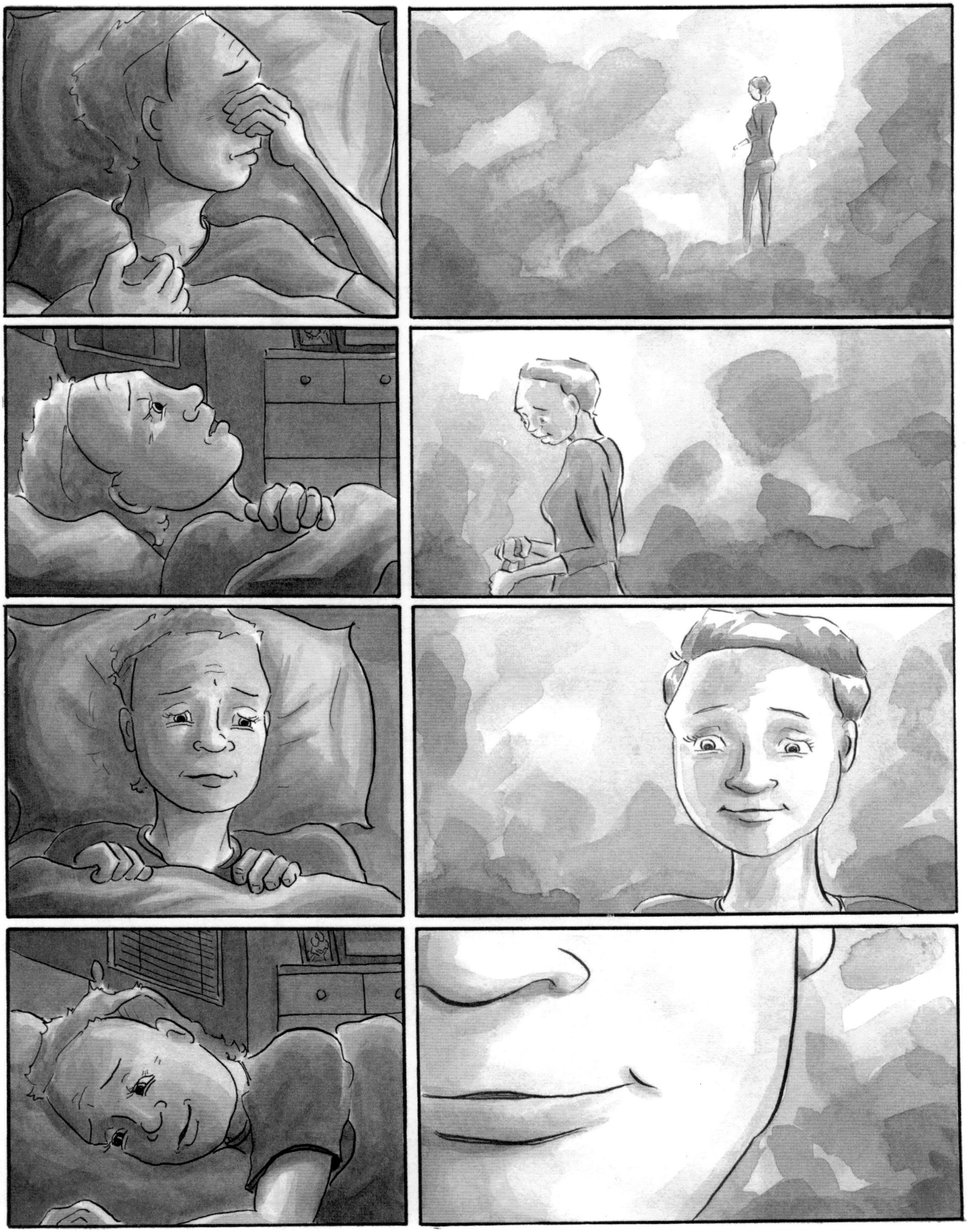

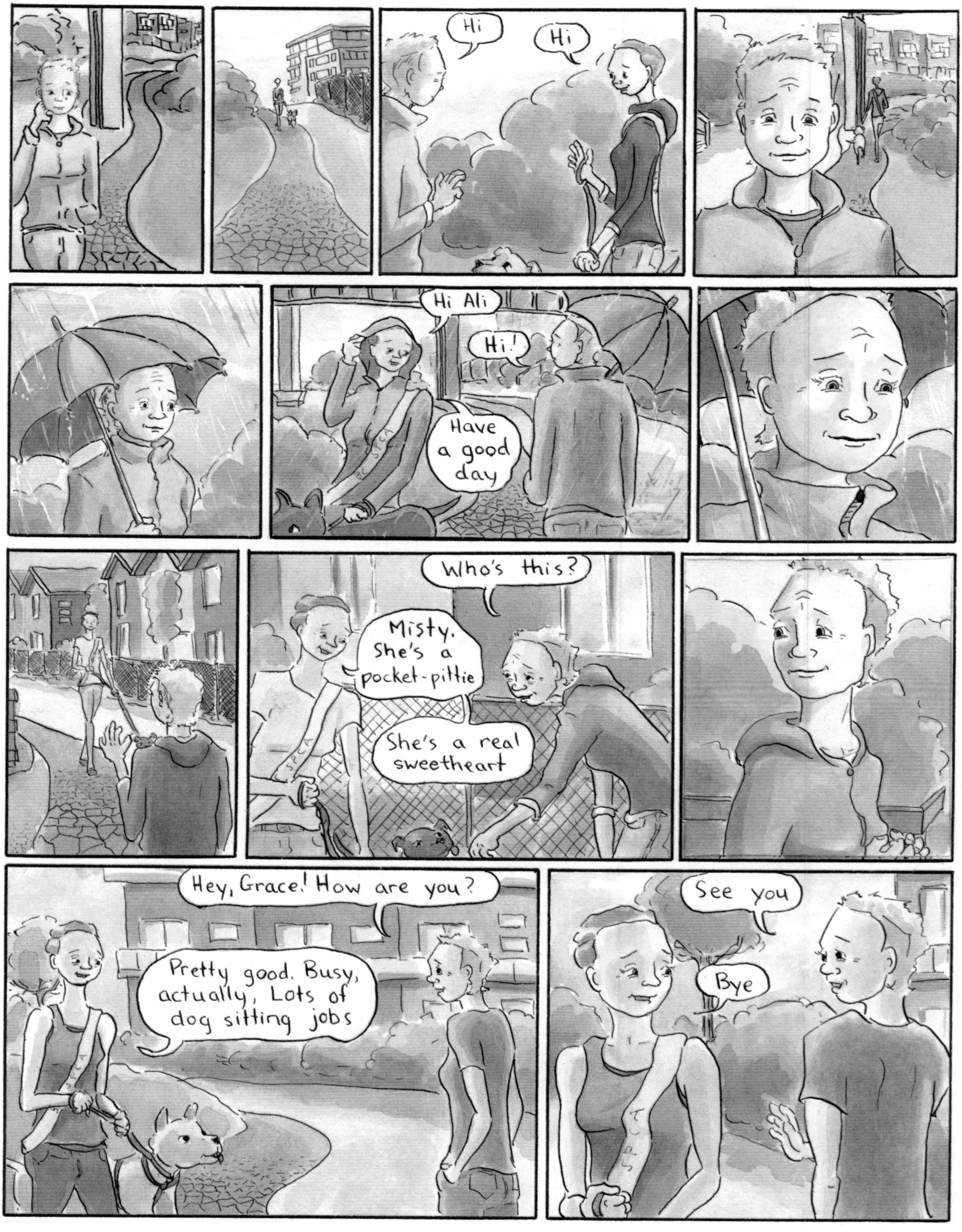
Hi
Hi
Hi Ali
Hi!
Have a good day
Who's this?
Misty. She's a pocket-pittie
She's a real sweetheart
Hey, Grace! How are you?
Pretty good. Busy, actually, Lots of dog sitting jobs
See you
Bye

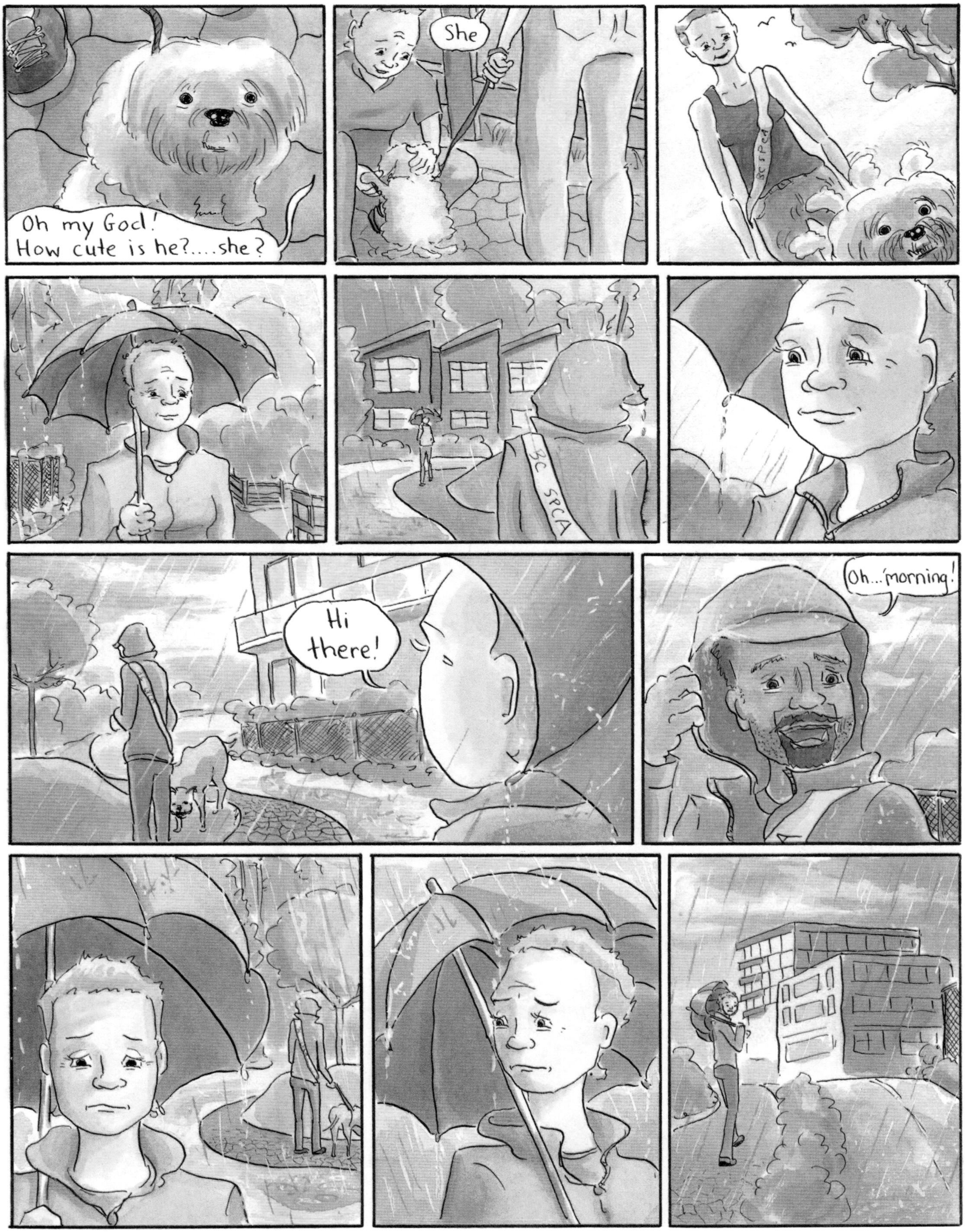
Oh my God!
How cute is he?....she?
She
Hi there!
Oh...morning!

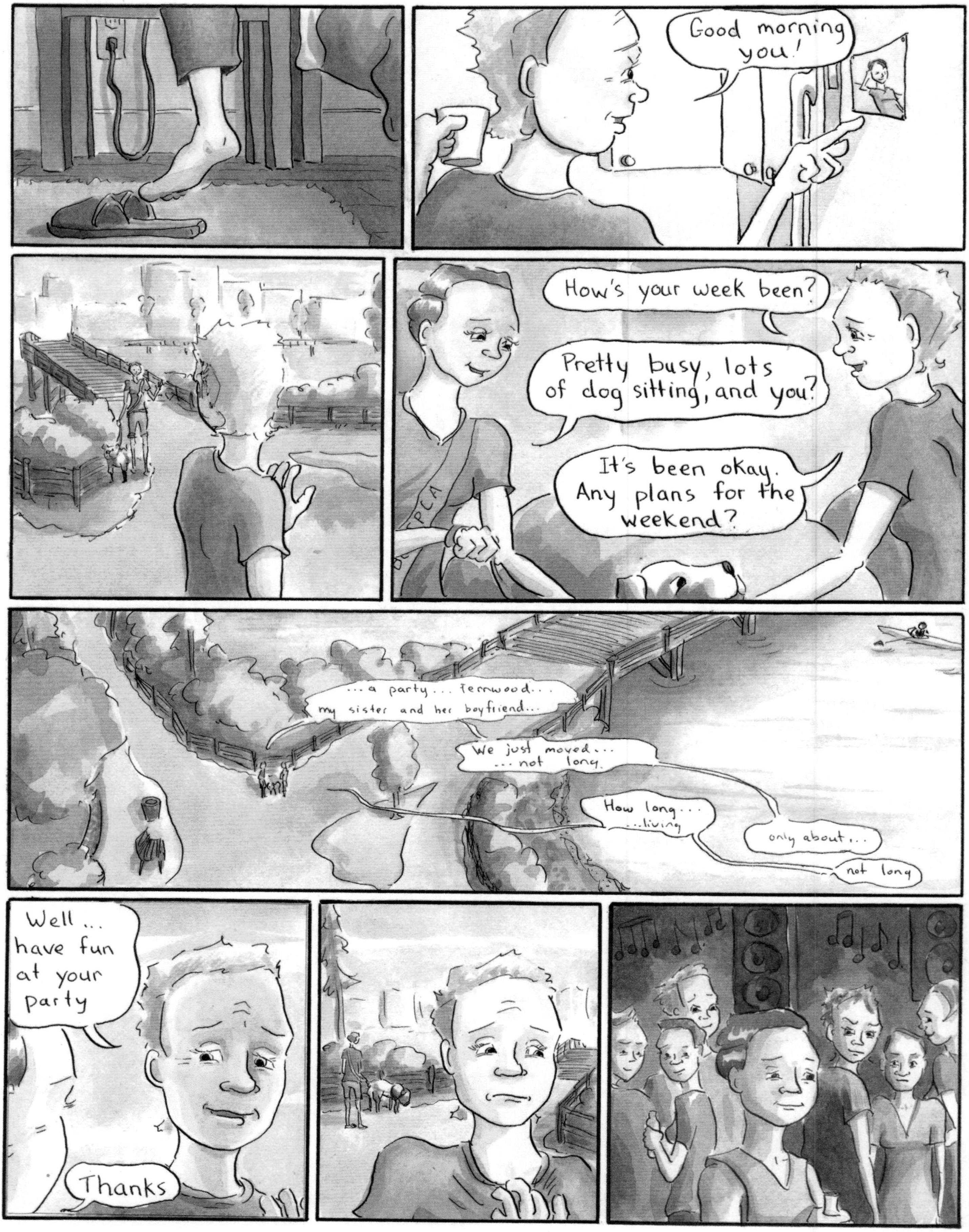
Good morning you!
How's your week been?
Pretty busy, lots of dog sitting, and you?
It's been okay. Any plans for the weekend?
PLA
... a party ... Fernwood... my sister and her boyfriend...
We just moved... ... not long.
How long... ...living
only about...
not long
Well ... have fun at your party
Thanks

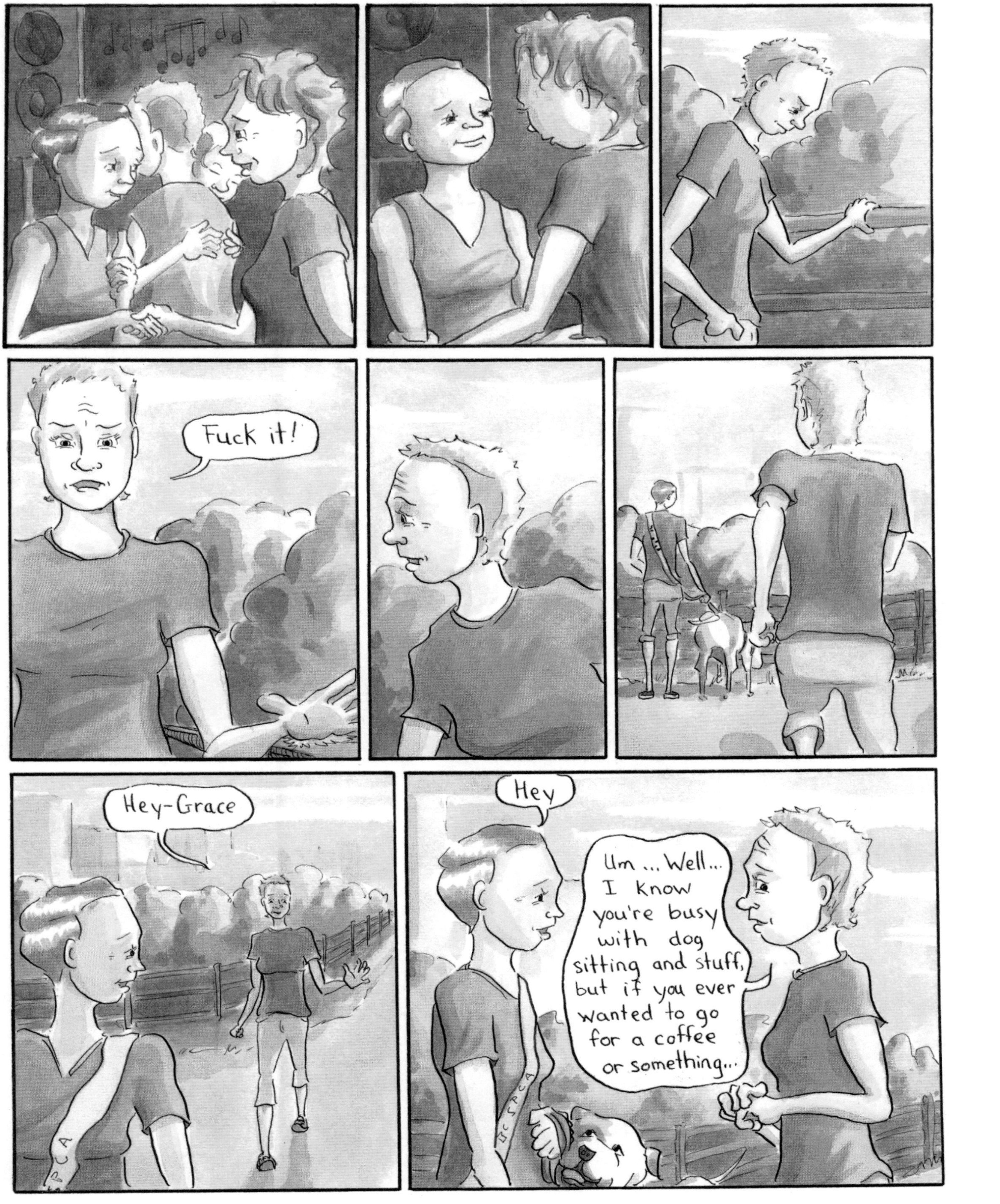
Fuck it!
Hey-Grace
Hey
Um ... Well... I know you're busy with dog sitting and stuff, but if you ever wanted to go for a coffee or something...

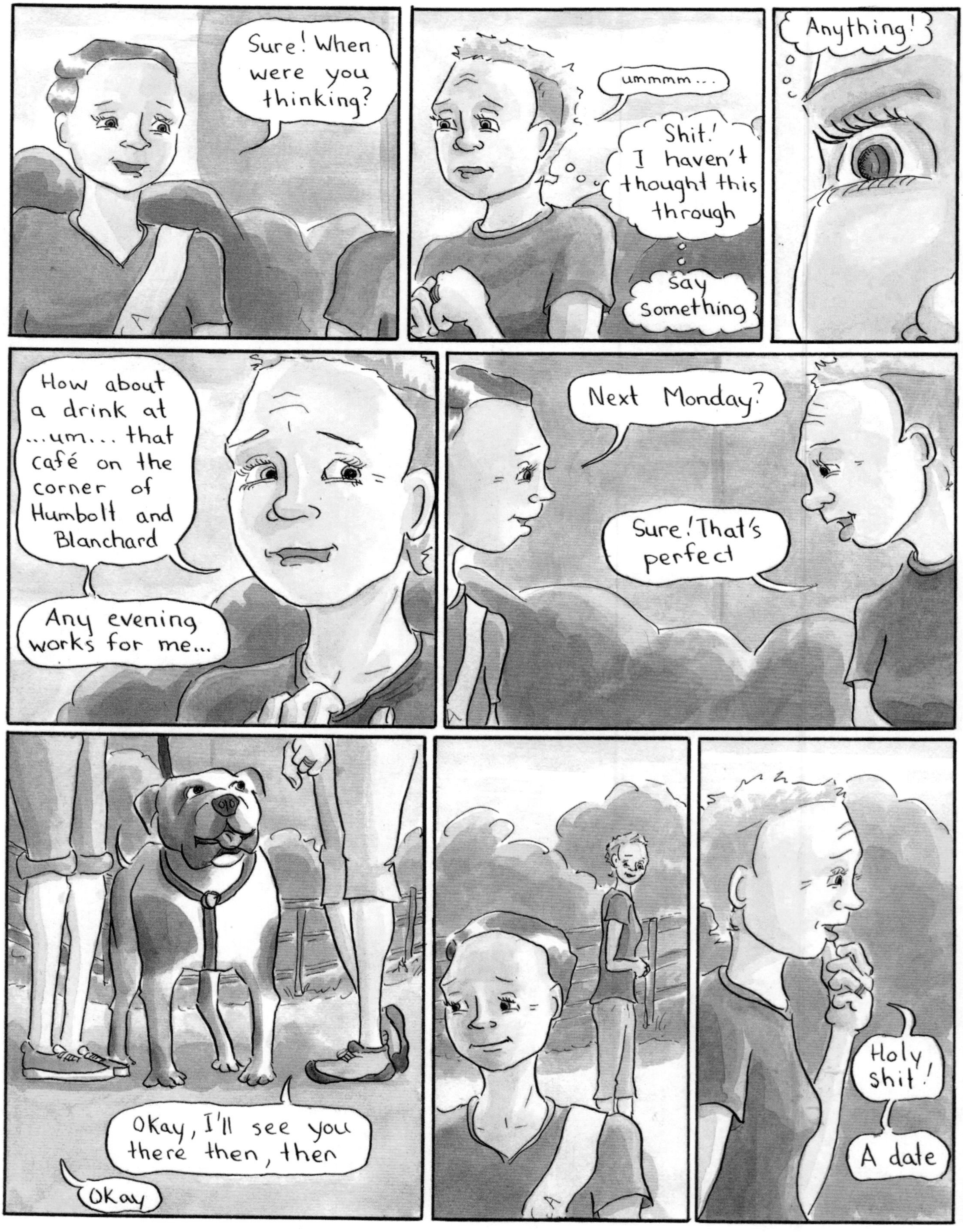
Sure! When were you thinking?
ummmm...
Shit! I haven't thought this through
say something
Anything!
How about a drink at ...um... that café on the corner of Humbolt and Blanchard
Any evening works for me...
Next Monday?
Sure! That's perfect
Okay, I'll see you there then, then
Okay
Holy shit!
A date

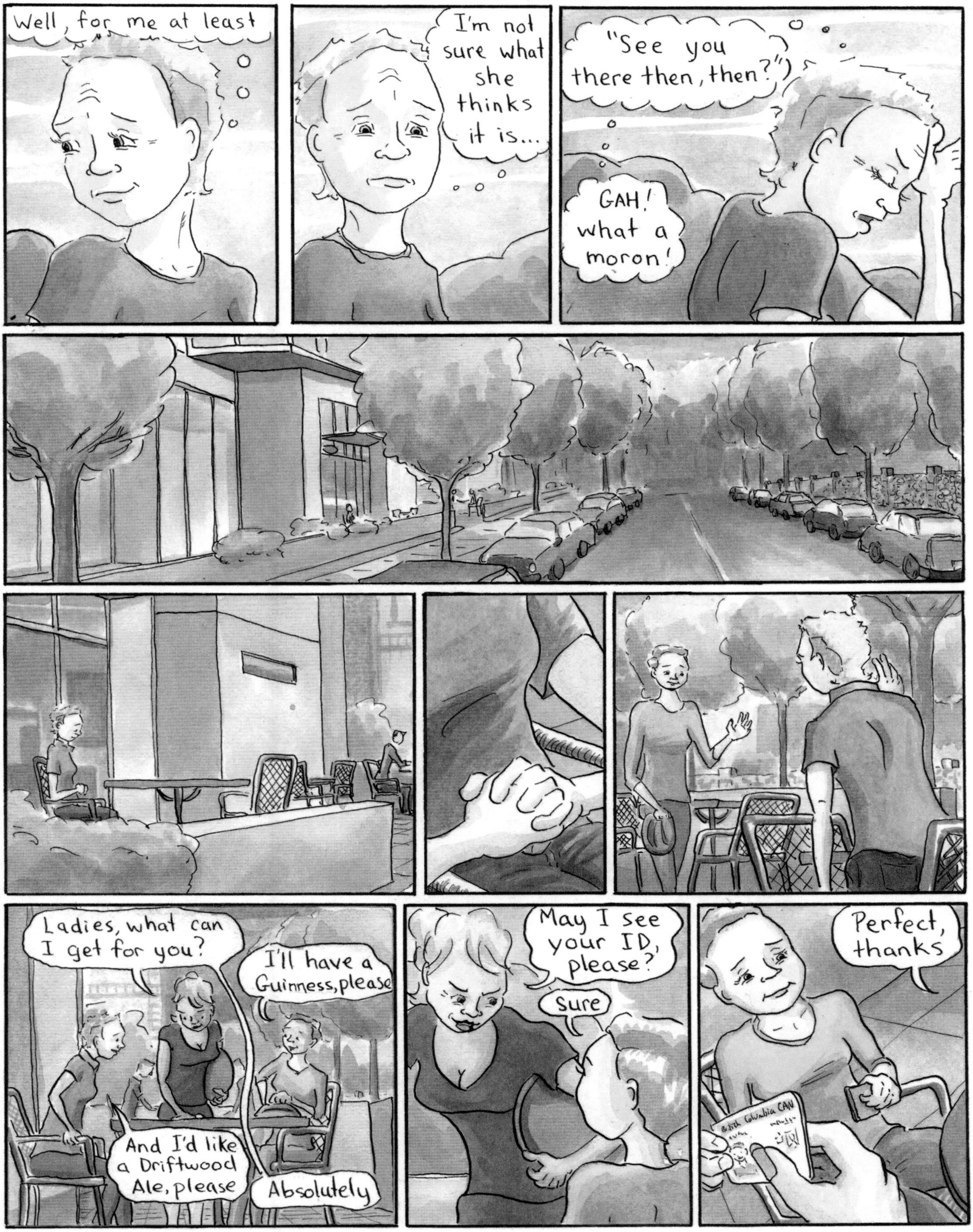
Well, for me at least
I'm not sure what she thinks it is...
"See you there then, then?"
GAH! what a moron!
Ladies, what can I get for you?
I'll have a Guinness, please
And I'd like a Driftwood Ale, please
Absolutely
May I see your ID, please?
Sure
Perfect, thanks

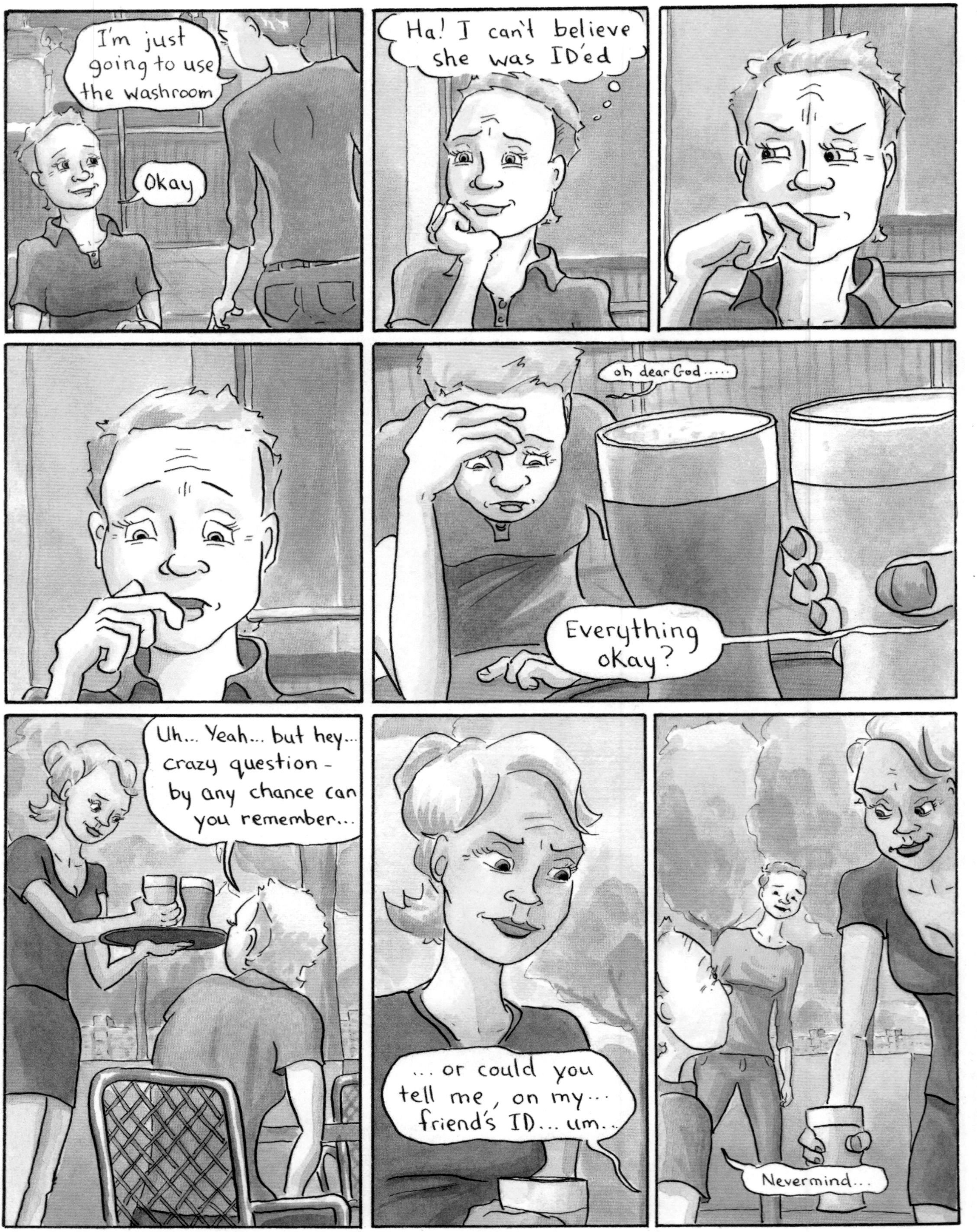
I'm just going to use the washroom
Okay
Ha! I can't believe she was ID'ed
oh dear God.....
Everything okay?
Uh... Yeah... but hey... crazy question - by any chance can you remember...
... or could you tell me, on my... friend's ID... um...
Nevermind...

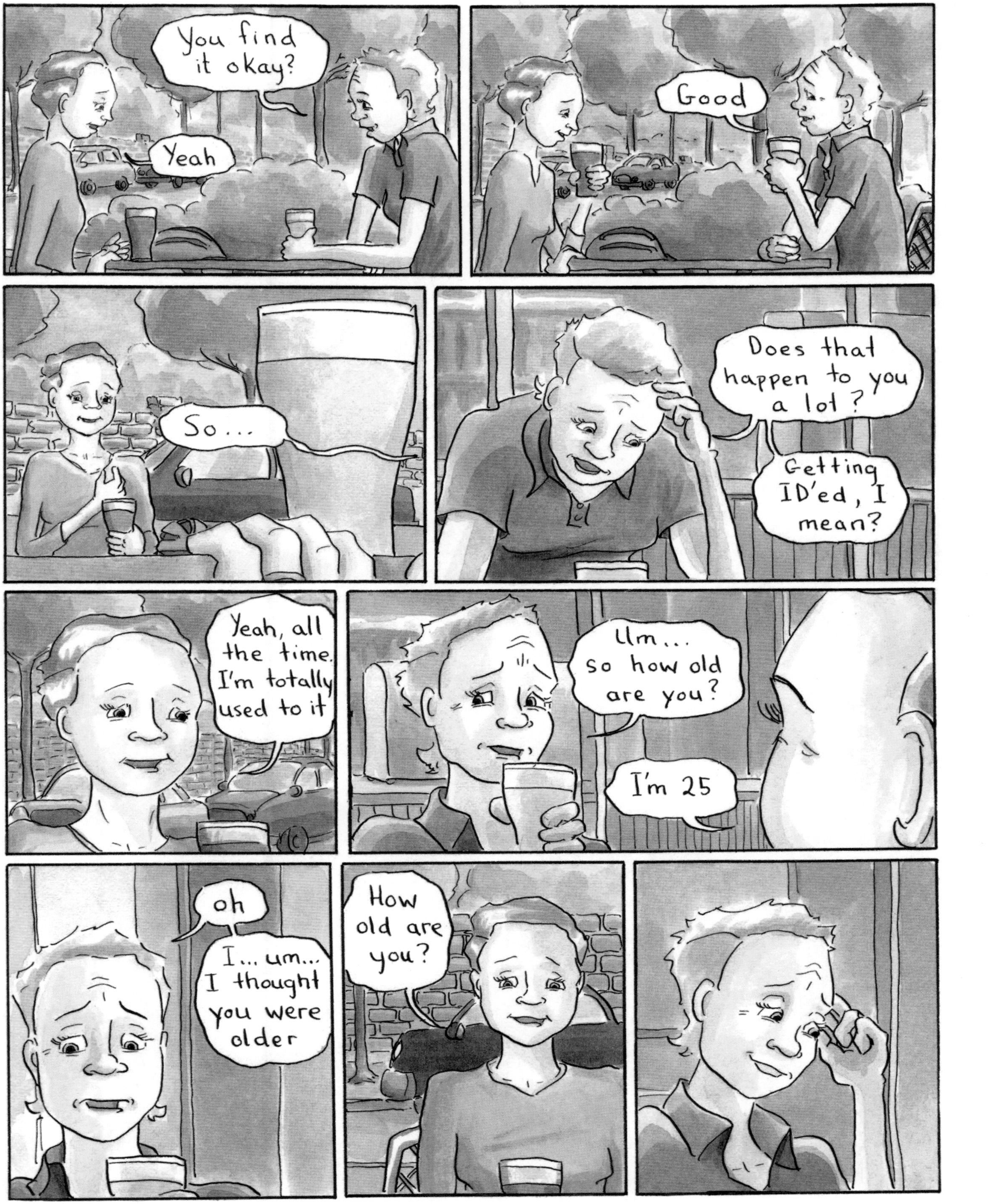
You find it okay?
Yeah
Good
So...
Does that happen to you a lot?
Getting ID'ed, I mean?
Yeah, all the time. I'm totally used to it
Um... so how old are you?
I'm 25
oh
I... um... I thought you were older
How old are you?

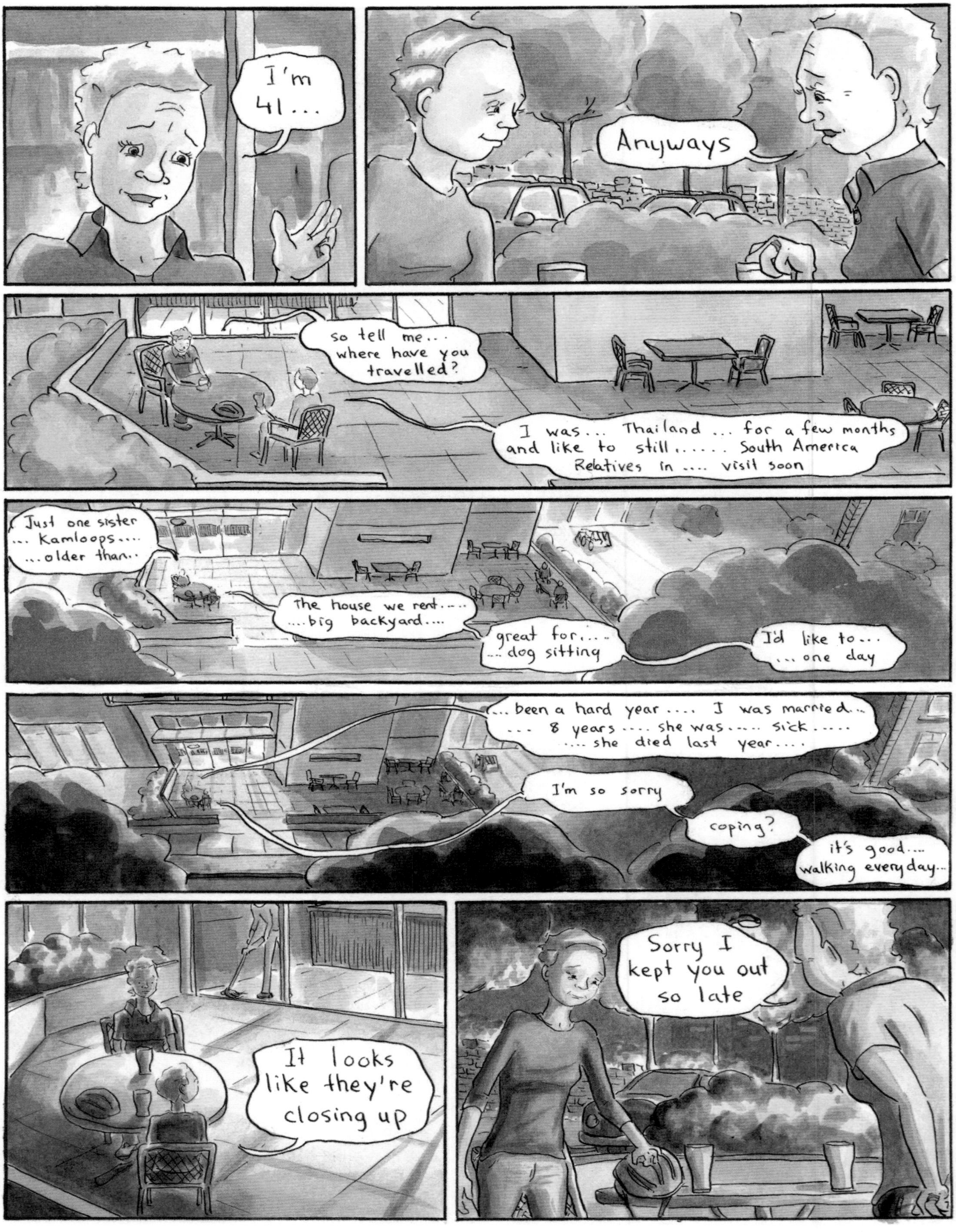
I'm 41...
Anyways
so tell me... where have you travelled?
I was... Thailand ... for a few months and like to still...... South America Relatives in .... visit soon
Just one sister ... Kamloops.... ...older than..
The house we rent... ...big backyard....
great for.... ...dog sitting
I'd like to... ...one day
...been a hard year.... I was married... ... 8 years.... she was.... sick..... ....she died last year....
I'm so sorry
coping?
it's good.... walking everyday...
It looks like they're closing up
Sorry I kept you out so late

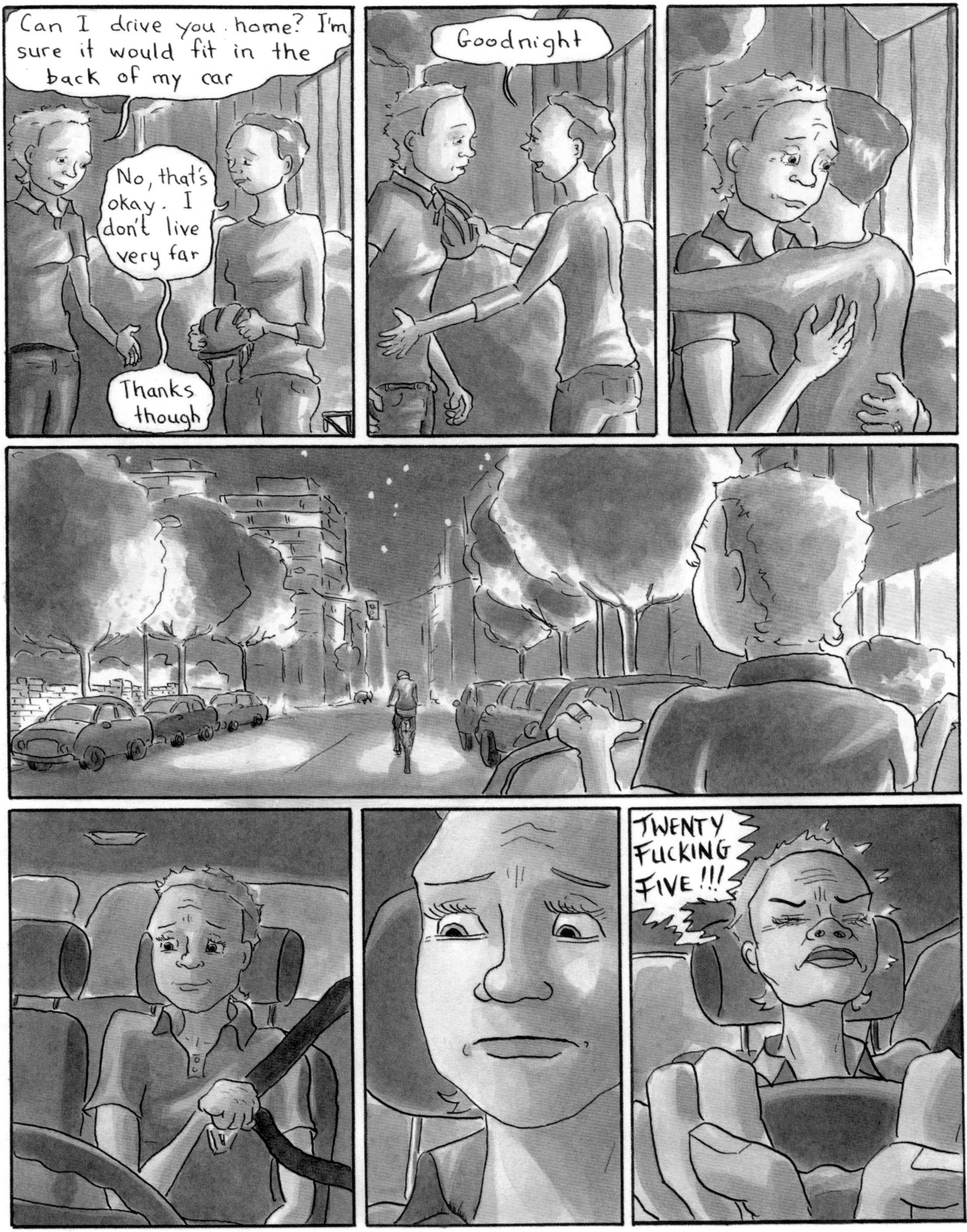
Can I drive you home? I'm sure it would fit in the back of my car
No, that's okay. I don't live very far
Thanks though
Goodnight
TWENTY FUCKING FIVE!!!

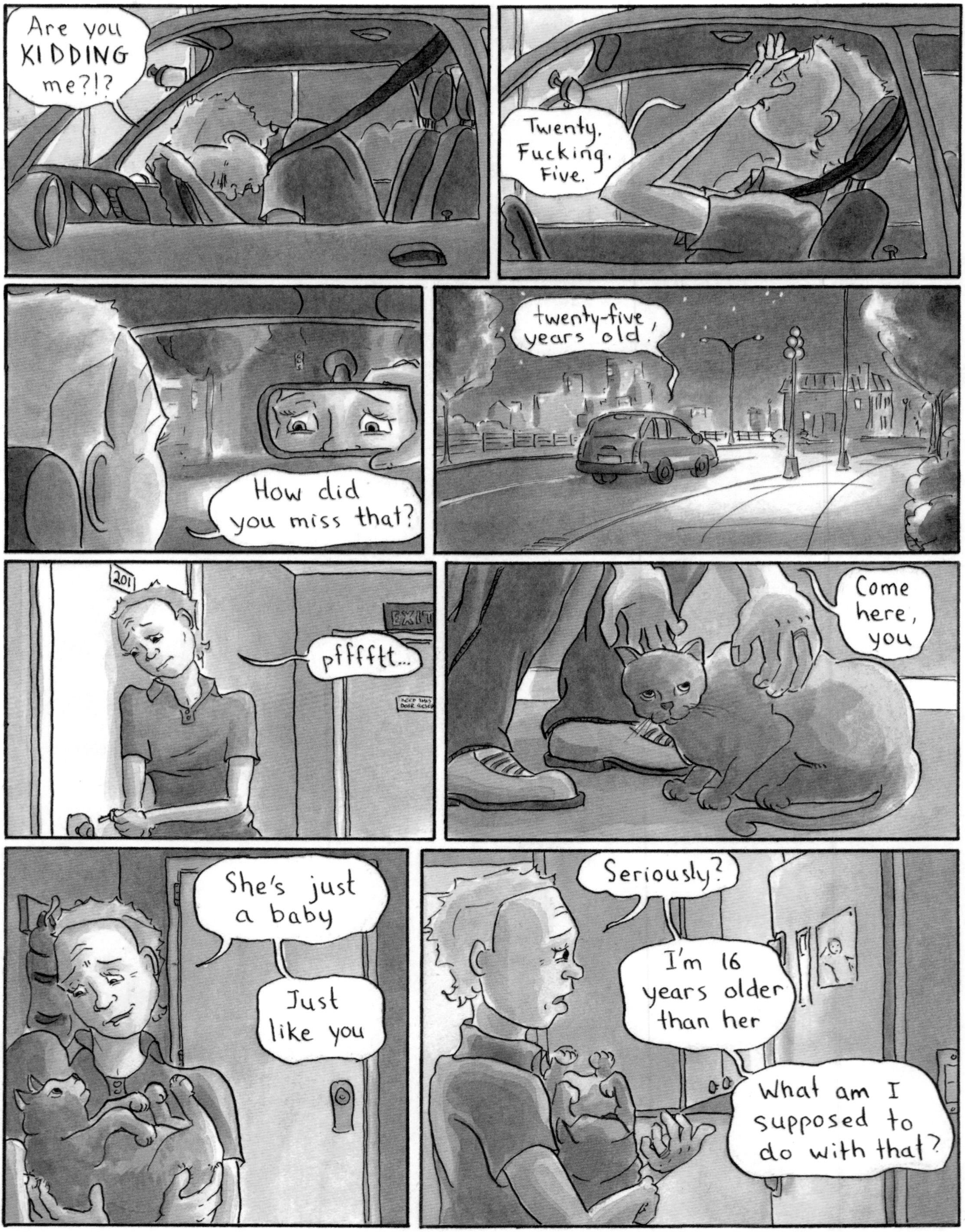
Are you KIDDING me?!?
Twenty. Fucking. Five.
How did you miss that?
twenty-five years old!
201
EXIT
pffffft...
Come here, you
She's just a baby
Just like you
Seriously?
I'm 16 years older than her
What am I supposed to do with that?

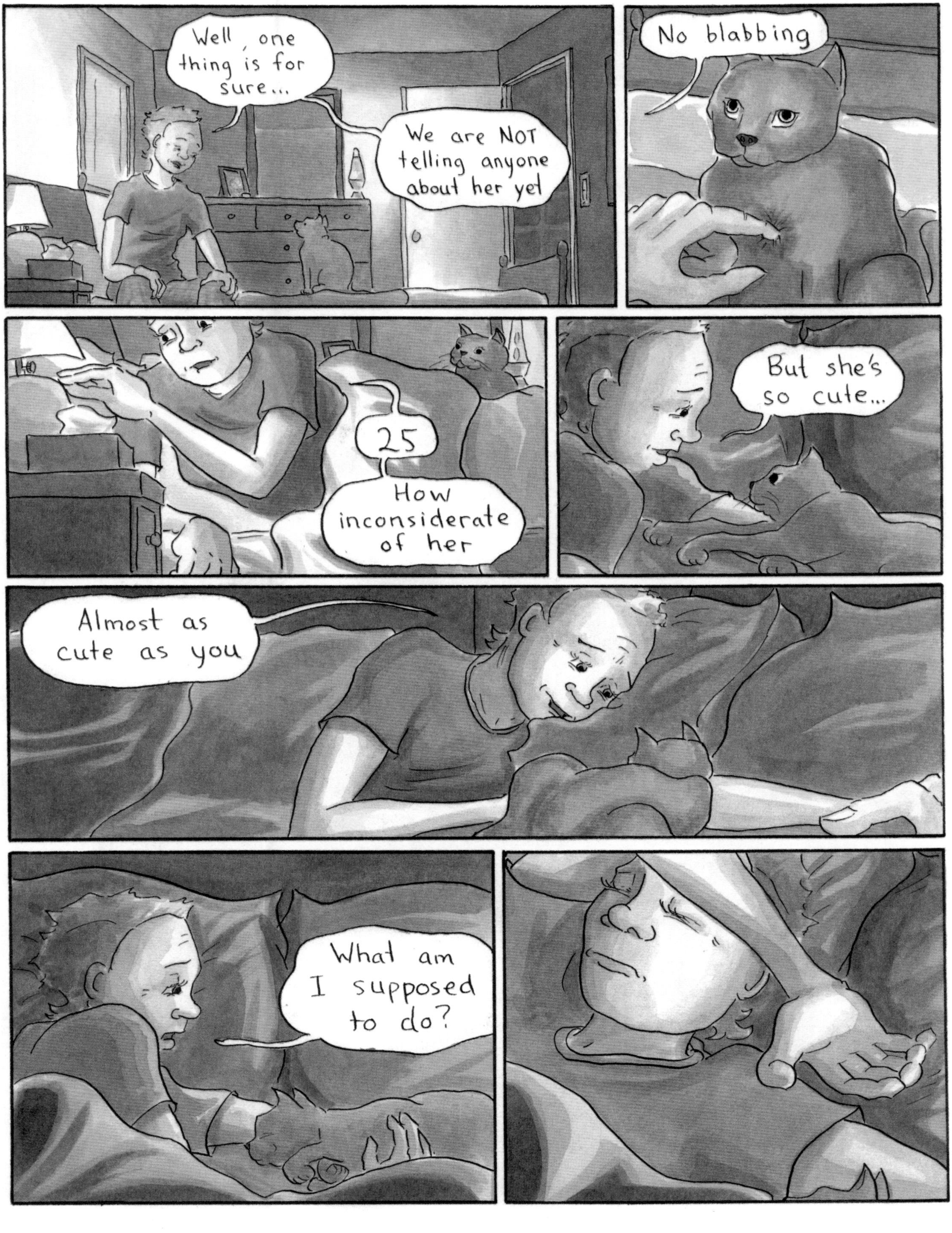
Well, one thing is for sure...
We are NOT telling anyone about her yet
No blabbing
25
How inconsiderate of her
But she's so cute...
Almost as cute as you
What am I supposed to do?

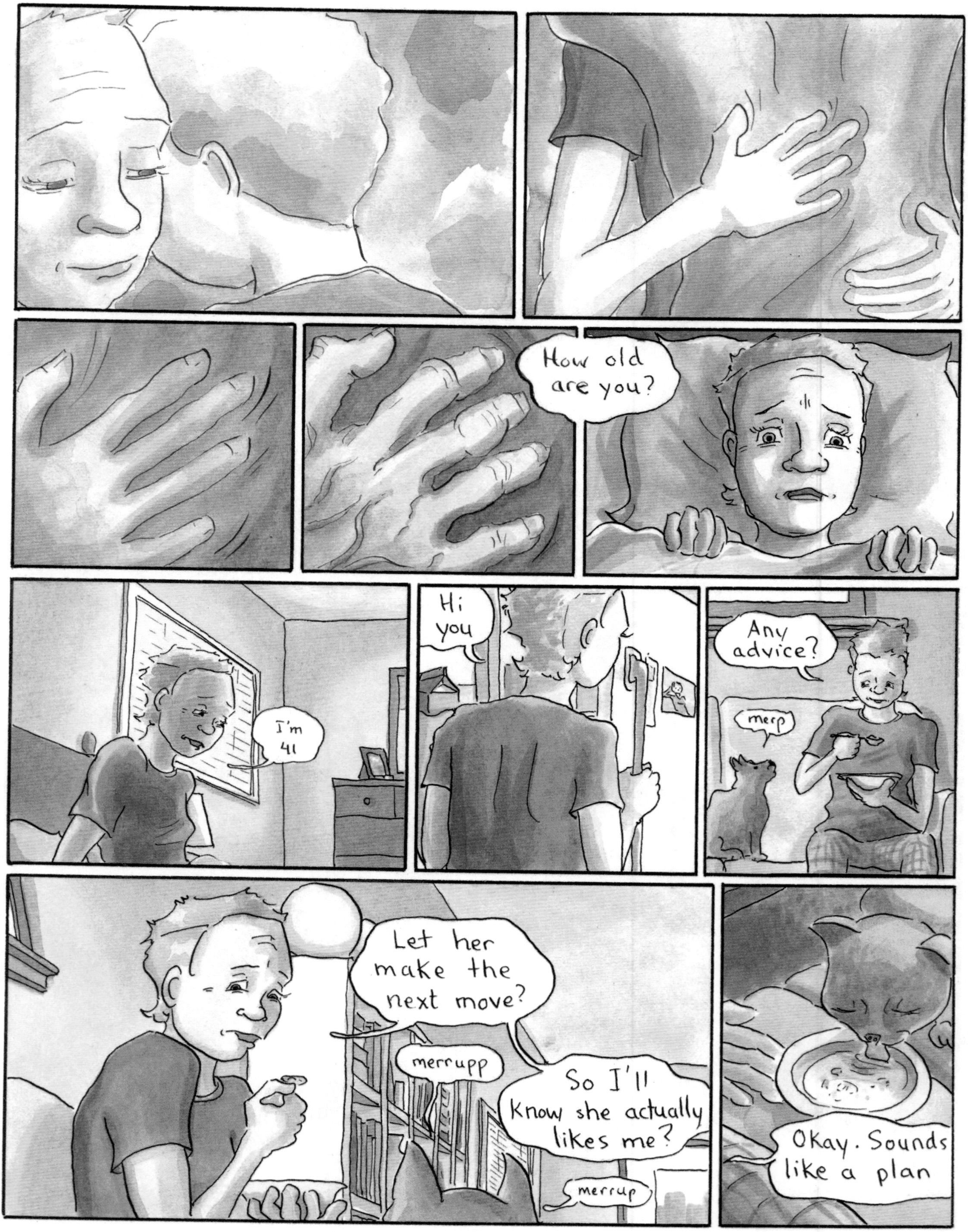
How old are you?
I'm 41
Hi you
Any advice?
merp
Let her make the next move?
merrupp
So I'll know she actually likes me?
merrup
Okay. Sounds like a plan

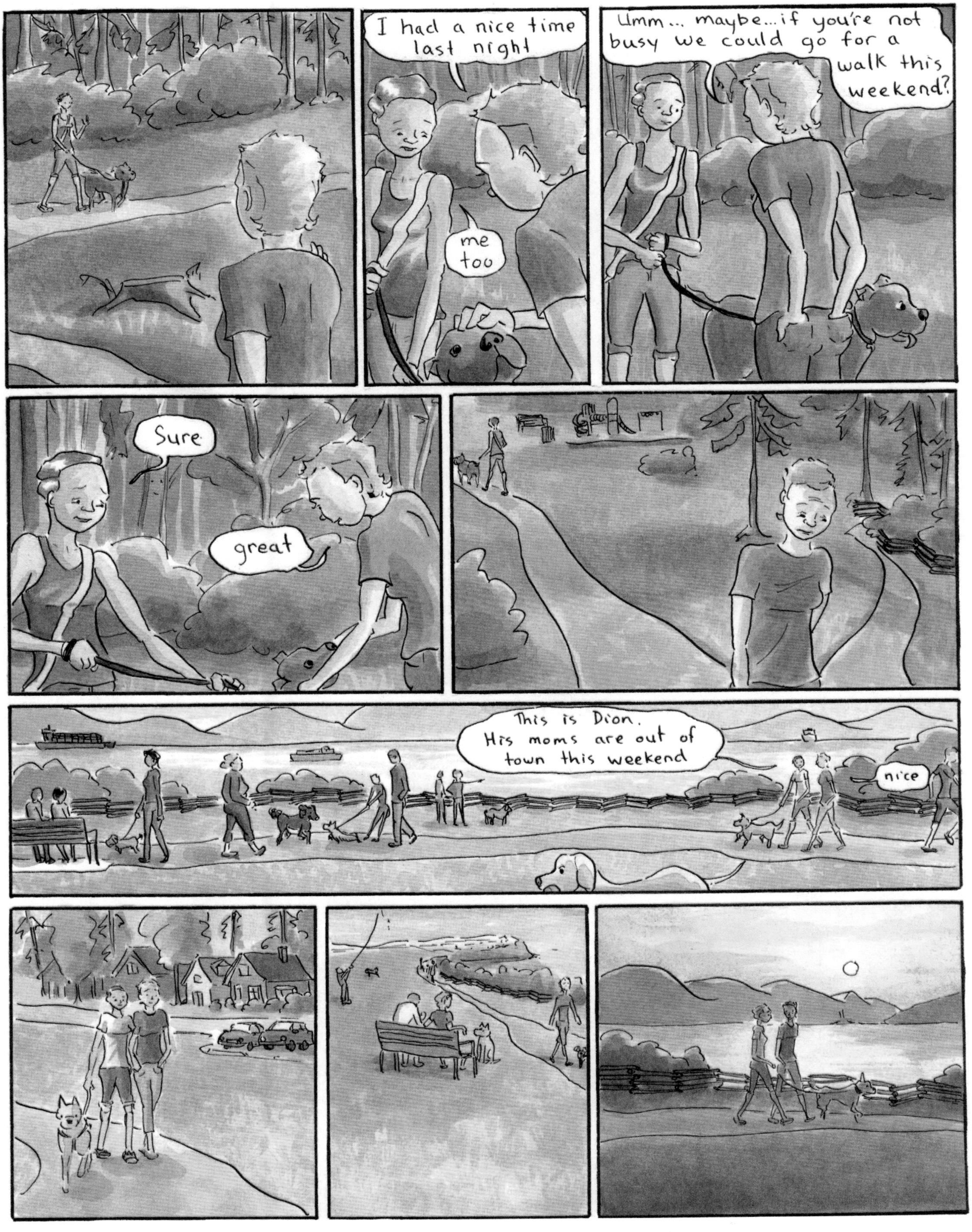
I had a nice time last night
me too
Umm... maybe...if you're not busy we could go for a walk this weekend?
Sure
great
This is Dion. His moms are out of town this weekend
nice

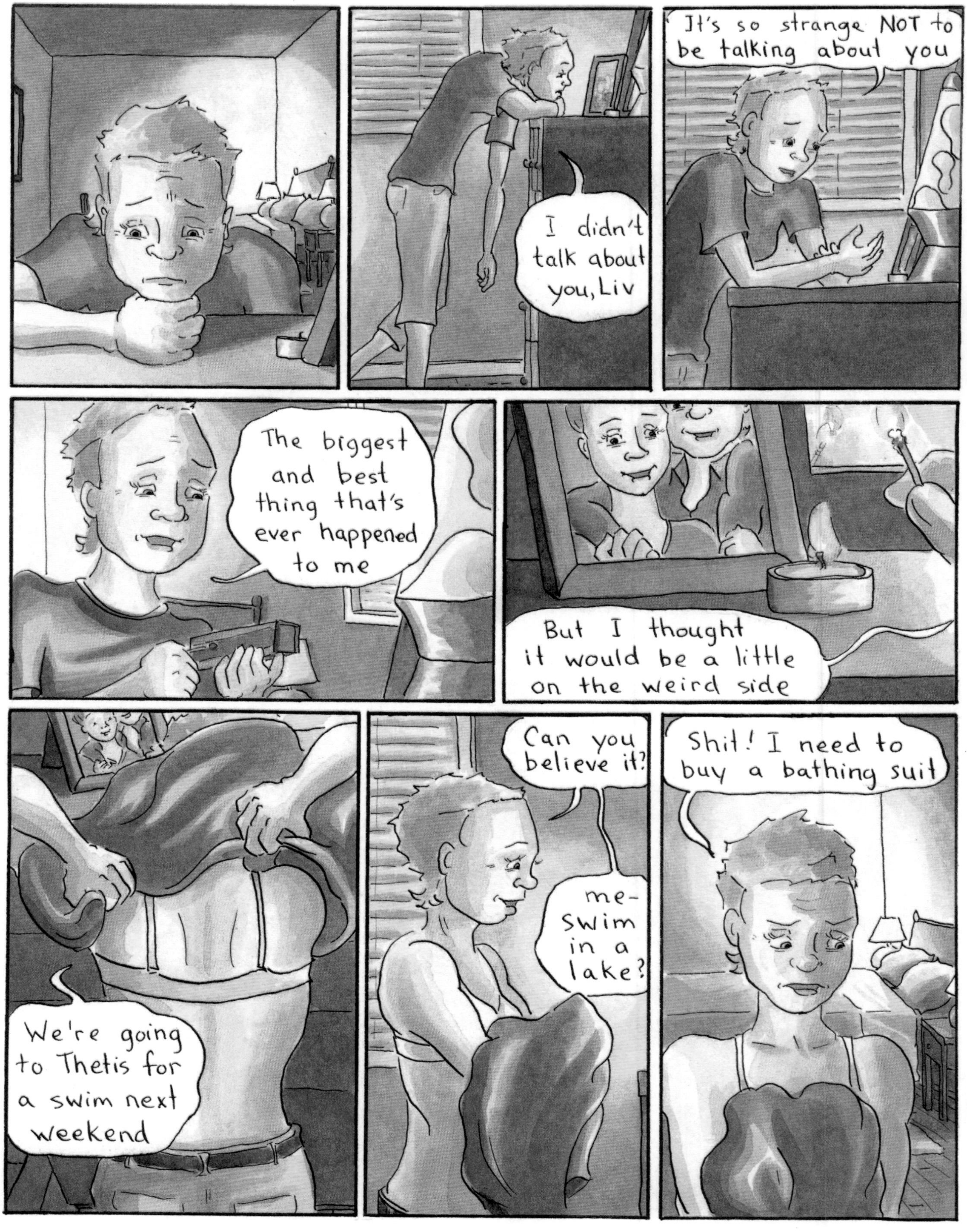
I didn't talk about you, Liv
It's so strange NOT to be talking about you
The biggest and best thing that's ever happened to me
But I thought it would be a little on the weird side
We're going to Thetis for a swim next weekend
Can you believe it?
me- swim in a lake?
Shit! I need to buy a bathing suit

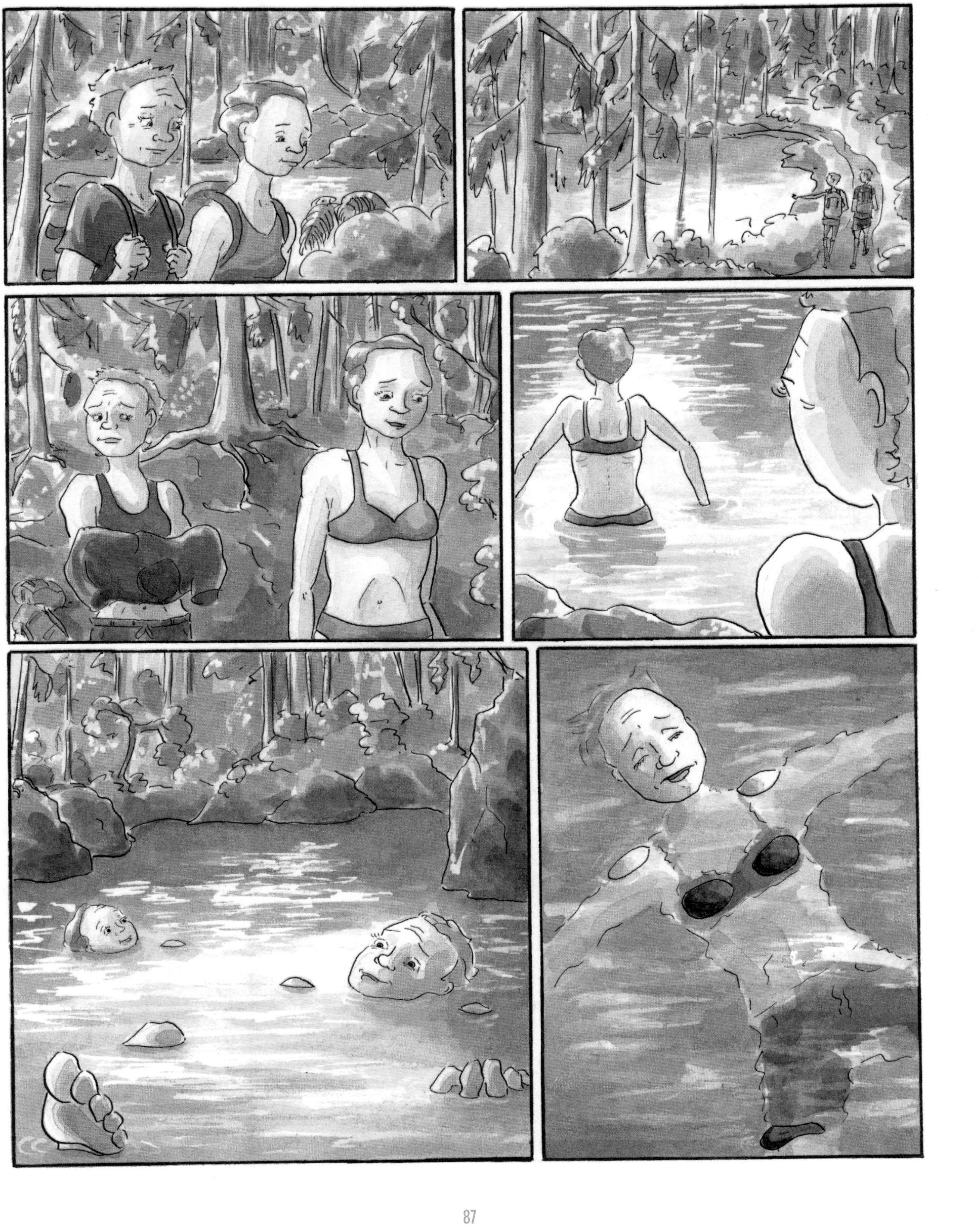

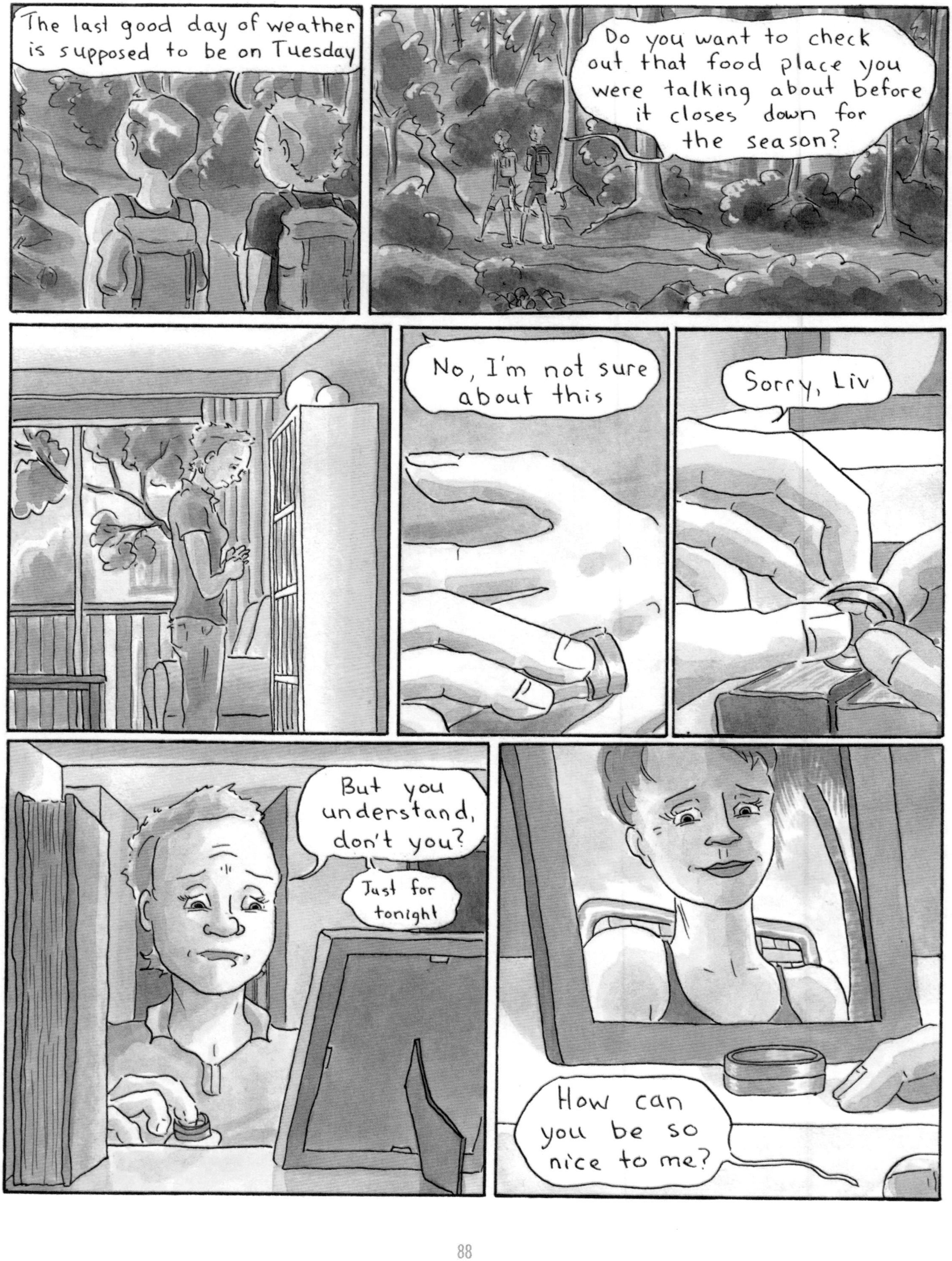
The last good day of weather is supposed to be on Tuesday
Do you want to check out that food place you were talking about before it closes down for the season?
No, I'm not sure about this
Sorry, Liv
But you understand, don't you?
Just for tonight
How can you be so nice to me?

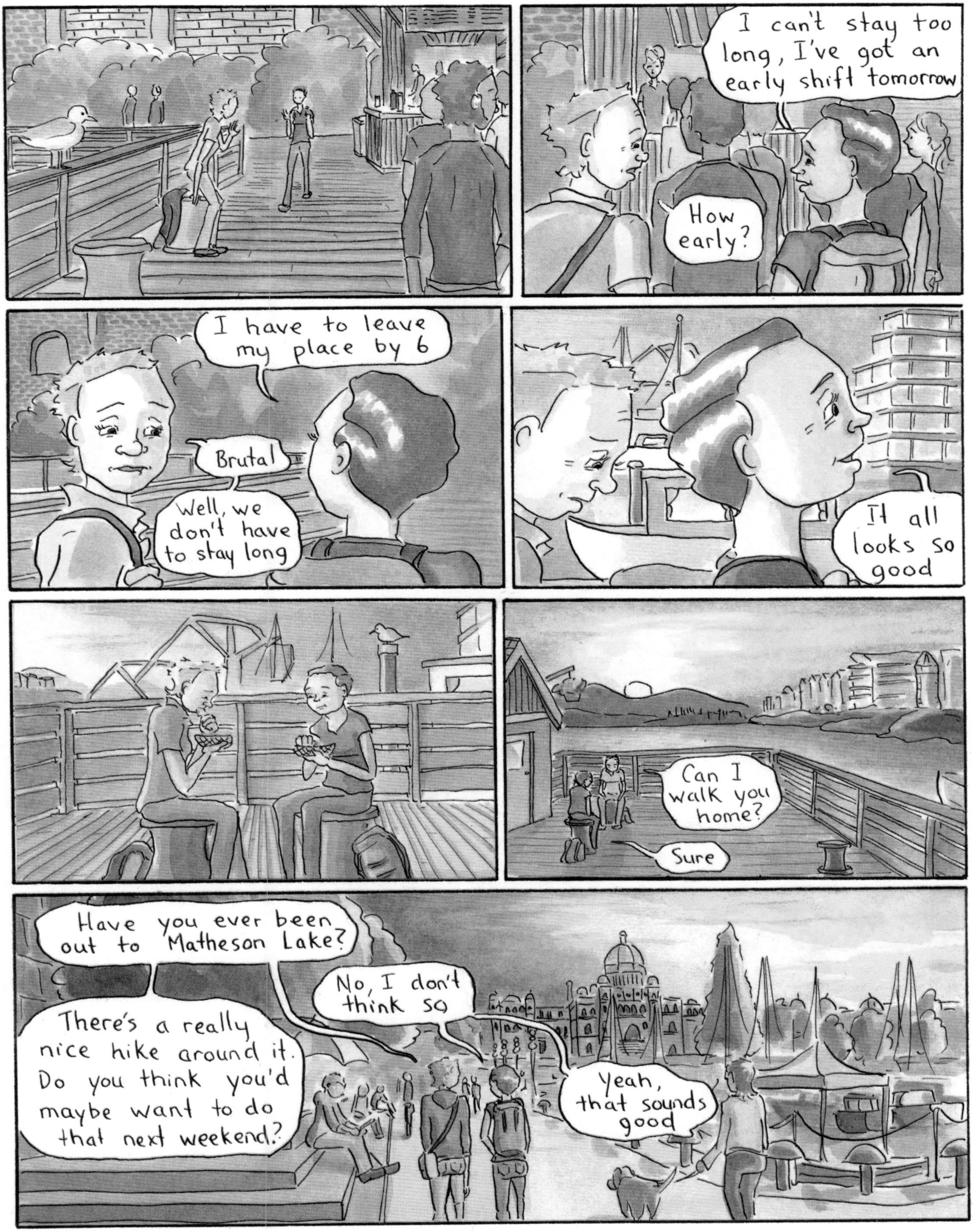
I can't stay too long, I've got an early shift tomorrow
How early?
I have to leave my place by 6
Brutal
Well, we don't have to stay long
It all looks so good
Can I walk you home?
Sure
Have you ever been out to Matheson Lake?
There's a really nice hike around it. Do you think you'd maybe want to do that next weekend?
No, I don't think so
Yeah, that sounds good

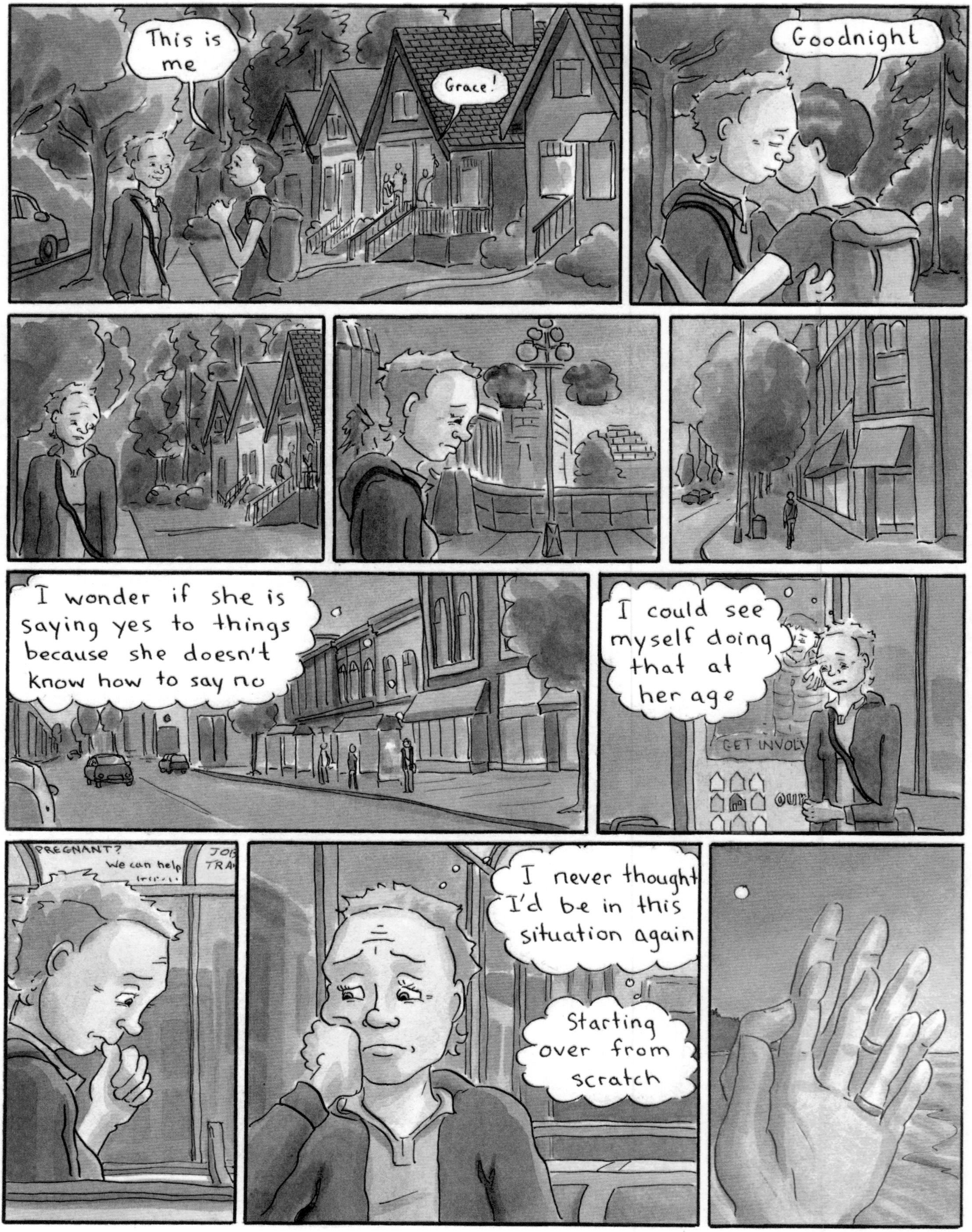
This is me
Grace!
Goodnight
I wonder if she is saying yes to things because she doesn't know how to say no
I could see myself doing that at her age
PREGNANT? We can help
I never thought I'd be in this situation again
Starting over from scratch

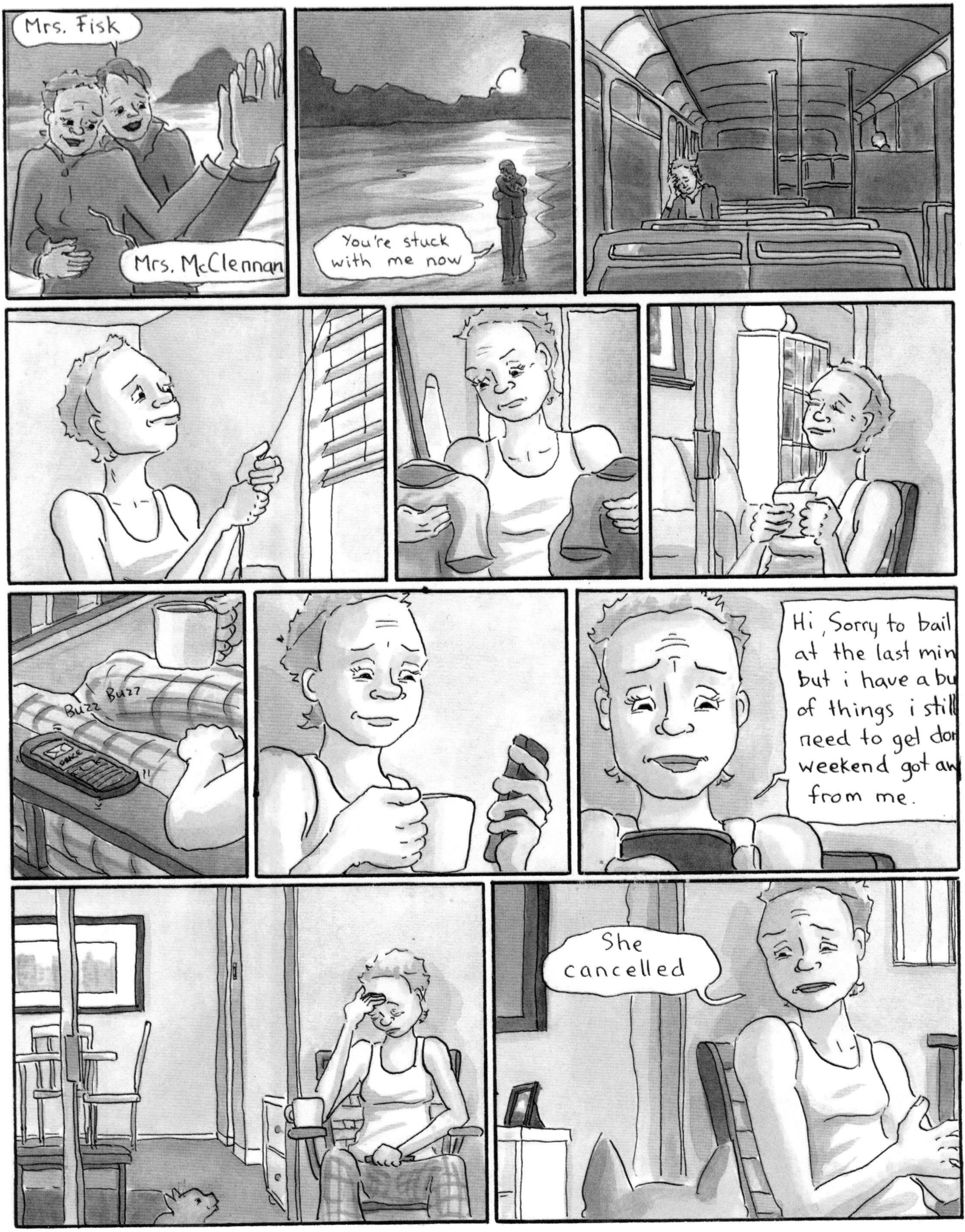
Mrs. Fisk
Mrs. McClennan
You're stuck with me now
Buzz Buzz
Hi, Sorry to bail at the last min but i have a bu of things i still need to get don weekend got aw from me.
She cancelled

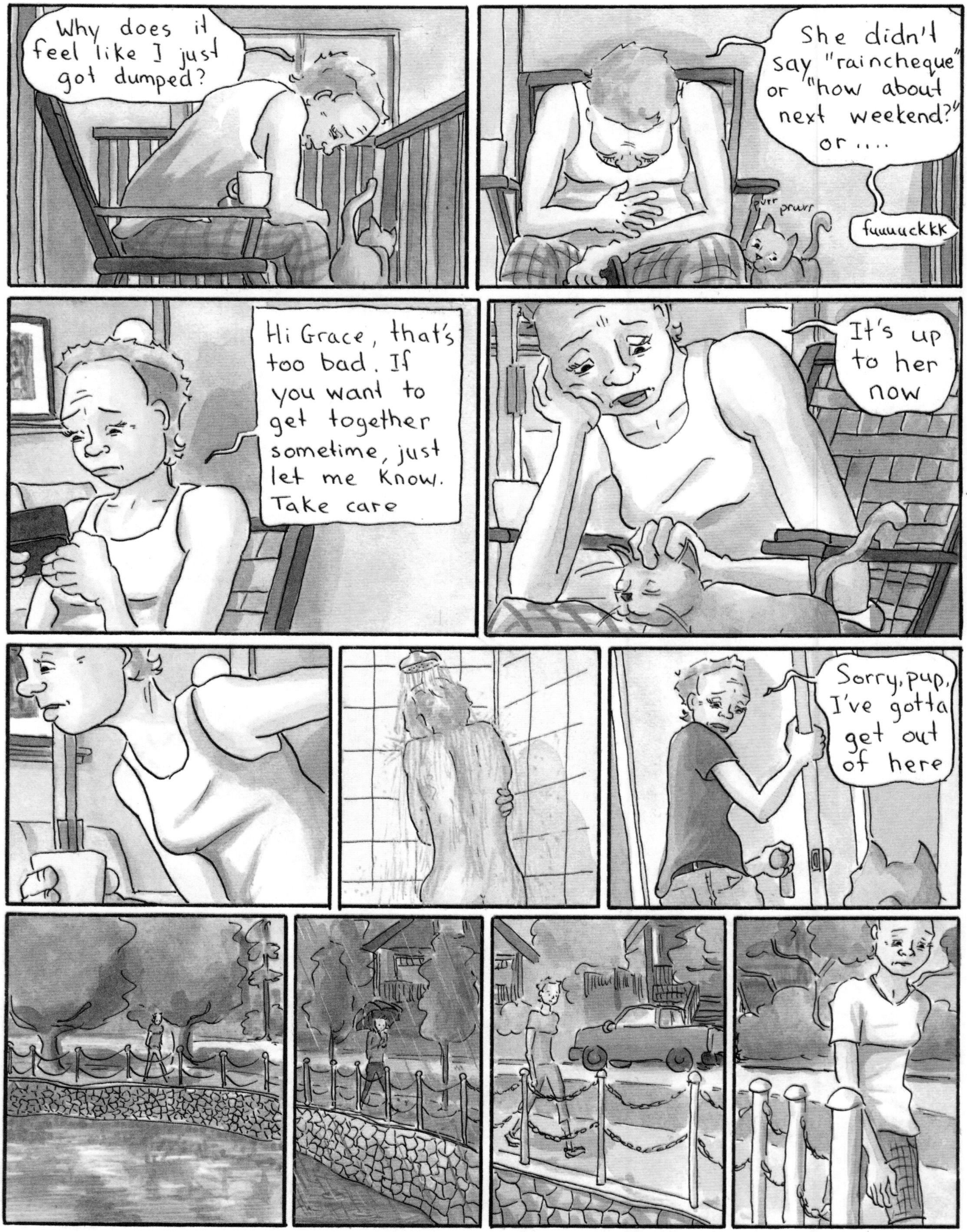
Why does it feel like I just got dumped?
She didn't say "raincheque" or "how about next weekend?" or....
prrr prurr
fuuuuckkk
Hi Grace, that's too bad. If you want to get together sometime, just let me know. Take care
It's up to her now
Sorry, pup, I've gotta get out of here

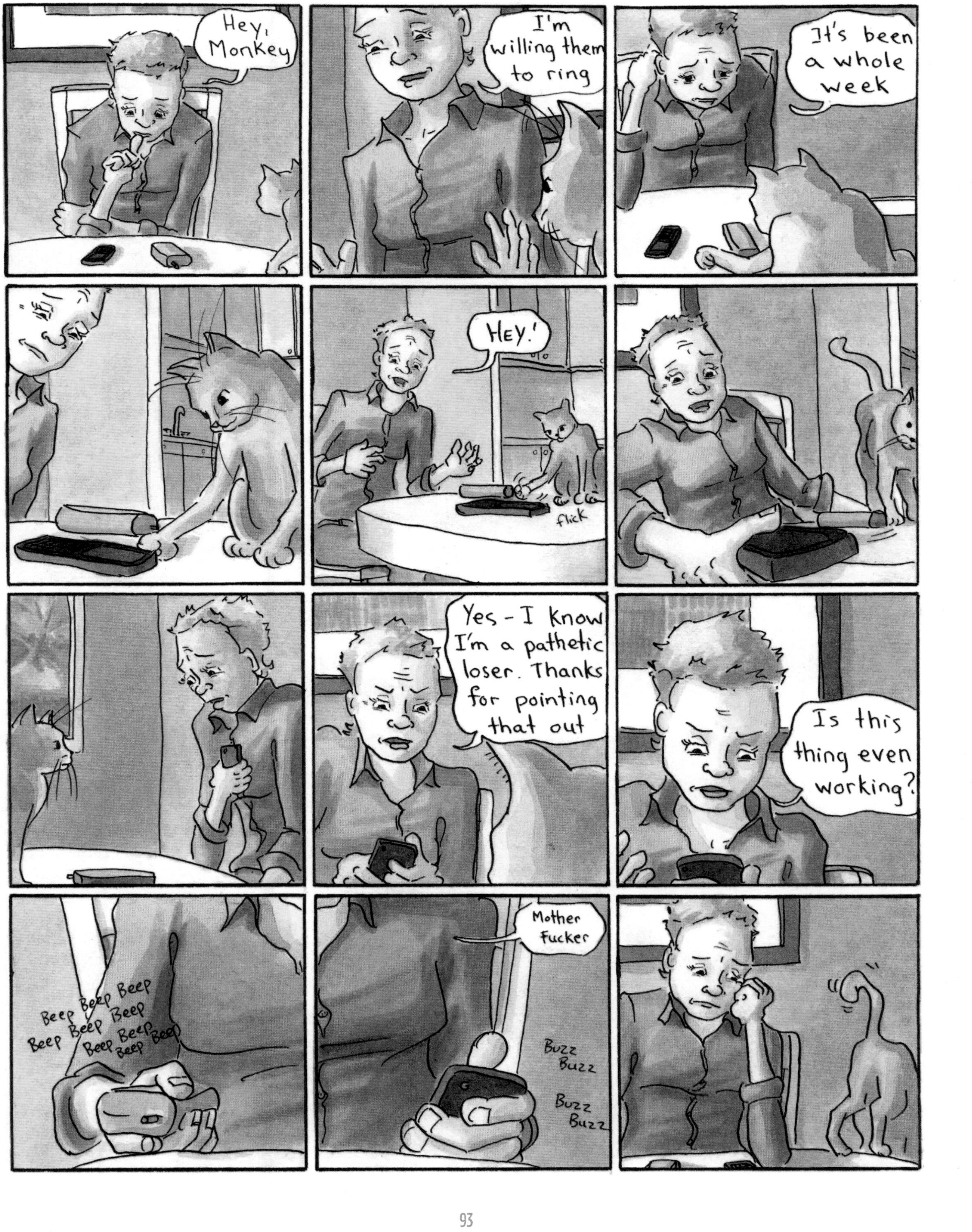
Hey, Monkey
I'm willing them to ring
It's been a whole week
Hey!
flick
Yes - I know I'm a pathetic loser. Thanks for pointing that out
Is this thing even working?
Beep Beep Beep Beep Beep Beep Beep Beep Beep Beep Beep
Mother Fucker
Buzz Buzz
Buzz Buzz

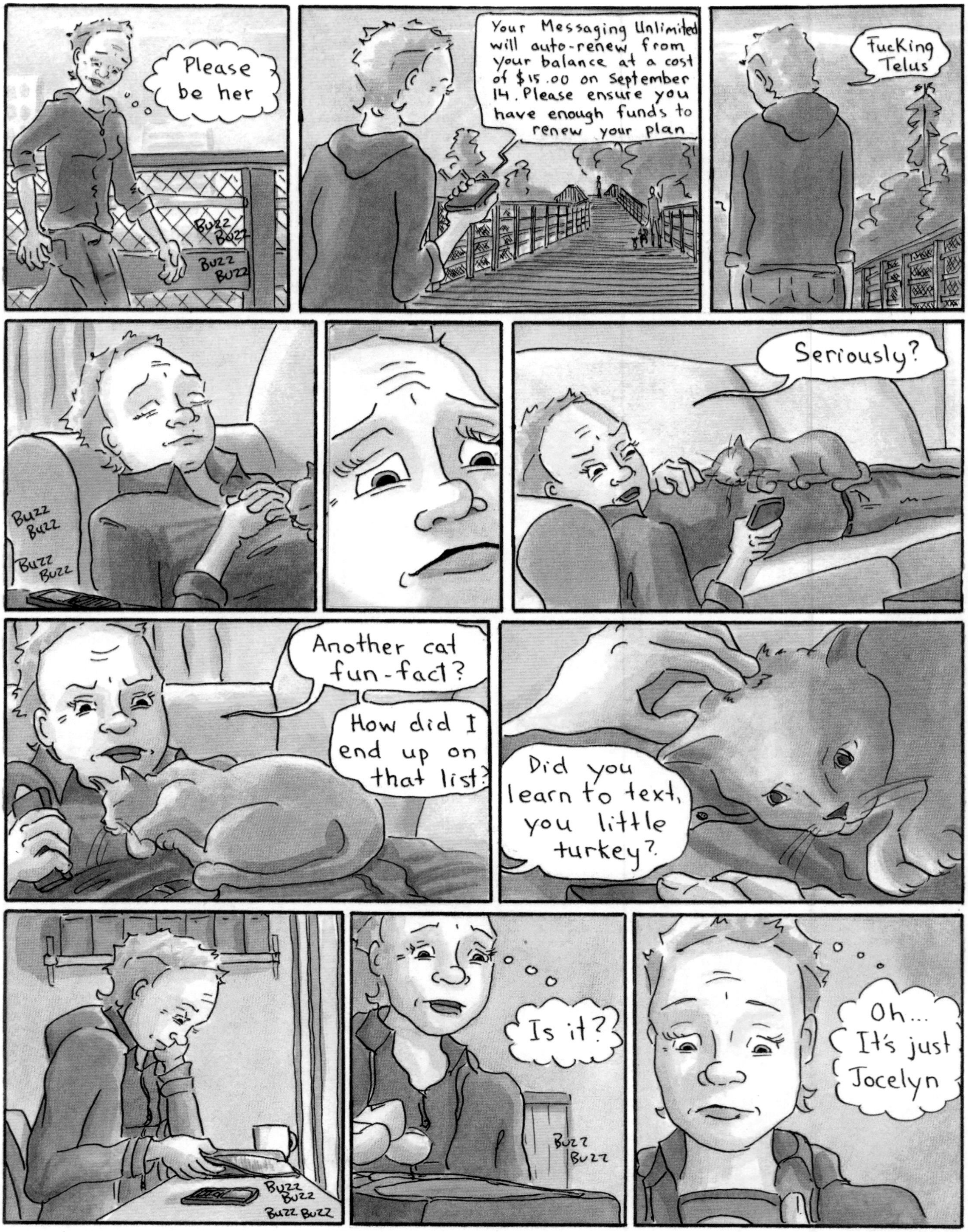
Please be her
BUZZ BUZZ
BUZZ BUZZ
Your Messaging Unlimited will auto-renew from your balance at a cost of $15.00 on September 14. Please ensure you have enough funds to renew your plan
Fucking Telus
BUZZ BUZZ
BUZZ BUZZ
Seriously?
Another cat fun-fact?
How did I end up on that list?
Did you learn to text, you little turkey?
BUZZ BUZZ
BUZZ BUZZ
Is it?
BUZZ BUZZ
Oh... It's just Jocelyn

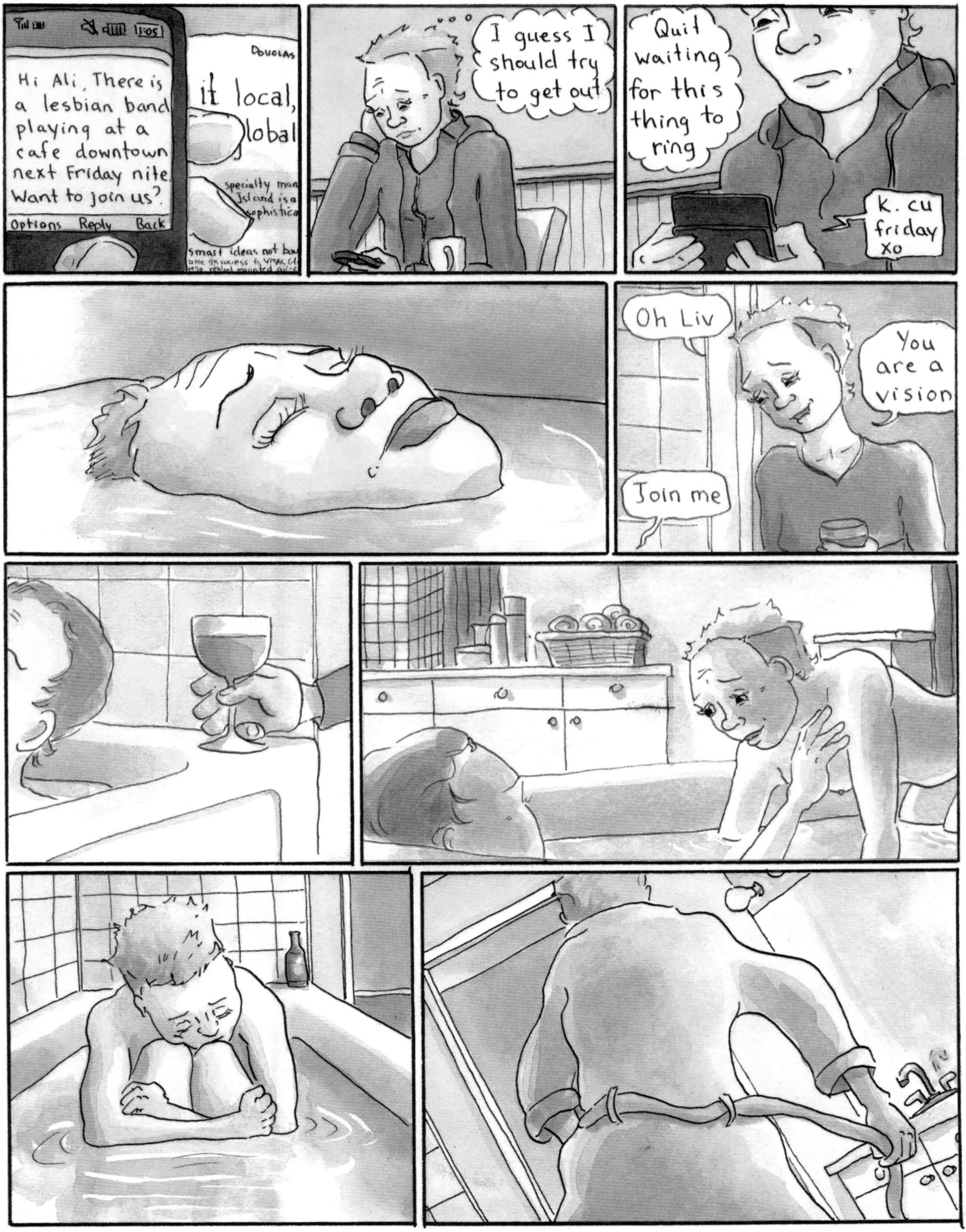
Hi Ali, There is a lesbian band playing at a cafe downtown next Friday nite. Want to join us?
Options Reply Back
DOUGLAS
it local,
I guess I should try to get out
Quit waiting for this thing to ring
k. cu friday xo
Oh Liv
You are a vision
Join me

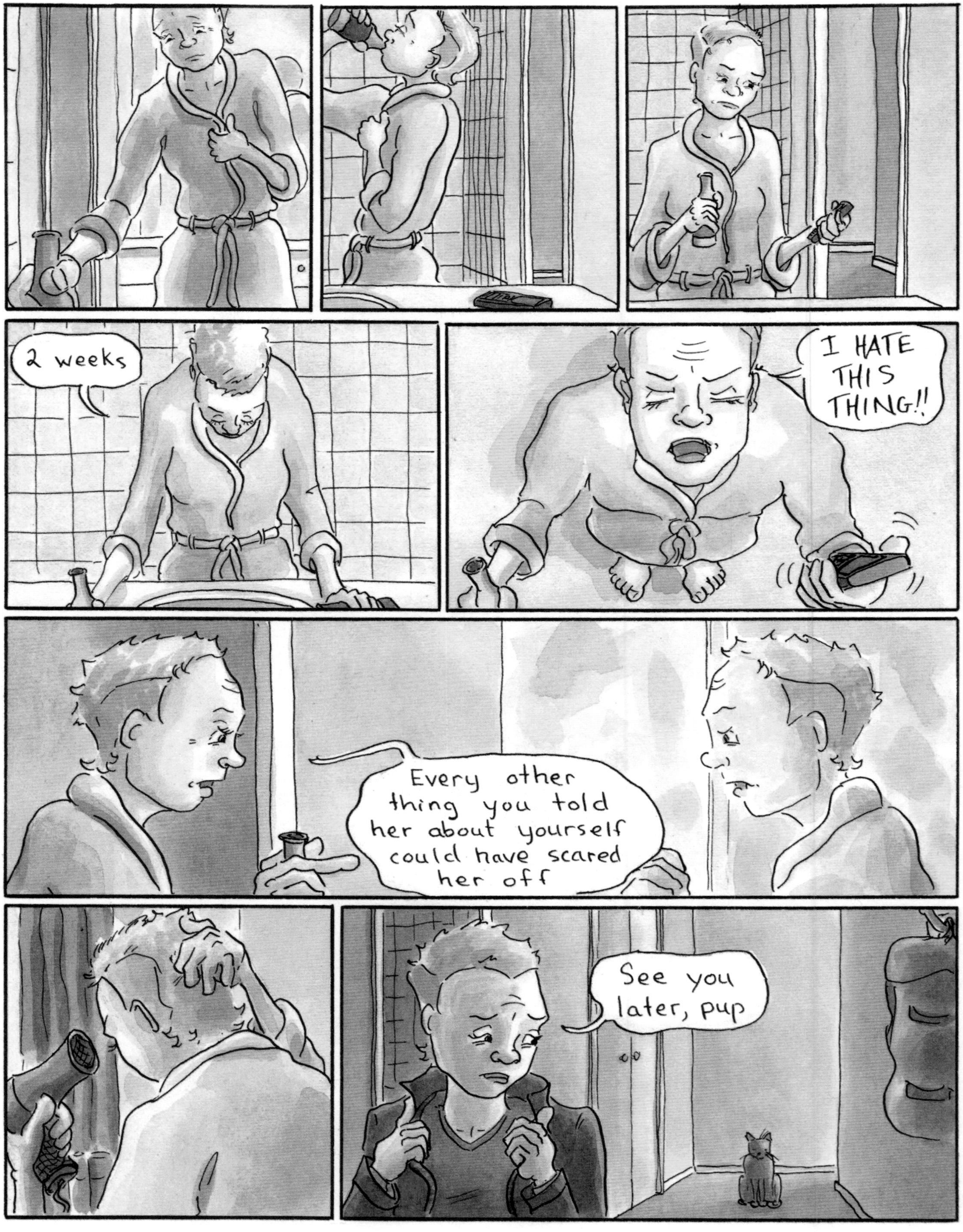
2 weeks
I HATE THIS THING!!
Every other thing you told her about yourself could have scared her off
See you later, pup

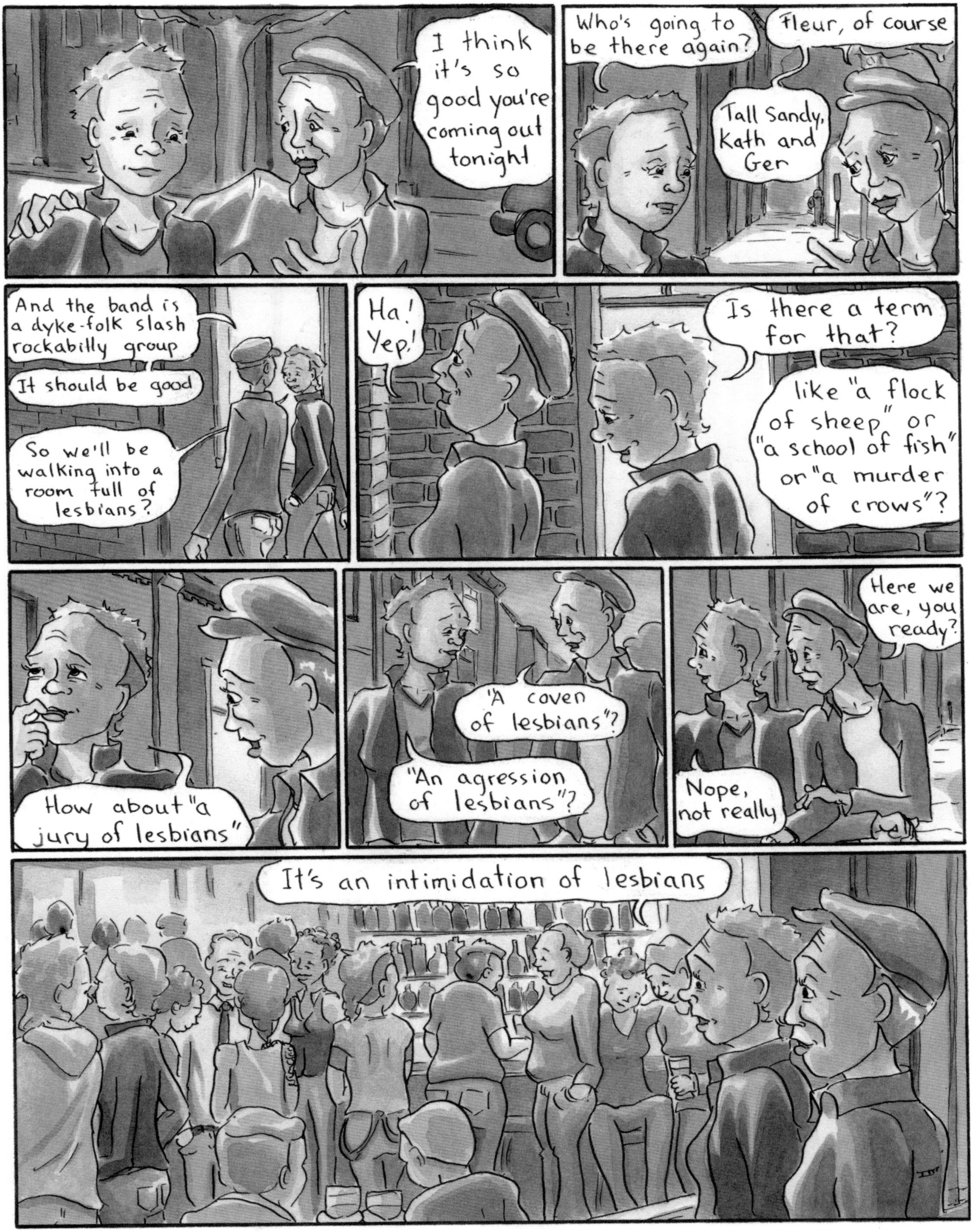
I think it's so good you're coming out tonight
Who's going to be there again?
Fleur, of course
Tall Sandy, Kath and Ger
And the band is a dyke-folk slash rockabilly group
It should be good
So we'll be walking into a room full of lesbians?
Ha! Yep!
Is there a term for that?
like "a flock of sheep" or "a school of fish" or "a murder of crows"?
How about "a jury of lesbians"
"A coven of lesbians"?
"An agression of lesbians"?
Nope, not really
Here we are, you ready?
It's an intimidation of lesbians

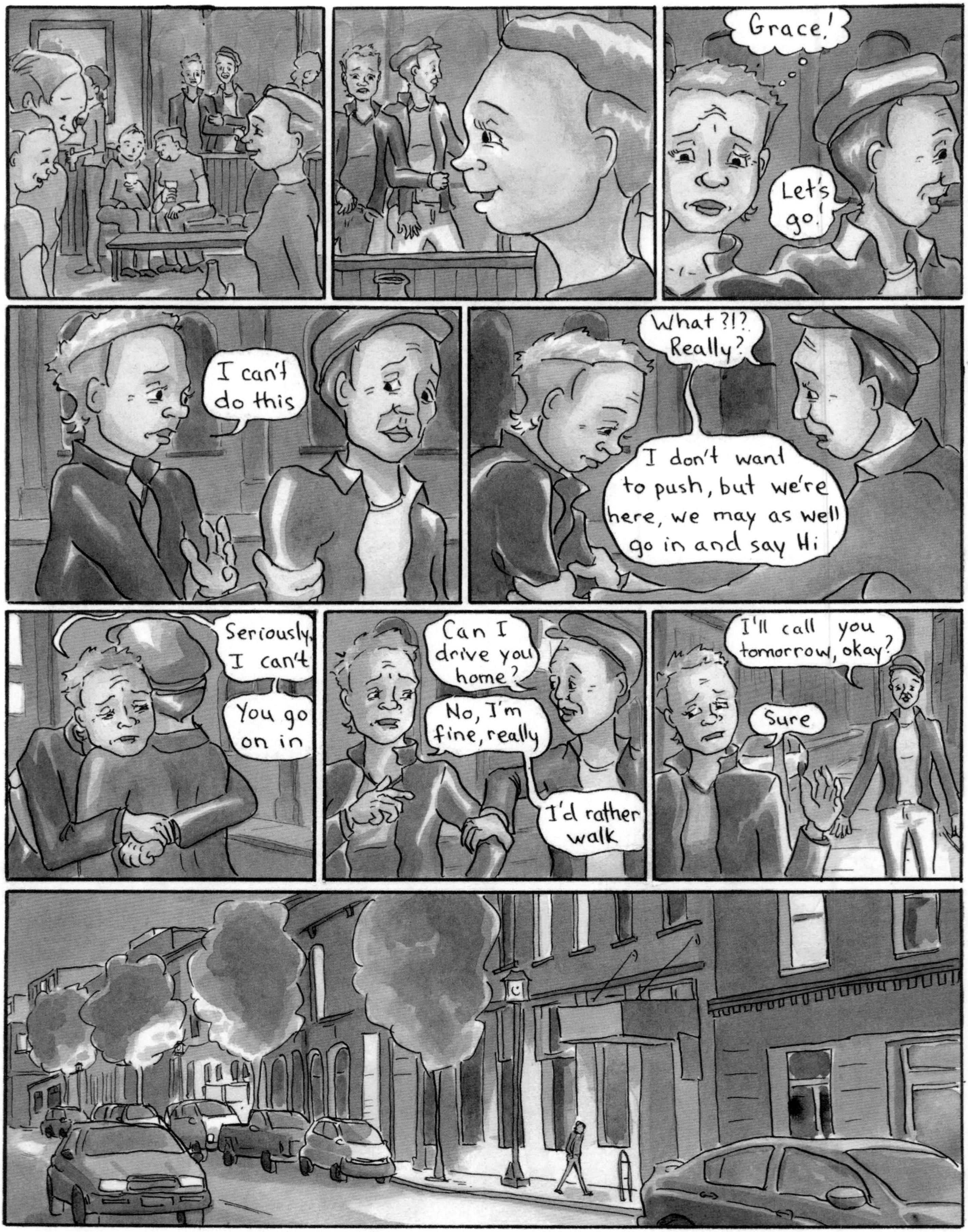
Grace!
Let's go!
I can't do this
What?!? Really?
I don't want to push, but we're here, we may as well go in and say Hi
Seriously, I can't
You go on in
Can I drive you home?
No, I'm fine, really
I'd rather walk
I'll call you tomorrow, okay?
Sure

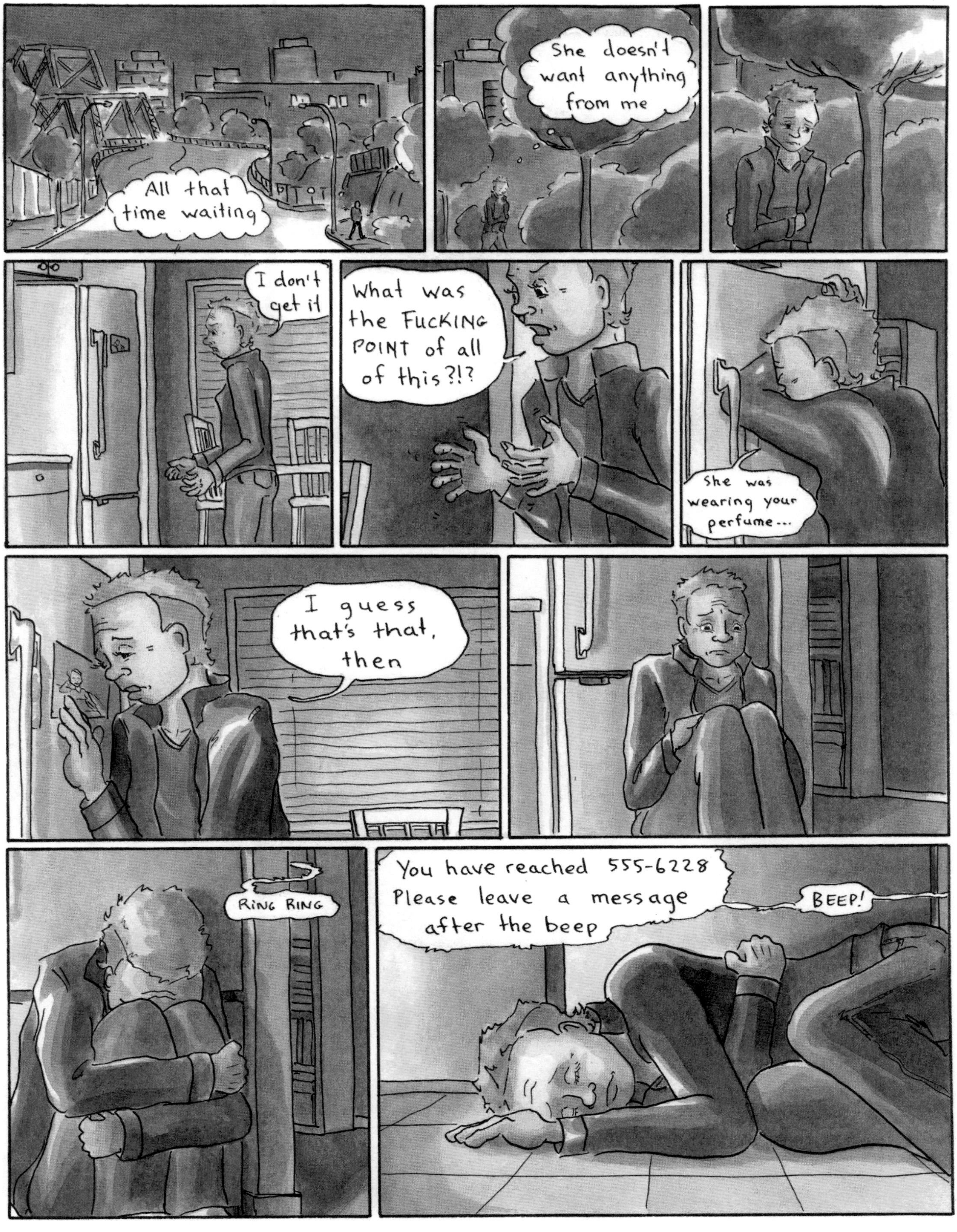
All that time waiting
She doesn't want anything from me
I don't get it
What was the FUCKING POINT of all of this?!?
She was wearing your perfume...
I guess that's that, then
RING RING
You have reached 555-6228 Please leave a message after the beep
BEEP!

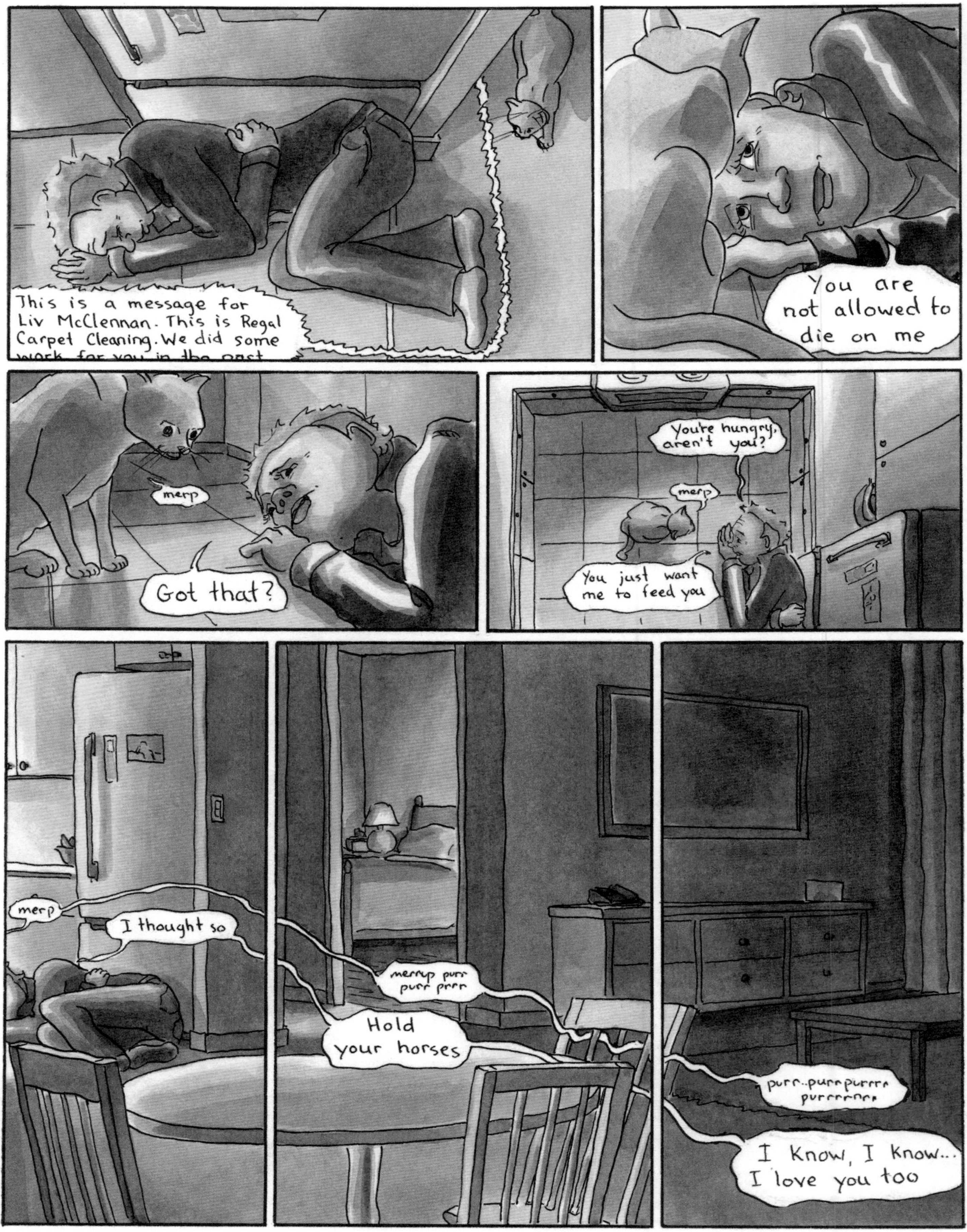
This is a message for Liv McClennan. This is Regal Carpet Cleaning. We did some
You are not allowed to die on me
merp
Got that?
You're hungry, aren't you?
merp
You just want me to feed you
merp
I thought so
merrup purr purr prrr
Hold your horses
purr..purrpurrrr purrrrrrrr
I Know, I Know...
I love you too

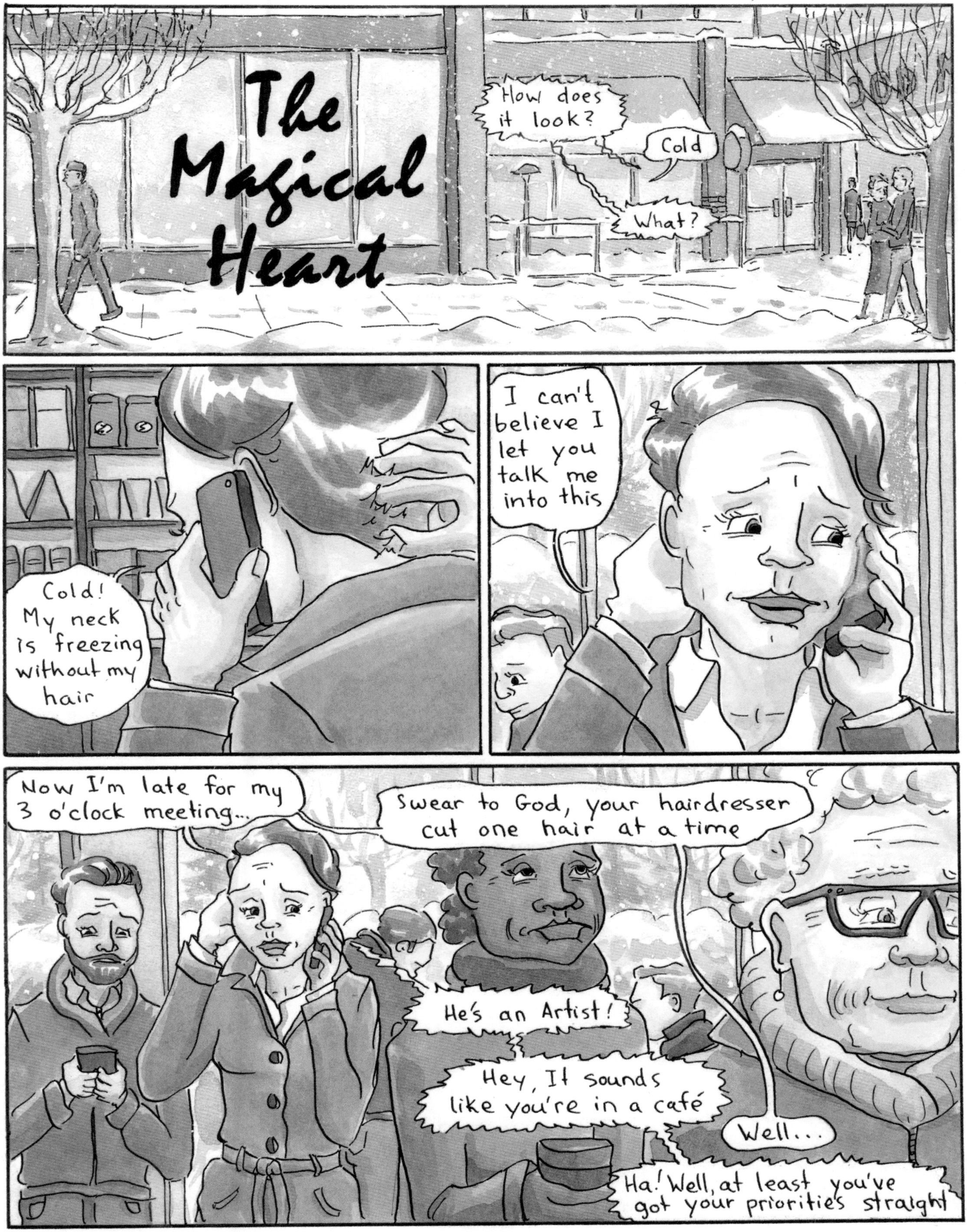
The Magical Heart
How does it look?
Cold
What?
Cold! My neck is freezing without my hair
I can't believe I let you talk me into this
Now I'm late for my 3 o'clock meeting...
Swear to God, your hairdresser cut one hair at a time
He's an Artist!
Hey, It sounds like you're in a café
Well...
Ha! Well, at least you've got your priorities straight

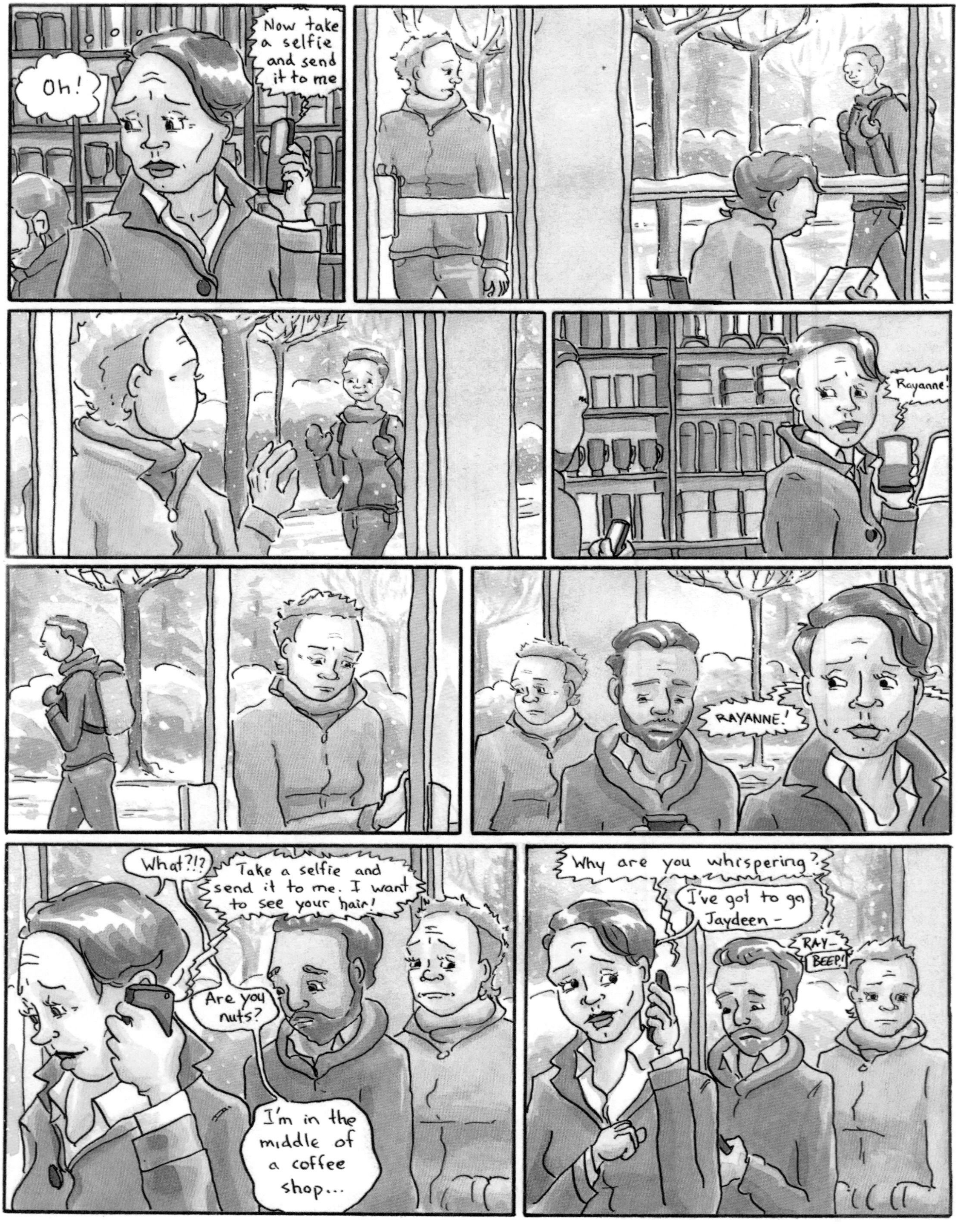
Now take a selfie and send it to me
Oh!
Rayanne!
RAYANNE!
What?!?
Take a selfie and send it to me. I want to see your hair!
Are you nuts?
I'm in the middle of a coffee shop...
Why are you whispering?
I've got to go Jaydeen –
RAY–
BEEP!

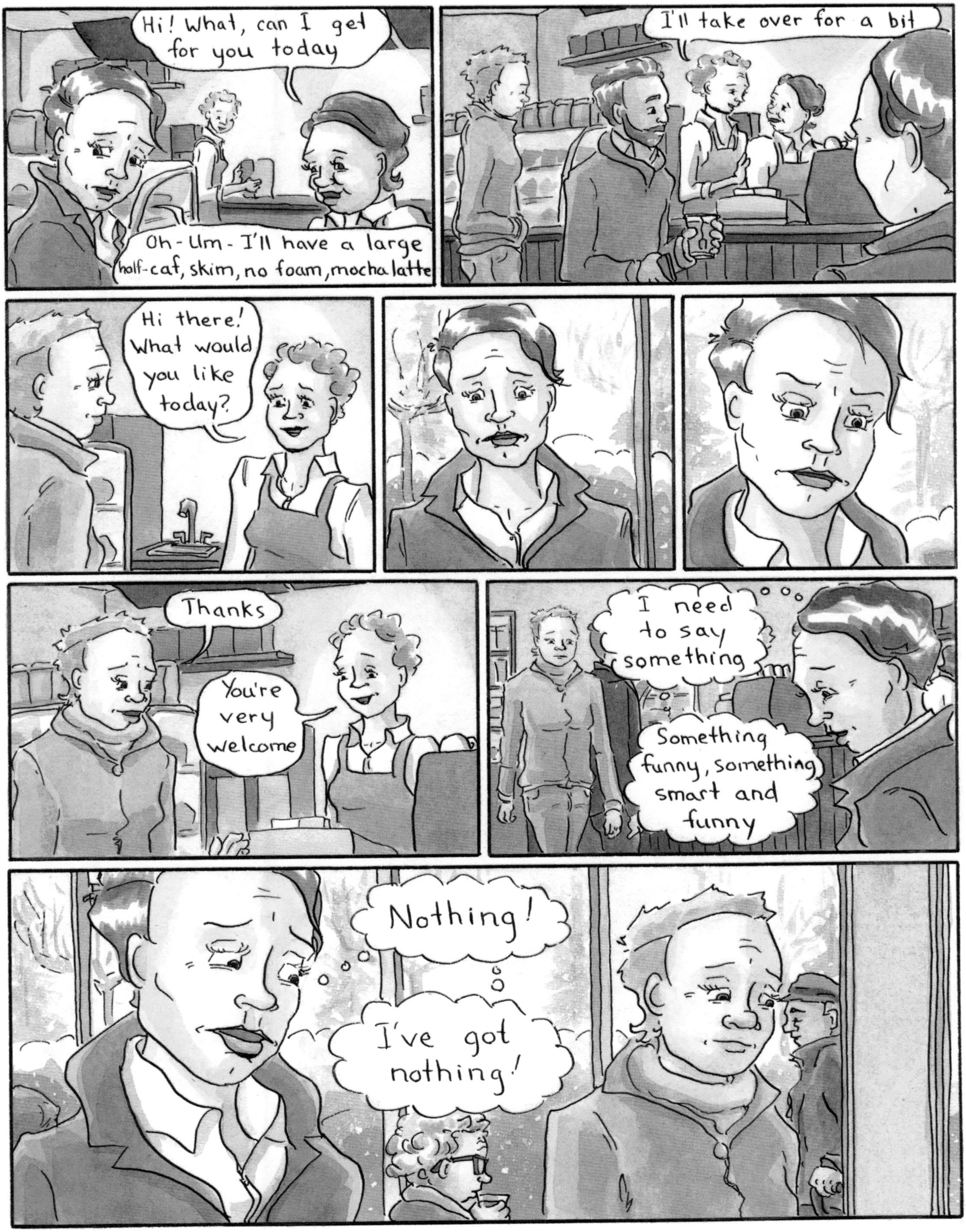
Hi! What, can I get for you today
Oh-Um- I'll have a large half-caf, skim, no foam, mocha latte
I'll take over for a bit
Hi there! What would you like today?
Thanks
You're very welcome
I need to say something
Something funny, something smart and funny
Nothing!
I've got nothing!

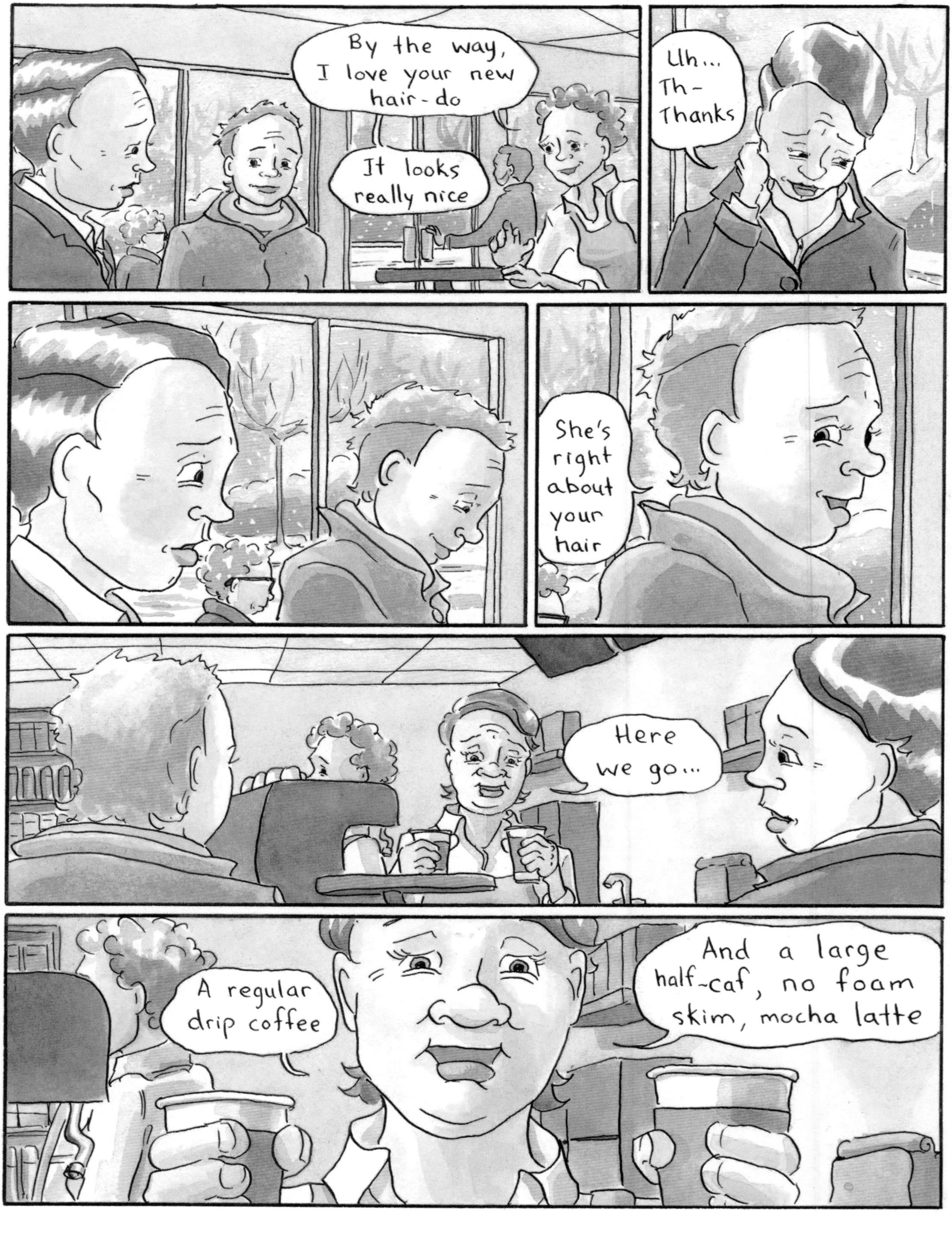
By the way, I love your new hair-do
It looks really nice
Uh... Th- Thanks
She's right about your hair
Here we go...
A regular drip coffee
And a large half-caf, no foam skim, mocha latte

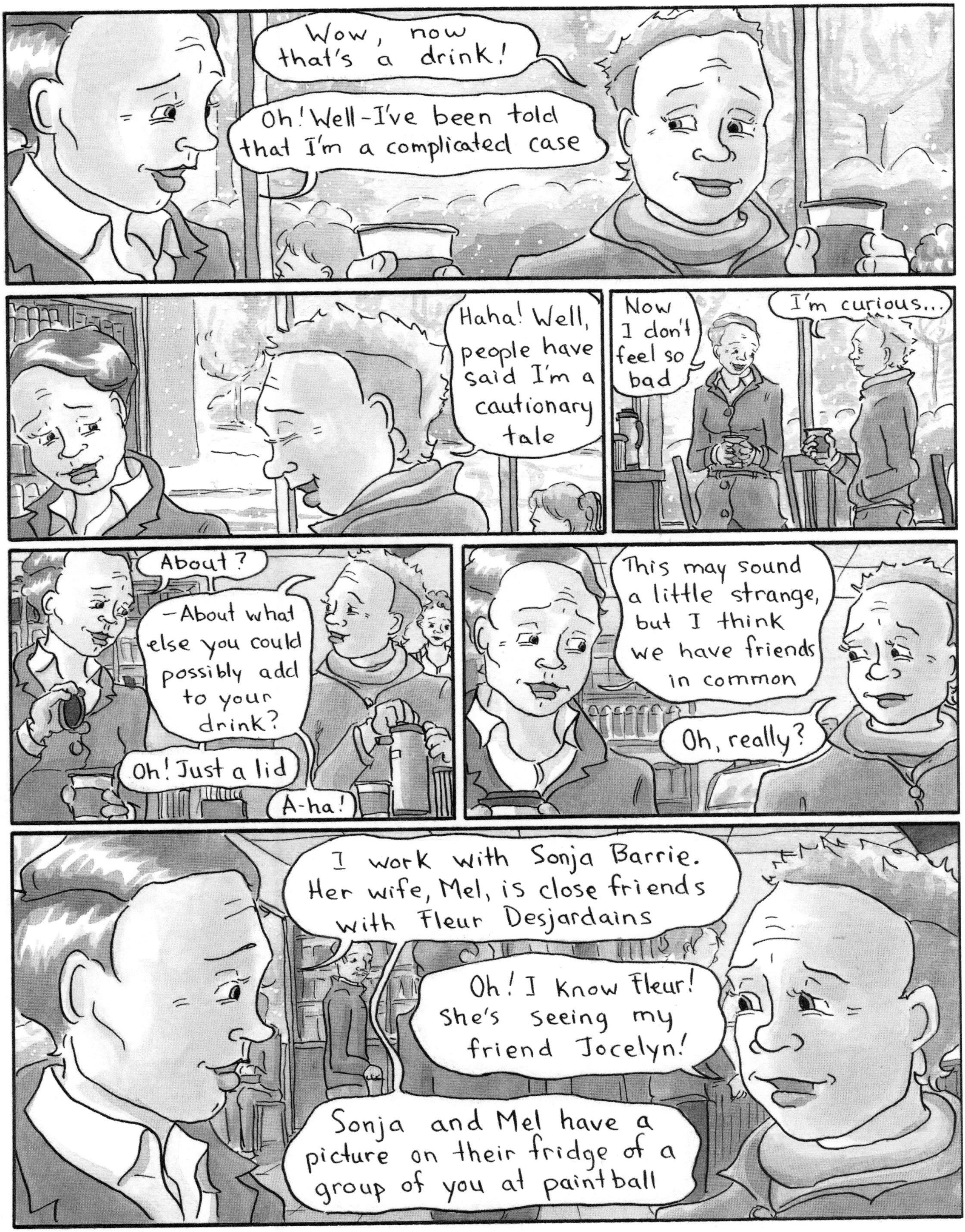
Wow, now that's a drink!
Oh! Well-I've been told that I'm a complicated case
Haha! Well, people have said I'm a cautionary tale
Now I don't feel so bad
I'm curious...
About?
-About what else you could possibly add to your drink?
Oh! Just a lid
A-ha!
This may sound a little strange, but I think we have friends in common
Oh, really?
I work with Sonja Barrie. Her wife, Mel, is close friends with Fleur Desjardains
Oh! I know Fleur! She's seeing my friend Jocelyn!
Sonja and Mel have a picture on their fridge of a group of you at paintball

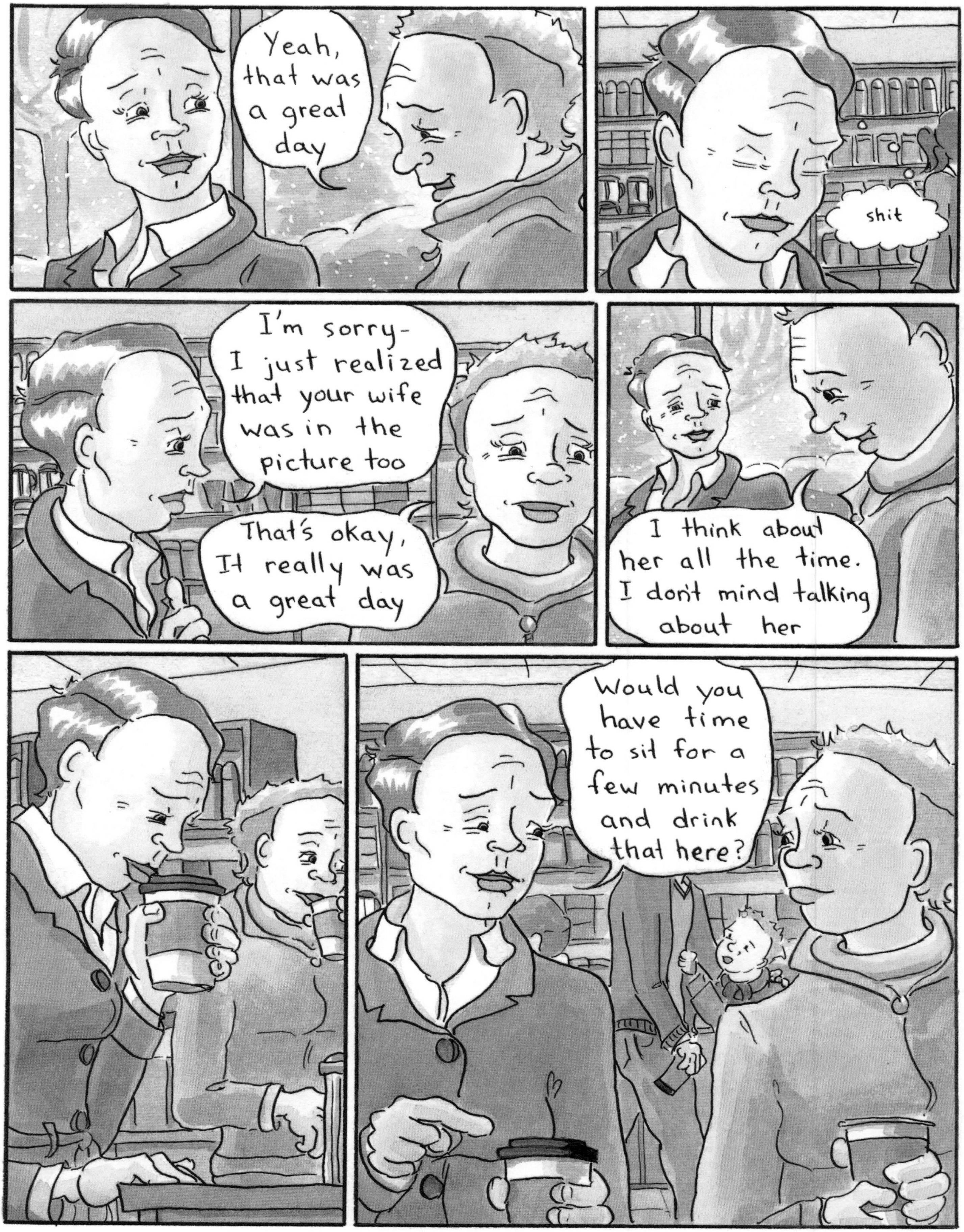
Yeah, that was a great day
shit
I'm sorry- I just realized that your wife was in the picture too
That's okay, It really was a great day
I think about her all the time. I don't mind talking about her
Would you have time to sit for a few minutes and drink that here?

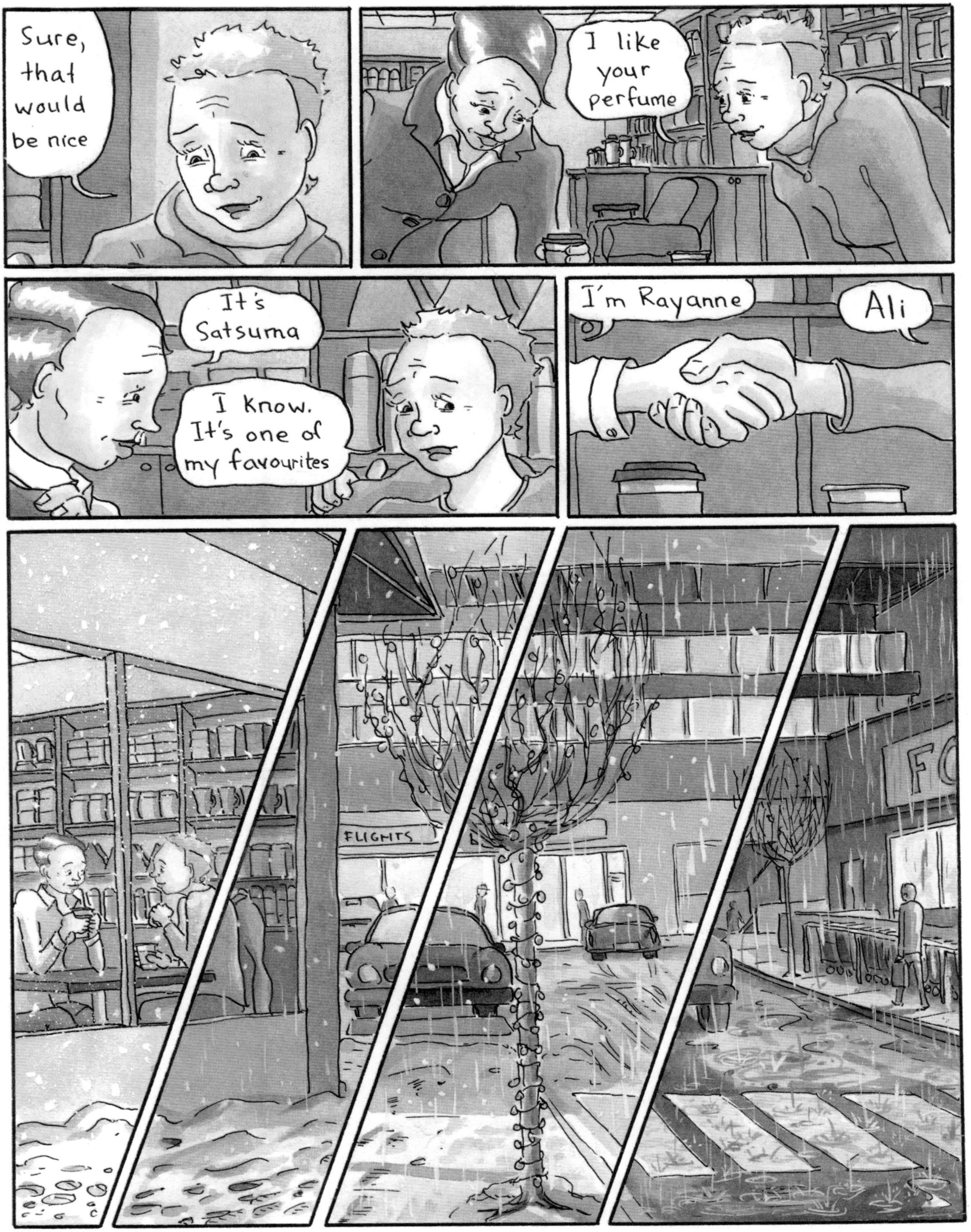
Sure, that would be nice
I like your perfume
It's Satsuma
I know. It's one of my favourites
I'm Rayanne
Ali
FLIGHTS

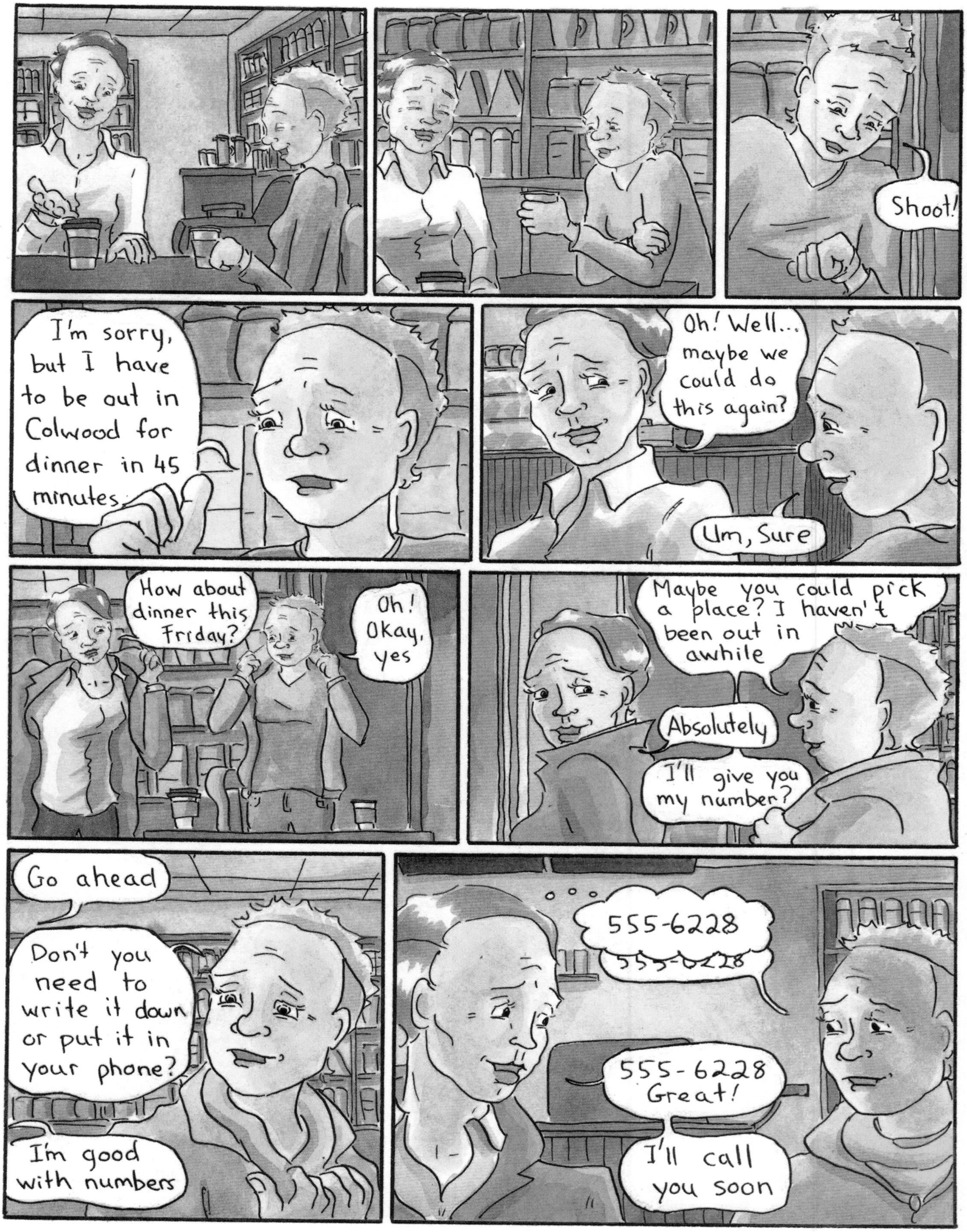
Shoot!
I'm sorry, but I have to be out in Colwood for dinner in 45 minutes.
Oh! Well... maybe we could do this again?
Um, Sure
How about dinner this Friday?
Oh! Okay, yes
Maybe you could pick a place? I haven't been out in awhile
Absolutely
I'll give you my number?
Go ahead
Don't you need to write it down or put it in your phone?
I'm good with numbers
555-6228
555-6228 Great!
I'll call you soon

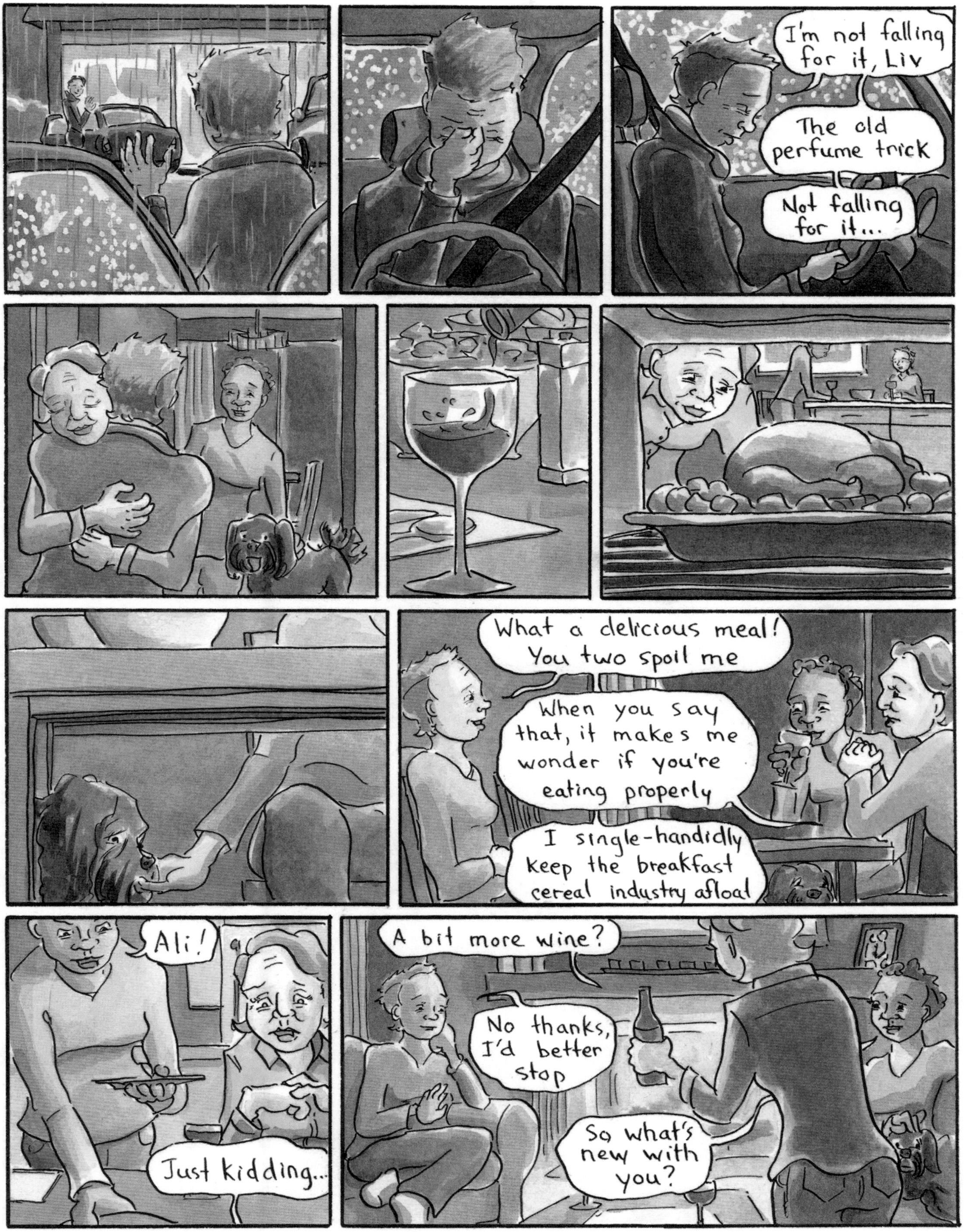
I'm not falling for it, Liv
The old perfume trick
Not falling for it...
What a delicious meal! You two spoil me
When you say that, it makes me wonder if you're eating properly
I single-handidly keep the breakfast cereal industry afloat
Ali!
Just kidding...
A bit more wine?
No thanks, I'd better stop
So what's new with you?

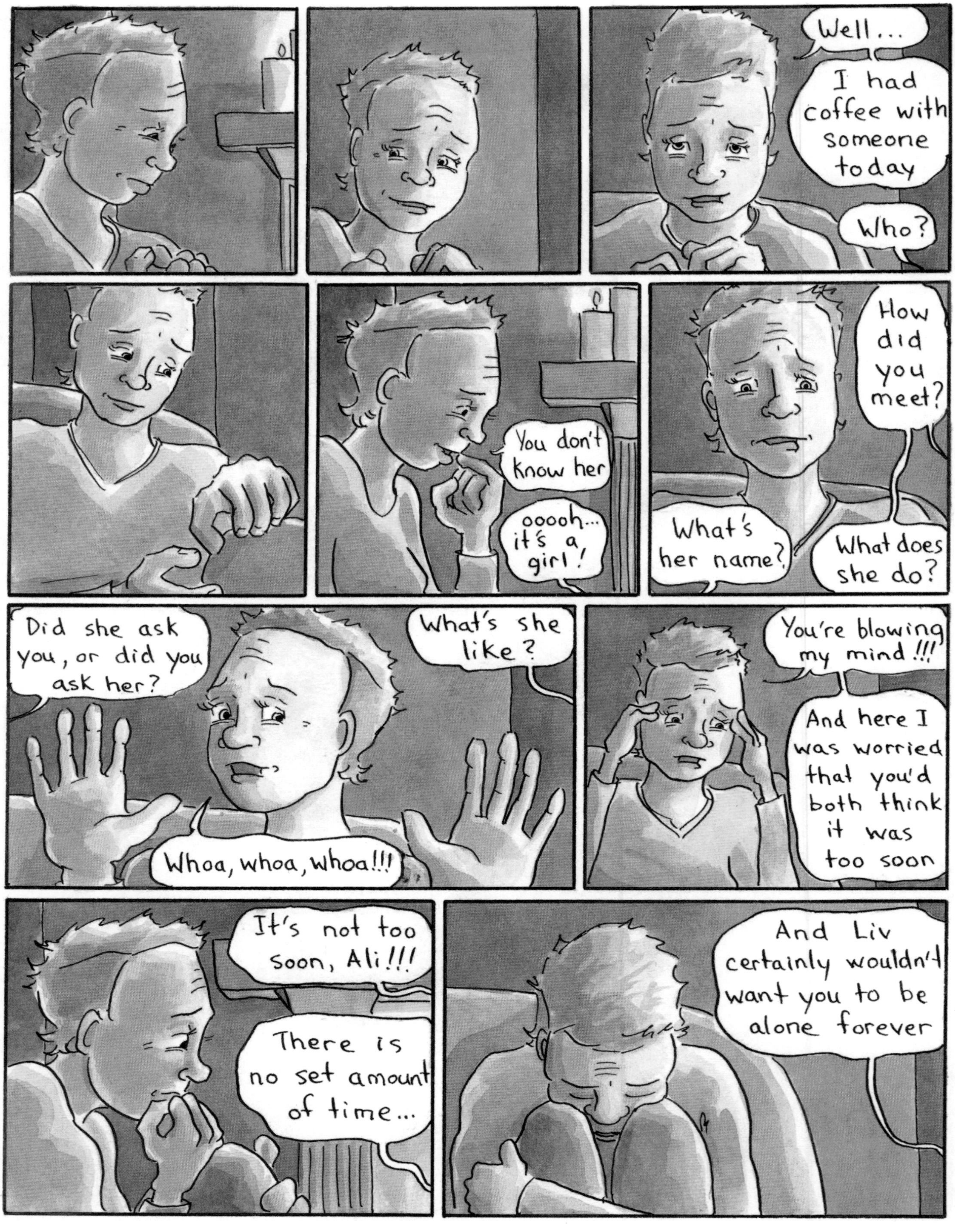
Well...
I had coffee with someone today
Who?
You don't know her
ooooh... it's a girl!
How did you meet?
What's her name?
What does she do?
Did she ask you, or did you ask her?
What's she like?
Whoa, whoa, whoa!!!
You're blowing my mind!!!
And here I was worried that you'd both think it was too soon
It's not too soon, Ali!!!
There is no set amount of time...
And Liv certainly wouldn't want you to be alone forever

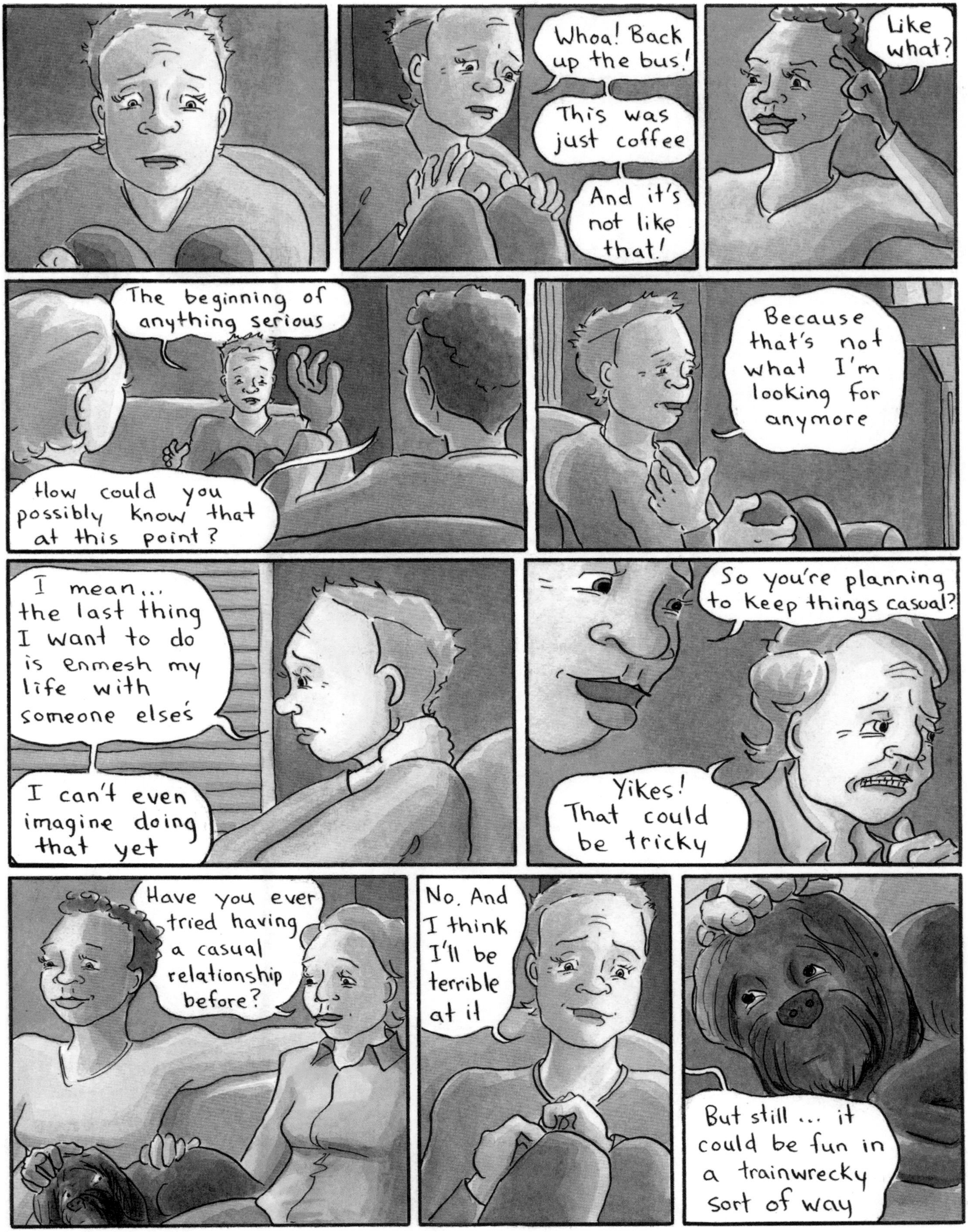
Whoa! Back up the bus!
This was just coffee
And it's not like that!
Like what?
The beginning of anything serious
How could you possibly know that at this point?
Because that's not what I'm looking for anymore
I mean... the last thing I want to do is enmesh my life with someone else's
I can't even imagine doing that yet
So you're planning to keep things casual?
Yikes! That could be tricky
Have you ever tried having a casual relationship before?
No. And I think I'll be terrible at it
But still ... it could be fun in a trainwrecky sort of way

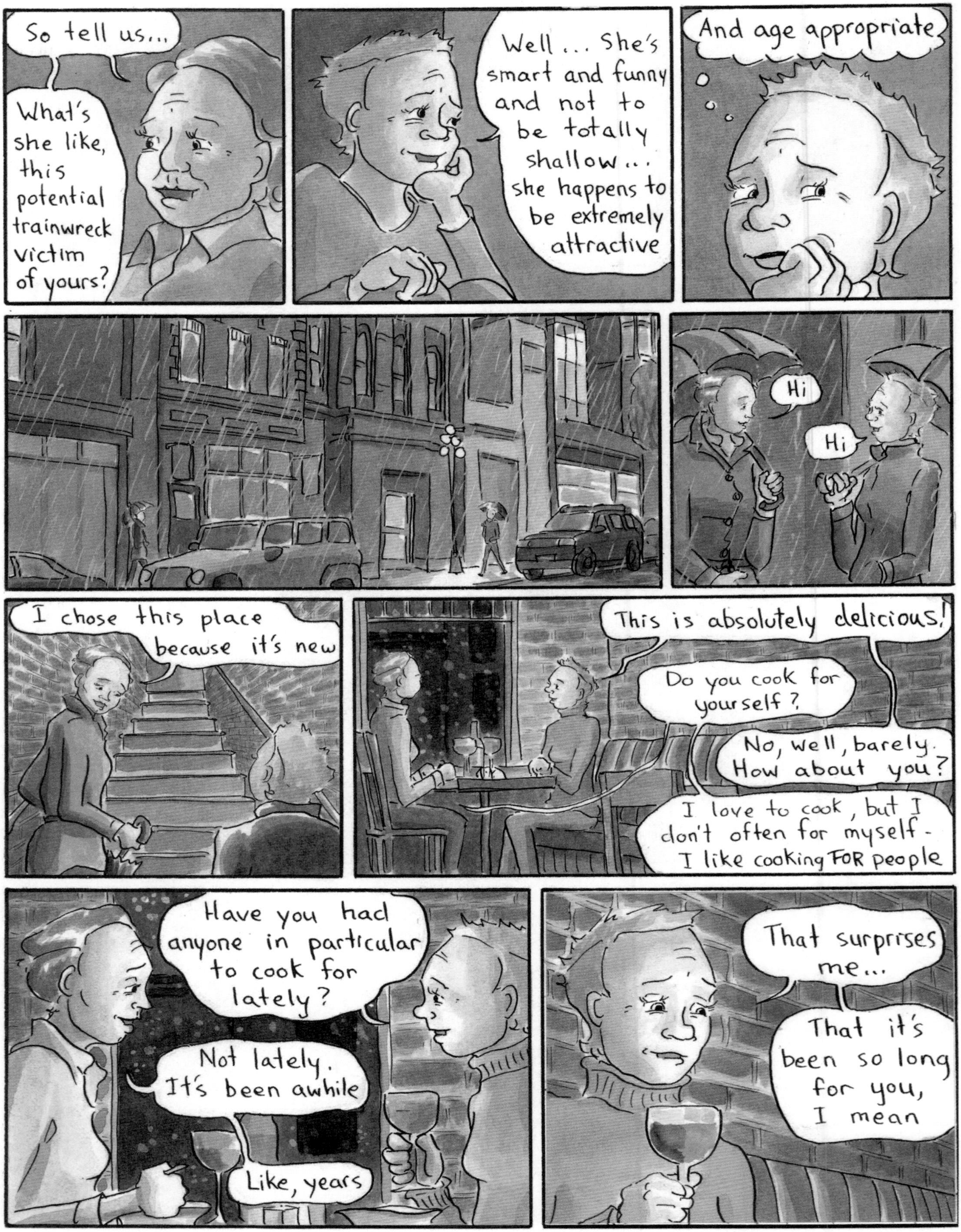
So tell us...
What's she like, this potential trainwreck victim of yours?
Well... She's smart and funny and not to be totally shallow... she happens to be extremely attractive
And age appropriate
Hi
Hi
I chose this place because it's new
This is absolutely delicious!
Do you cook for yourself?
No, well, barely. How about you?
I love to cook, but I don't often for myself - I like cooking FOR people
Have you had anyone in particular to cook for lately?
Not lately. It's been awhile
Like, years
That surprises me...
That it's been so long for you, I mean

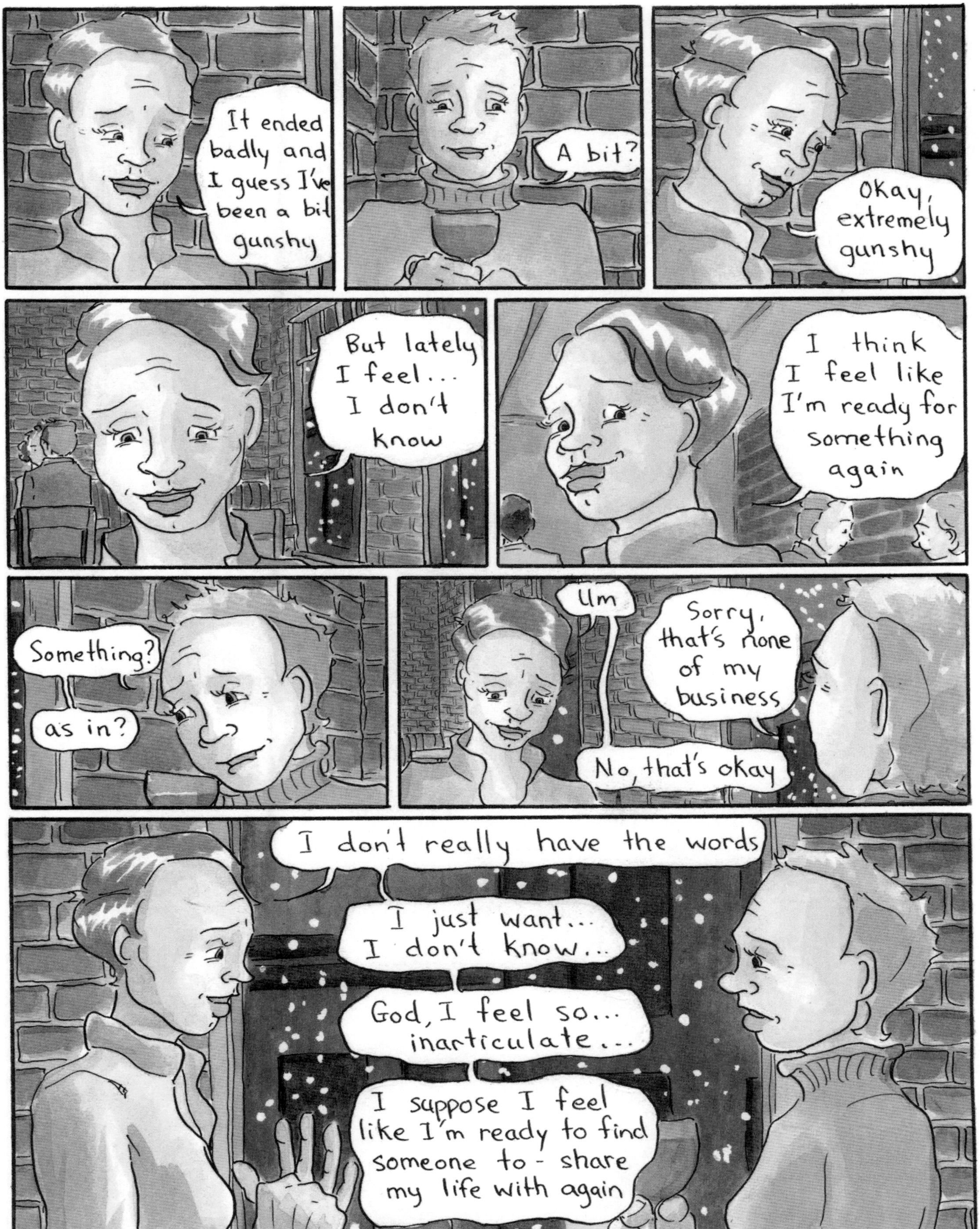
It ended badly and I guess I've been a bit gunshy
A bit?
Okay, extremely gunshy
But lately I feel... I don't know
I think I feel like I'm ready for something again
Something?
as in?
Um
Sorry, that's none of my business
No, that's okay
I don't really have the words
I just want... I don't know...
God, I feel so... inarticulate...
I suppose I feel like I'm ready to find someone to - share my life with again

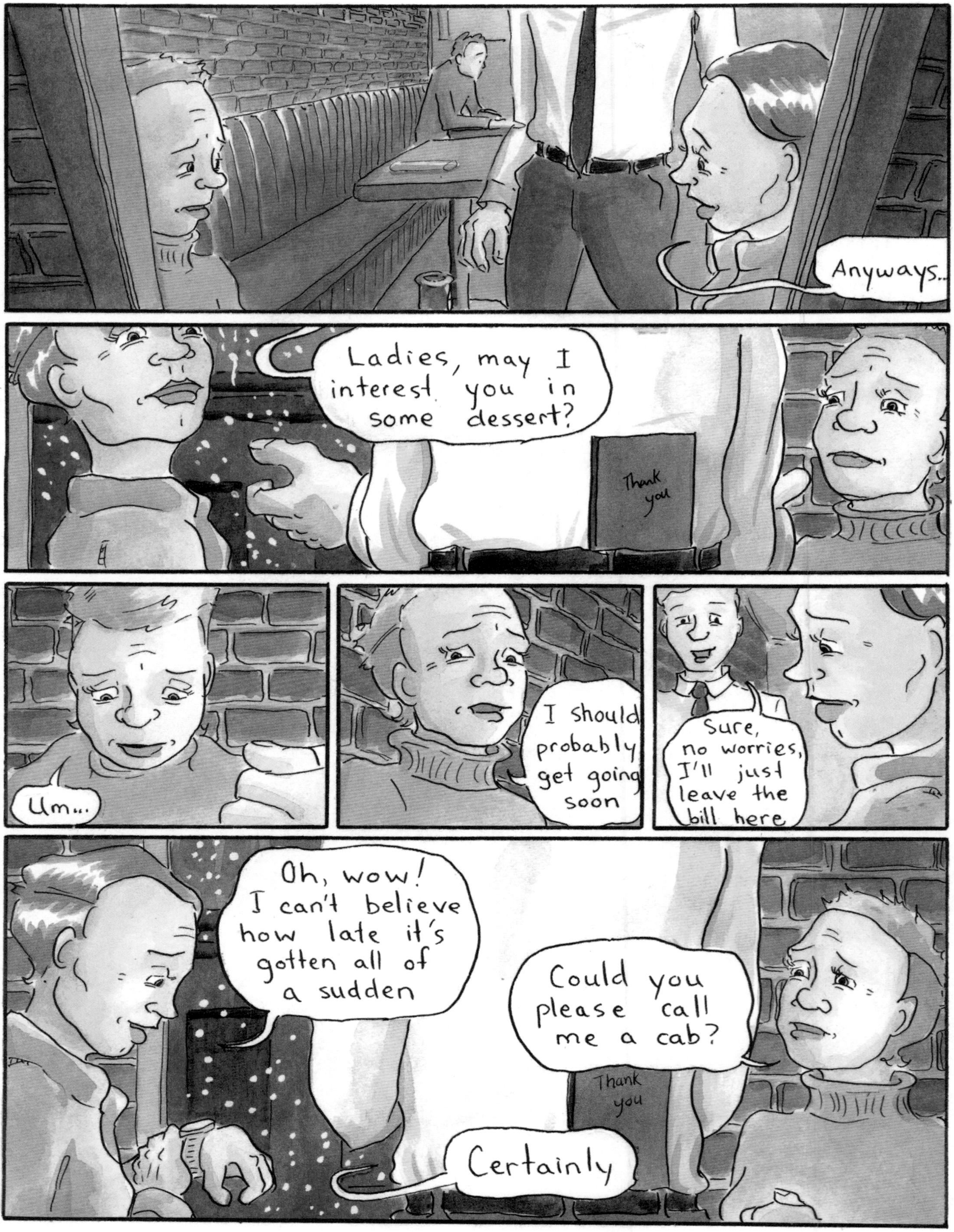
Anyways...
Ladies, may I interest you in some dessert?
Thank you
Um...
I should probably get going soon
Sure, no worries, I'll just leave the bill here
Oh, wow! I can't believe how late it's gotten all of a sudden
Could you please call me a cab?
Thank you
Certainly

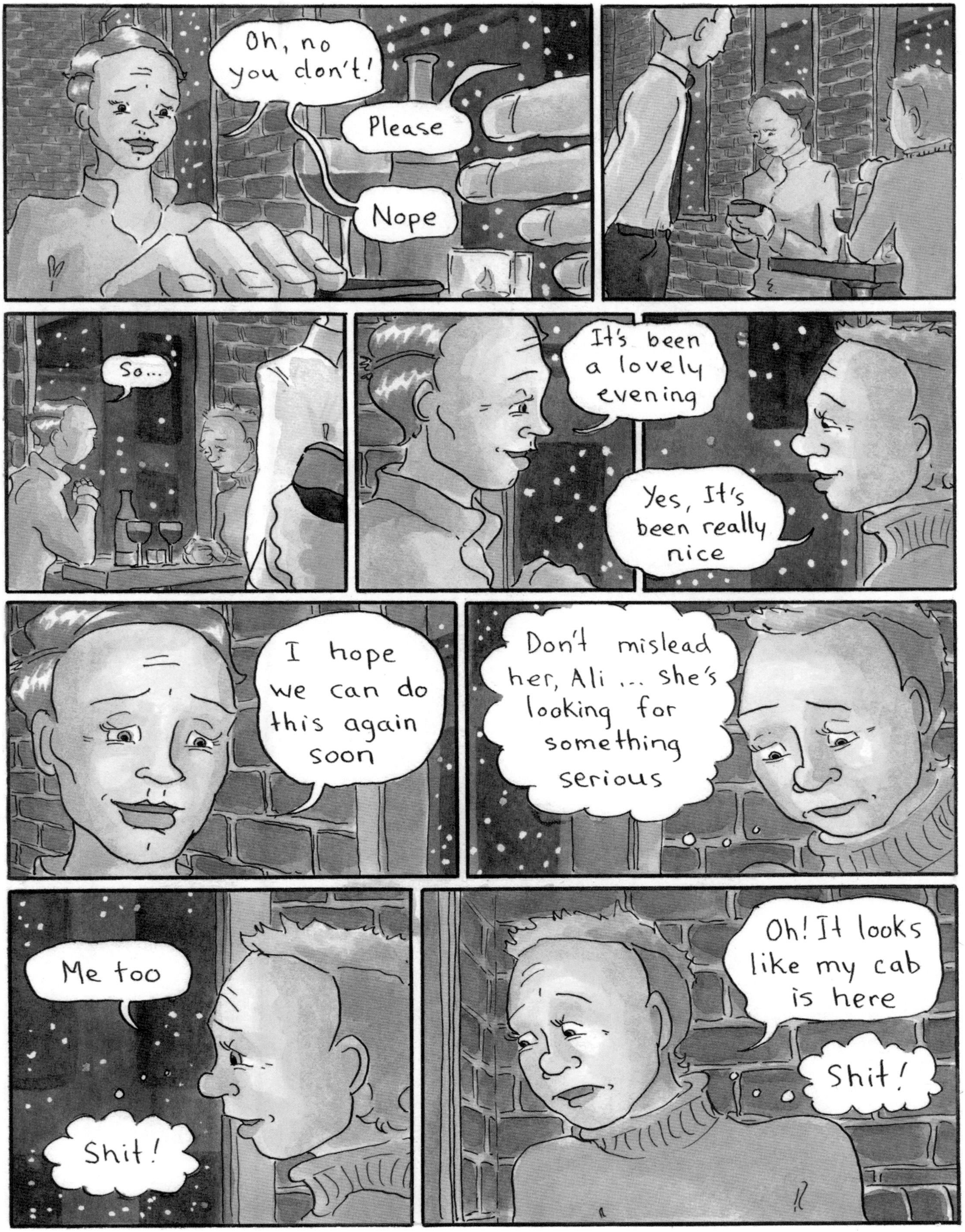
Oh, no you don't!
Please
Nope
So...
It's been a lovely evening
Yes, It's been really nice
I hope we can do this again soon
Don't mislead her, Ali ... she's looking for something serious
Me too
Shit!
Oh! It looks like my cab is here
Shit!

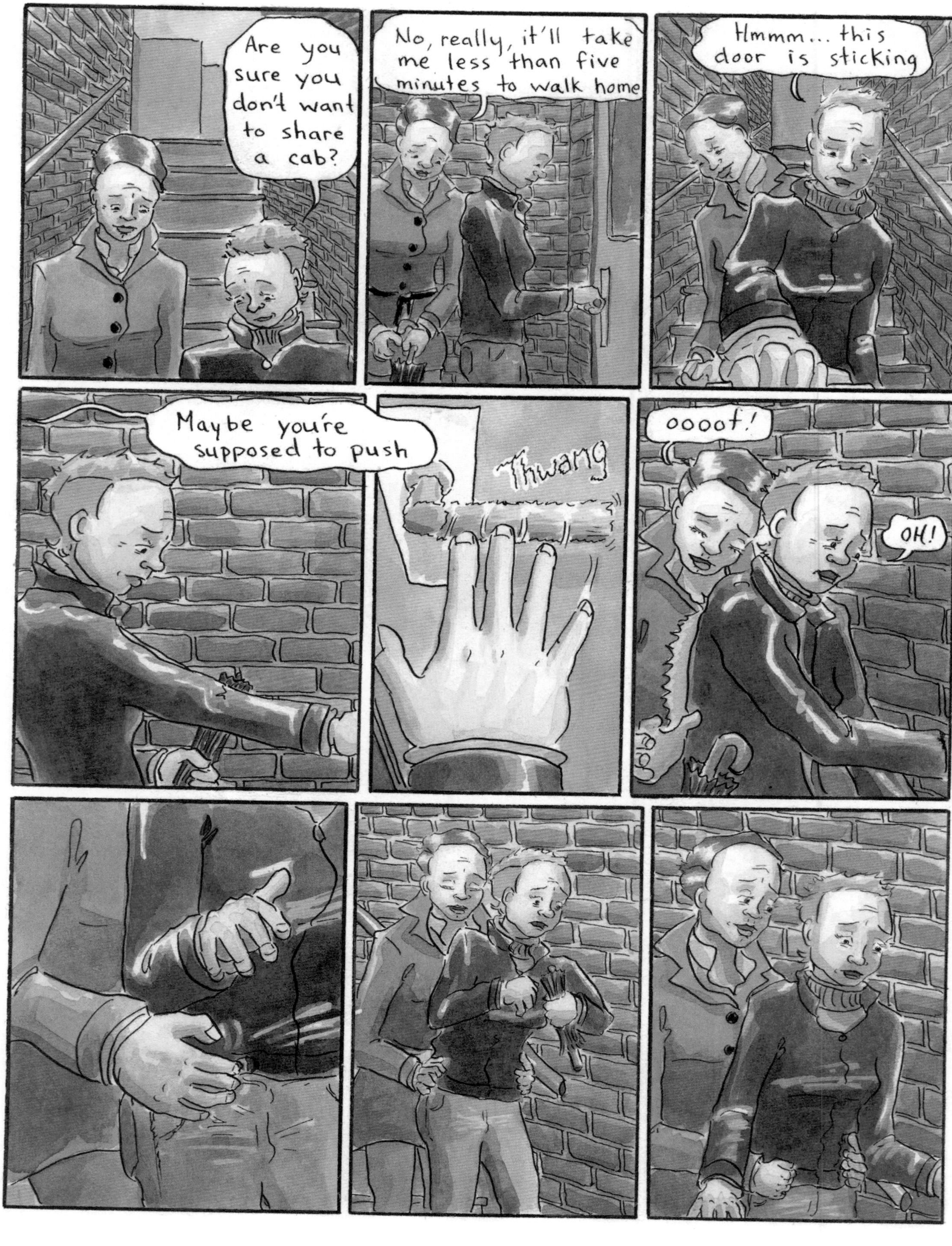
Are you sure you don't want to share a cab?
No, really, it'll take me less than five minutes to walk home
Hmmm... this door is sticking
Maybe you're supposed to push
Thwang
oooof!
OH!

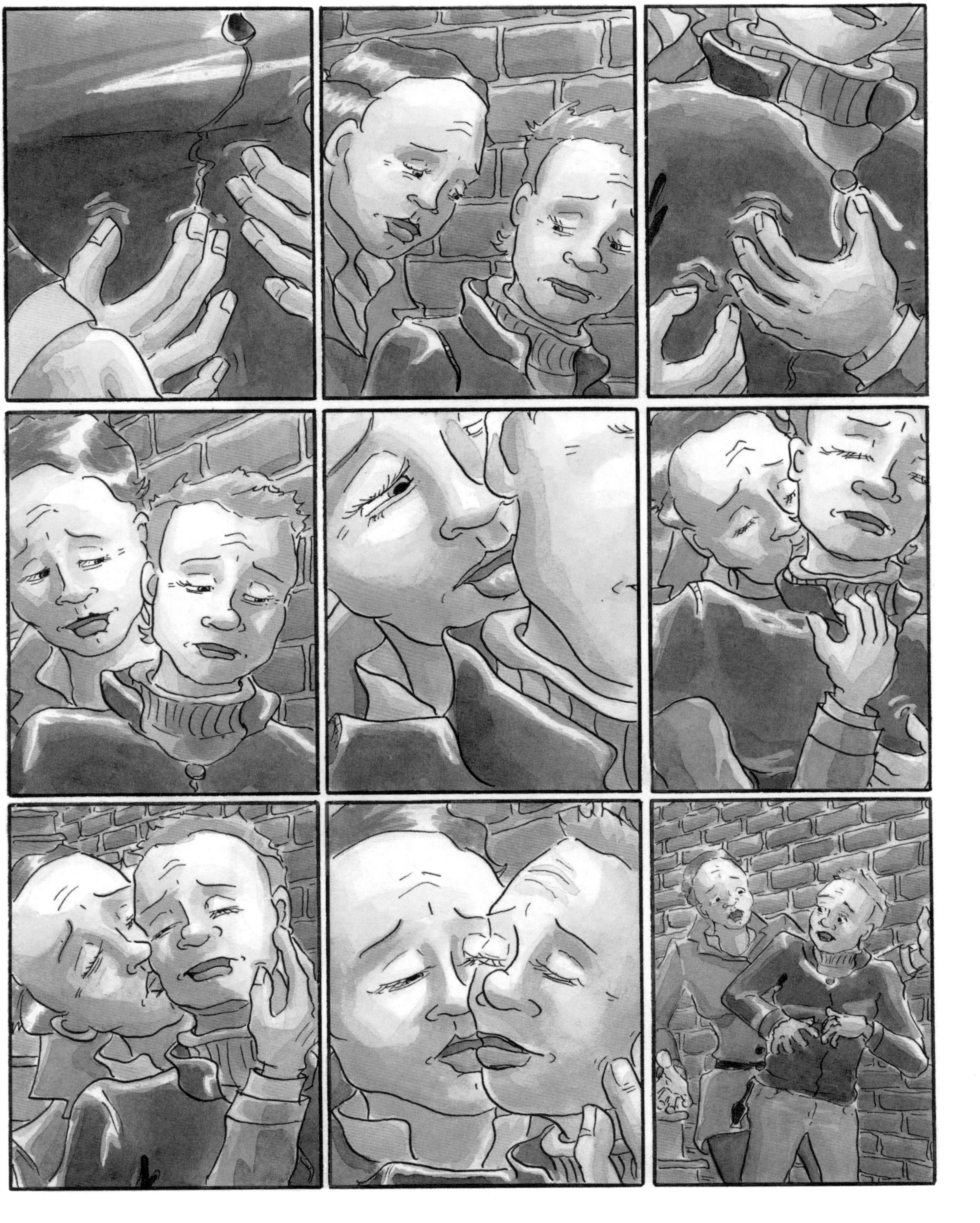

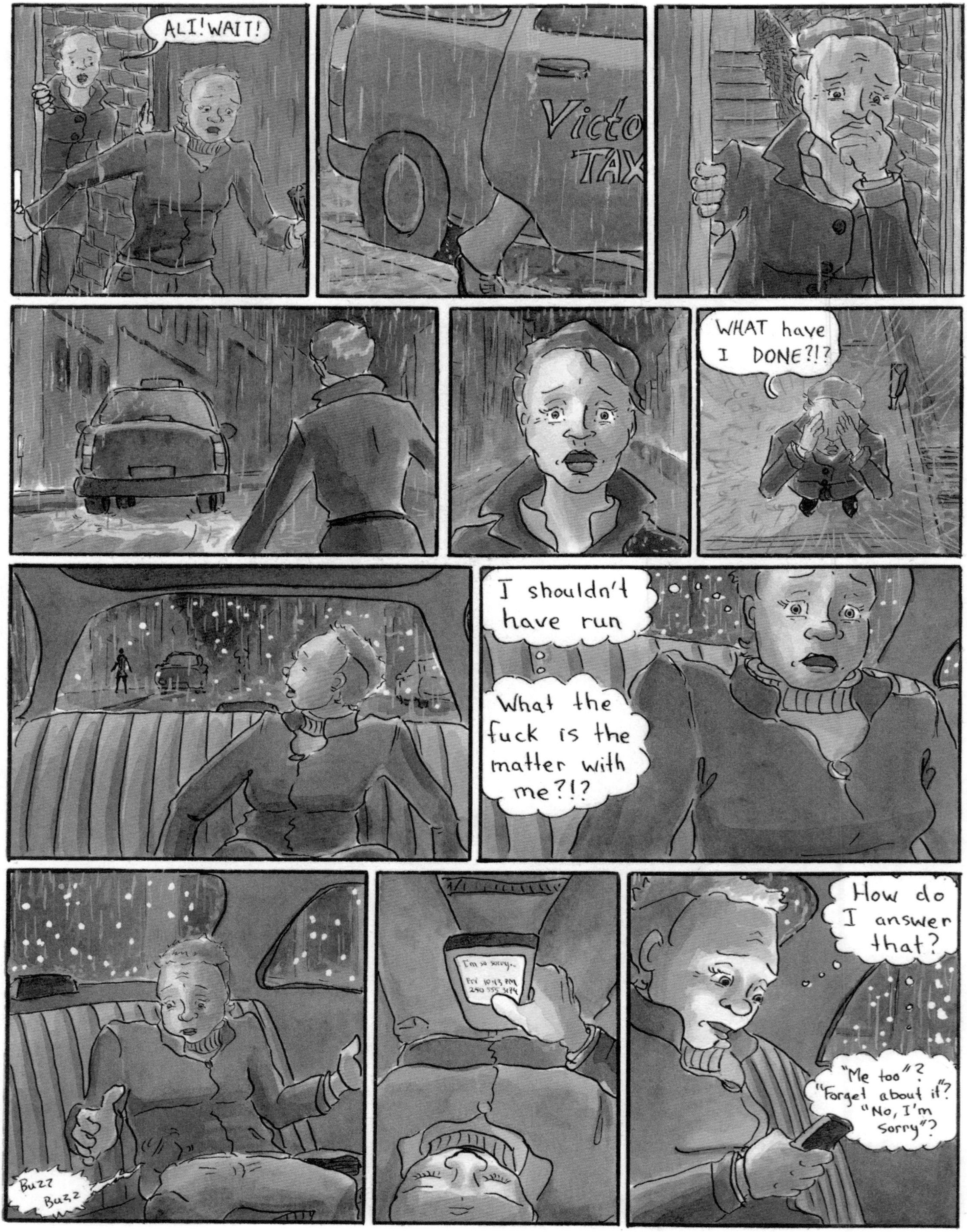
ALI! WAIT!
Victo
TAX
WHAT have I DONE?!?
I shouldn't have run
What the fuck is the matter with me?!?
Buzz Buzz
I'm so sorry..
Fri 10:13 PM
240 555 3174
How do I answer that?
"Me too"? "Forget about it"? "No, I'm sorry"?

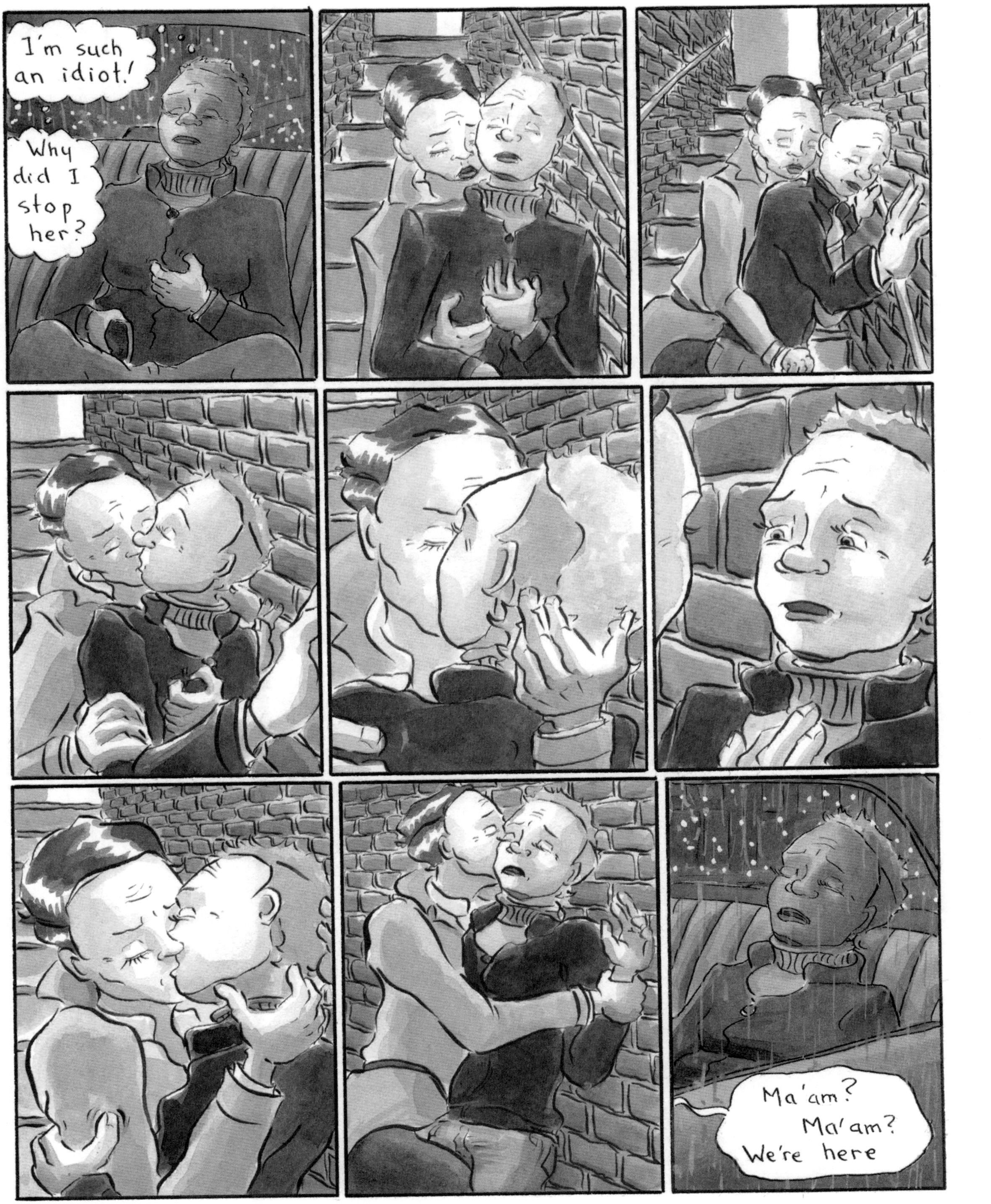
I'm such an idiot!
Why did I stop her?
Ma'am? Ma'am? We're here

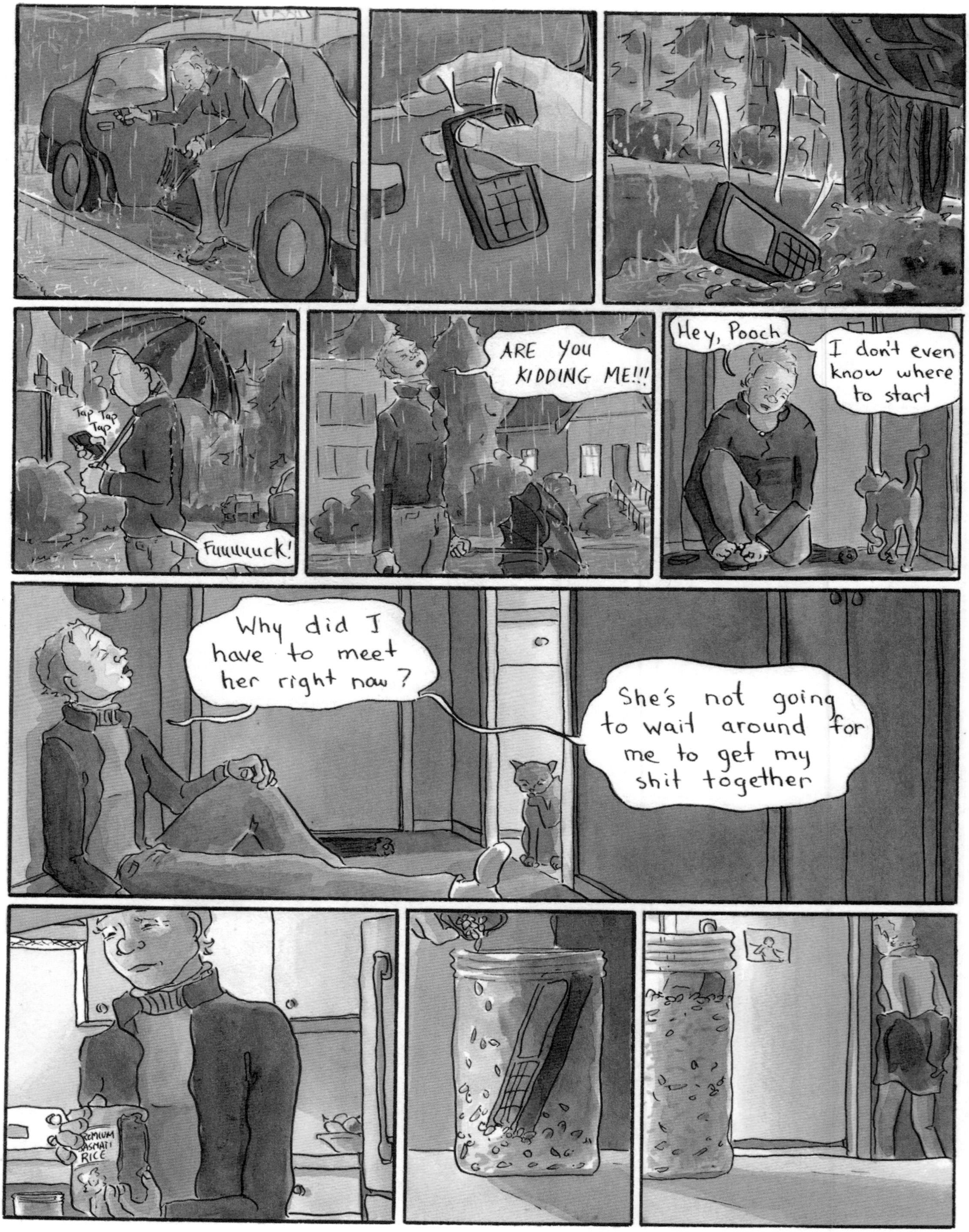
Tap Tap Tap
Fuuuuuck!
ARE YOU KIDDING ME!!!
Hey, Pooch
I don't even know where to start
Why did I have to meet her right now?
She's not going to wait around for me to get my shit together
PREMIUM BASMATI RICE

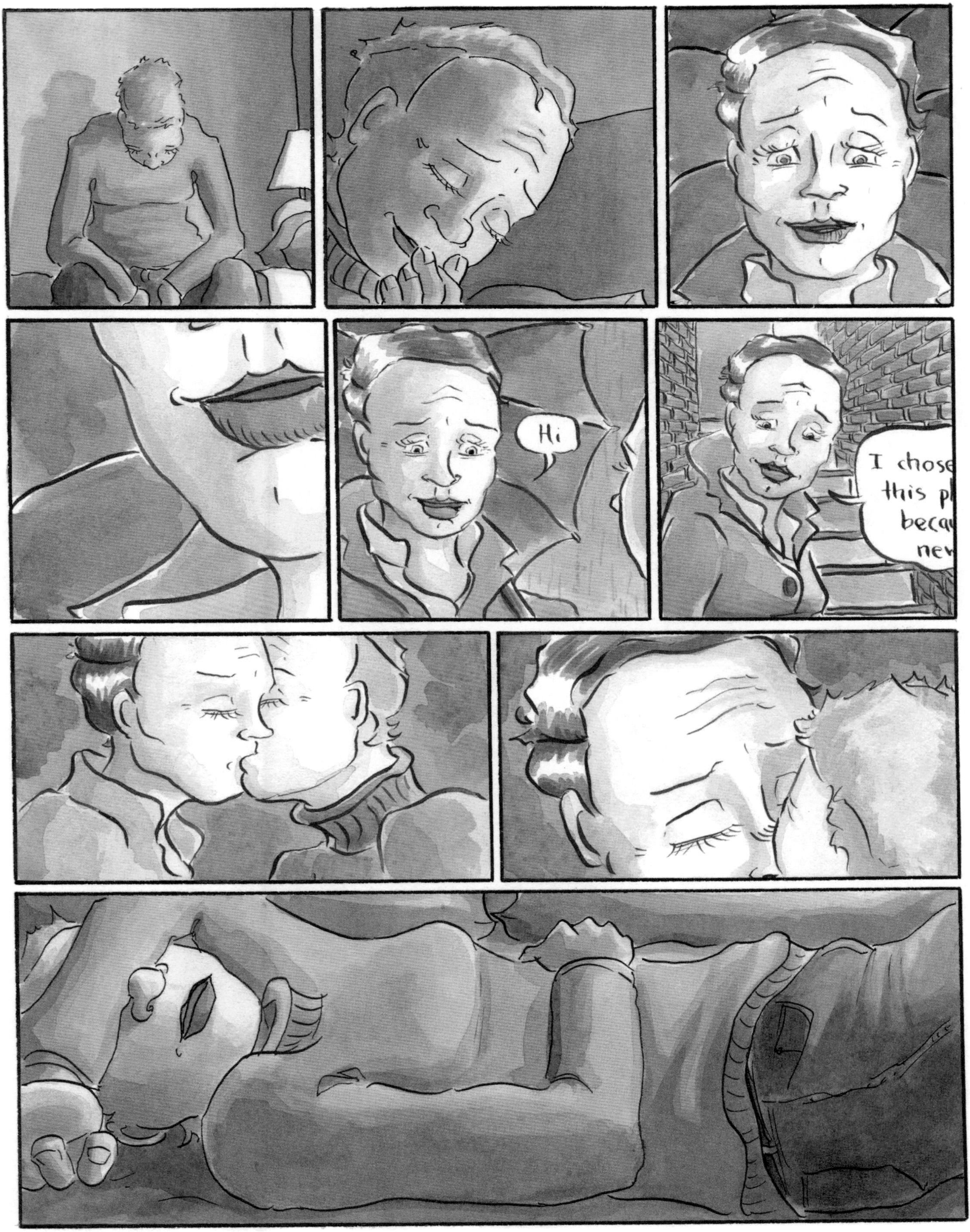
Hi
I chose this

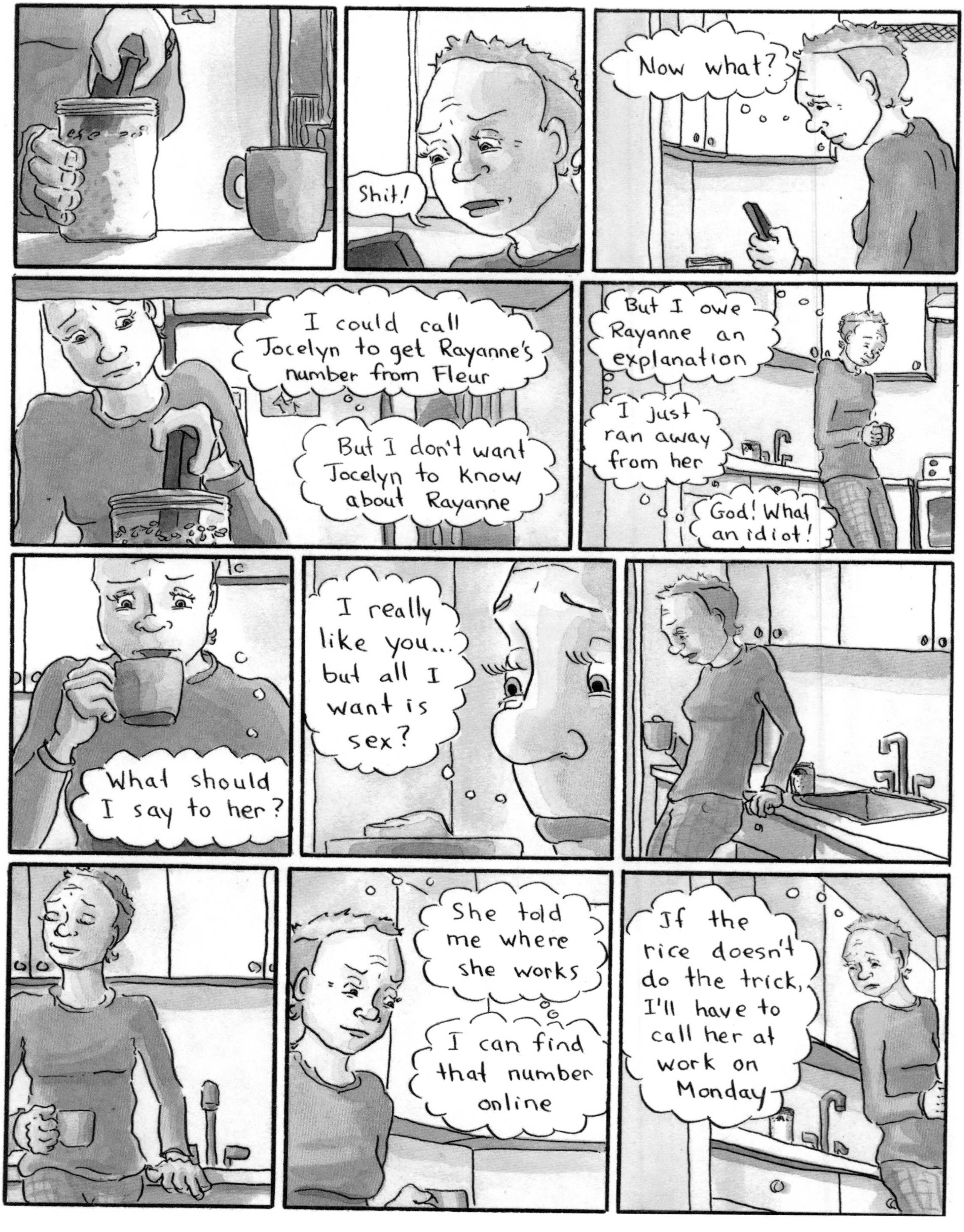
Shit!
Now what?
I could call Jocelyn to get Rayanne's number from Fleur
But I don't want Jocelyn to know about Rayanne
But I owe Rayanne an explanation
I just ran away from her
God! What an idiot!
What should I say to her?
I really like you... but all I want is sex?
She told me where she works
I can find that number online
If the rice doesn't do the trick, I'll have to call her at work on Monday

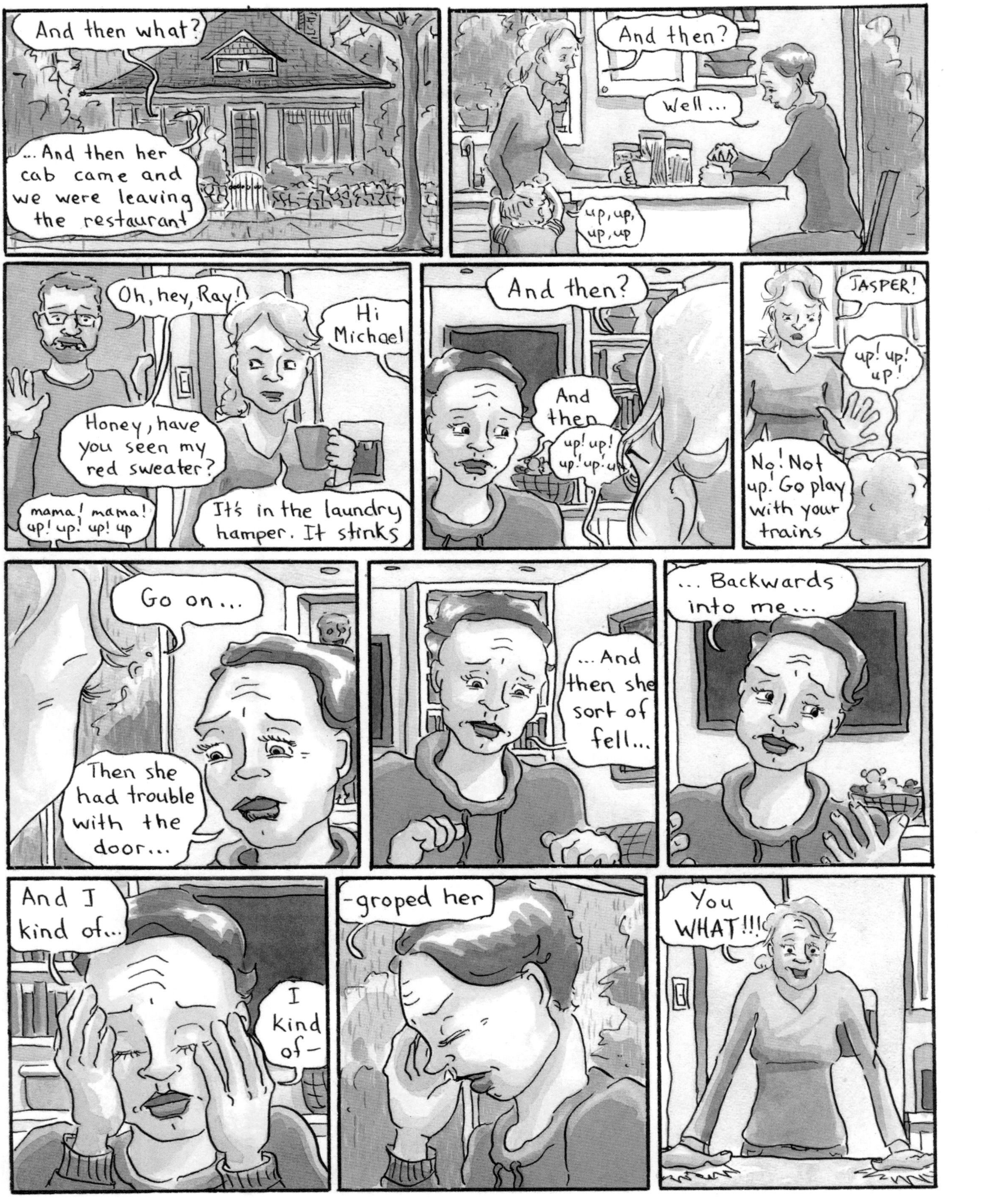
And then what?
...And then her cab came and we were leaving the restaurant
And then?
Well...
up, up, up, up
Oh, hey, Ray!
Hi Michael
Honey, have you seen my red sweater?
mama! mama! up! up! up! up
It's in the laundry hamper. It stinks
And then?
And then
up! up! up! up! up
JASPER!
up! up! up!
No! Not up! Go play with your trains
Go on...
Then she had trouble with the door...
...And then she sort of fell...
... Backwards into me...
And I kind of...
I kind of-
-groped her
You WHAT!!!

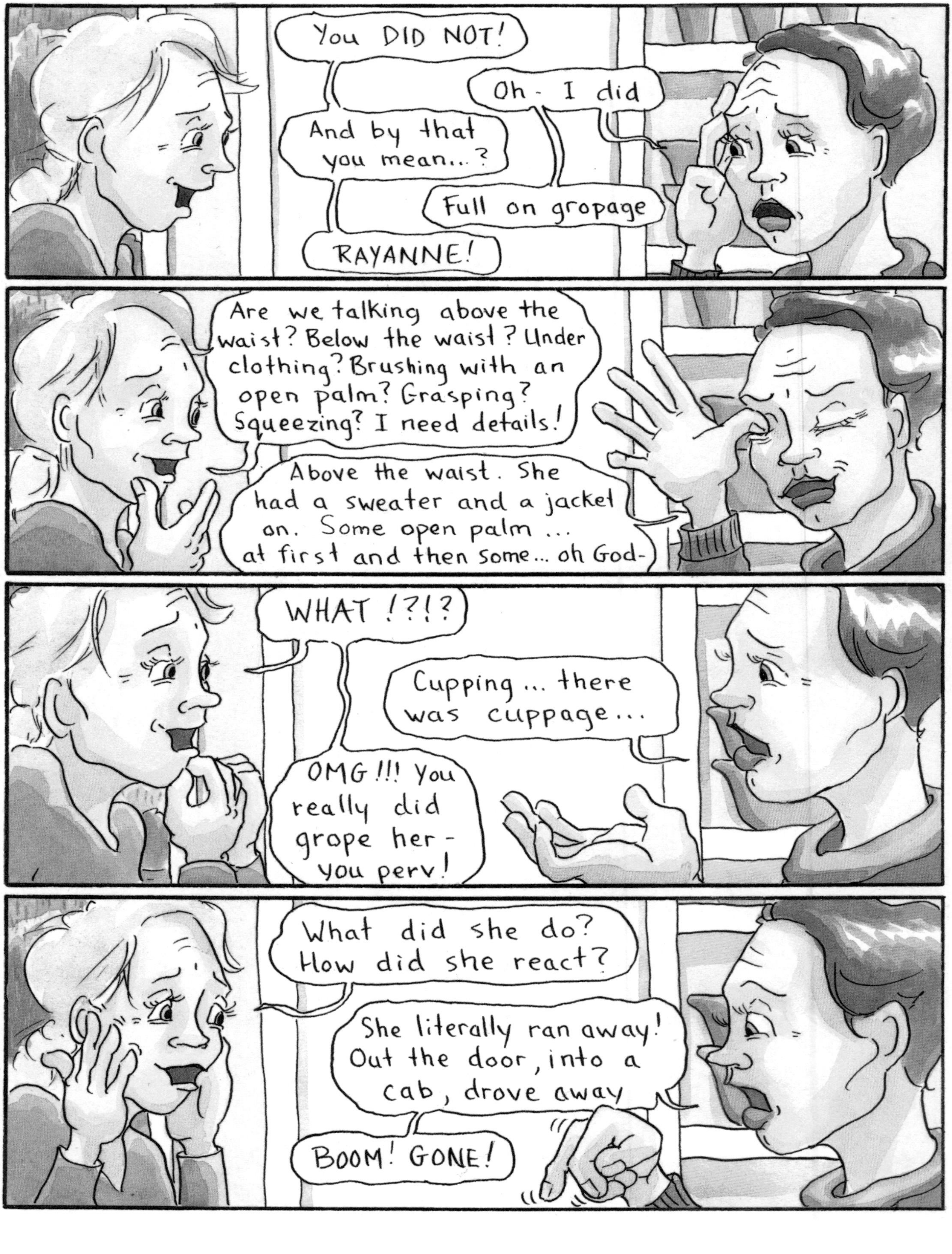

You DID NOT!
Oh - I did
And by that you mean...?
Full on gropage
RAYANNE!
Are we talking above the waist? Below the waist? Under clothing? Brushing with an open palm? Grasping? Squeezing? I need details!
Above the waist. She had a sweater and a jacket on. Some open palm ... at first and then some... oh God-
WHAT!?!?
Cupping... there was cuppage...
OMG!!! You really did grope her - you perv!
What did she do? How did she react?
She literally ran away! Out the door, into a cab, drove away
BOOM! GONE!

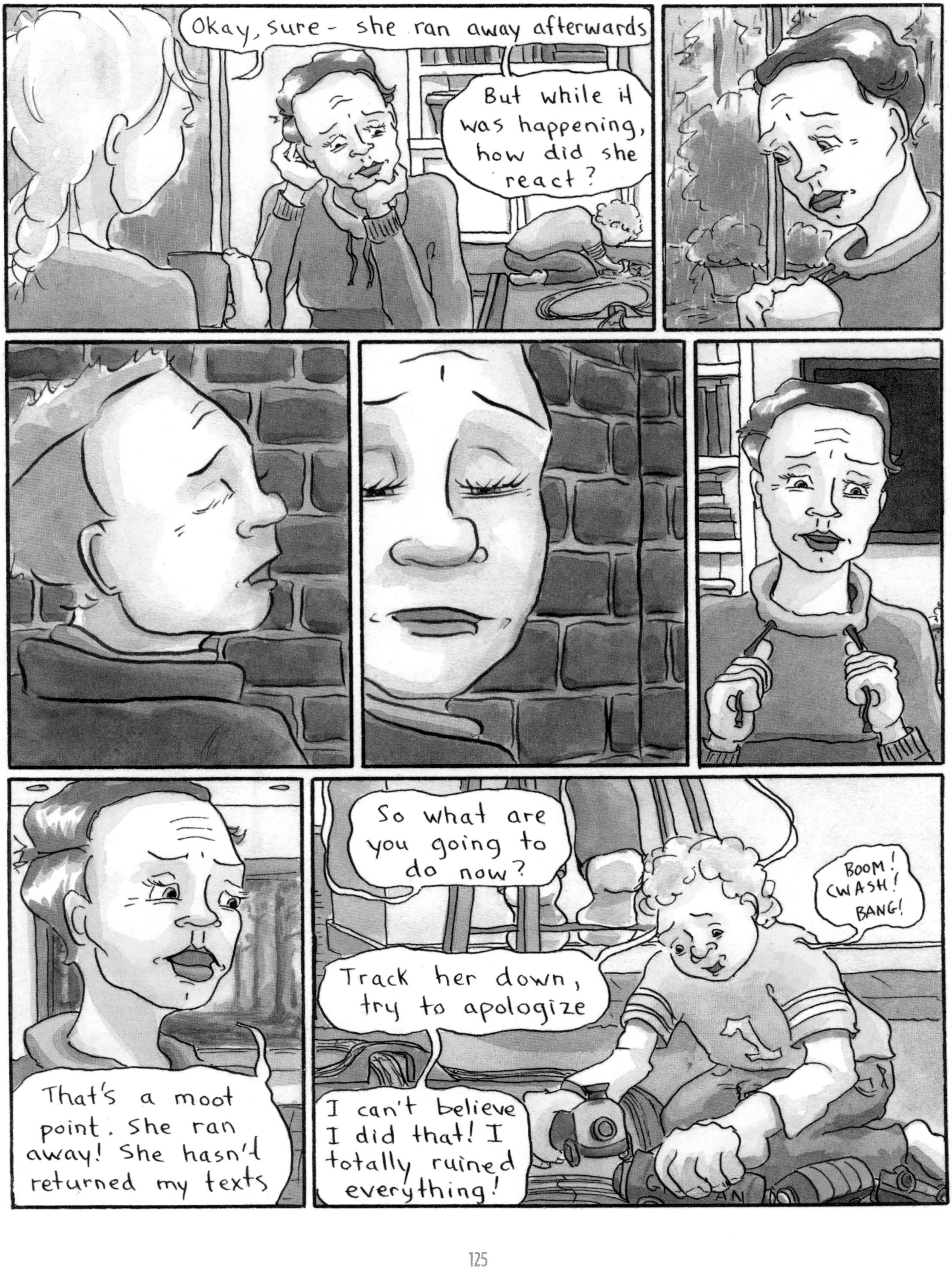
Okay, sure - she ran away afterwards
But while it was happening, how did she react?
So what are you going to do now?
BOOM! CWASH! BANG!
Track her down, try to apologize
That's a moot point. She ran away! She hasn't returned my texts
I can't believe I did that! I totally ruined everything!

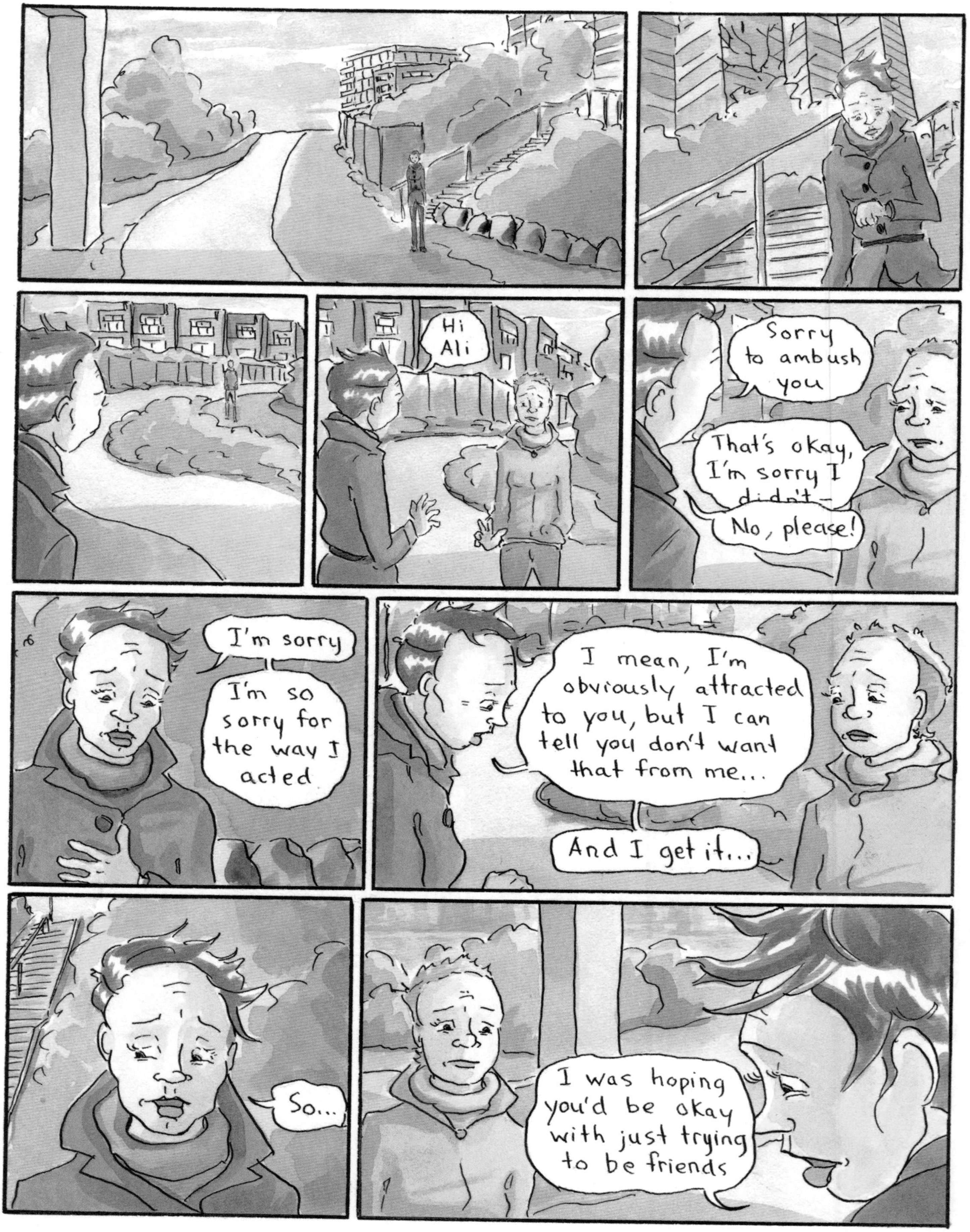
Hi Ali
Sorry to ambush you
That's okay, I'm sorry I didn't—
No, please!
I'm sorry
I'm so sorry for the way I acted
I mean, I'm obviously attracted to you, but I can tell you don't want that from me...
And I get it...
So...
I was hoping you'd be okay with just trying to be friends

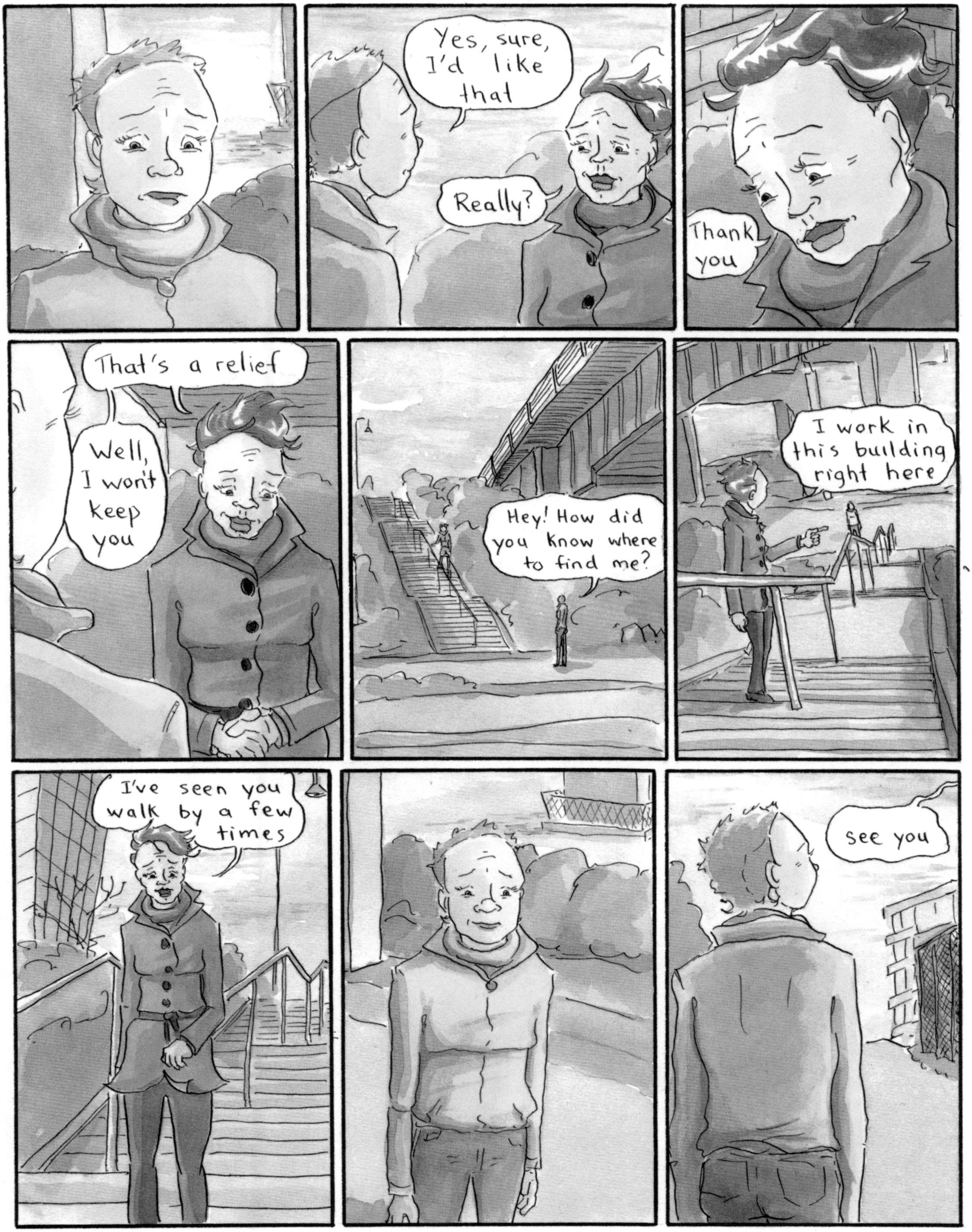

Yes, sure, I'd like that
Really?
Thank you
That's a relief
Well, I won't keep you
Hey! How did you know where to find me?
I work in this building right here
I've seen you walk by a few times
see you

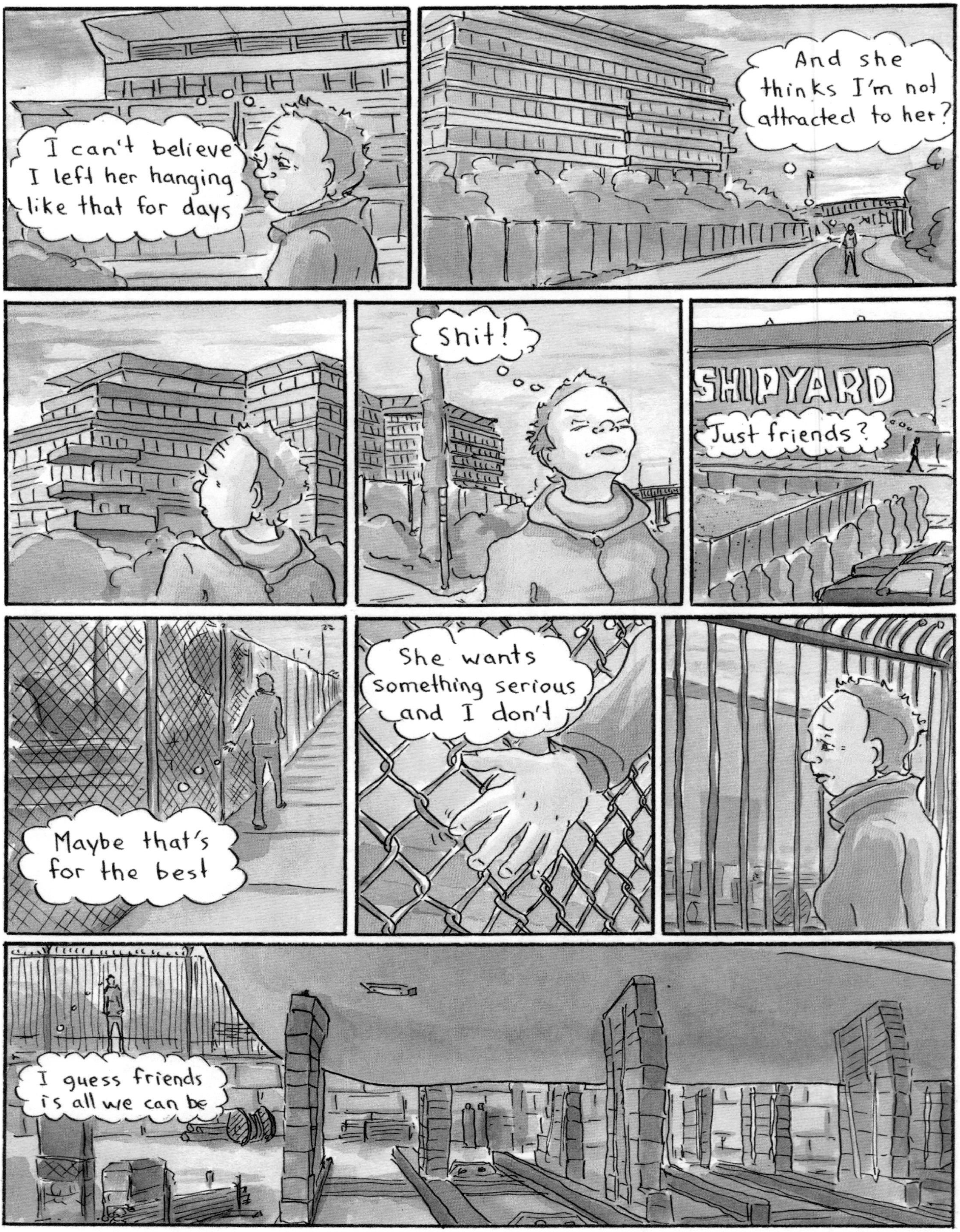
I can't believe I left her hanging like that for days
And she thinks I'm not attracted to her?
Shit!
SHIPYARD
Just friends?
Maybe that's for the best
She wants something serious and I don't
I guess friends is all we can be

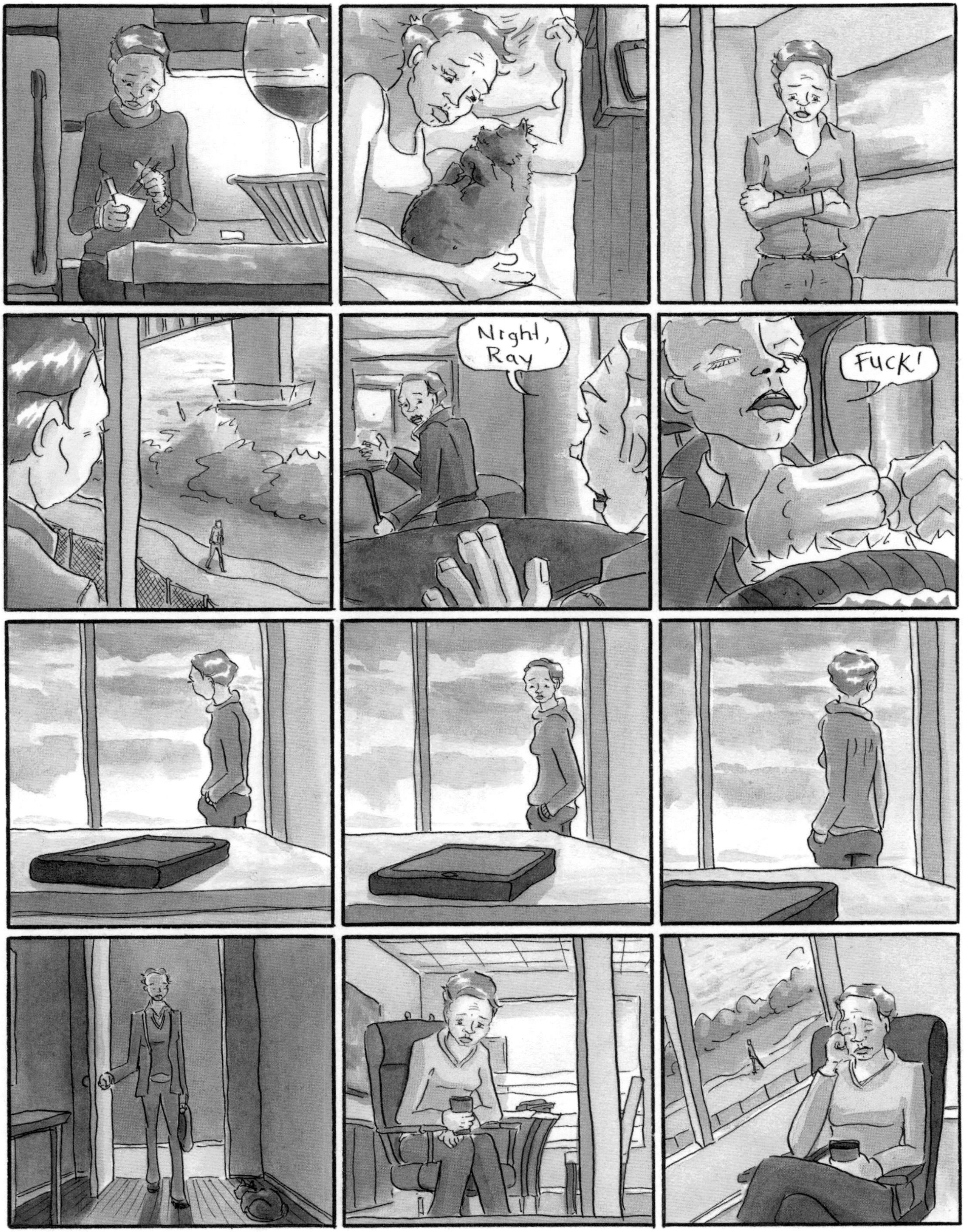
Night, Ray
FUCK!

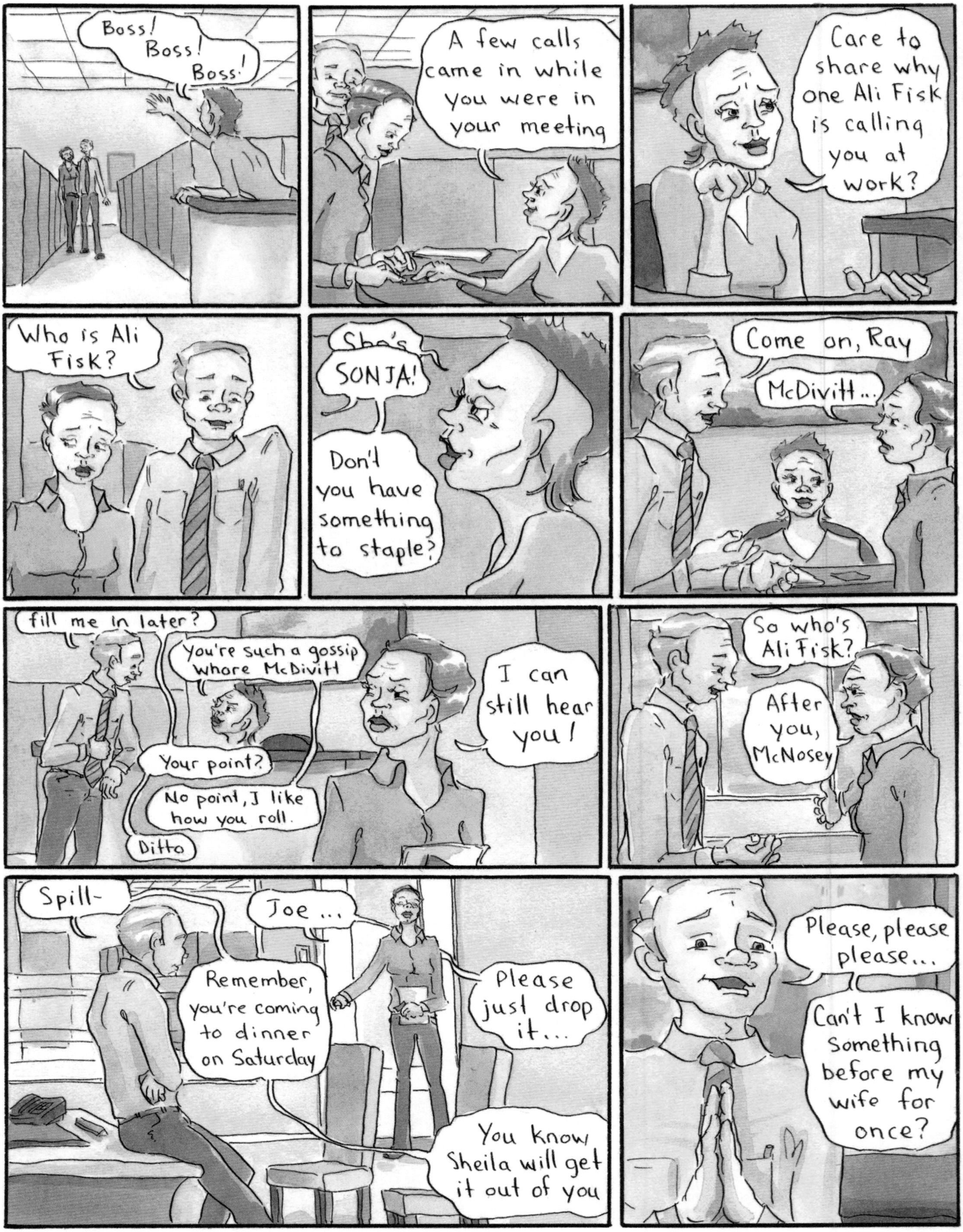
Boss! Boss! Boss!
A few calls came in while you were in your meeting
Care to share why one Ali Fisk is calling you at work?
Who is Ali Fisk?
She's
SONJA!
Don't you have something to staple?
Come on, Ray
McDivitt...
fill me in later?
You're such a gossip whore McDivitt
I can still hear you!
Your point?
No point, I like how you roll.
Ditto
So who's Ali Fisk?
After you, McNosey
Spill-
Joe ...
Remember, you're coming to dinner on Saturday
Please just drop it...
You know Sheila will get it out of you
Please, please please...
Can't I know something before my wife for once?

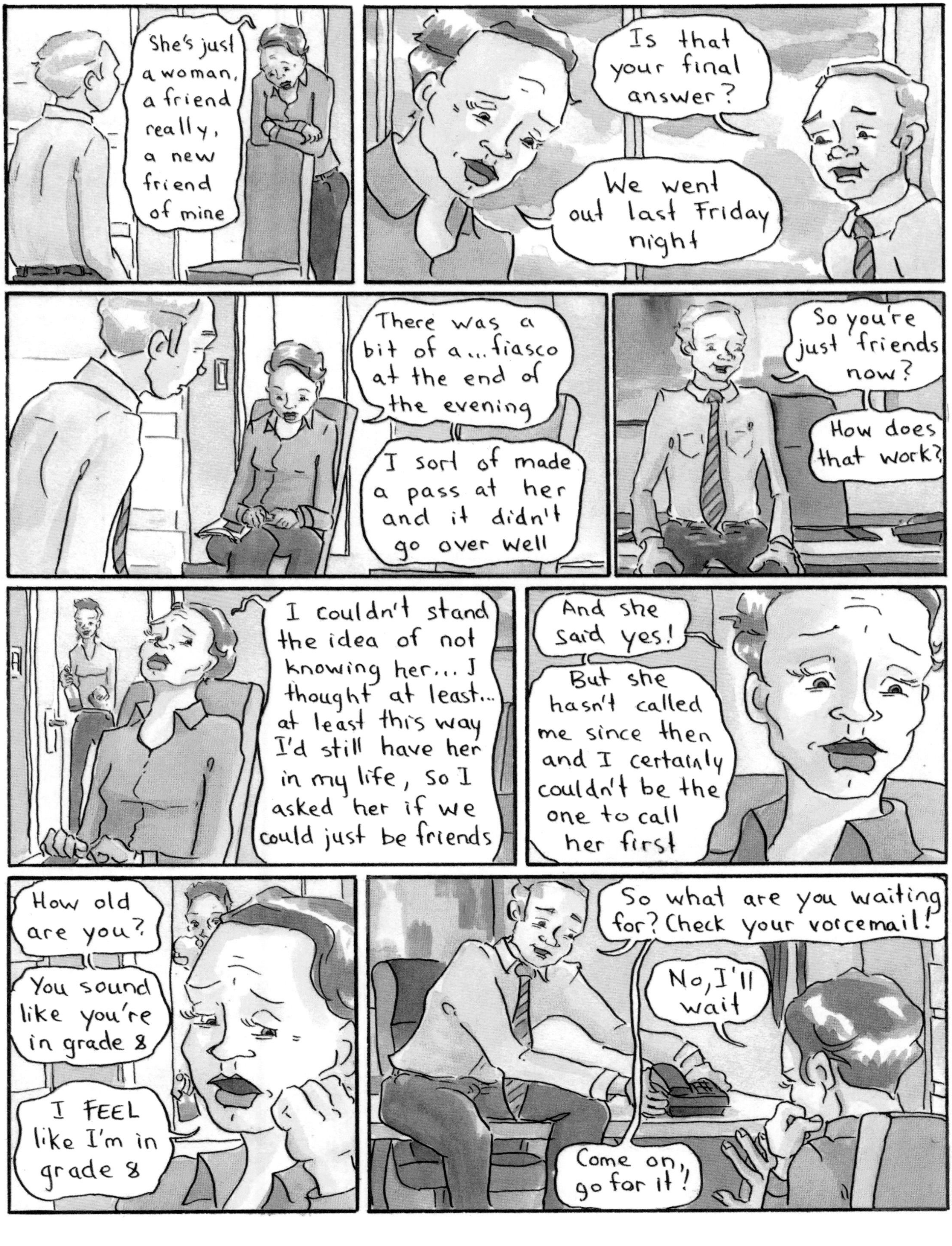
She's just a woman, a friend really, a new friend of mine
Is that your final answer?
We went out last Friday night
There was a bit of a... fiasco at the end of the evening
I sort of made a pass at her and it didn't go over well
So you're just friends now?
How does that work?
I couldn't stand the idea of not knowing her... I thought at least... at least this way I'd still have her in my life, so I asked her if we could just be friends
And she said yes!
But she hasn't called me since then and I certainly couldn't be the one to call her first
How old are you?
You sound like you're in grade 8
I FEEL like I'm in grade 8
So what are you waiting for? Check your voicemail!
No, I'll wait
Come on, go for it!

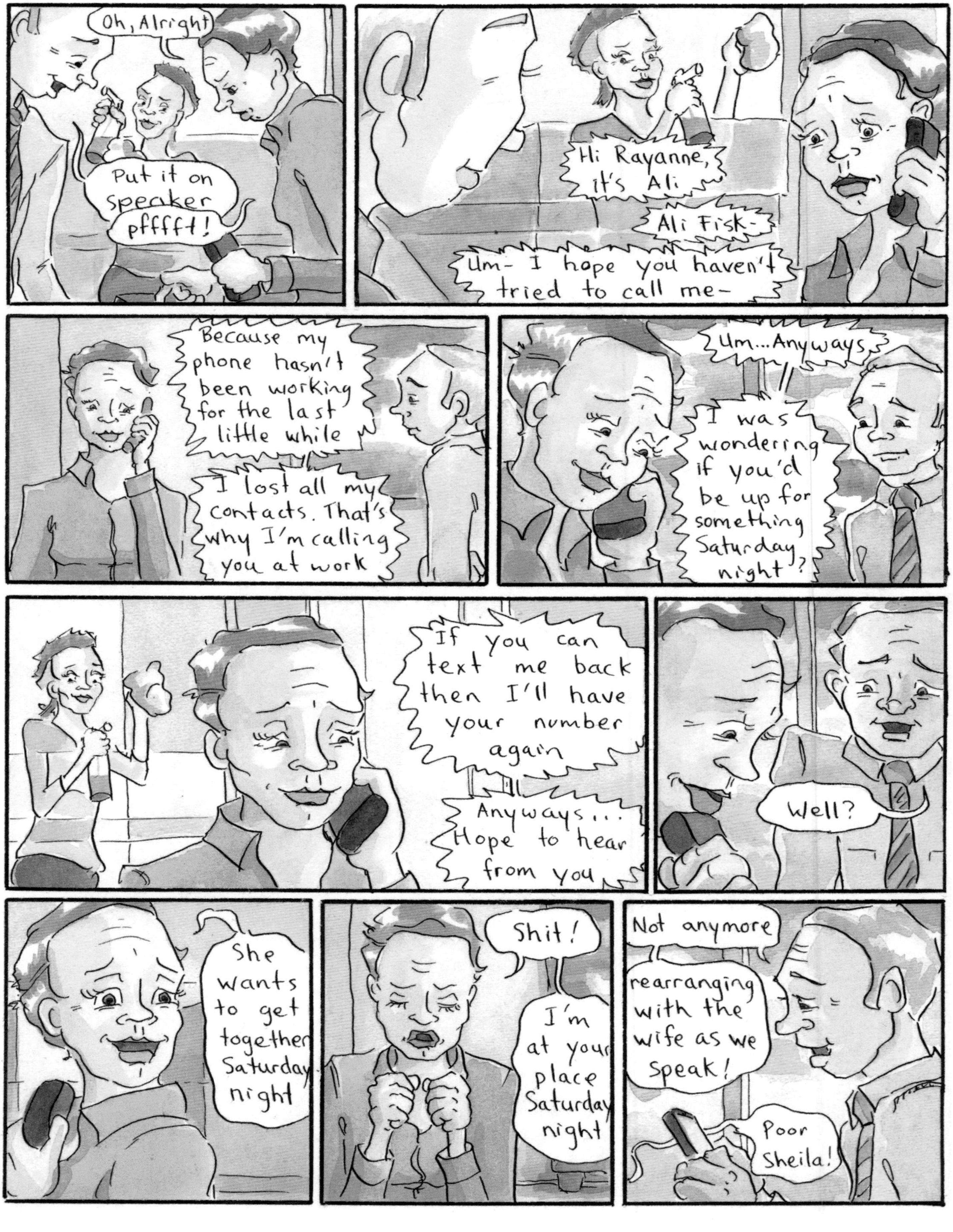
Oh, Alright
Put it on speaker pfffft!
Hi Rayanne, it's Ali
Ali Fisk-
Um- I hope you haven't tried to call me-
Because my phone hasn't been working for the last little while
I lost all my contacts. That's why I'm calling you at work
Um... Anyways
I was wondering if you'd be up for something Saturday night?
If you can text me back then I'll have your number again
Anyways... Hope to hear from you
Well?
She wants to get together Saturday night
Shit!
I'm at your place Saturday night
Not anymore
rearranging with the wife as we speak!
Poor Sheila!

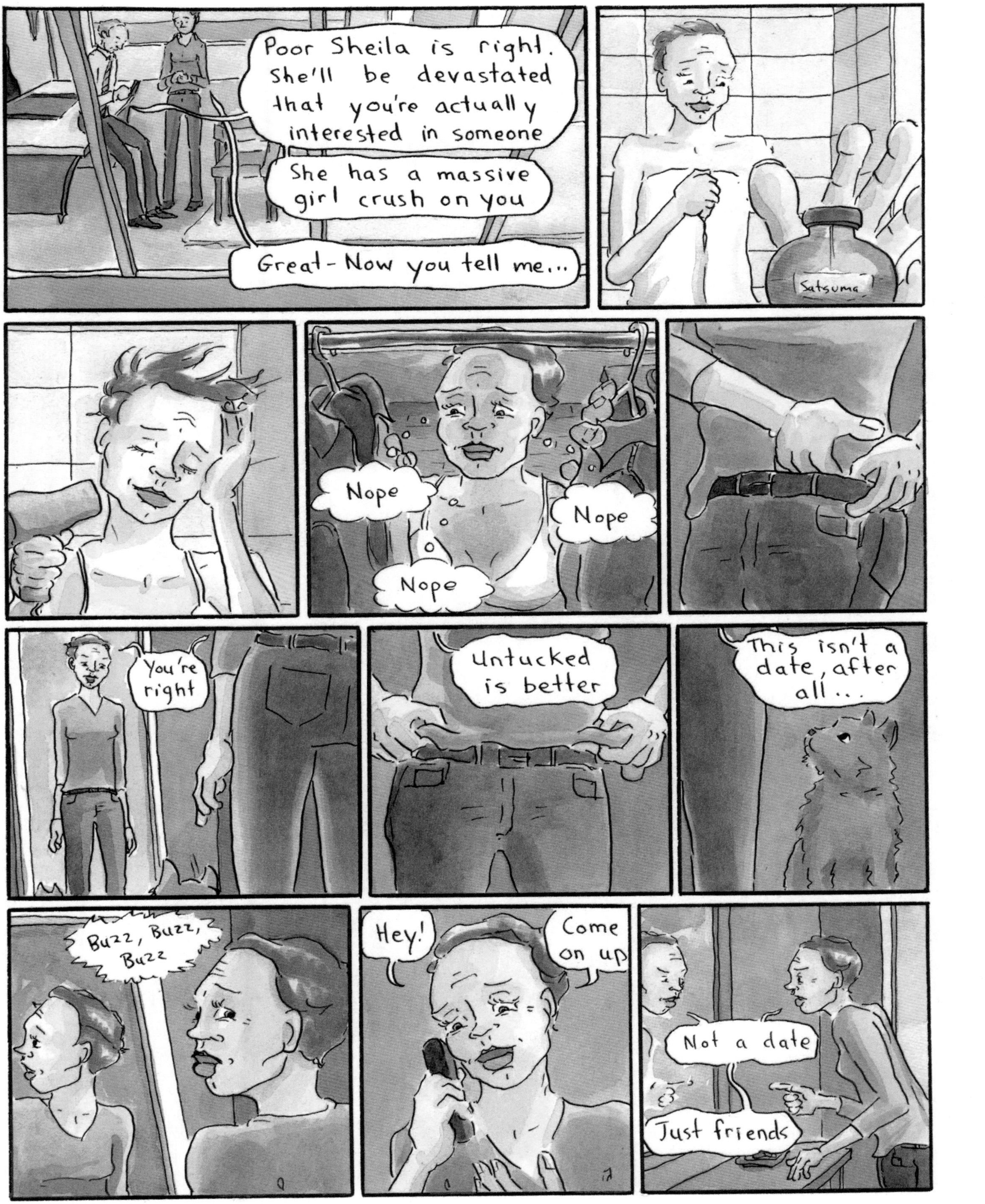
Poor Sheila is right. She'll be devastated that you're actually interested in someone
She has a massive girl crush on you
Great - Now you tell me...
Satsuma
Nope
Nope
Nope
You're right
Untucked is better
This isn't a date, after all...
Buzz, Buzz, Buzz
Hey!
Come on up
Not a date
Just friends

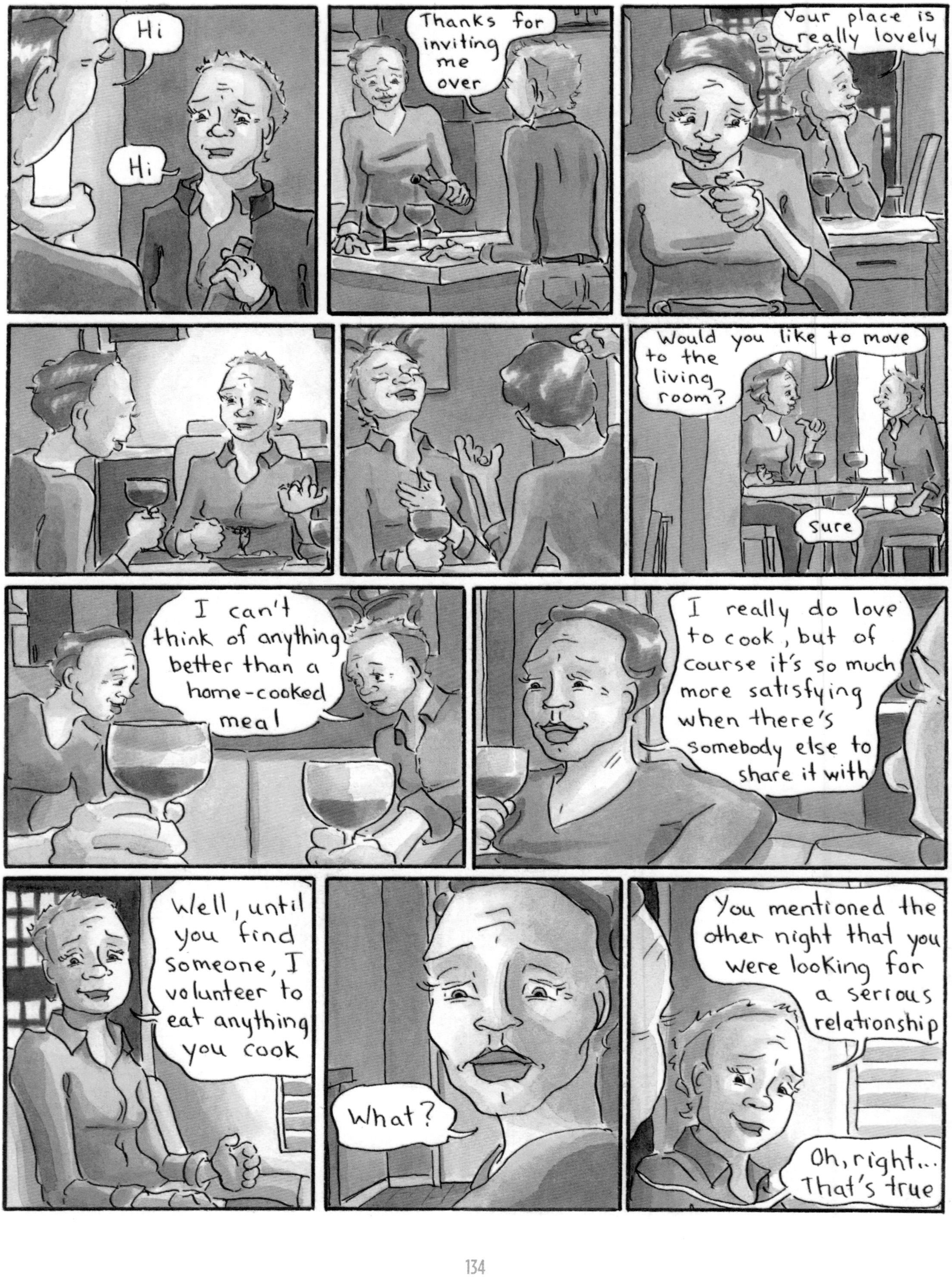
Hi
Hi
Thanks for inviting me over
Your place is really lovely
Would you like to move to the living room?
Sure
I can't think of anything better than a home-cooked meal
I really do love to cook, but of course it's so much more satisfying when there's somebody else to share it with
Well, until you find someone, I volunteer to eat anything you cook
What?
You mentioned the other night that you were looking for a serious relationship
Oh, right... That's true

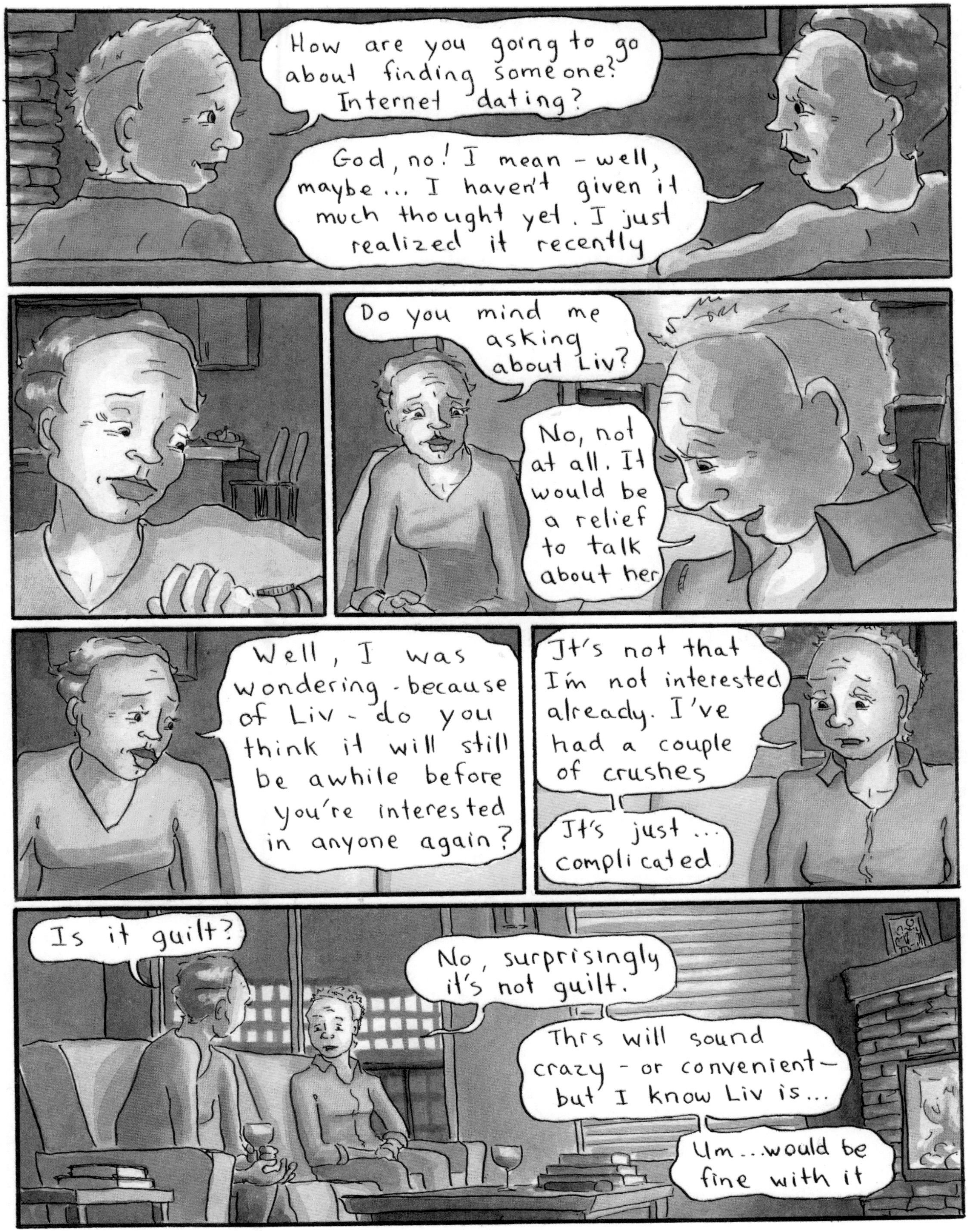
How are you going to go about finding someone? Internet dating?
God, no! I mean - well, maybe... I haven't given it much thought yet. I just realized it recently
Do you mind me asking about Liv?
No, not at all. It would be a relief to talk about her
Well, I was wondering - because of Liv - do you think it will still be awhile before you're interested in anyone again?
It's not that I'm not interested already. I've had a couple of crushes
It's just... complicated
Is it guilt?
No, surprisingly it's not guilt.
This will sound crazy - or convenient - but I know Liv is...
Um...would be fine with it

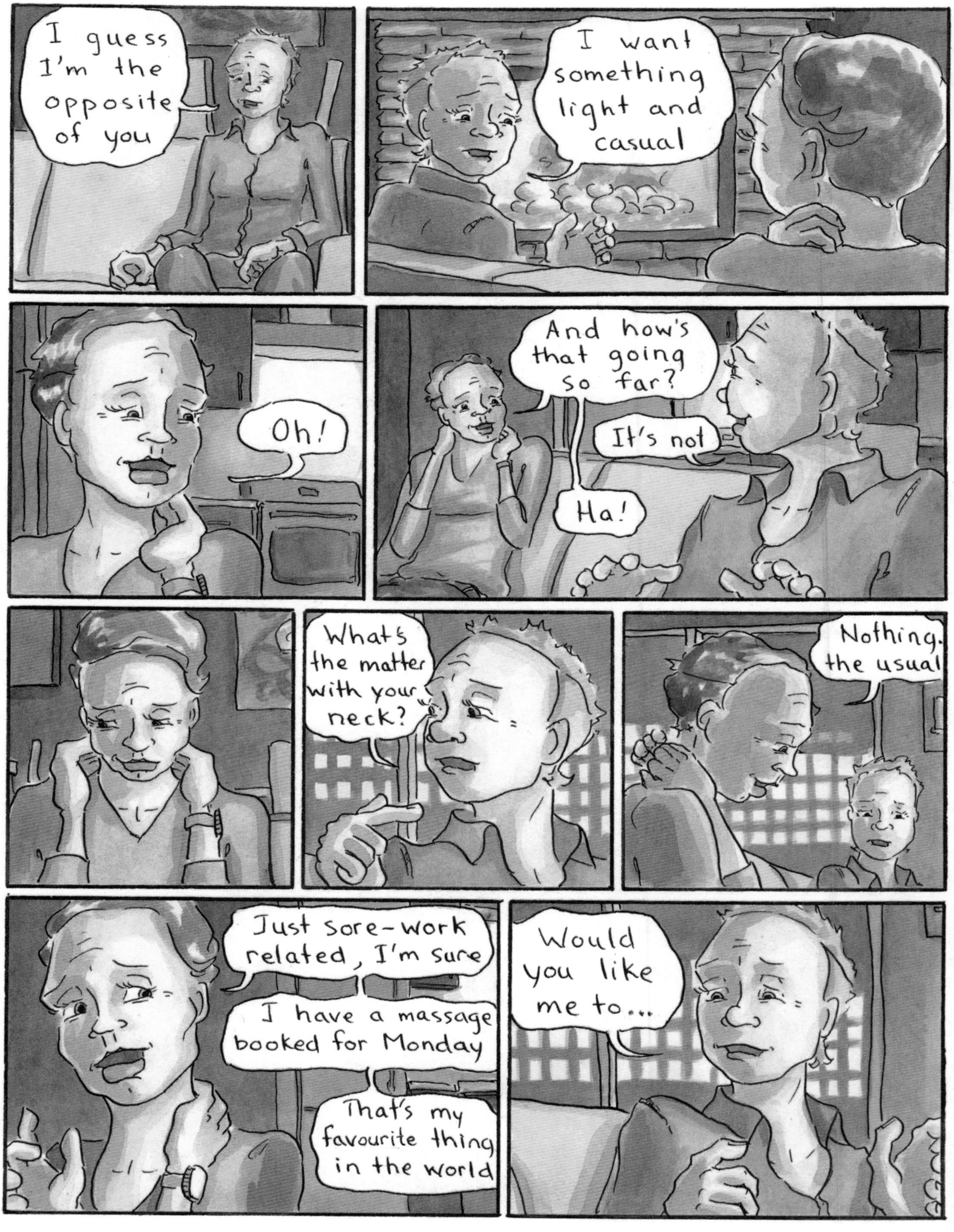
I guess I'm the opposite of you
I want something light and casual
Oh!
And how's that going so far?
It's not
Ha!
What's the matter with your neck?
Nothing. the usual
Just sore-work related, I'm sure
I have a massage booked for Monday
That's my favourite thing in the world
Would you like me to...

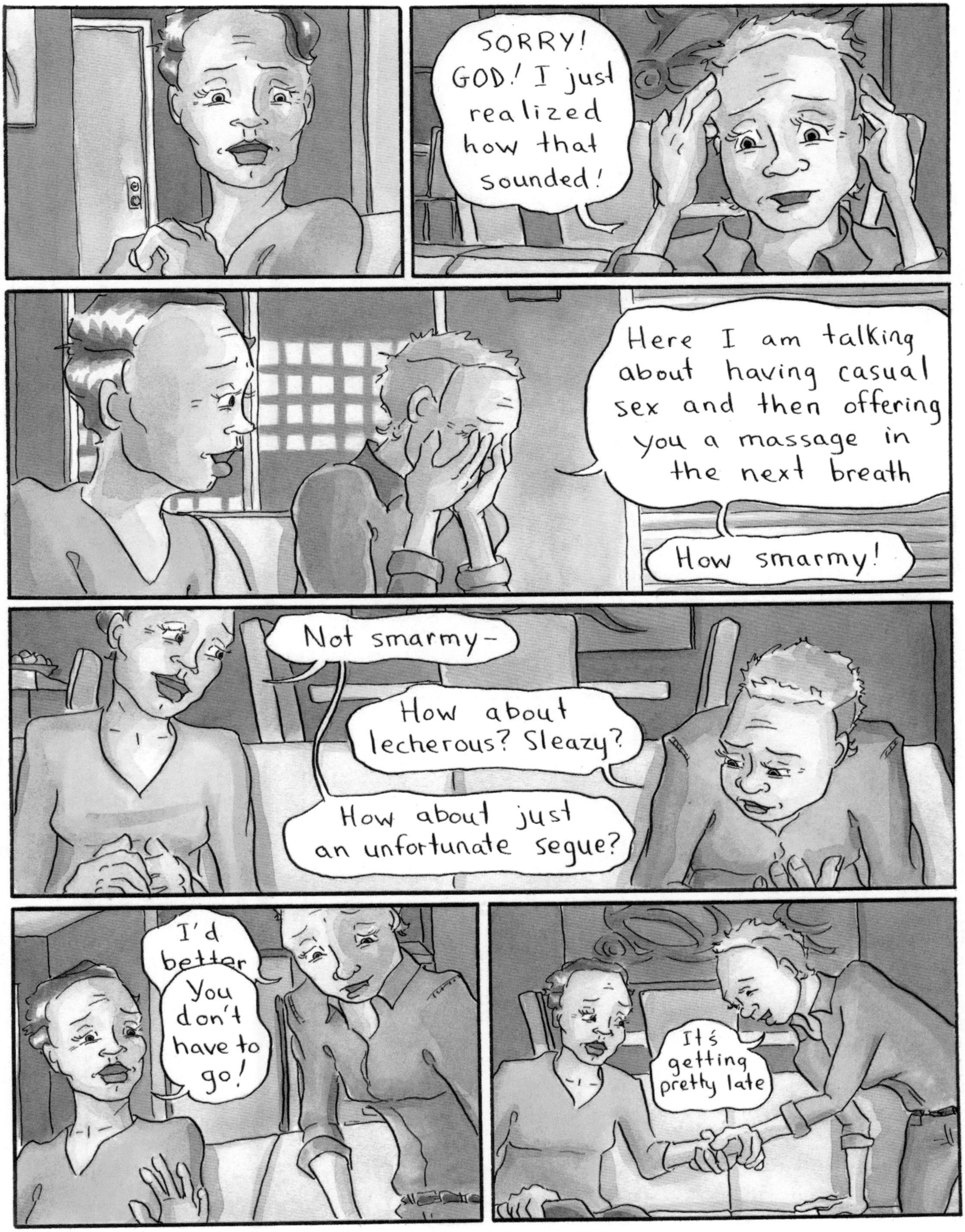
SORRY! GOD! I just realized how that sounded!
Here I am talking about having casual sex and then offering you a massage in the next breath
How smarmy!
Not smarmy-
How about lecherous? Sleazy?
How about just an unfortunate segue?
I'd better
You don't have to go!
It's getting pretty late

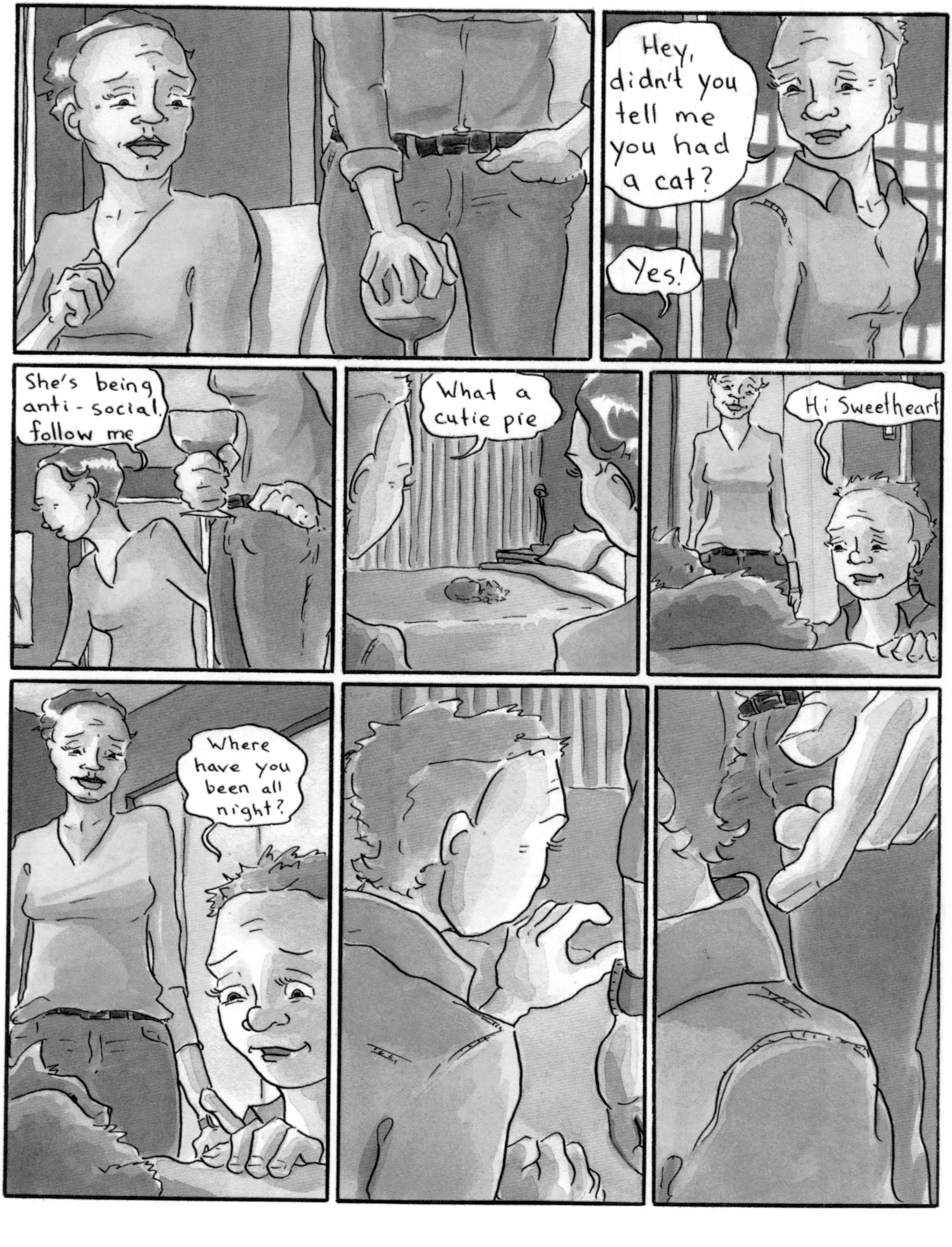
Hey, didn't you tell me you had a cat?
Yes!
She's being anti-social, follow me
What a cutie pie
Hi Sweetheart
Where have you been all night?

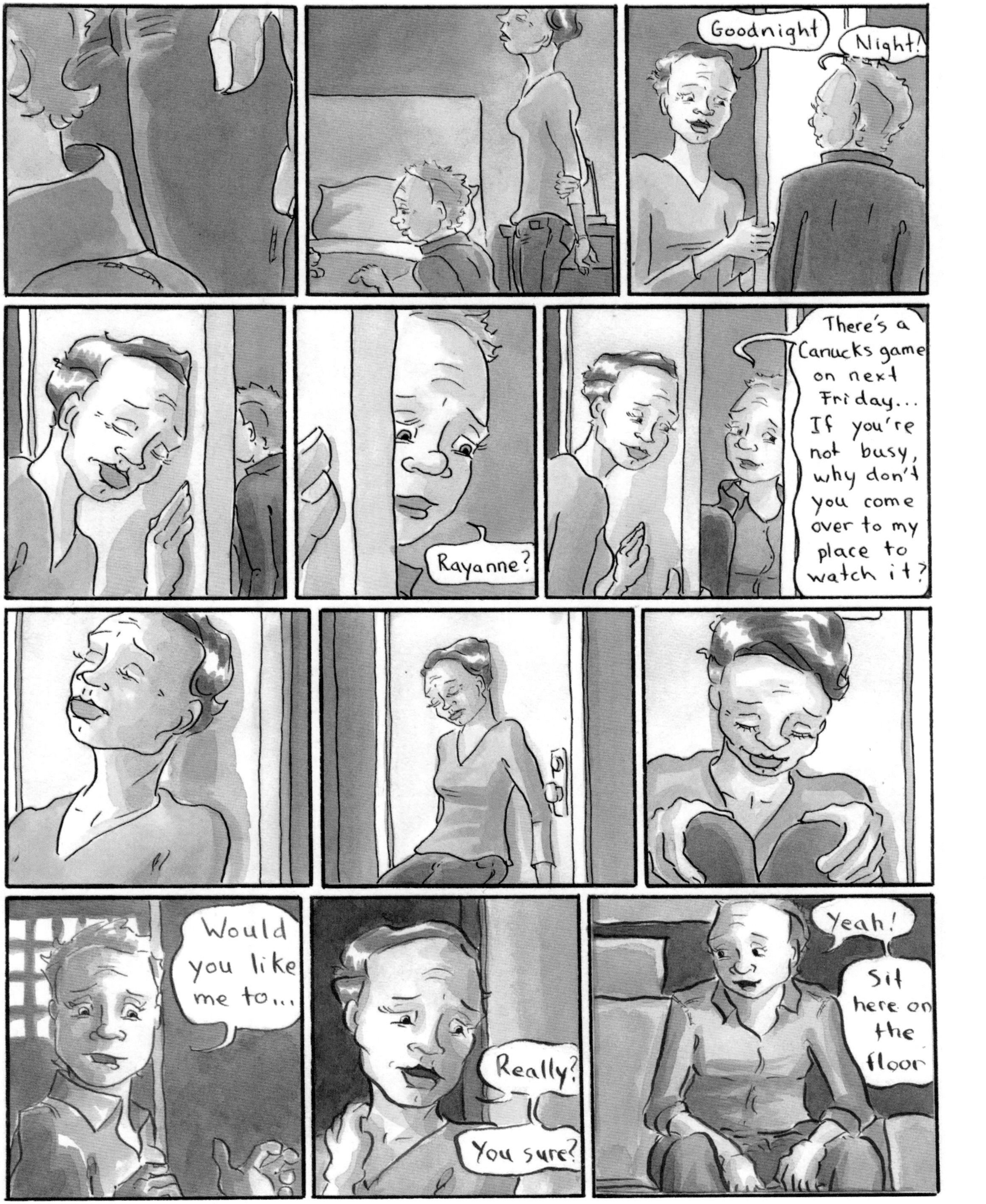
Goodnight
Night!
Rayanne?
There's a Canucks game on next Friday... If you're not busy, why don't you come over to my place to watch it?
Would you like me to...
Really?
You sure?
Yeah!
Sit here on the floor

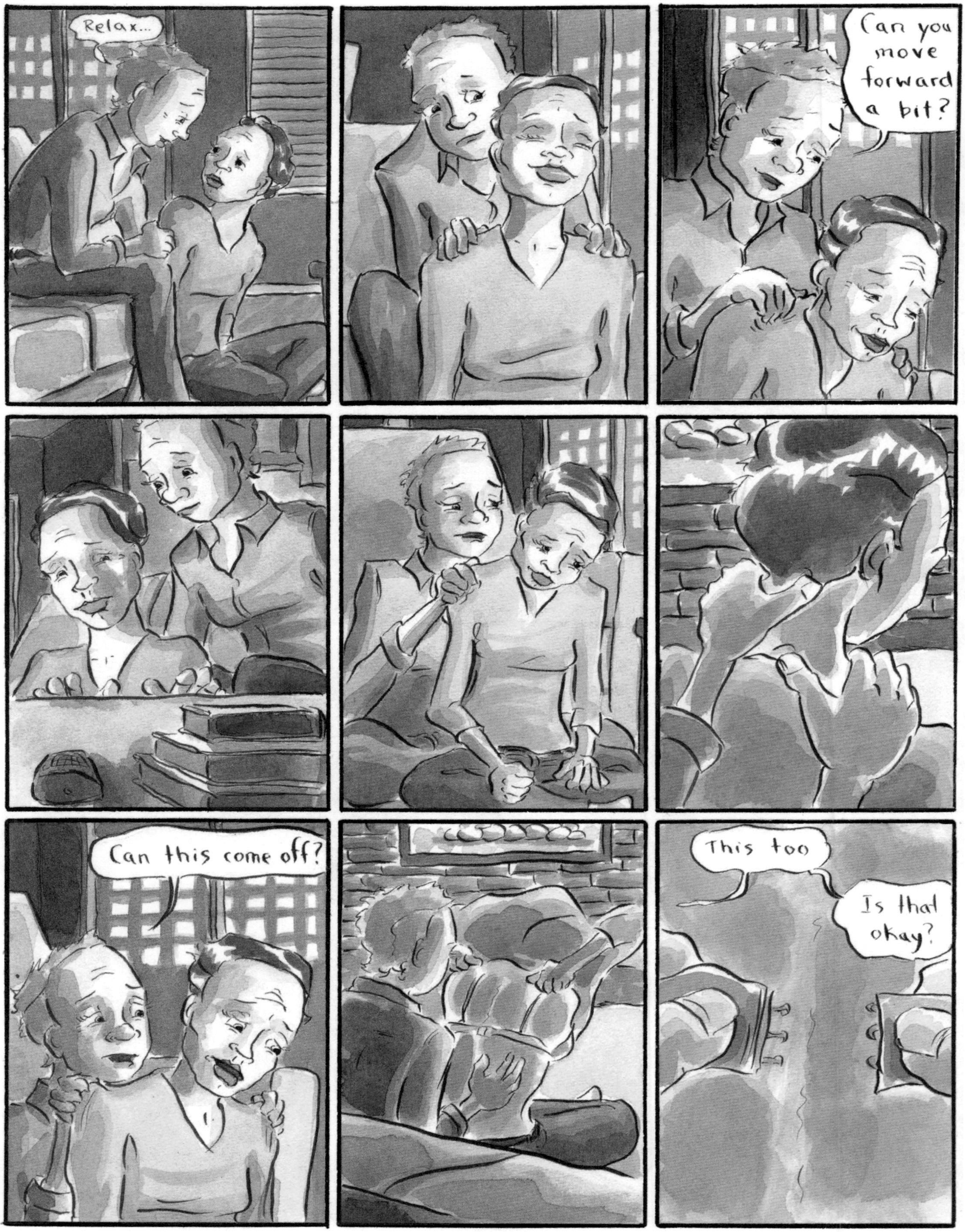

Relax...
Can you move forward a bit?
Can this come off?
This too
Is that okay?

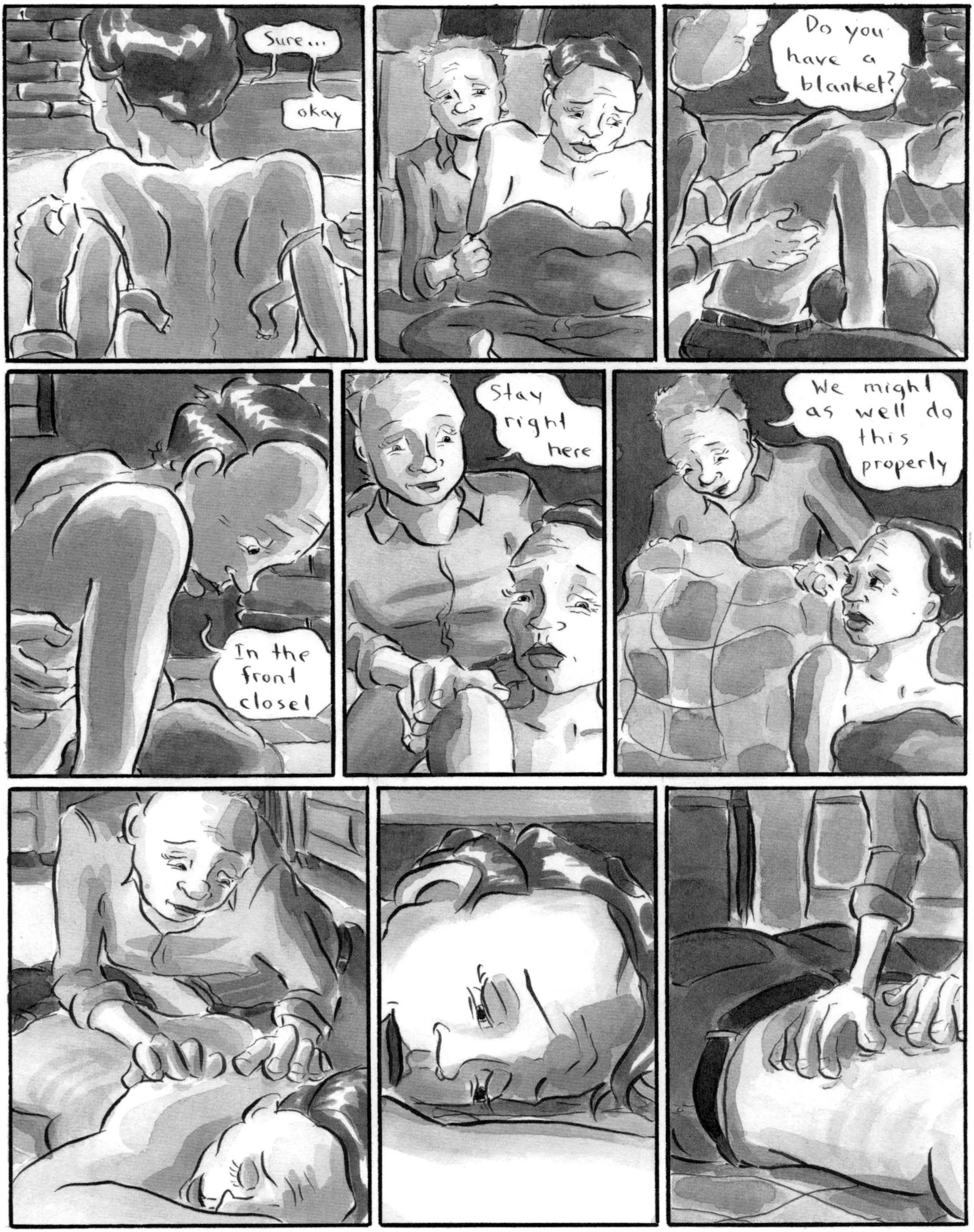
Sure...
okay
Do you have a blanket?
In the front closet
Stay right here
We might as well do this properly

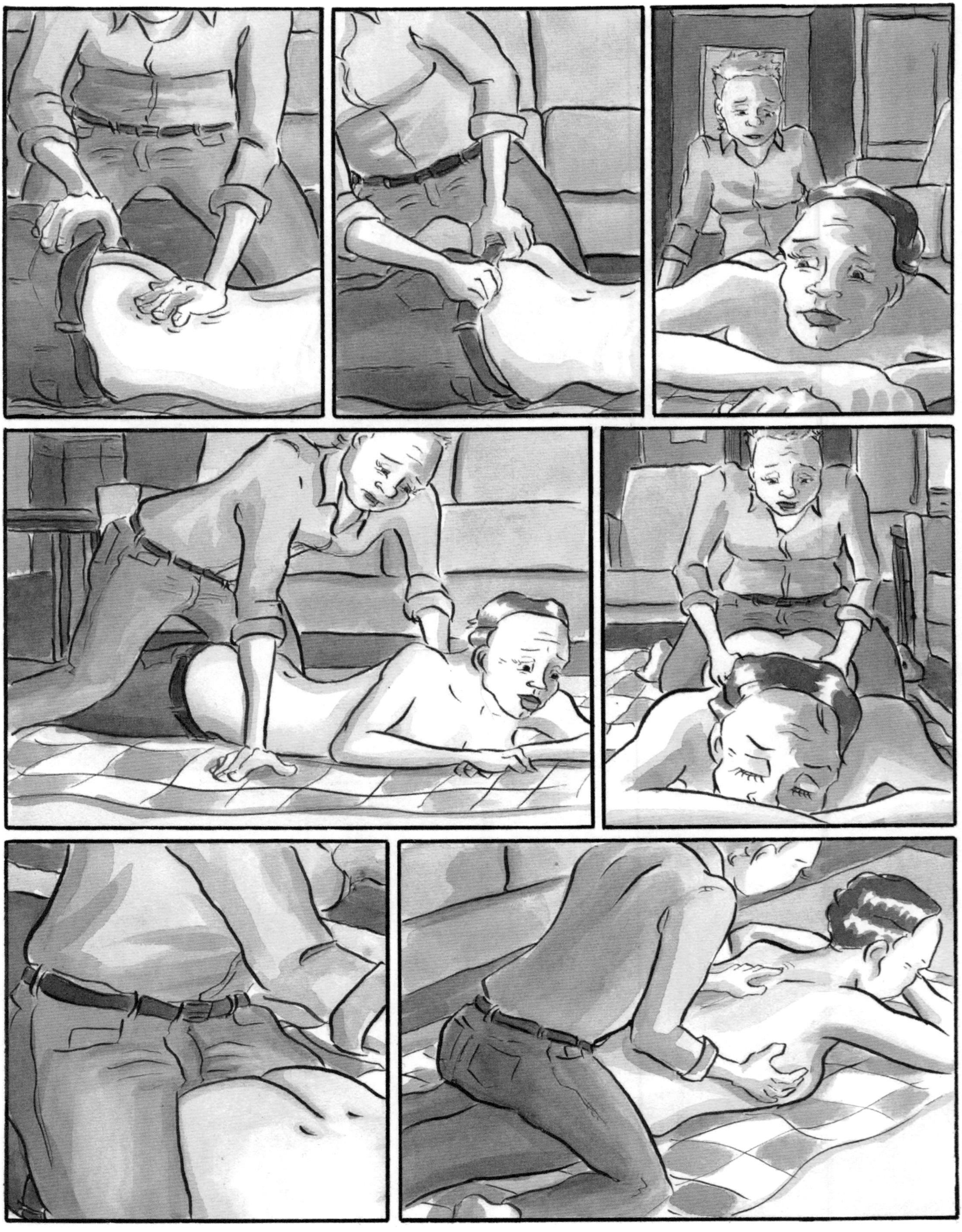

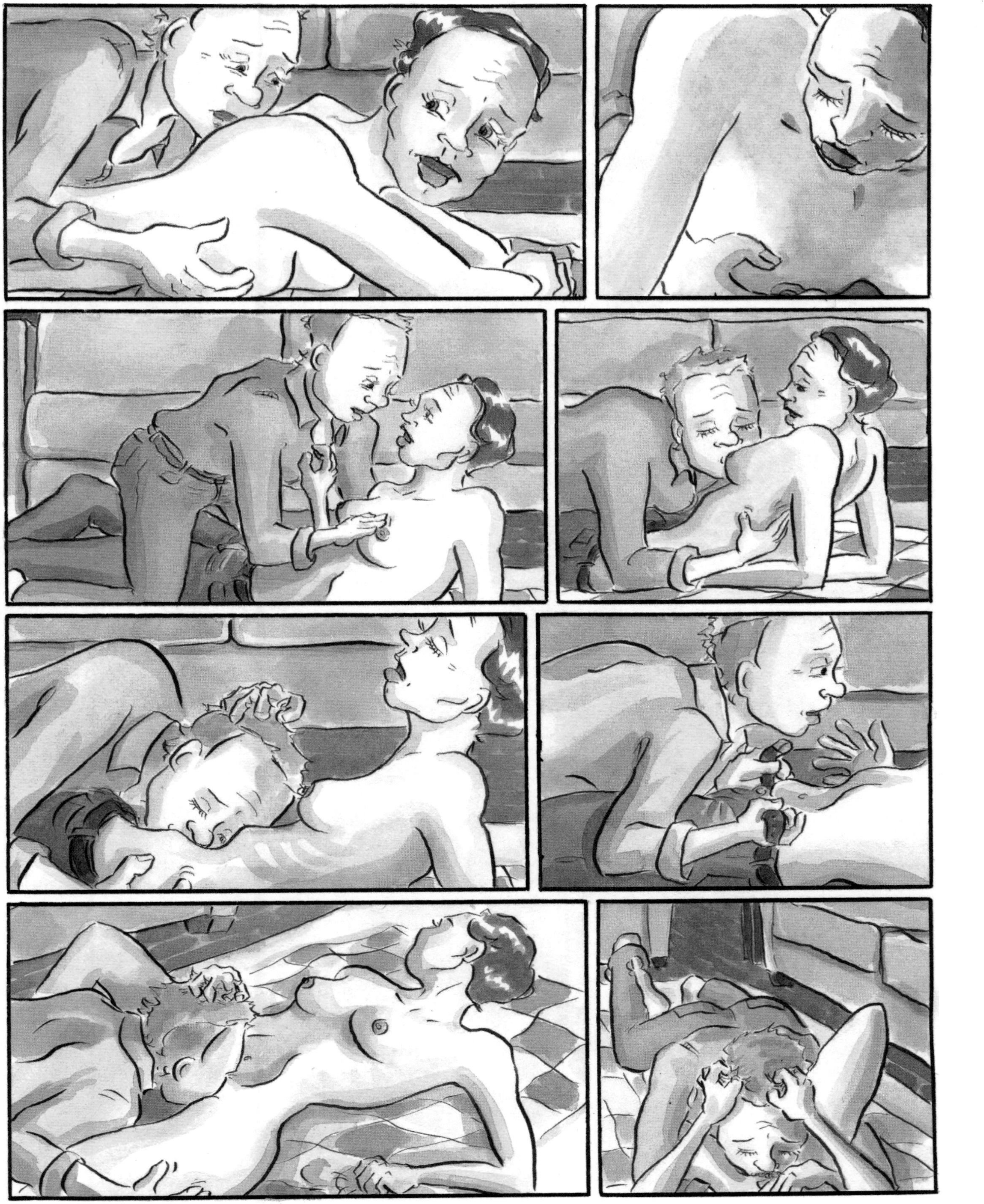

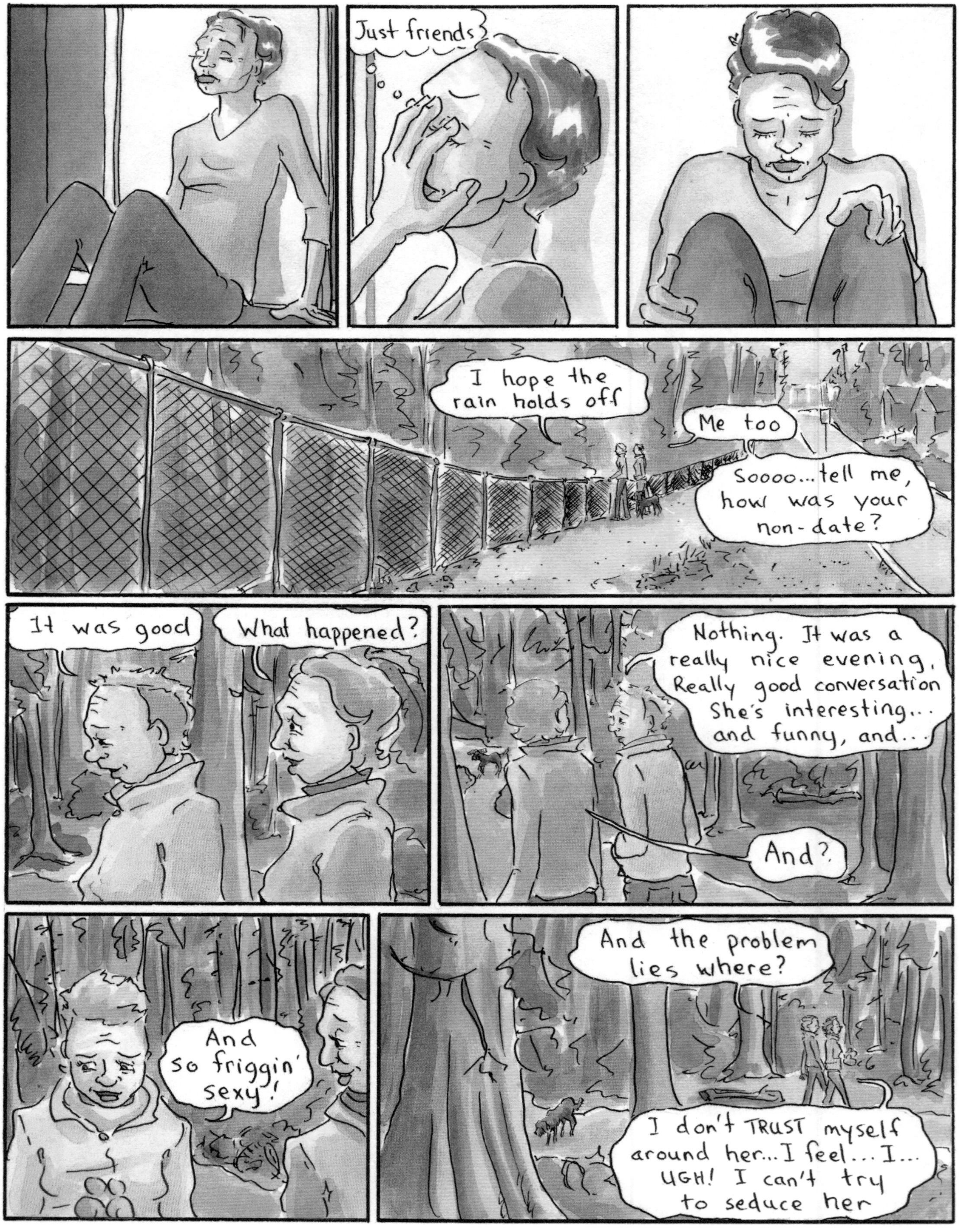
Just friends
I hope the rain holds off
Me too
Soooo... tell me, how was your non-date?
It was good
What happened?
Nothing. It was a really nice evening. Really good conversation She's interesting... and funny, and...
And?
And so friggin' sexy!
And the problem lies where?
I don't TRUST myself around her... I feel... I... UGH! I can't try to seduce her

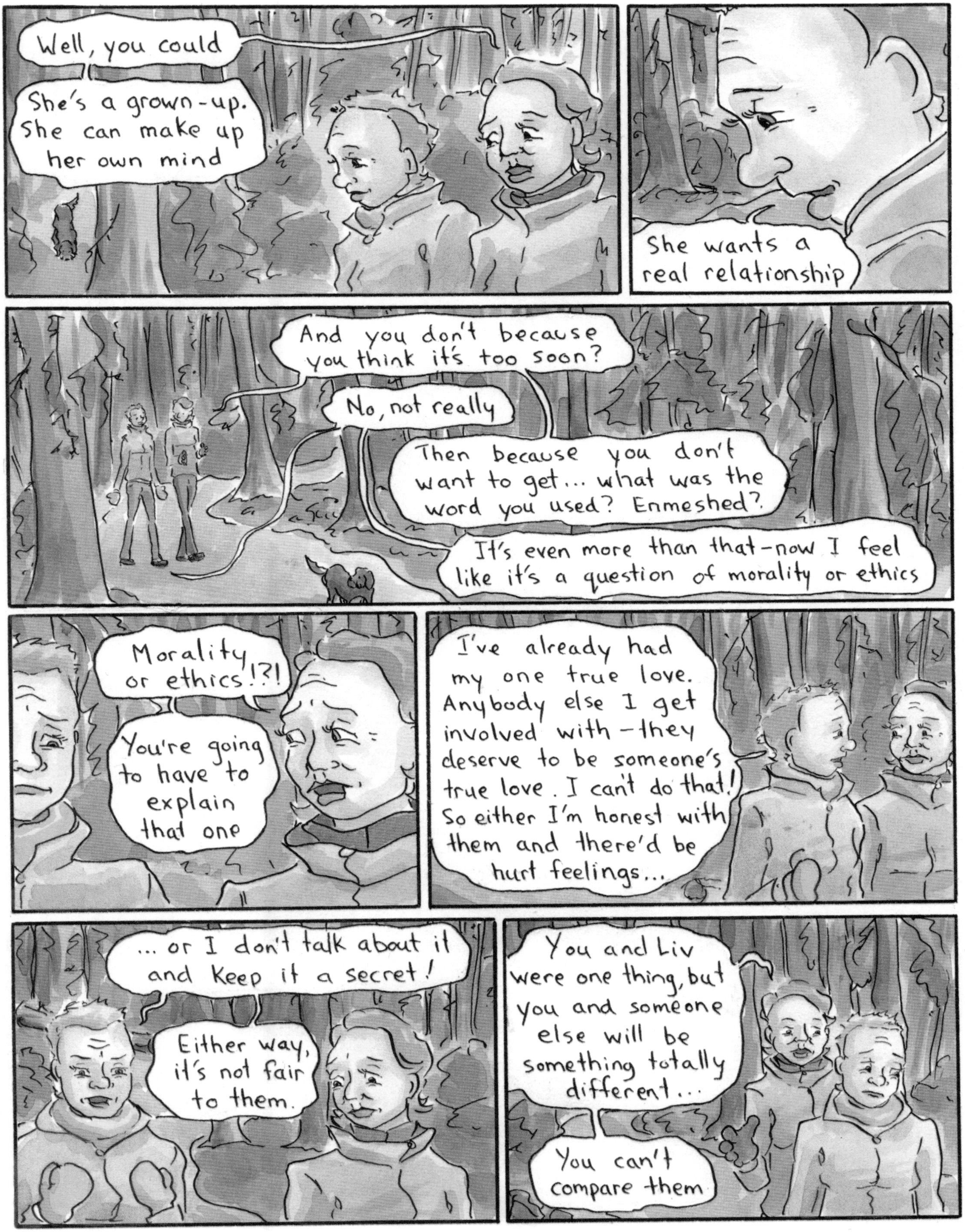
Well, you could
She's a grown-up. She can make up her own mind
She wants a real relationship
And you don't because you think it's too soon?
No, not really
Then because you don't want to get... what was the word you used? Enmeshed?
It's even more than that—now I feel like it's a question of morality or ethics
Morality or ethics!?!
You're going to have to explain that one
I've already had my one true love. Anybody else I get involved with—they deserve to be someone's true love. I can't do that! So either I'm honest with them and there'd be hurt feelings...
... or I don't talk about it and keep it a secret!
Either way, it's not fair to them.
You and Liv were one thing, but you and someone else will be something totally different...
You can't compare them

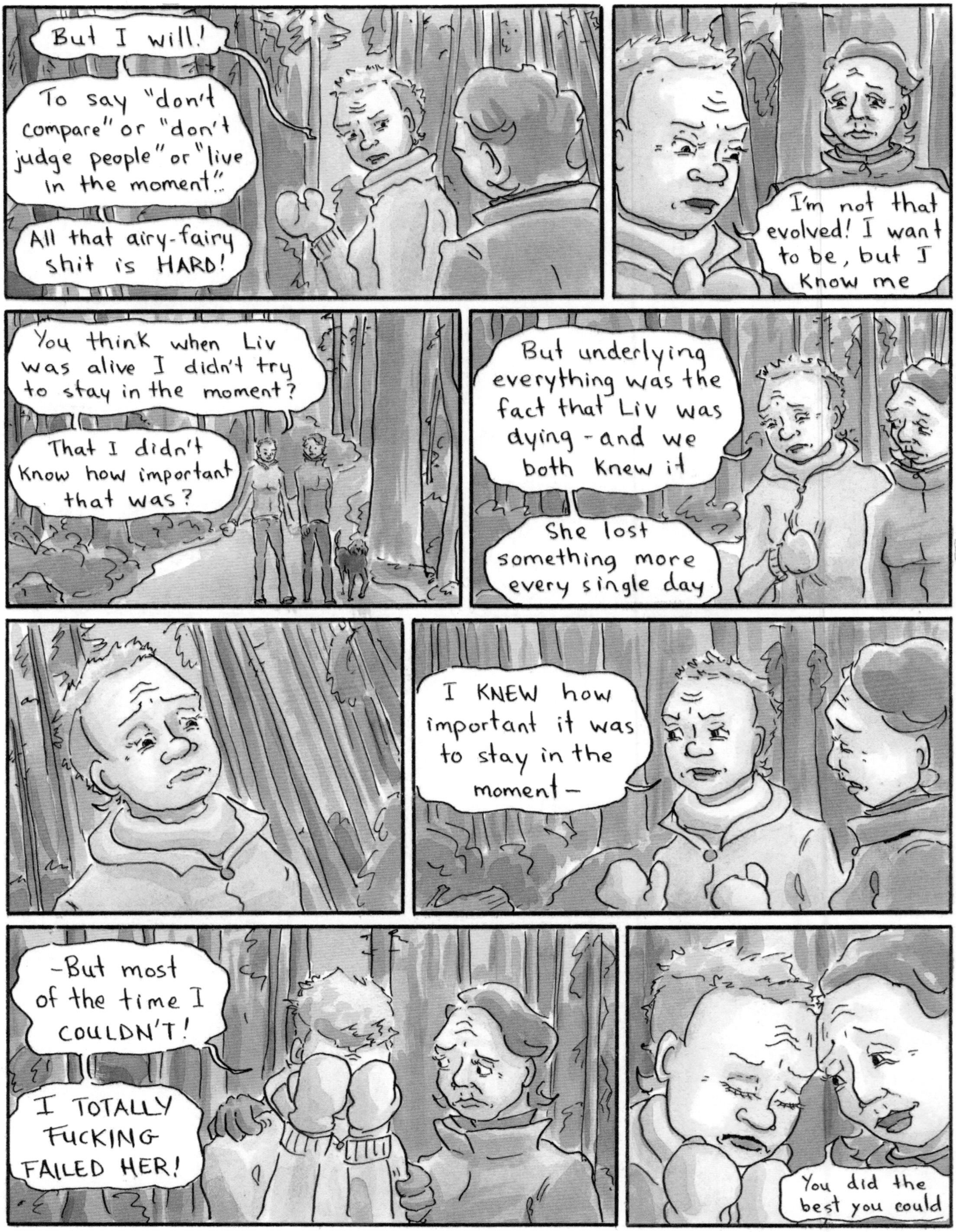

But I will!
To say "don't compare" or "don't judge people" or "live in the moment"...
All that airy-fairy shit is HARD!
I'm not that evolved! I want to be, but I know me
You think when Liv was alive I didn't try to stay in the moment?
That I didn't know how important that was?
But underlying everything was the fact that Liv was dying - and we both knew it
She lost something more every single day
I KNEW how important it was to stay in the moment-
-But most of the time I COULDN'T!
I TOTALLY FUCKING FAILED HER!
You did the best you could

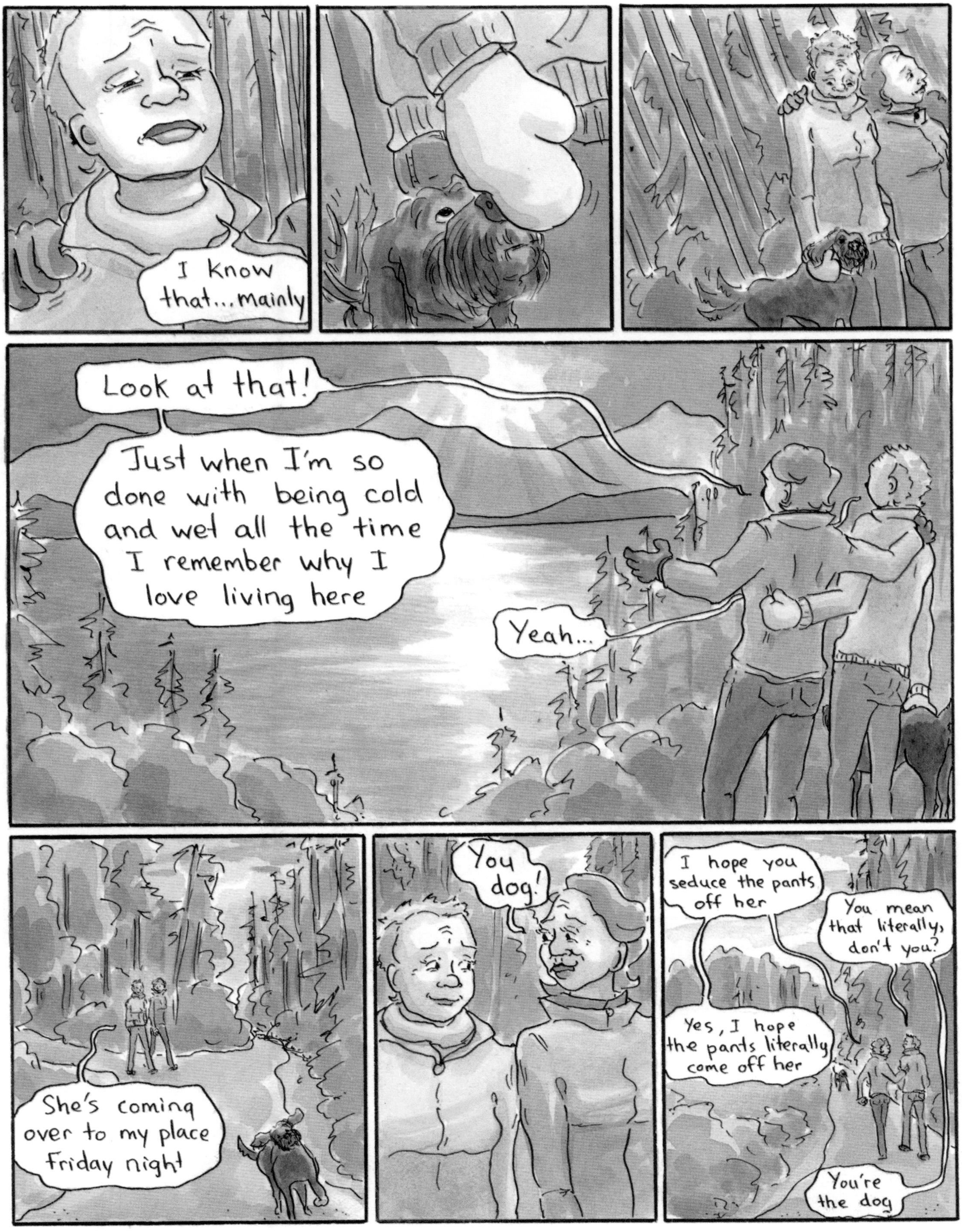
I know that...mainly
Look at that!
Just when I'm so done with being cold and wet all the time I remember why I love living here
Yeah...
She's coming over to my place Friday night
You dog!
I hope you seduce the pants off her
You mean that literally, don't you?
Yes, I hope the pants literally come off her
You're the dog

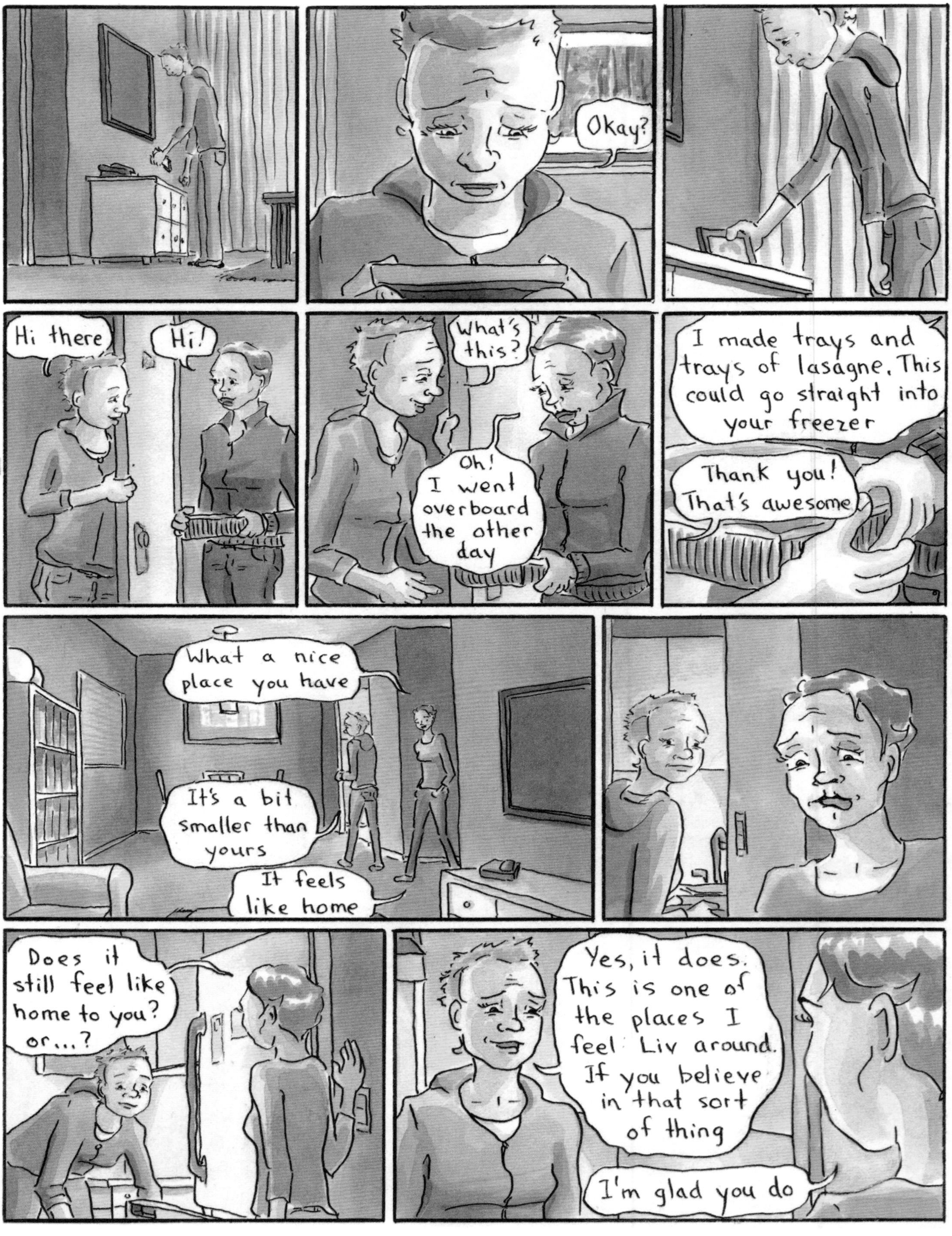
Okay?
Hi there
Hi!
What's this?
Oh! I went overboard the other day
I made trays and trays of lasagne. This could go straight into your freezer
Thank you! That's awesome
What a nice place you have
It's a bit smaller than yours
It feels like home
Does it still feel like home to you? or...?
Yes, it does. This is one of the places I feel Liv around. If you believe in that sort of thing
I'm glad you do

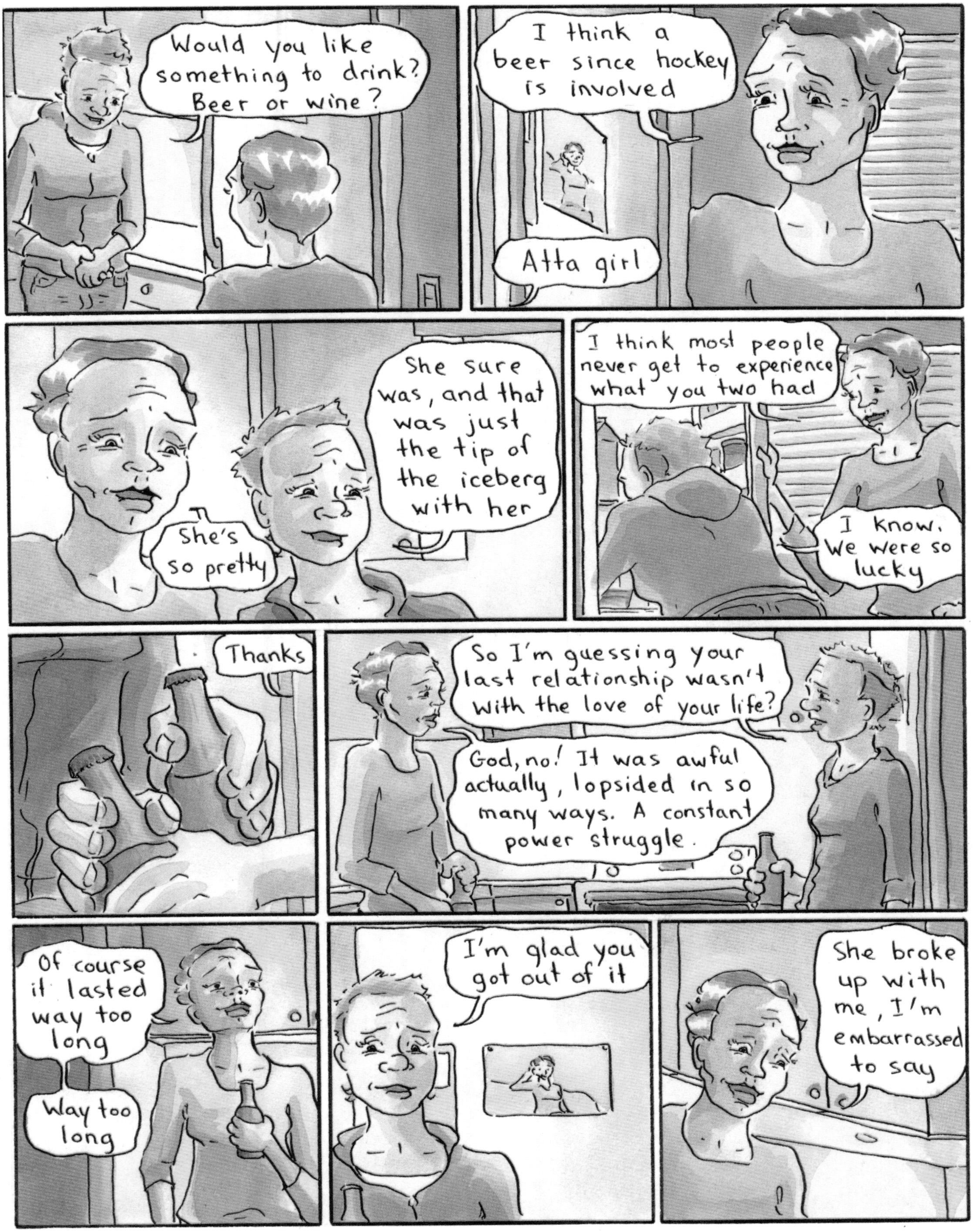
Would you like something to drink? Beer or wine?
I think a beer since hockey is involved
Atta girl
She's so pretty
She sure was, and that was just the tip of the iceberg with her
I think most people never get to experience what you two had
I know. We were so lucky
Thanks
So I'm guessing your last relationship wasn't with the love of your life?
God, no! It was awful actually, lopsided in so many ways. A constant power struggle.
Of course it lasted way too long
Way too long
I'm glad you got out of it
She broke up with me, I'm embarrassed to say

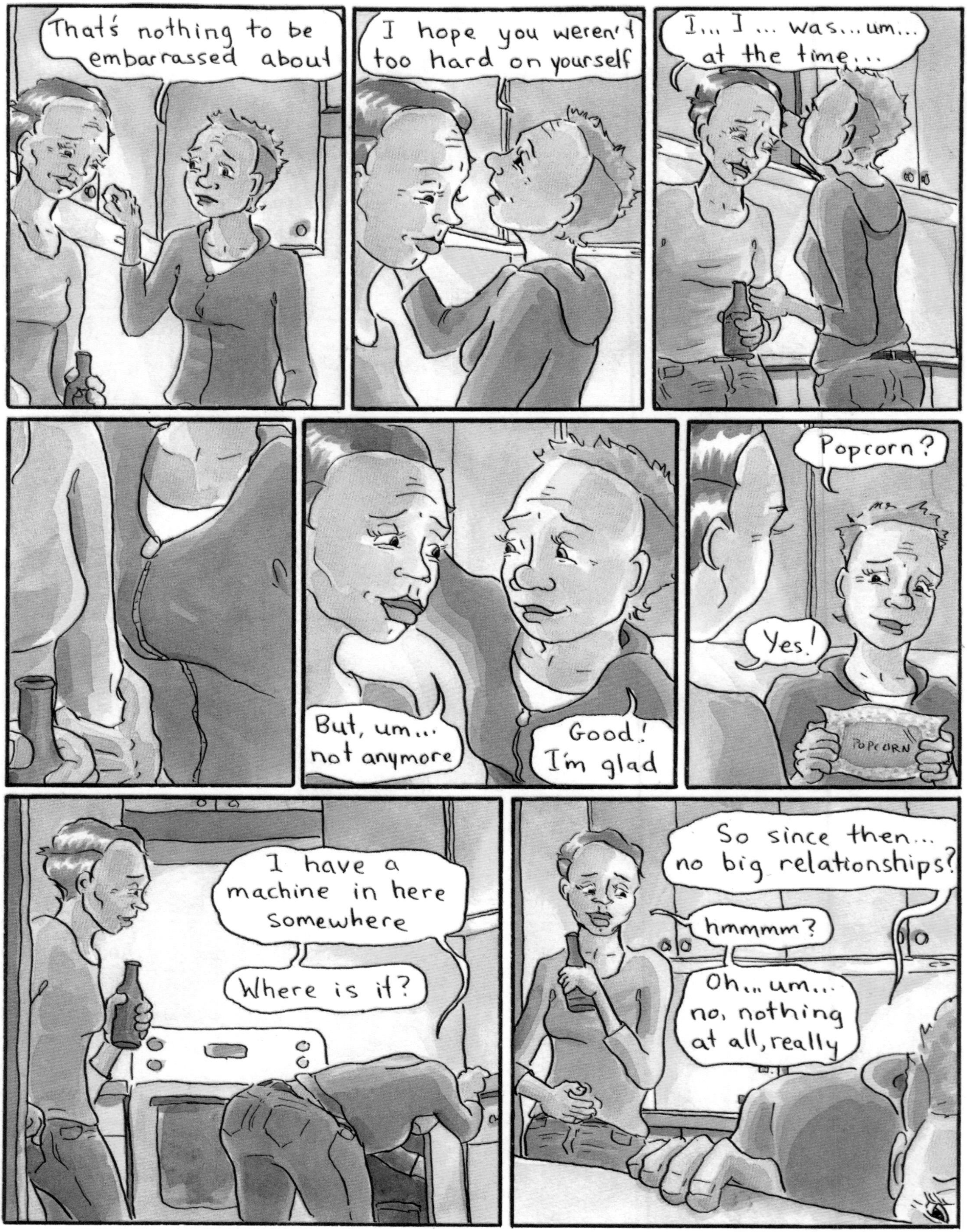
That's nothing to be embarrassed about
I hope you weren't too hard on yourself
I... I ... was... um... at the time...
But, um... not anymore
Good! I'm glad
Popcorn?
Yes!
POPCORN
I have a machine in here somewhere
Where is it?
So since then... no big relationships?
hmmmm?
Oh... um... no, nothing at all, really

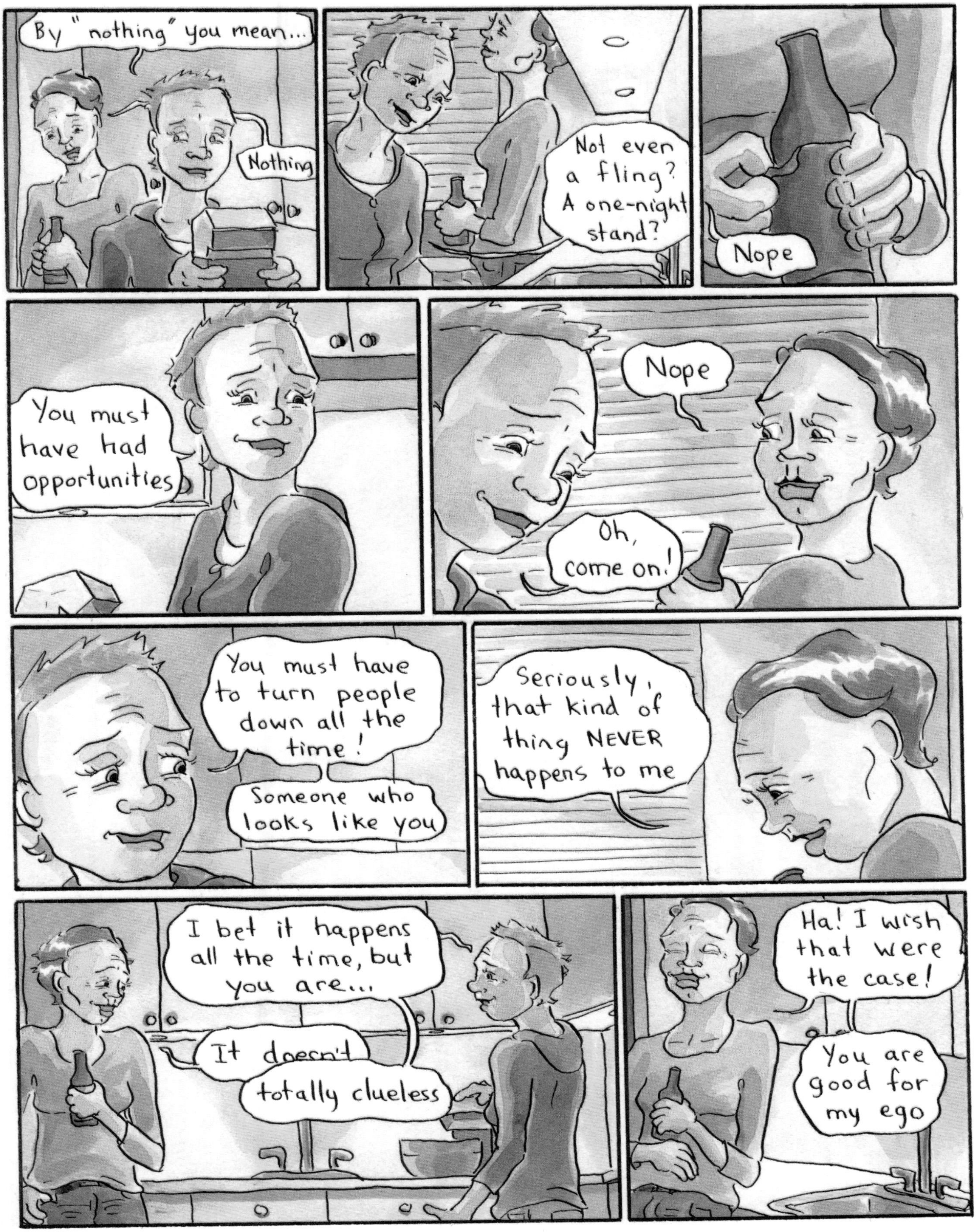
By "nothing" you mean...
Nothing
Not even a fling? A one-night stand?
Nope
You must have had opportunities
Nope
Oh, come on!
You must have to turn people down all the time!
Someone who looks like you
Seriously, that kind of thing NEVER happens to me
I bet it happens all the time, but you are...
It doesn't
totally clueless
Ha! I wish that were the case!
You are good for my ego

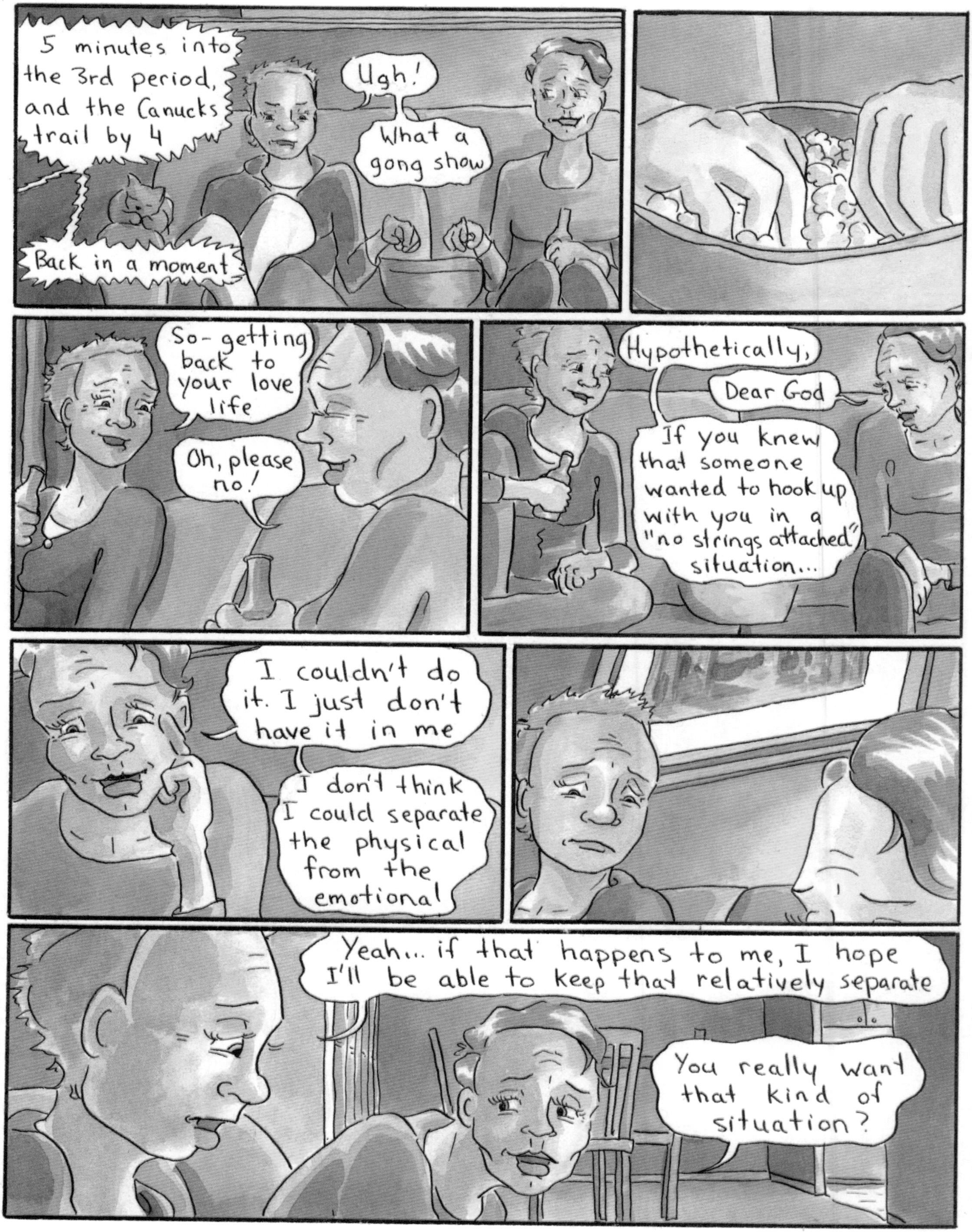
5 minutes into the 3rd period, and the Canucks trail by 4
Back in a moment
Ugh!
What a gong show
So- getting back to your love life
Oh, please no!
Hypothetically,
Dear God
If you knew that someone wanted to hook up with you in a "no strings attached" situation...
I couldn't do it. I just don't have it in me
I don't think I could separate the physical from the emotional
Yeah... if that happens to me, I hope I'll be able to keep that relatively separate
You really want that kind of situation?

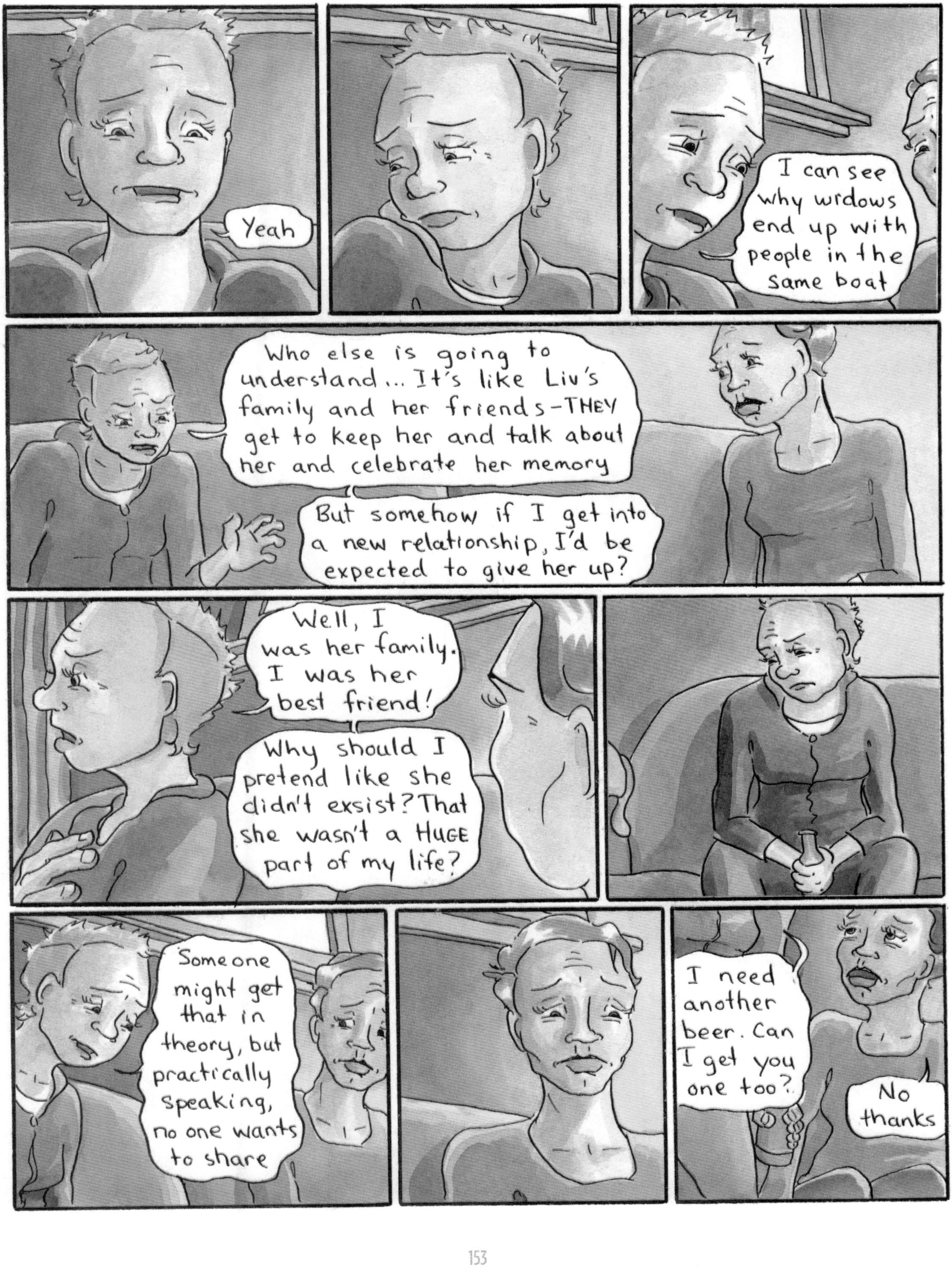
Yeah
I can see why widows end up with people in the same boat
Who else is going to understand... It's like Liv's family and her friends-THEY get to keep her and talk about her and celebrate her memory
But somehow if I get into a new relationship, I'd be expected to give her up?
Well, I was her family. I was her best friend!
Why should I pretend like she didn't exsist? That she wasn't a HUGE part of my life?
Someone might get that in theory, but practically speaking, no one wants to share
I need another beer. Can I get you one too?
No thanks

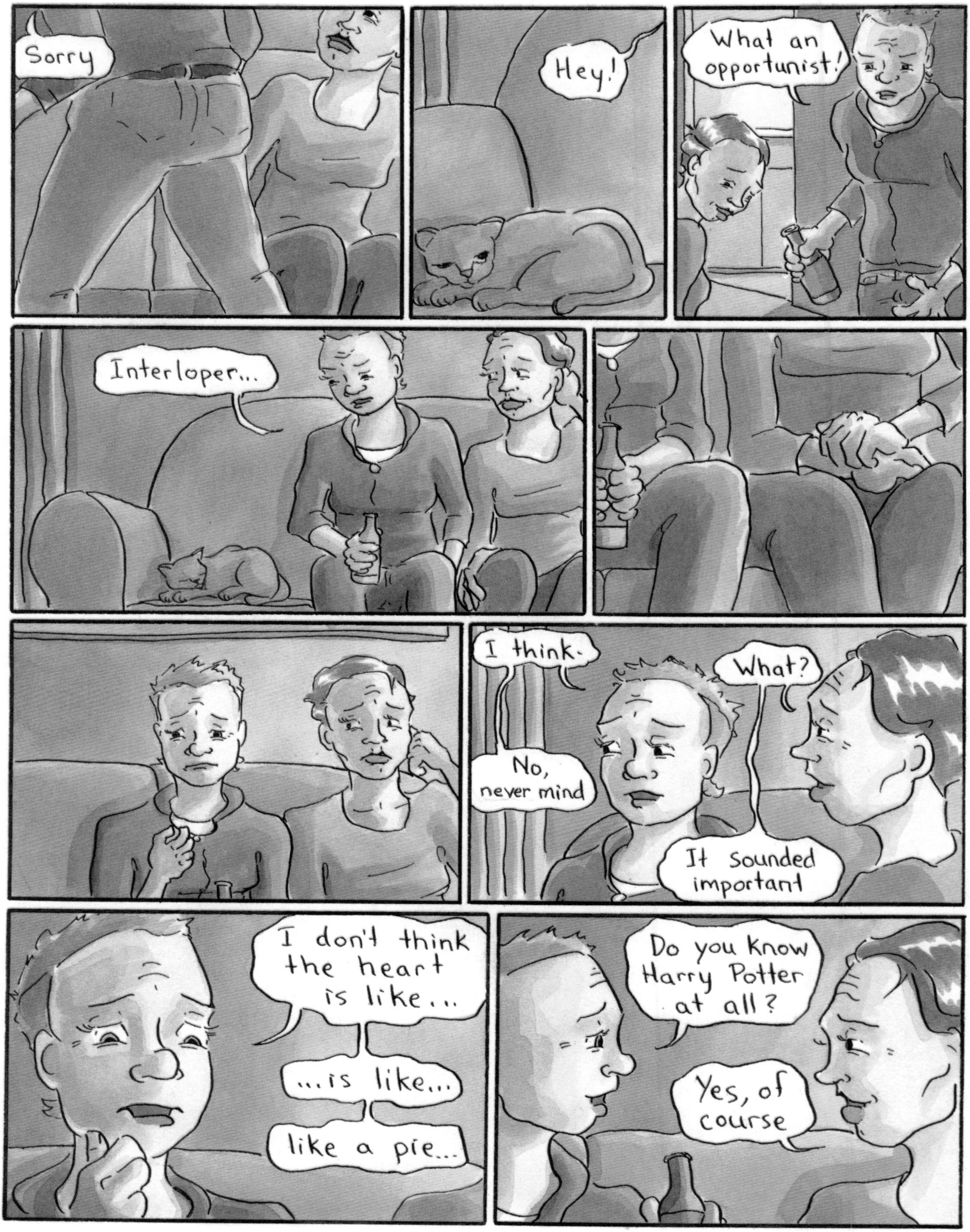
Sorry
Hey!
What an opportunist!
Interloper...
I think.
No, never mind
What?
It sounded important
I don't think the heart is like...
...is like...
like a pie...
Do you know Harry Potter at all?
Yes, of course

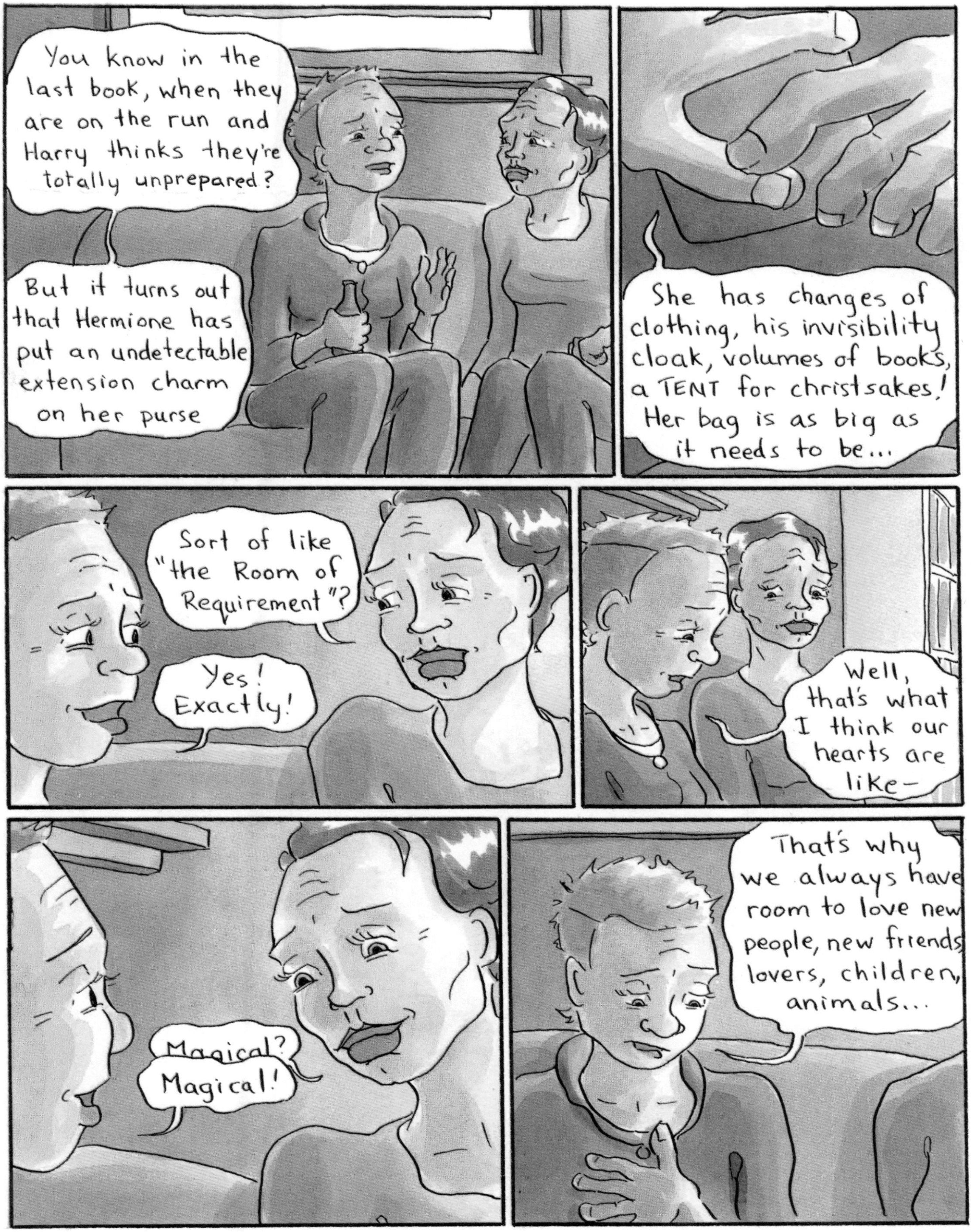
You know in the last book, when they are on the run and Harry thinks they're totally unprepared?
But it turns out that Hermione has put an undetectable extension charm on her purse
She has changes of clothing, his invisibility cloak, volumes of books, a TENT for christsakes! Her bag is as big as it needs to be...
Sort of like "the Room of Requirement"?
Yes! Exactly!
Well, that's what I think our hearts are like–
Magical?
Magical!
That's why we always have room to love new people, new friends, lovers, children, animals...

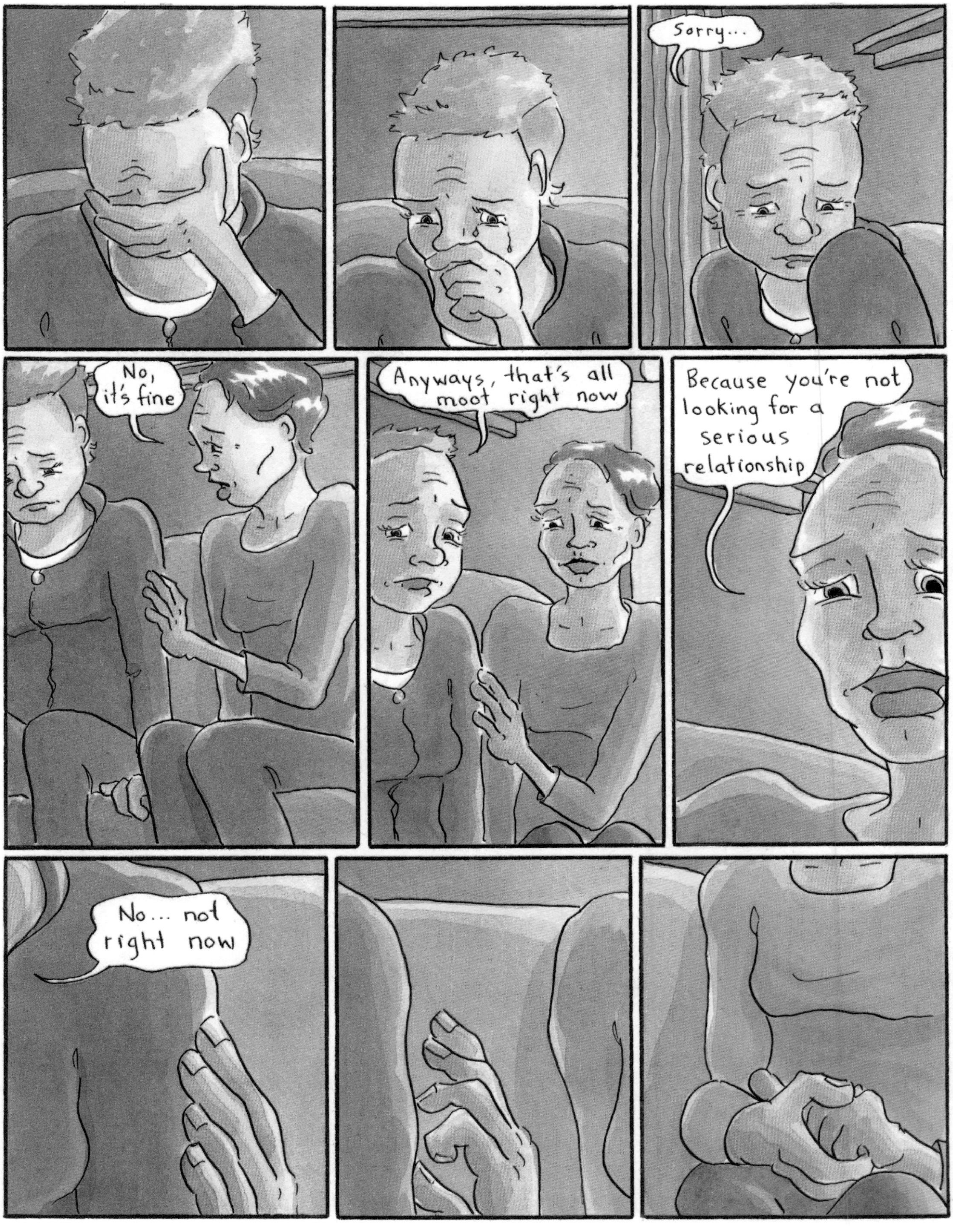
Sorry...
No, it's fine
Anyways, that's all moot right now
Because you're not looking for a serious relationship
No... not right now

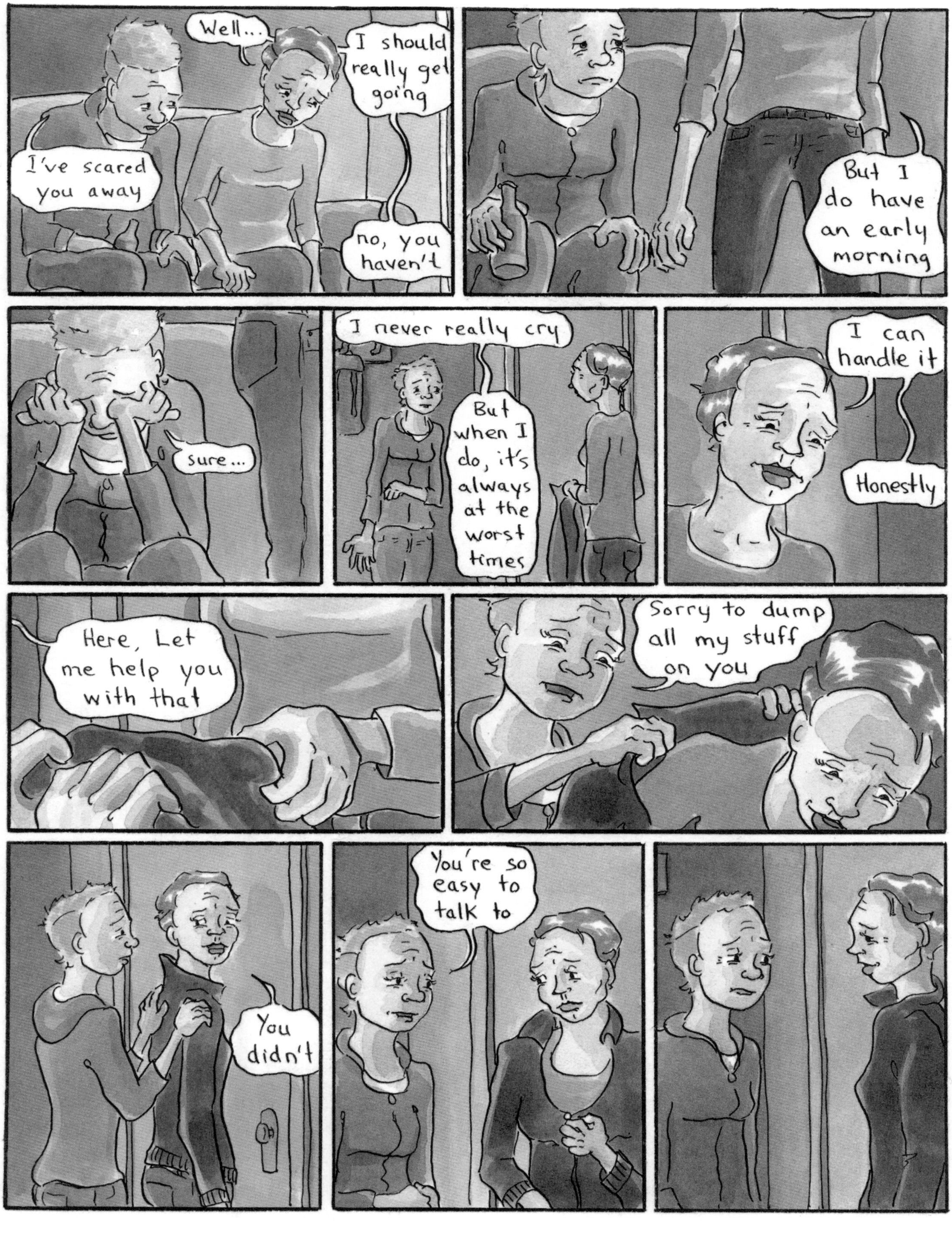
Well...
I should really get going
I've scared you away
no, you haven't
But I do have an early morning
sure...
I never really cry
But when I do, it's always at the worst times
I can handle it
Honestly
Here, Let me help you with that
Sorry to dump all my stuff on you
You didn't
You're so easy to talk to

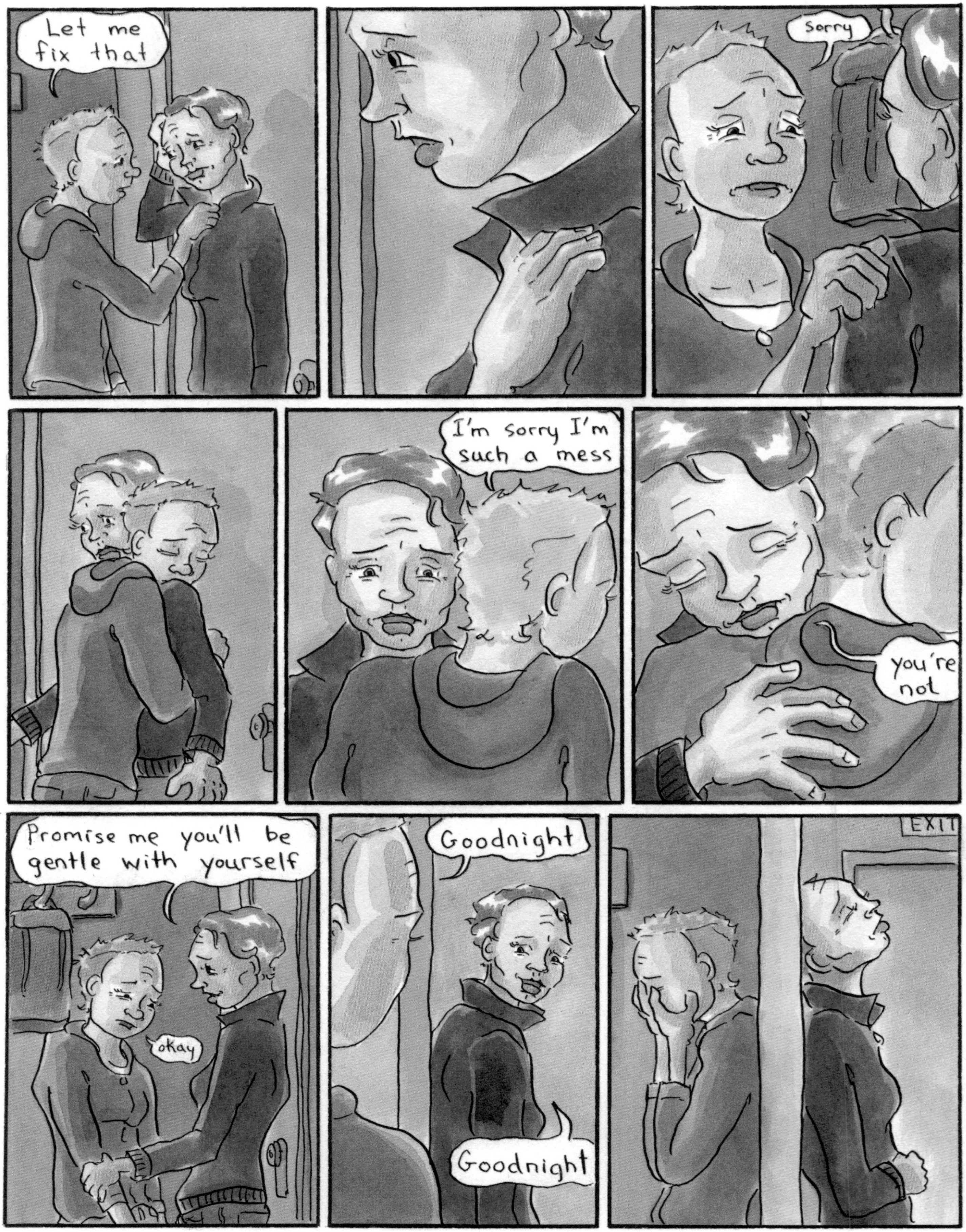
Let me fix that
Sorry
I'm sorry I'm such a mess
you're not
Promise me you'll be gentle with yourself
okay
Goodnight
Goodnight
EXIT

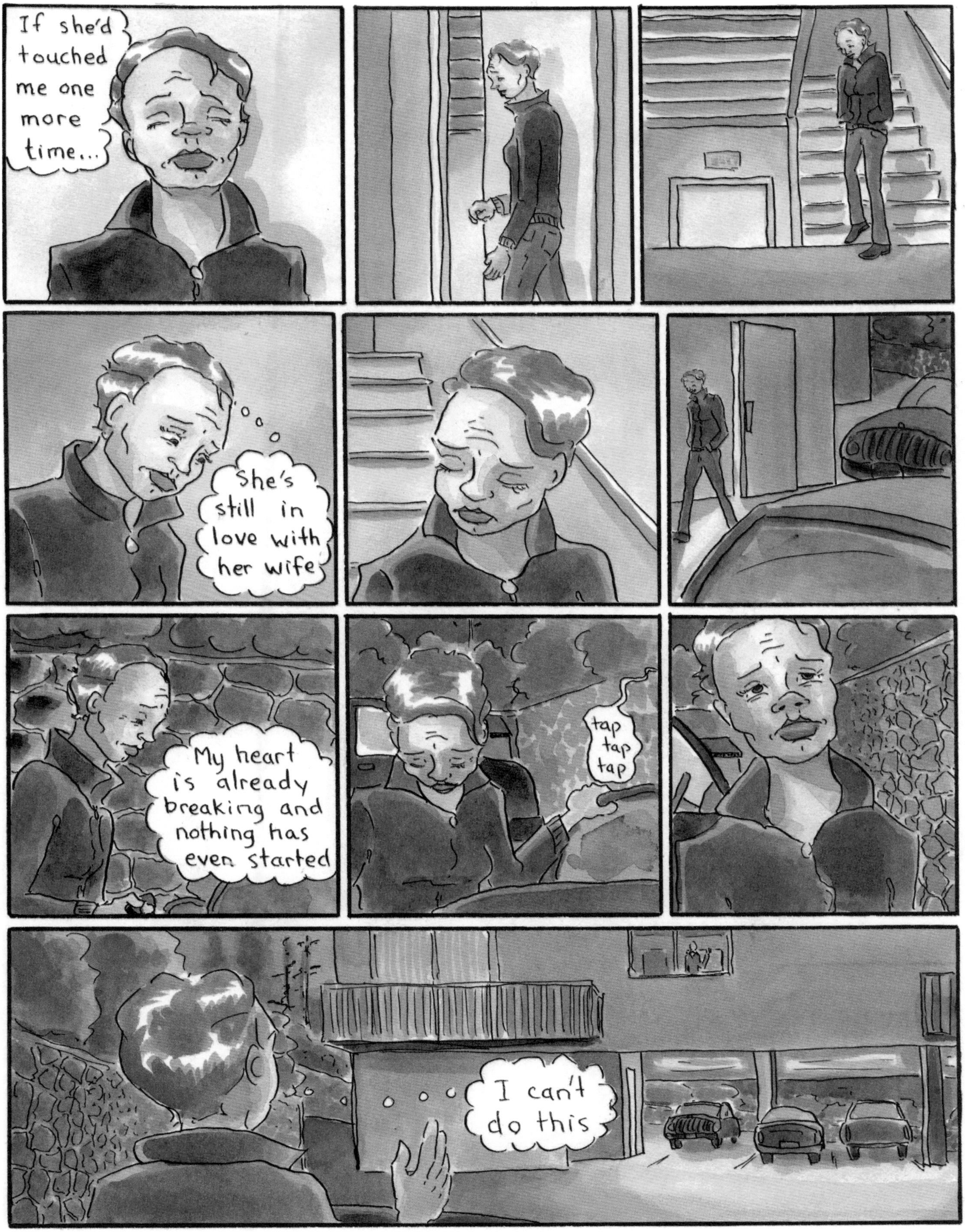
If she'd touched me one more time...
She's still in love with her wife
My heart is already breaking and nothing has even started
tap tap tap
I can't do this

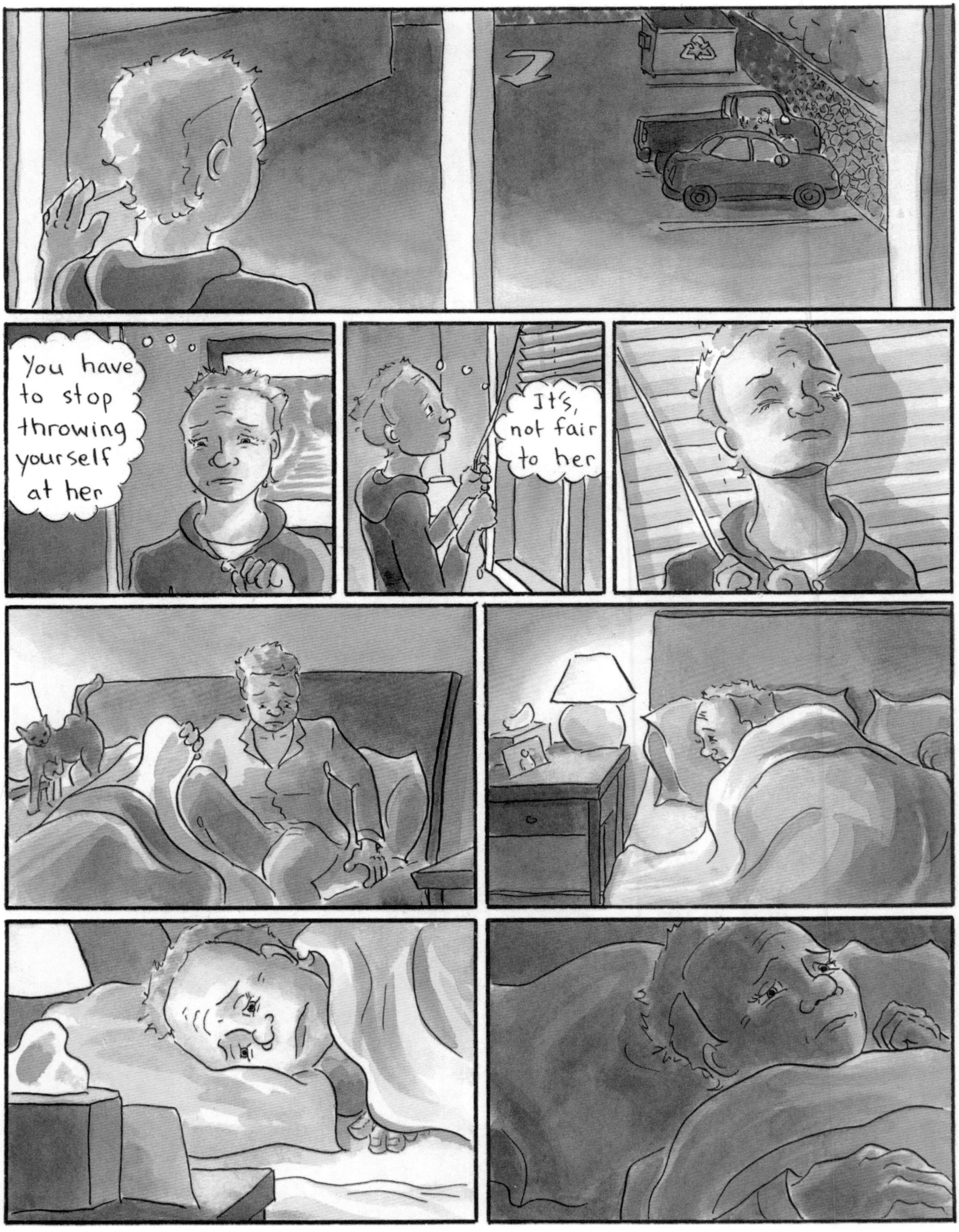
You have to stop throwing yourself at her
It's, not fair to her

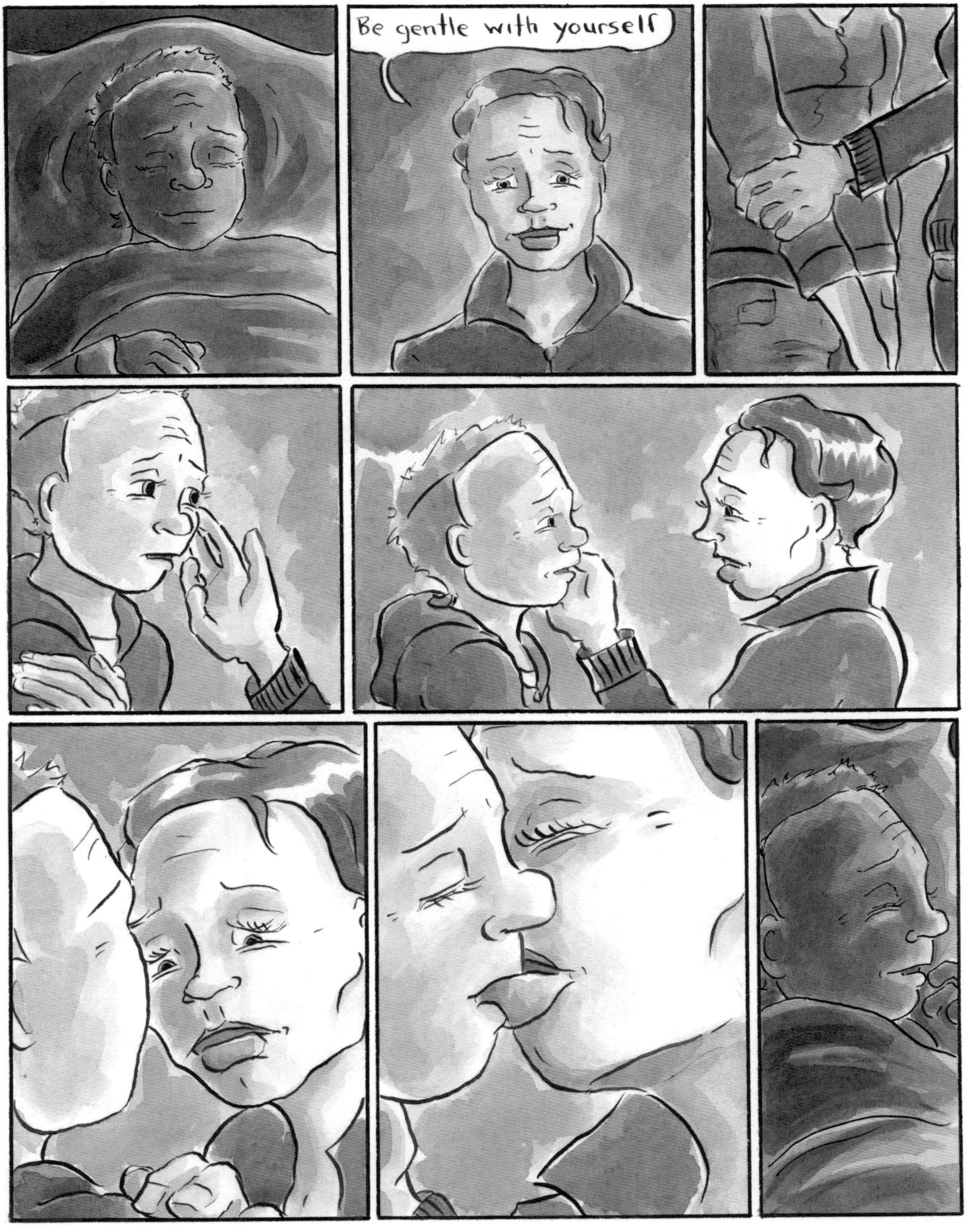
Be gentle with yourself

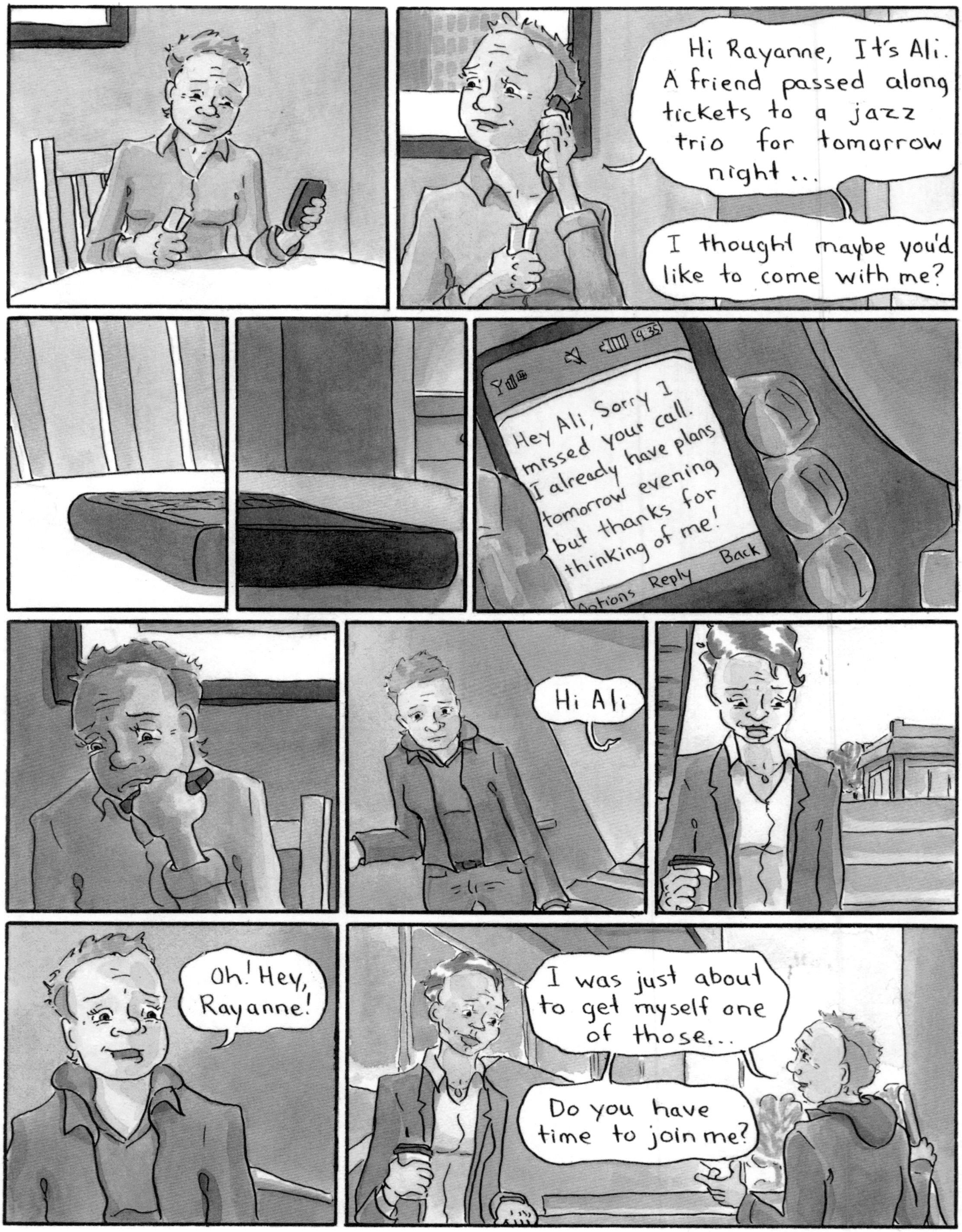
Hi Rayanne, It's Ali. A friend passed along tickets to a jazz trio for tomorrow night...
I thought maybe you'd like to come with me?
4:35
Hey Ali, Sorry I missed your call. I already have plans tomorrow evening but thanks for thinking of me!
Options Reply Back
Hi Ali
Oh! Hey, Rayanne!
I was just about to get myself one of those...
Do you have time to join me?

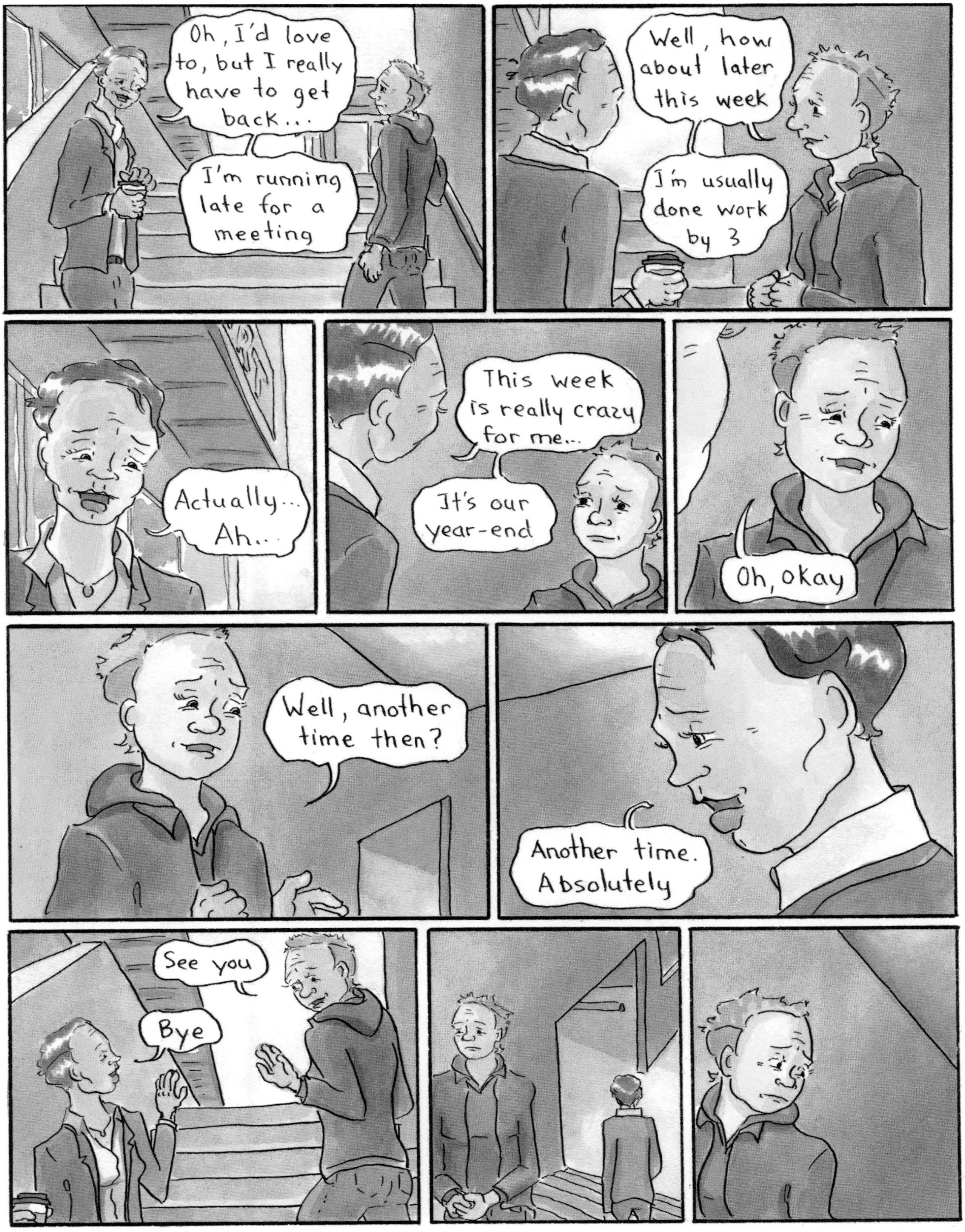
Oh, I'd love to, but I really have to get back...
I'm running late for a meeting
Well, how about later this week
I'm usually done work by 3
Actually... Ah...
This week is really crazy for me...
It's our year-end
Oh, okay
Well, another time then?
Another time. Absolutely
See you
Bye

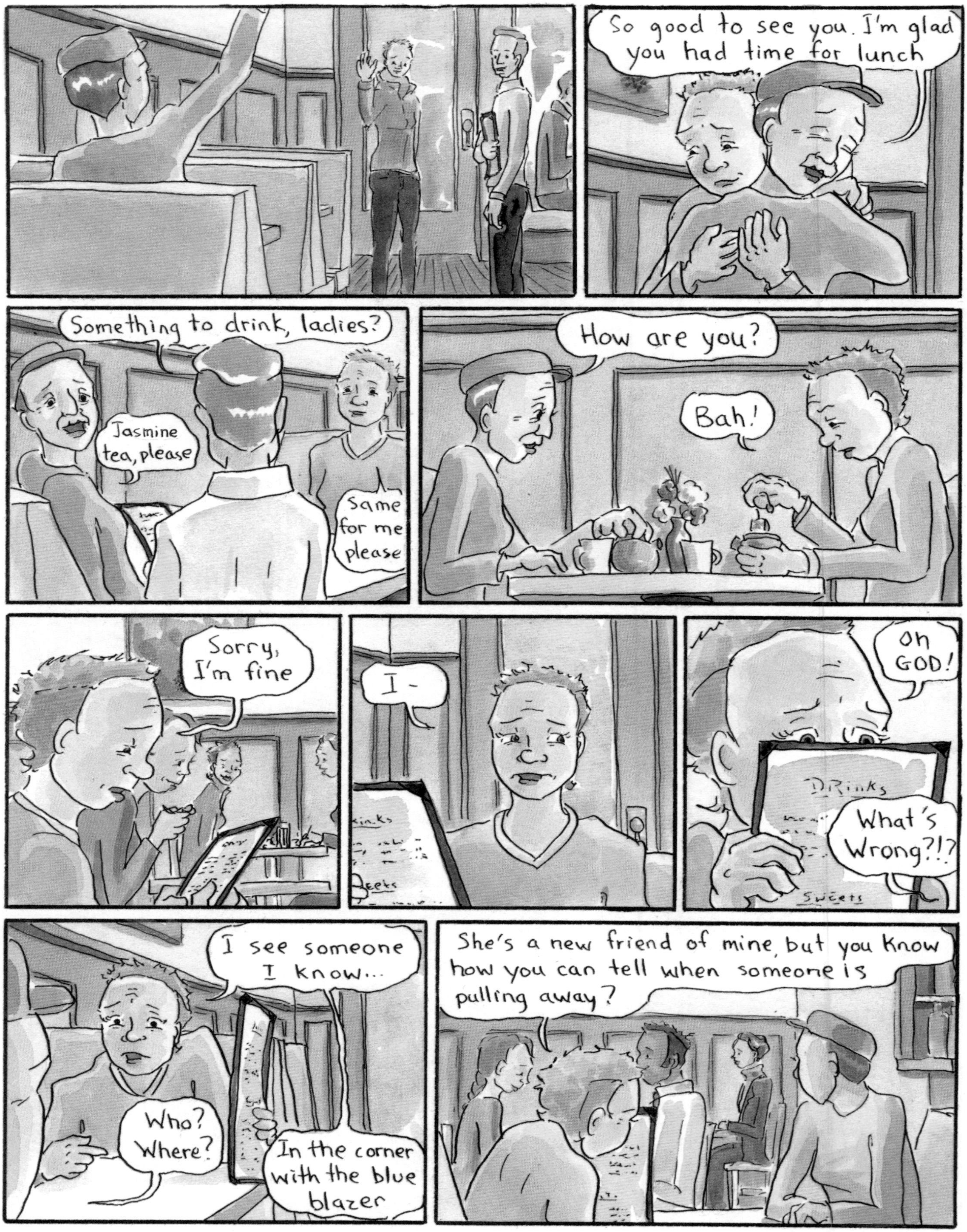
So good to see you. I'm glad you had time for lunch
Something to drink, ladies?
Jasmine tea, please
Same for me please
How are you?
Bah!
Sorry, I'm fine
I -
Oh GOD!
DRinks
What's Wrong?!?
Sweets
I see someone I know...
Who? Where?
In the corner with the blue blazer
She's a new friend of mine, but you know how you can tell when someone is pulling away?

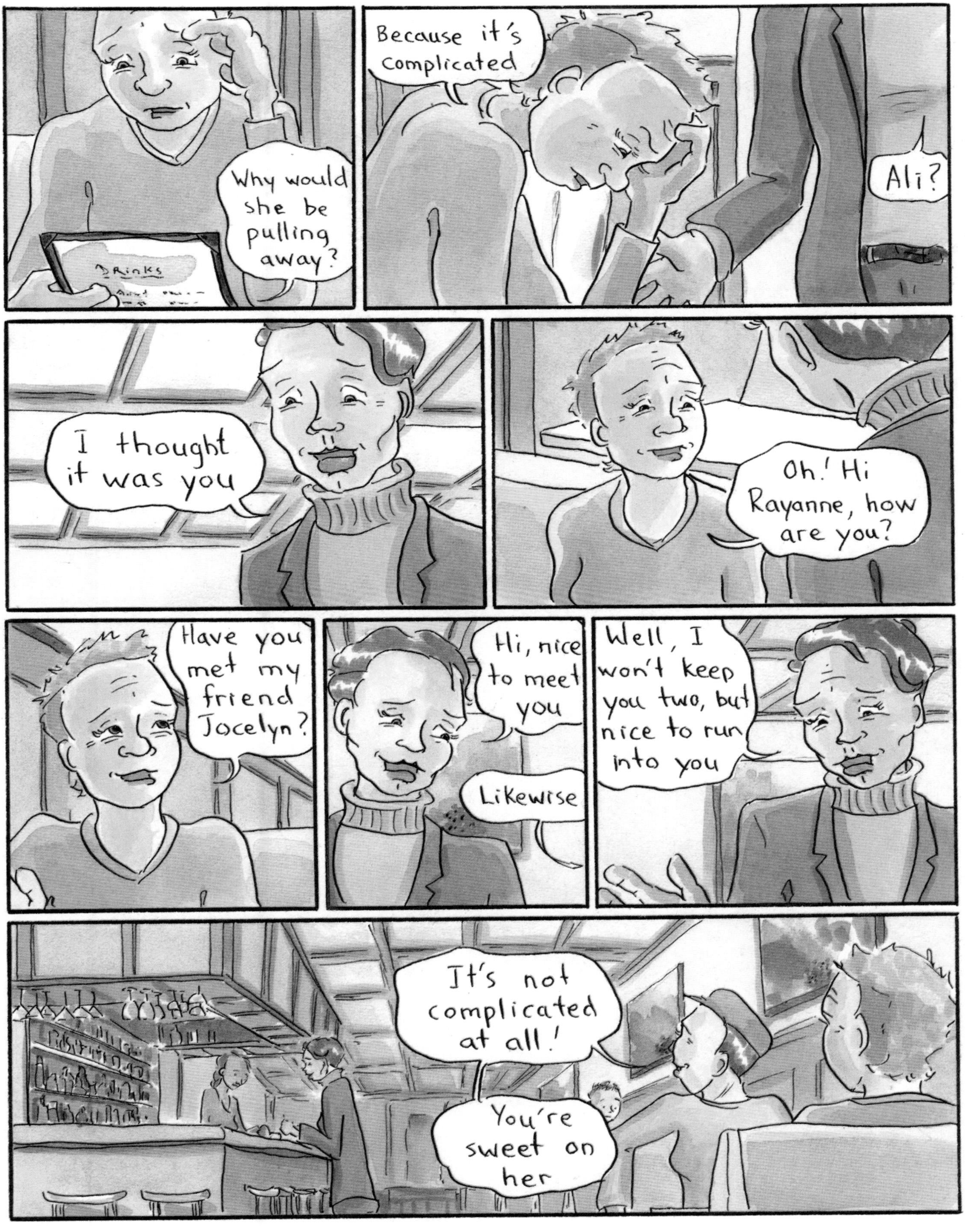
Why would she be pulling away?
Because it's complicated
Ali?
I thought it was you
Oh! Hi Rayanne, how are you?
Have you met my friend Jocelyn?
Hi, nice to meet you
Likewise
Well, I won't keep you two, but nice to run into you
It's not complicated at all!
You're sweet on her

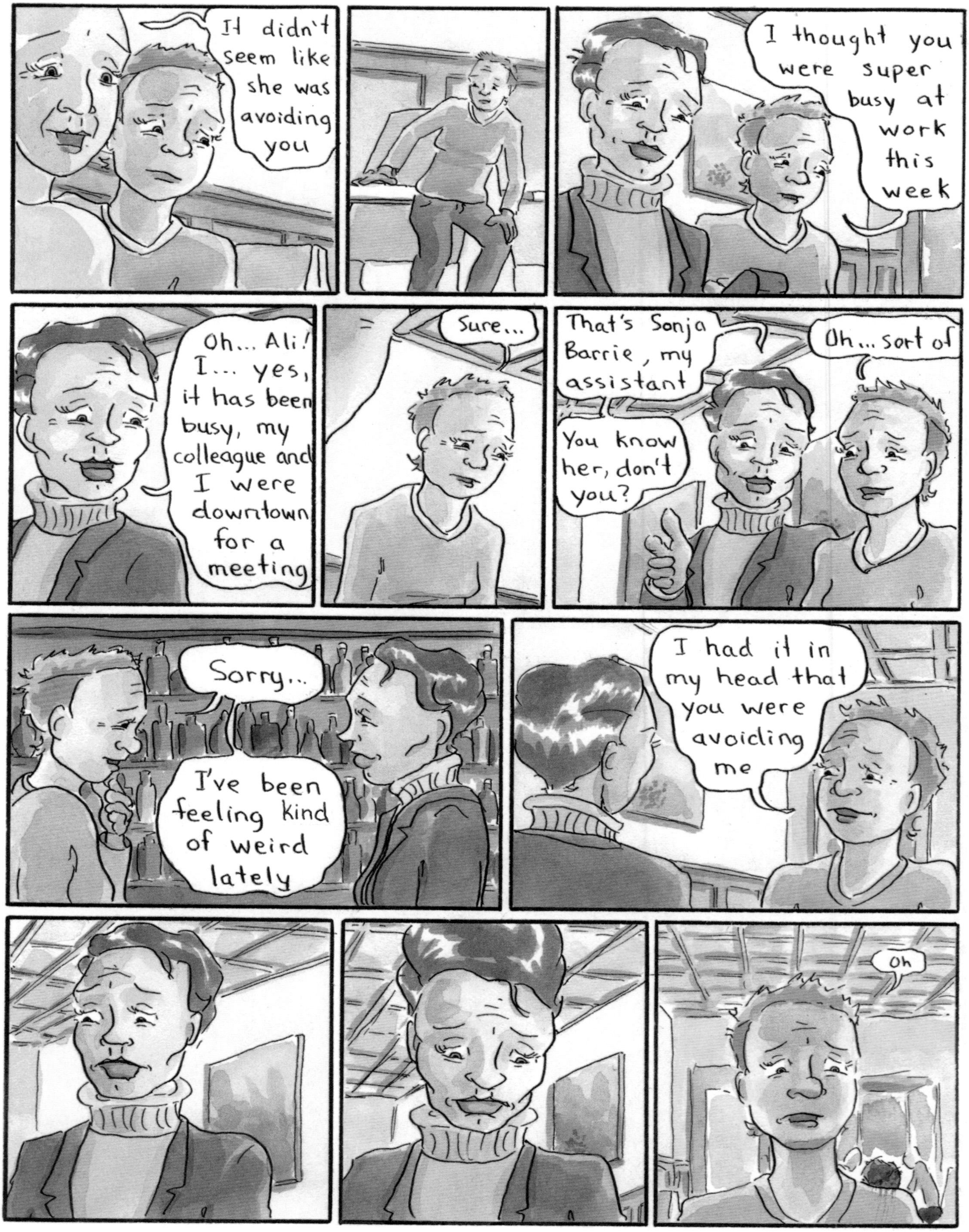
It didn't seem like she was avoiding you
I thought you were super busy at work this week
Oh... Ali! I... yes, it has been busy, my colleague and I were downtown for a meeting
Sure...
That's Sonja Barrie, my assistant
You know her, don't you?
Oh... sort of
Sorry..
I've been feeling kind of weird lately
I had it in my head that you were avoiding me
Oh

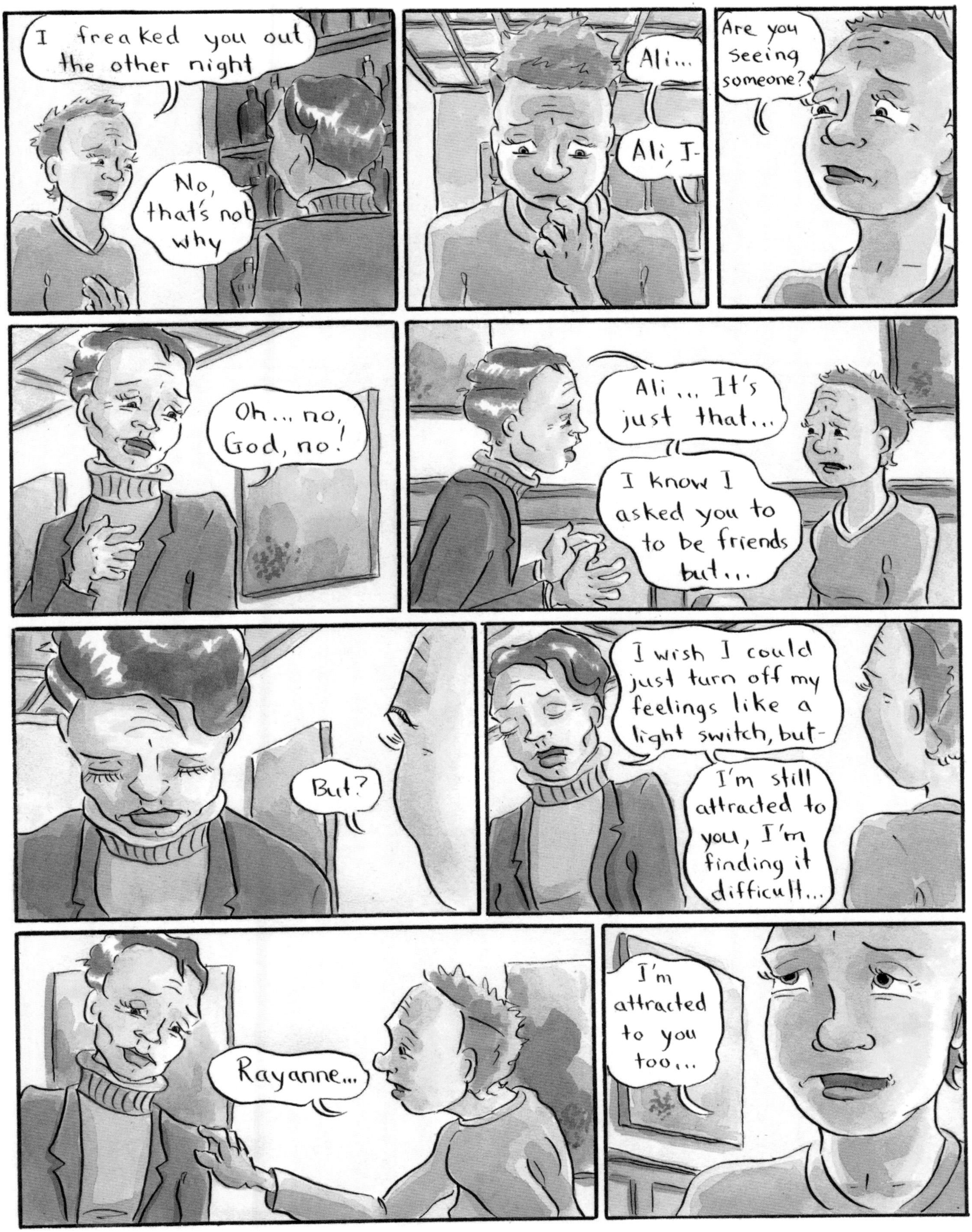
I freaked you out the other night
No, that's not why
Ali...
Ali, I-
Are you seeing someone?
Oh... no, God, no!
Ali... It's just that...
I know I asked you to to be friends but...
But?
I wish I could just turn off my feelings like a light switch, but-
I'm still attracted to you, I'm finding it difficult...
Rayanne...
I'm attracted to you too...

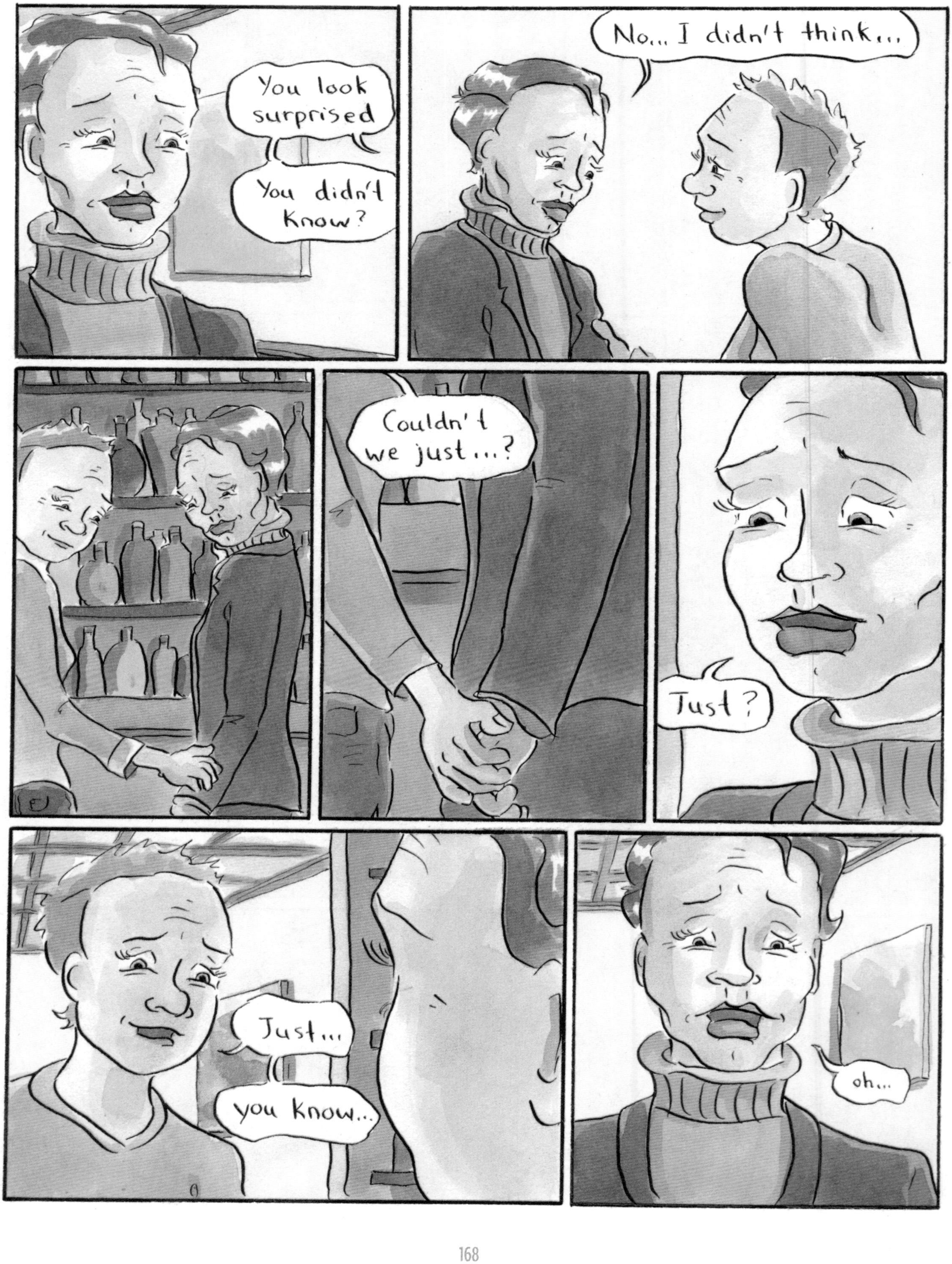
You look surprised
You didn't know?
No... I didn't think...
Couldn't we just...?
Just?
Just...
you know...
oh...

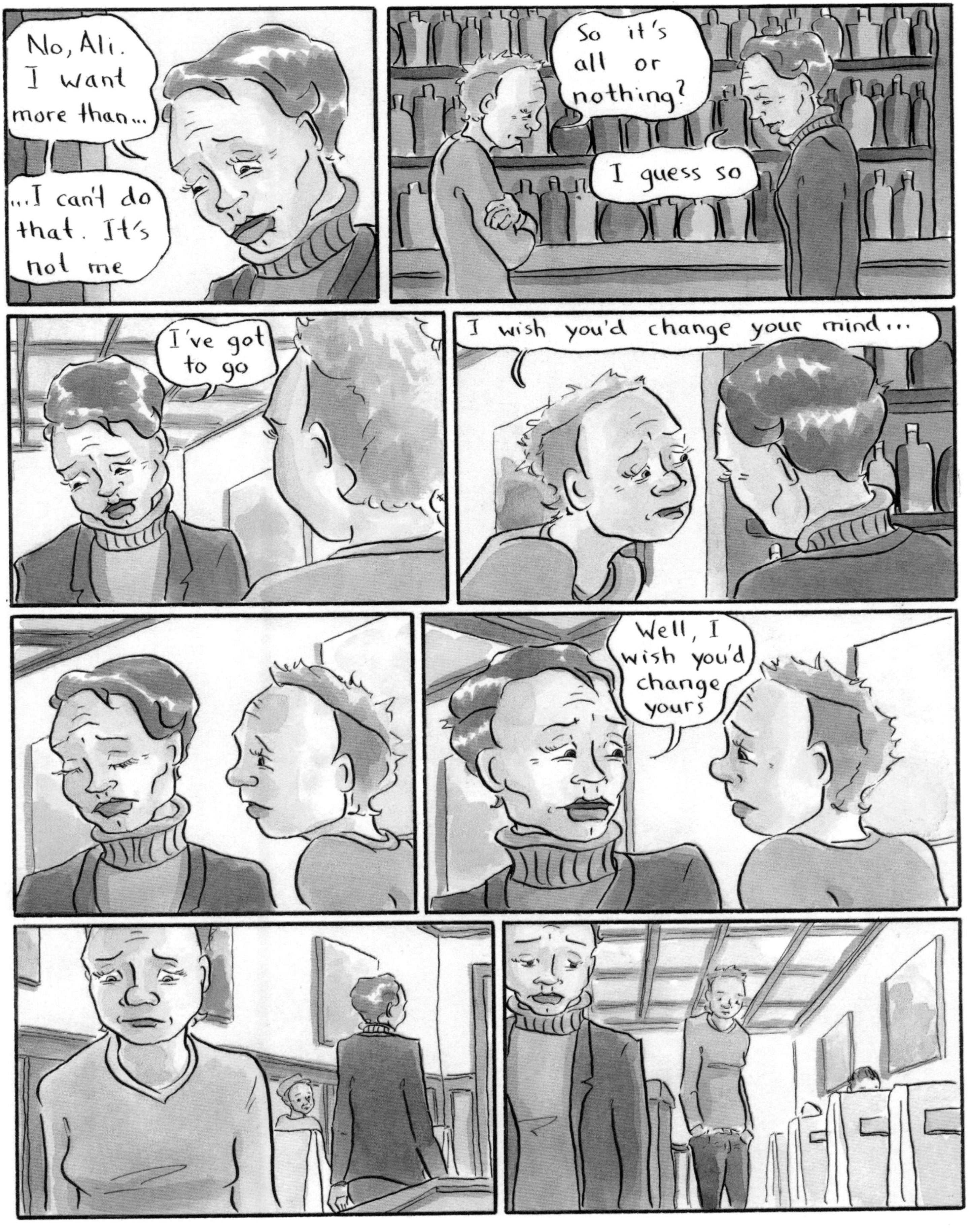
No, Ali. I want more than...
...I can't do that. It's not me
So it's all or nothing?
I guess so
I've got to go
I wish you'd change your mind...
Well, I wish you'd change yours

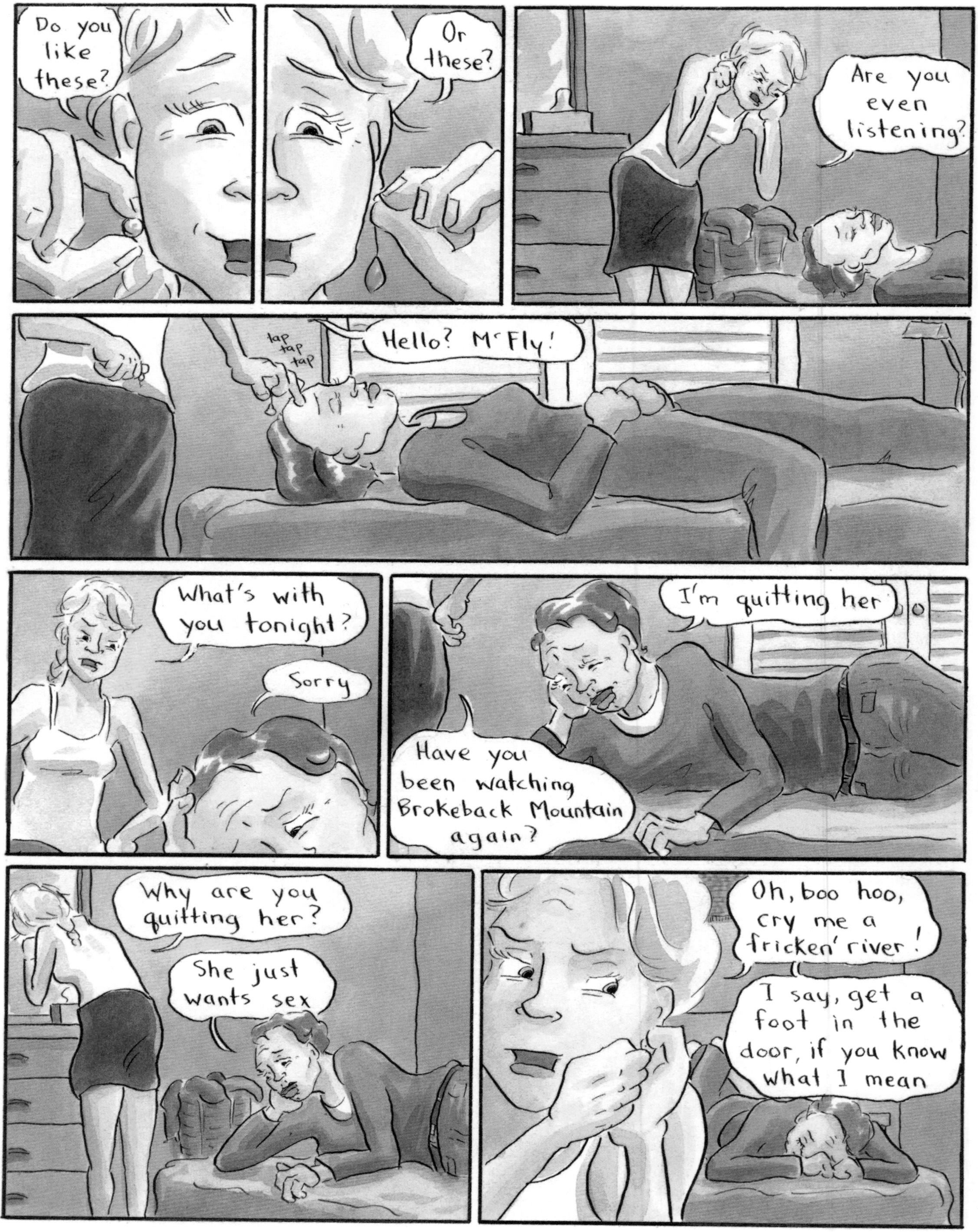

Do you like these?
Or these?
Are you even listening?
tap tap tap
Hello? McFly!
What's with you tonight?
Sorry
I'm quitting her
Have you been watching Brokeback Mountain again?
Why are you quitting her?
She just wants sex
Oh, boo hoo, cry me a fricken' river!
I say, get a foot in the door, if you know what I mean

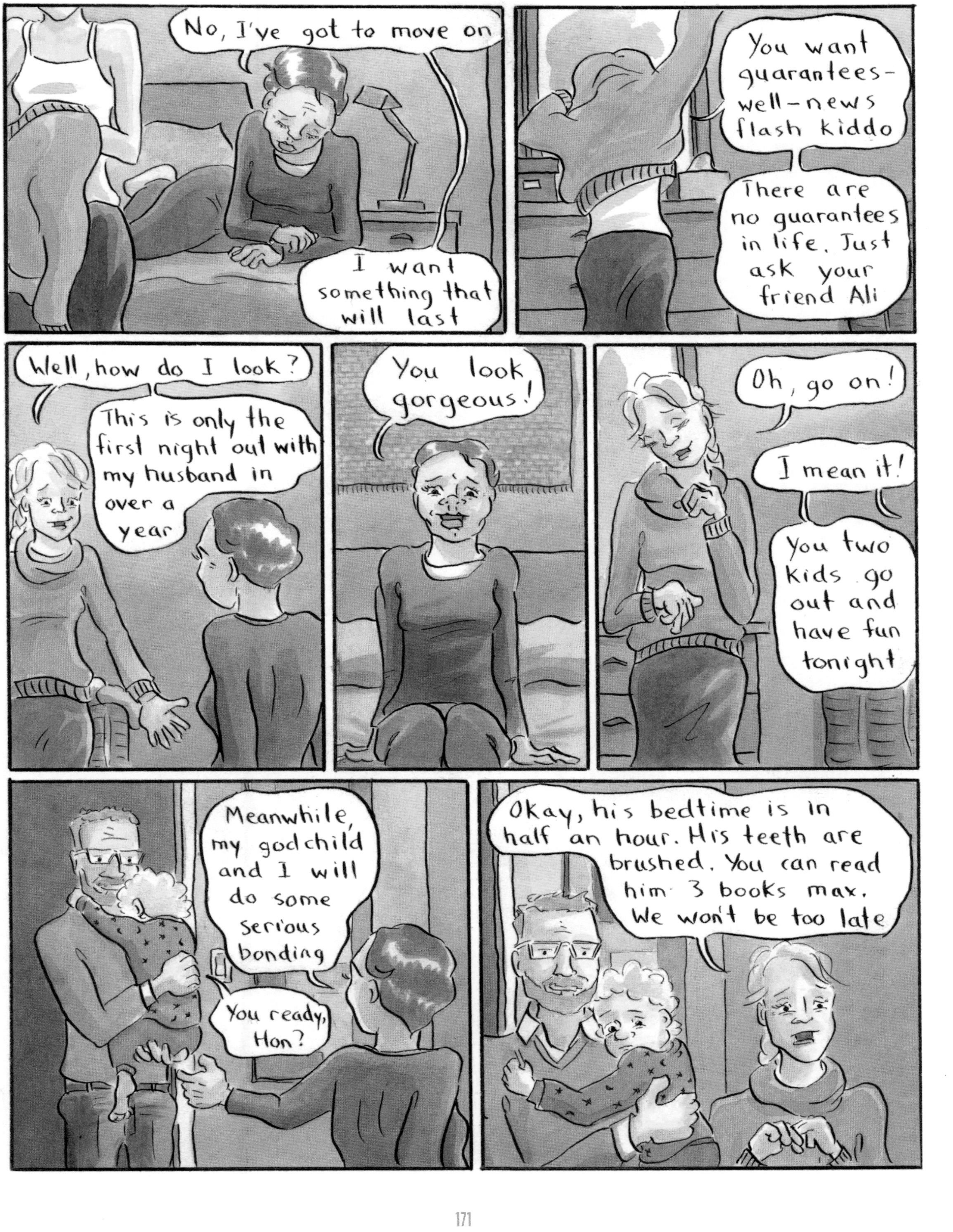
No, I've got to move on
I want something that will last
You want guarantees- well-news flash kiddo
There are no guarantees in life. Just ask your friend Ali
Well, how do I look?
This is only the first night out with my husband in over a year
You look gorgeous!
Oh, go on!
I mean it!
You two kids go out and have fun tonight
Meanwhile, my godchild and I will do some serious bonding
You ready, Hon?
Okay, his bedtime is in half an hour. His teeth are brushed. You can read him 3 books max. We won't be too late

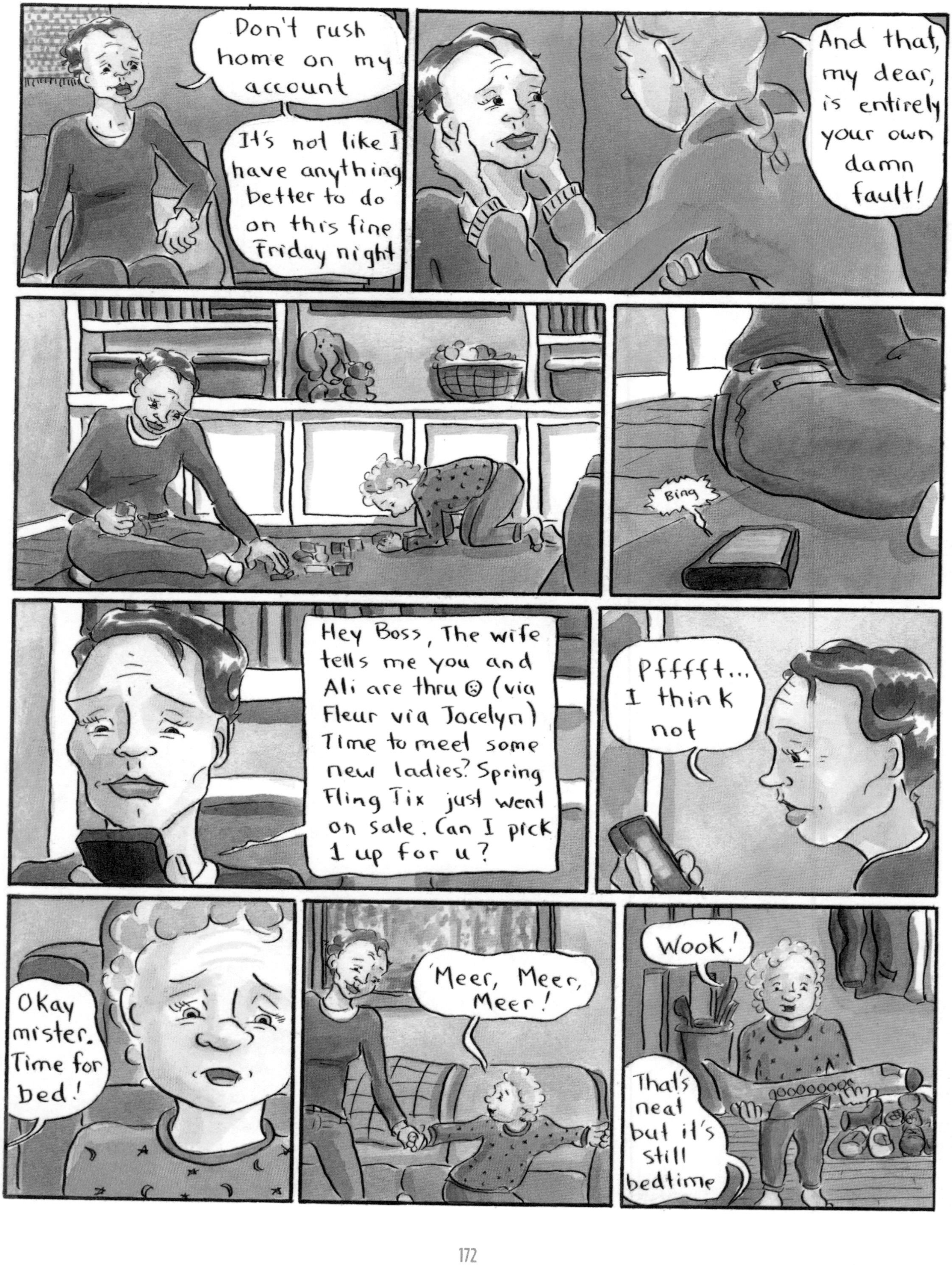
Don't rush home on my account
It's not like I have anything better to do on this fine Friday night
And that, my dear, is entirely your own damn fault!
Bing
Hey Boss, The wife tells me you and Ali are thru ☹ (via Fleur via Jocelyn) Time to meet some new ladies? Spring Fling Tix just went on sale. Can I pick 1 up for u?
Pfffft... I think not
Okay mister. Time for bed!
'Meer, Meer, Meer!
Wook!
That's neat but it's still bedtime

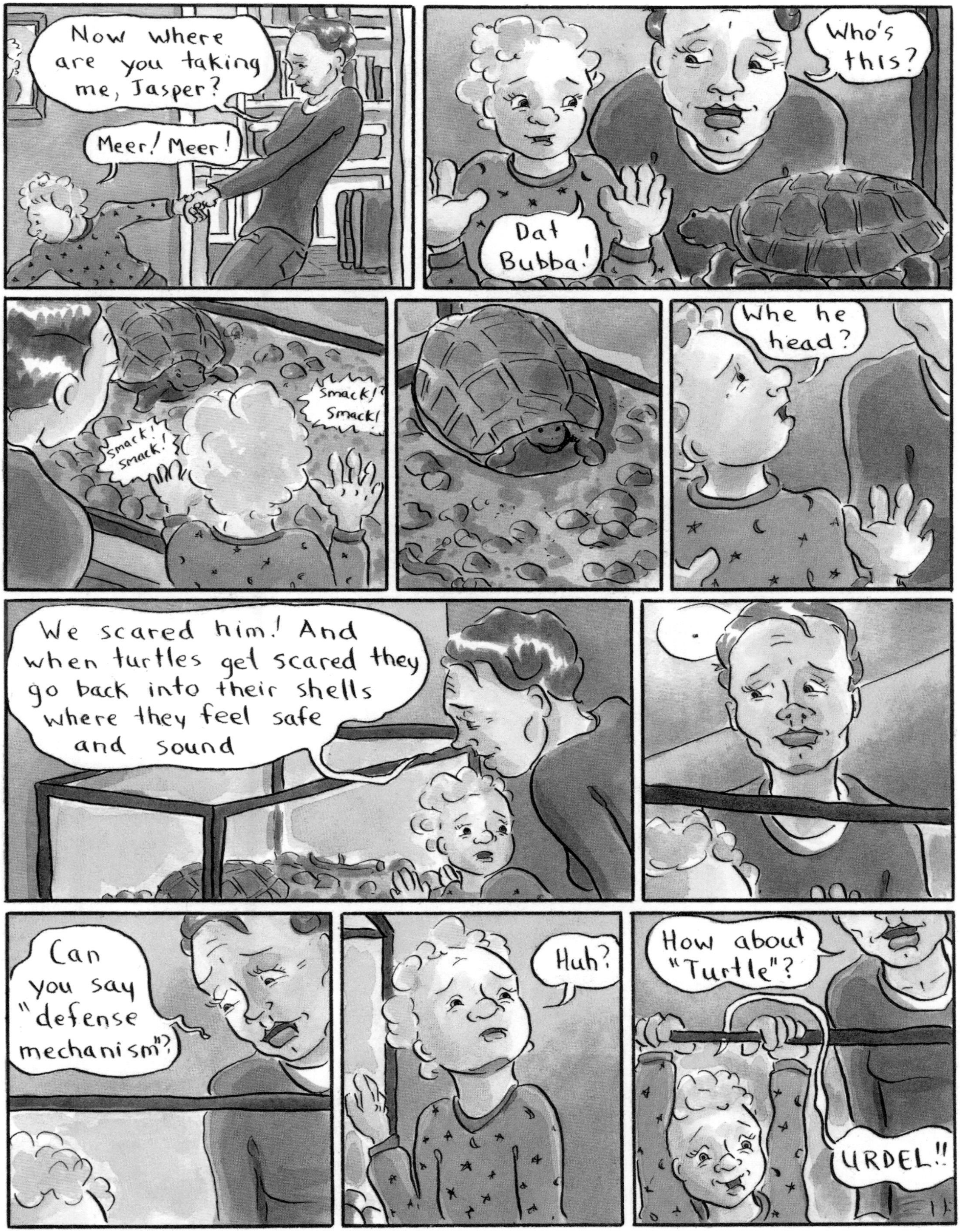

Now where are you taking me, Jasper?
Meer! Meer!
Who's this?
Dat Bubba!
Smack! Smack!
Smack! Smack!
Whe he head?
We scared him! And when turtles get scared they go back into their shells where they feel safe and sound
Can you say "defense mechanism"?
Huh?
How about "Turtle"?
URDEL!!

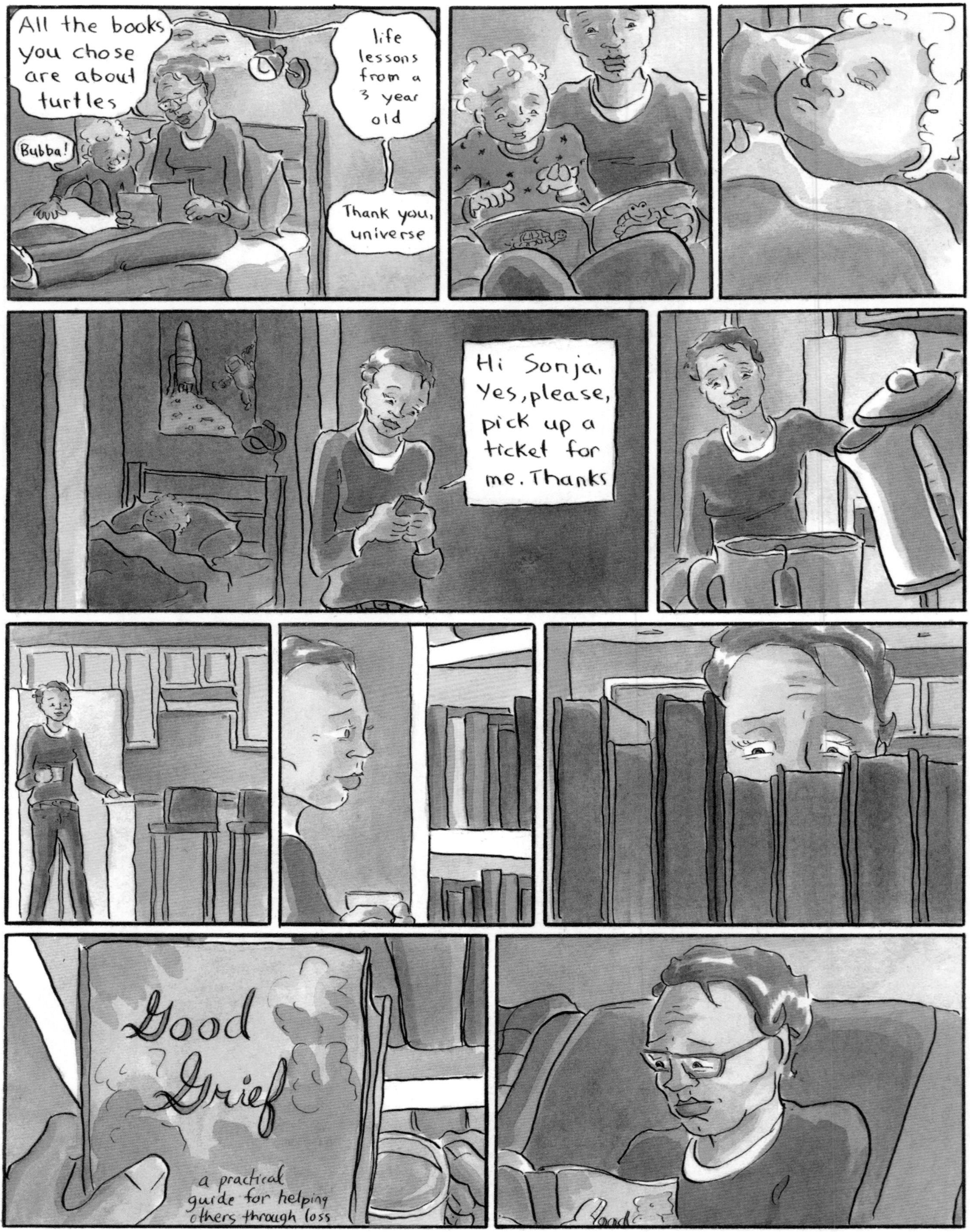
All the books you chose are about turtles
Bubba!
life lessons from a 3 year old
Thank you, universe
Hi Sonja, Yes, please, pick up a ticket for me. Thanks
Good Grief
a practical guide for helping others through loss

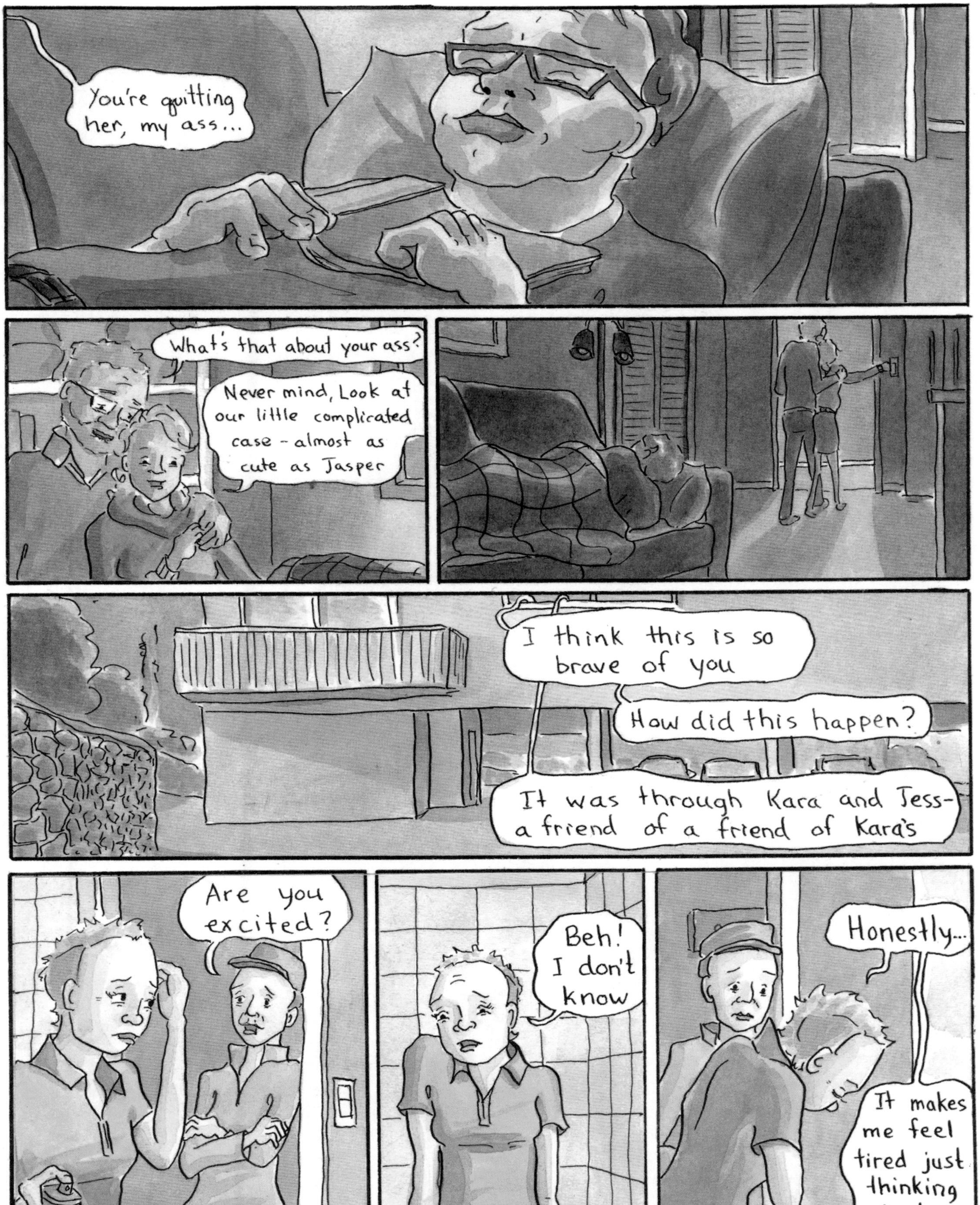
You're quitting her, my ass...
What's that about your ass?
Never mind, Look at our little complicated case - almost as cute as Jasper
I think this is so brave of you
How did this happen?
It was through Kara and Jess- a friend of a friend of Kara's
Are you excited?
Beh! I don't know
Honestly...
It makes me feel tired just thinking about it

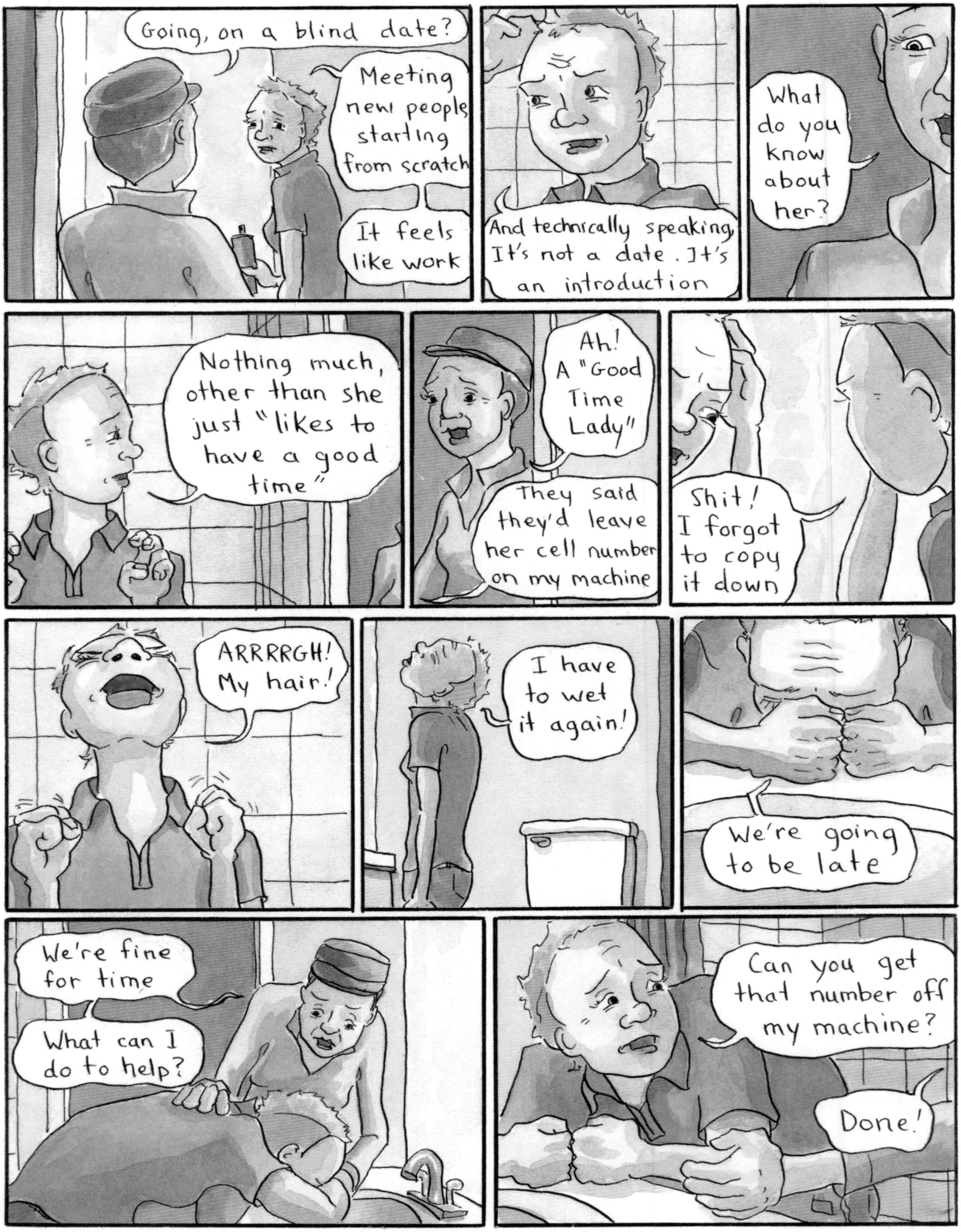
Going, on a blind date?
Meeting new people starting from scratch
It feels like work
And technically speaking, It's not a date. It's an introduction
What do you know about her?
Nothing much, other than she just "likes to have a good time"
Ah! A "Good Time Lady"
They said they'd leave her cell number on my machine
Shit! I forgot to copy it down
ARRRRGH! My hair!
I have to wet it again!
We're going to be late
We're fine for time
What can I do to help?
Can you get that number off my machine?
Done!

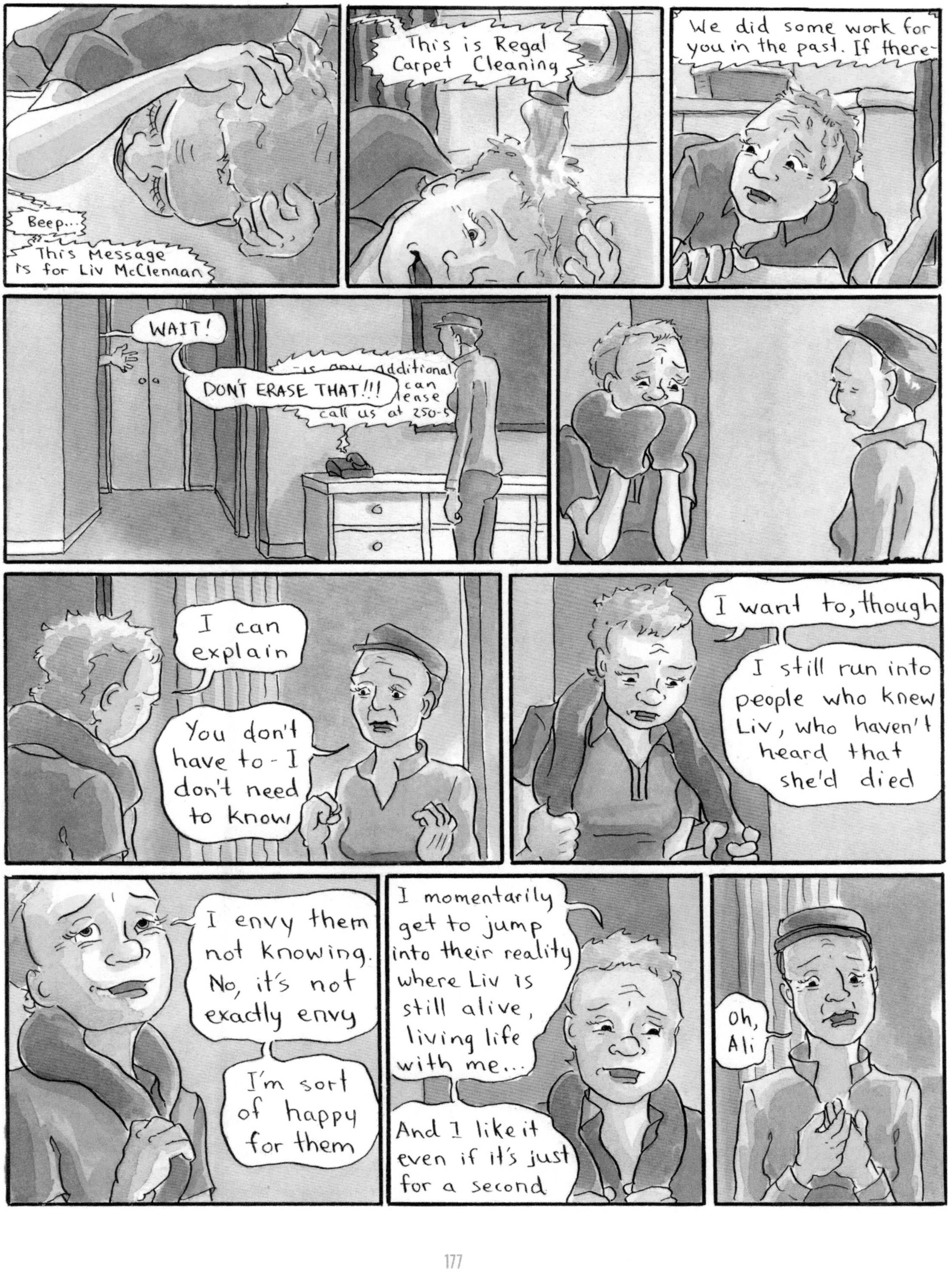
Beep...
This Message is for Liv McClennan
This is Regal Carpet Cleaning
We did some work for you in the past. If there-
WAIT!
DON'T ERASE THAT!!!
is any additional can lease call us at 250-5
I can explain
You don't have to - I don't need to know
I want to, though
I still run into people who knew Liv, who haven't heard that she'd died
I envy them not knowing. No, it's not exactly envy
I'm sort of happy for them
I momentarily get to jump into their reality where Liv is still alive, living life with me...
And I like it even if it's just for a second
Oh, Ali

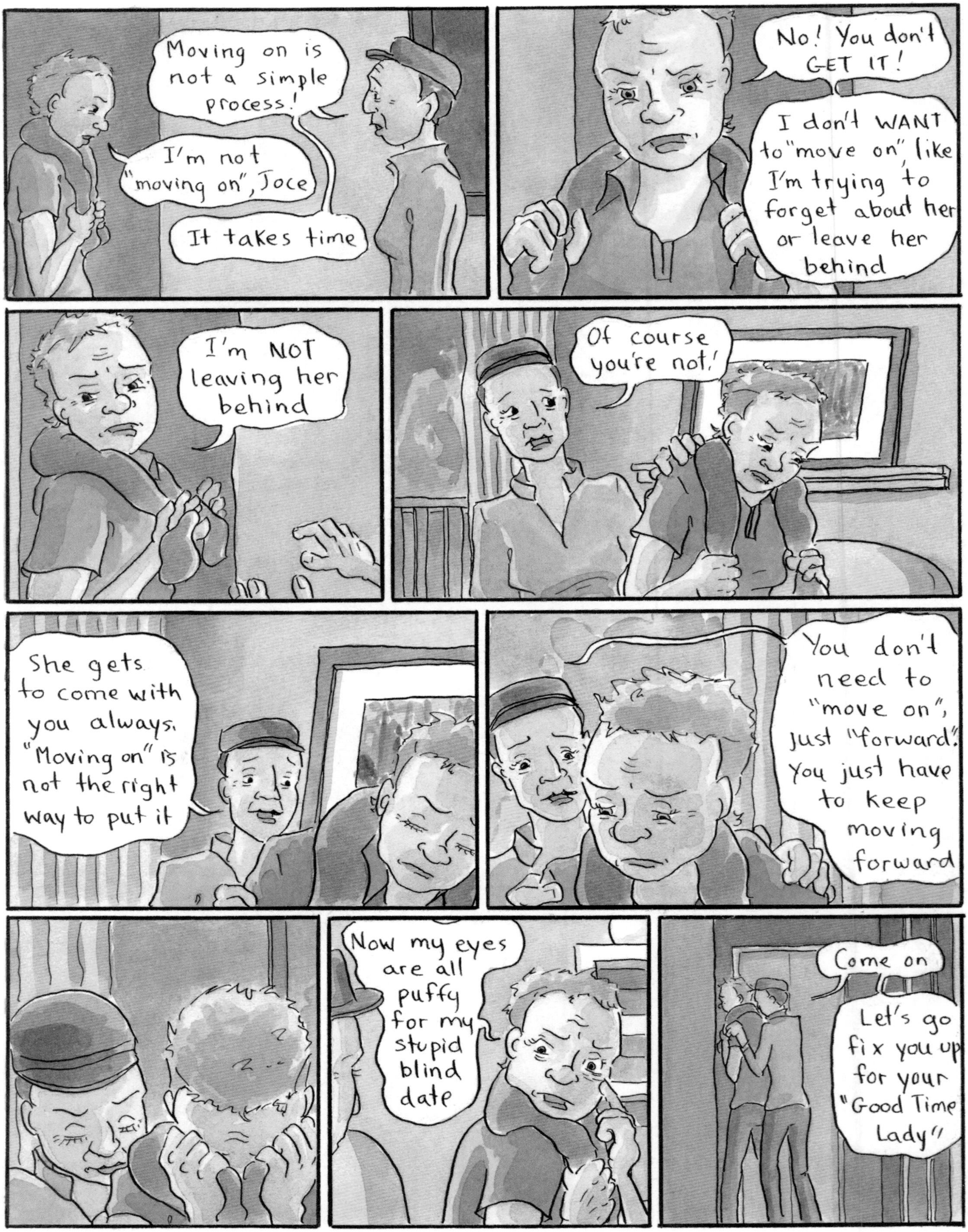
Moving on is not a simple process!
I'm not "moving on", Joce
It takes time
No! You don't GET IT!
I don't WANT to "move on", like I'm trying to forget about her or leave her behind
I'm NOT leaving her behind
Of course you're not!
She gets to come with you always. "Moving on" is not the right way to put it
You don't need to "move on", just "forward". You just have to keep moving forward
Now my eyes are all puffy for my stupid blind date
Come on
Let's go fix you up for your "Good Time Lady"

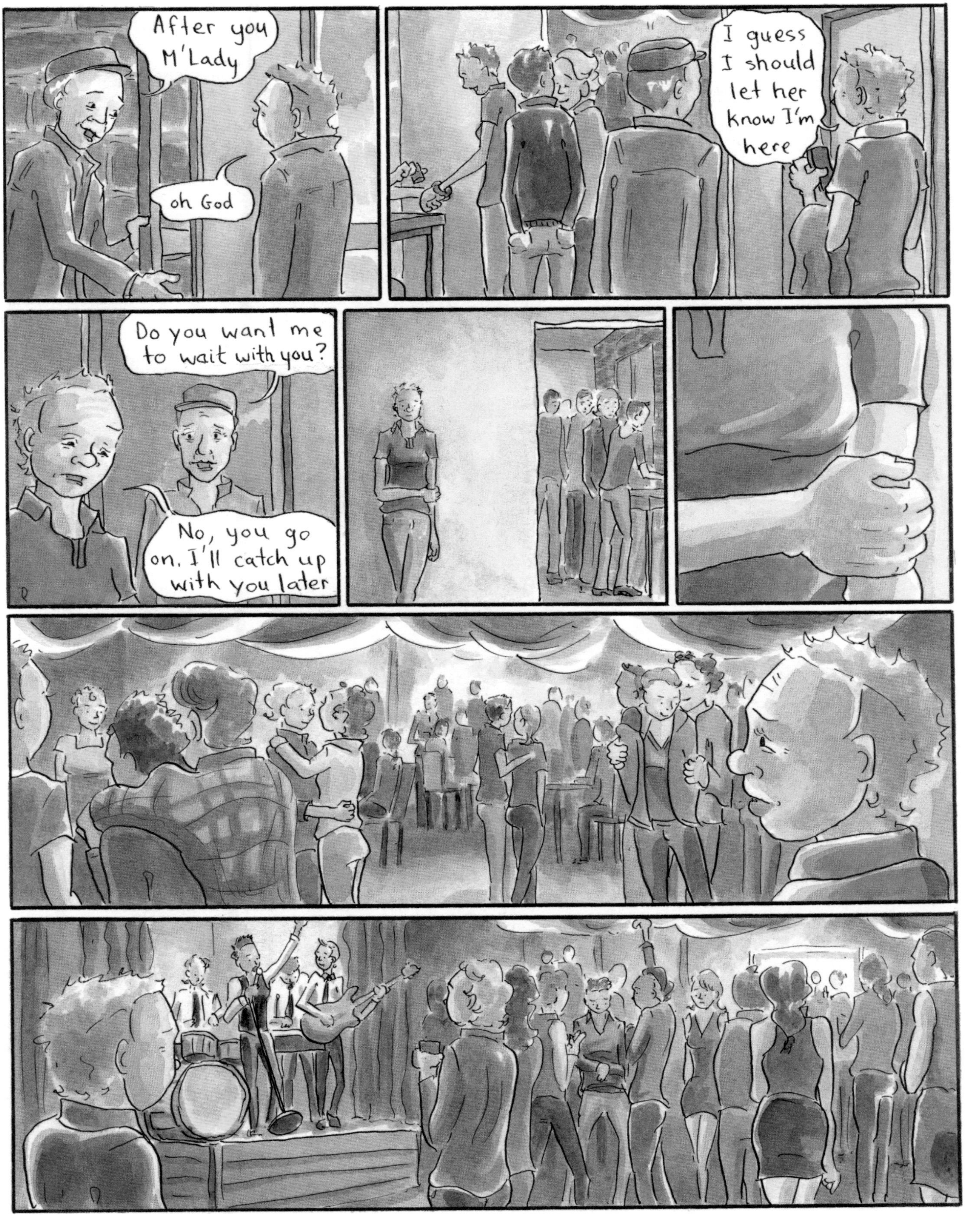
After you M'Lady
oh God
I guess I should let her know I'm here
Do you want me to wait with you?
No, you go on. I'll catch up with you later

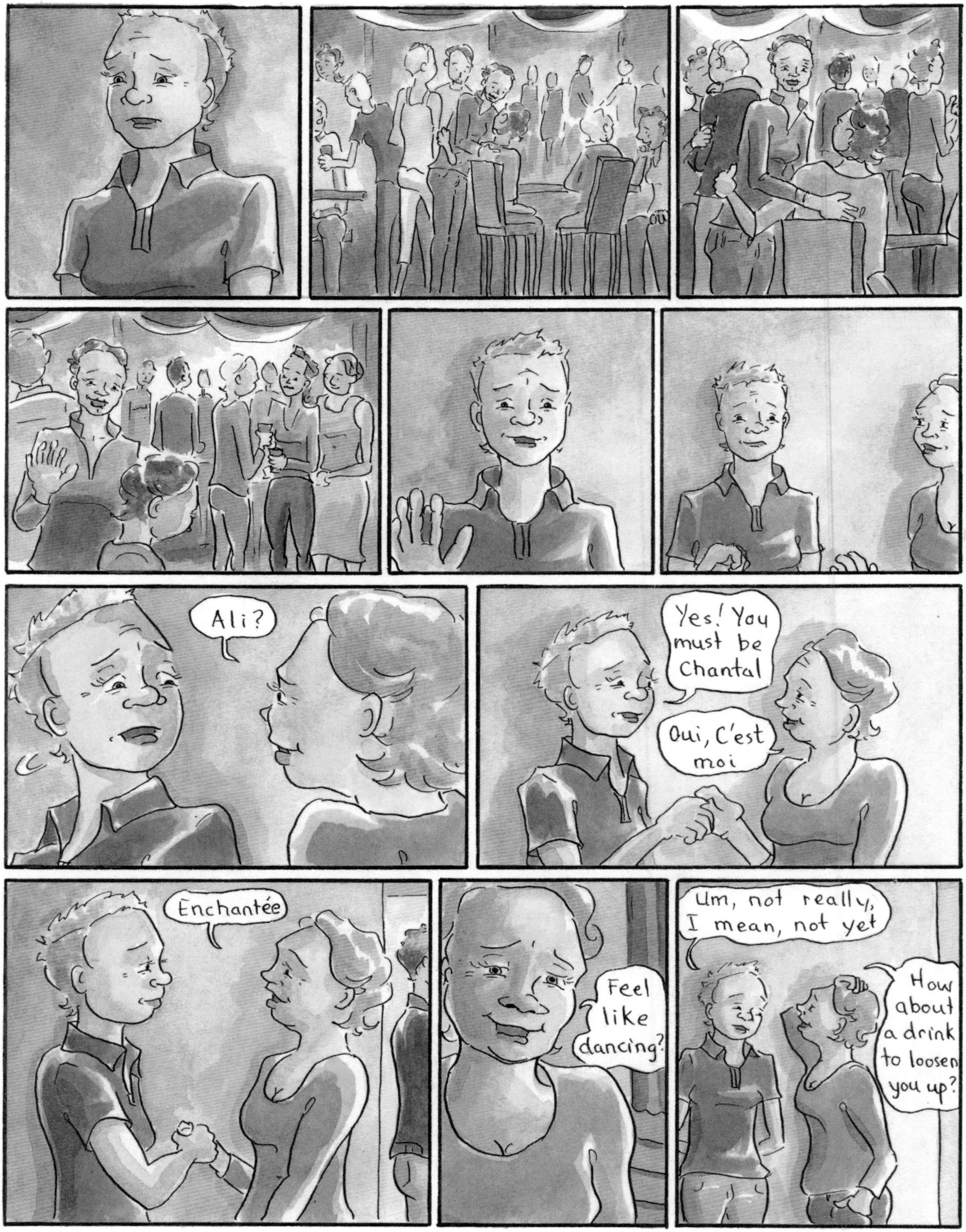
Ali?
Yes! You must be Chantal
Oui, C'est moi
Enchantée
Feel like dancing?
Um, not really, I mean, not yet
How about a drink to loosen you up?

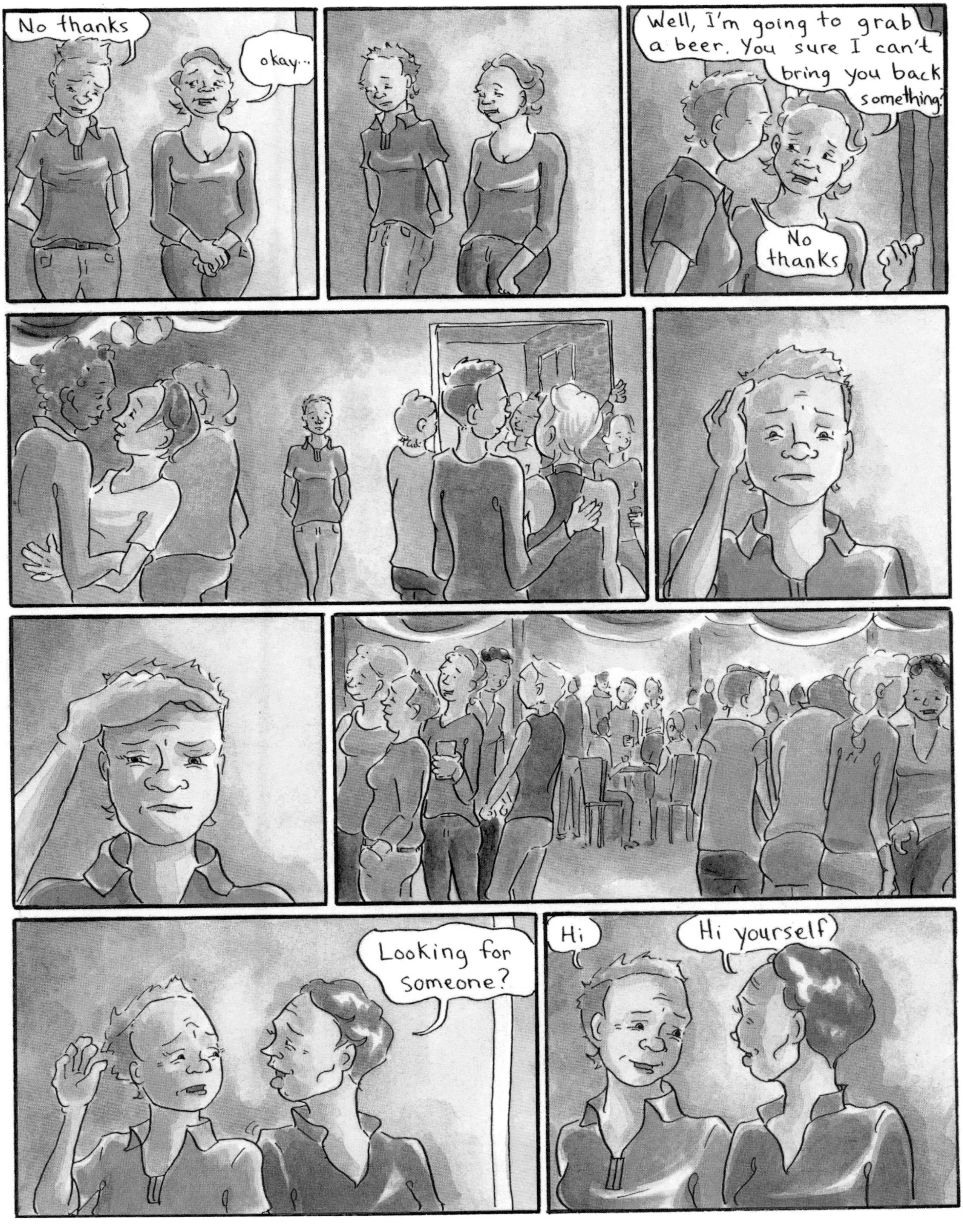
No thanks
okay...
Well, I'm going to grab a beer. You sure I can't bring you back something?
No thanks
Looking for someone?
Hi
Hi yourself

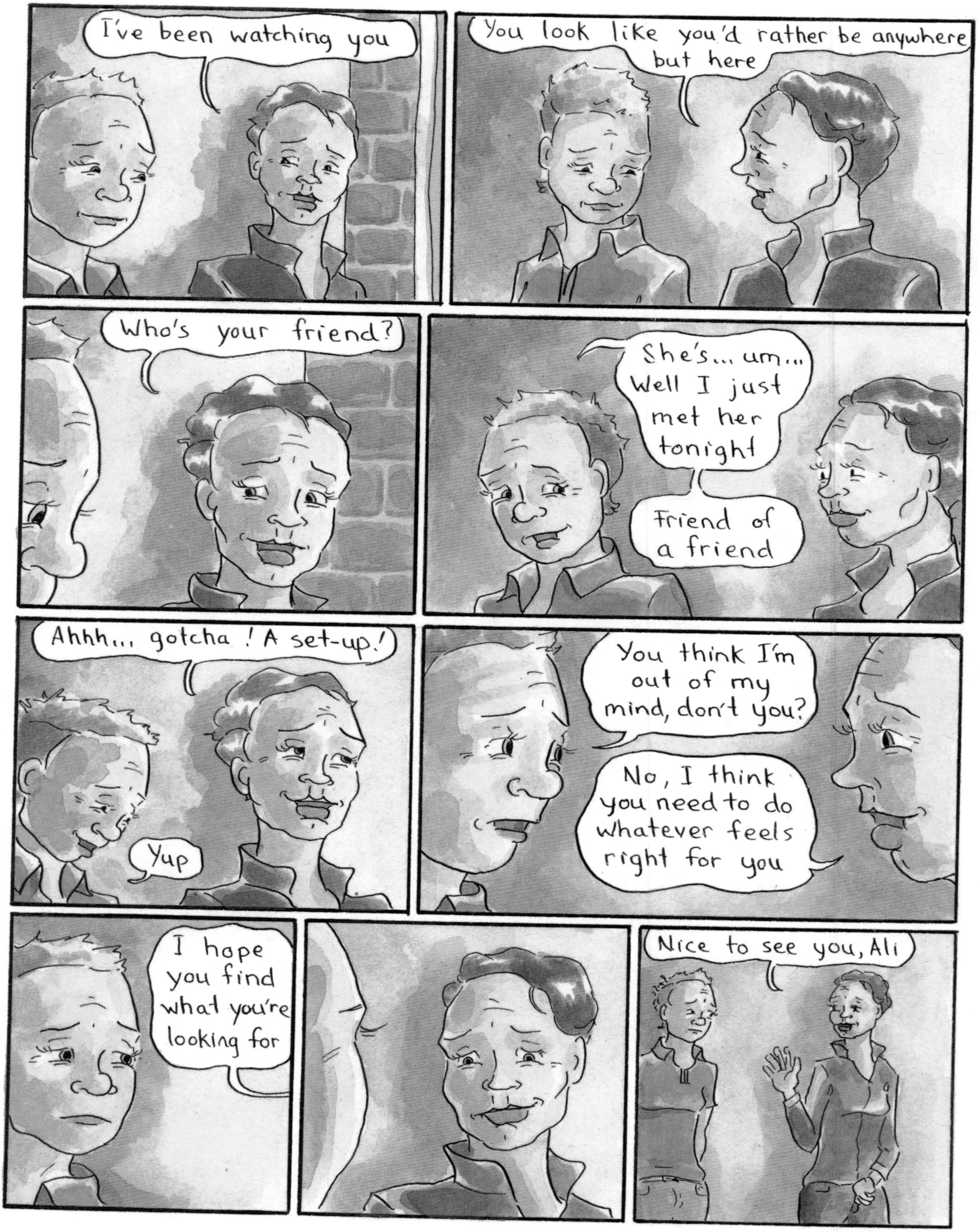
I've been watching you
You look like you'd rather be anywhere but here
Who's your friend?
She's... um... Well I just met her tonight
Friend of a friend
Ahhh... gotcha! A set-up!
Yup
You think I'm out of my mind, don't you?
No, I think you need to do whatever feels right for you
I hope you find what you're looking for
Nice to see you, Ali

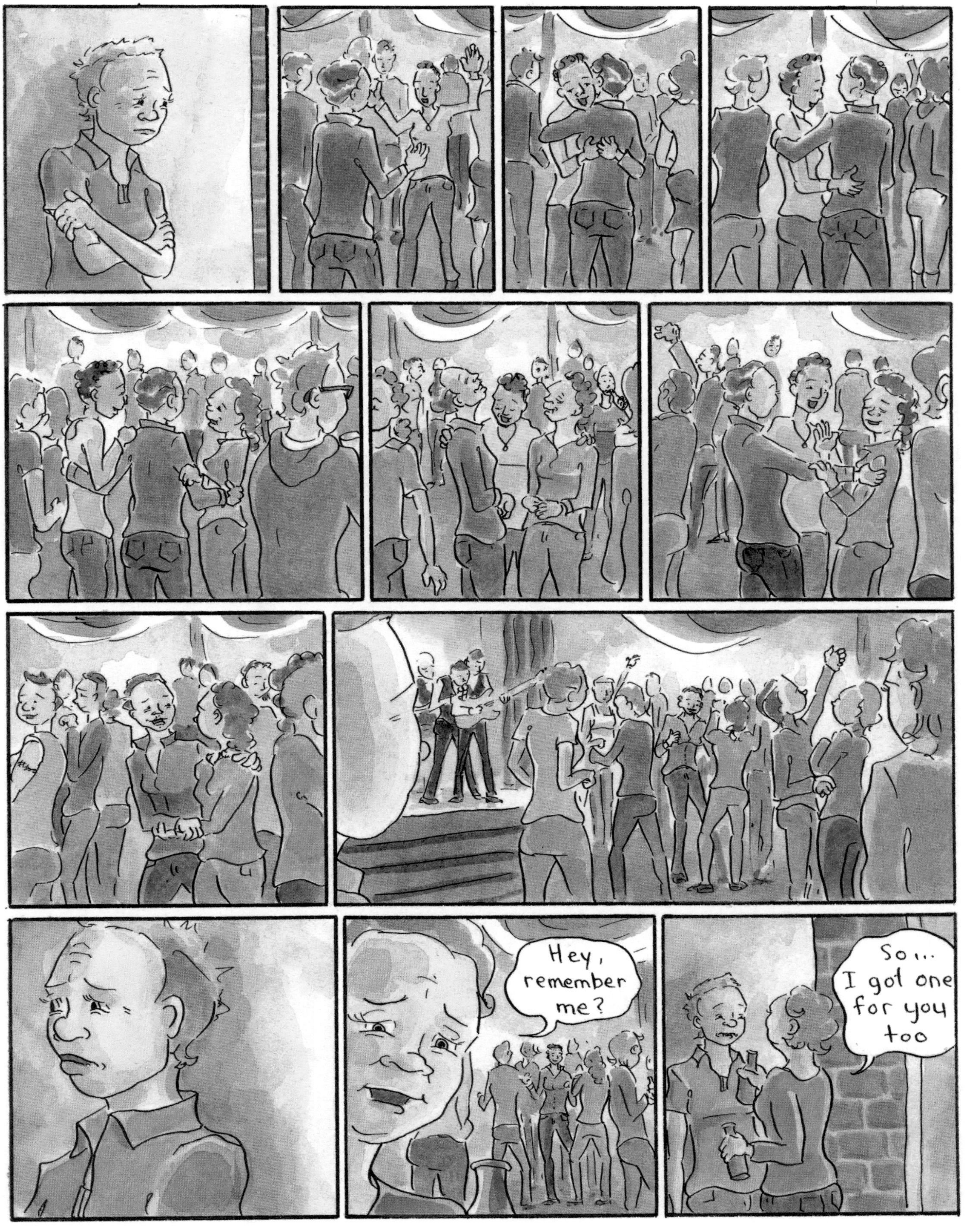
Hey, remember me?
So... I got one for you too

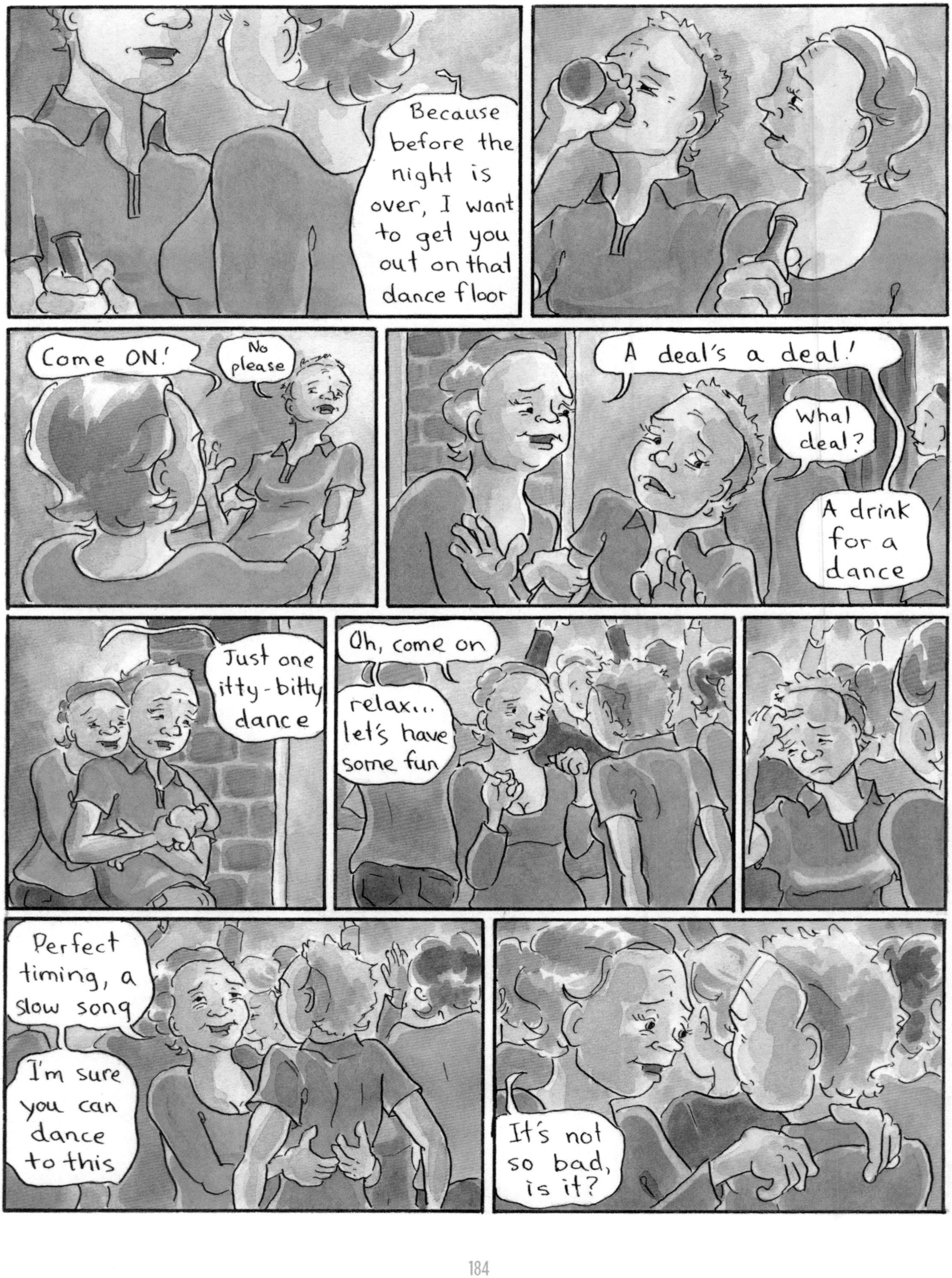
Because before the night is over, I want to get you out on that dance floor
Come ON!
No please
A deal's a deal!
What deal?
A drink for a dance
Just one itty-bitty dance
Oh, come on
relax... let's have some fun
Perfect timing, a slow song
I'm sure you can dance to this
It's not so bad, is it?

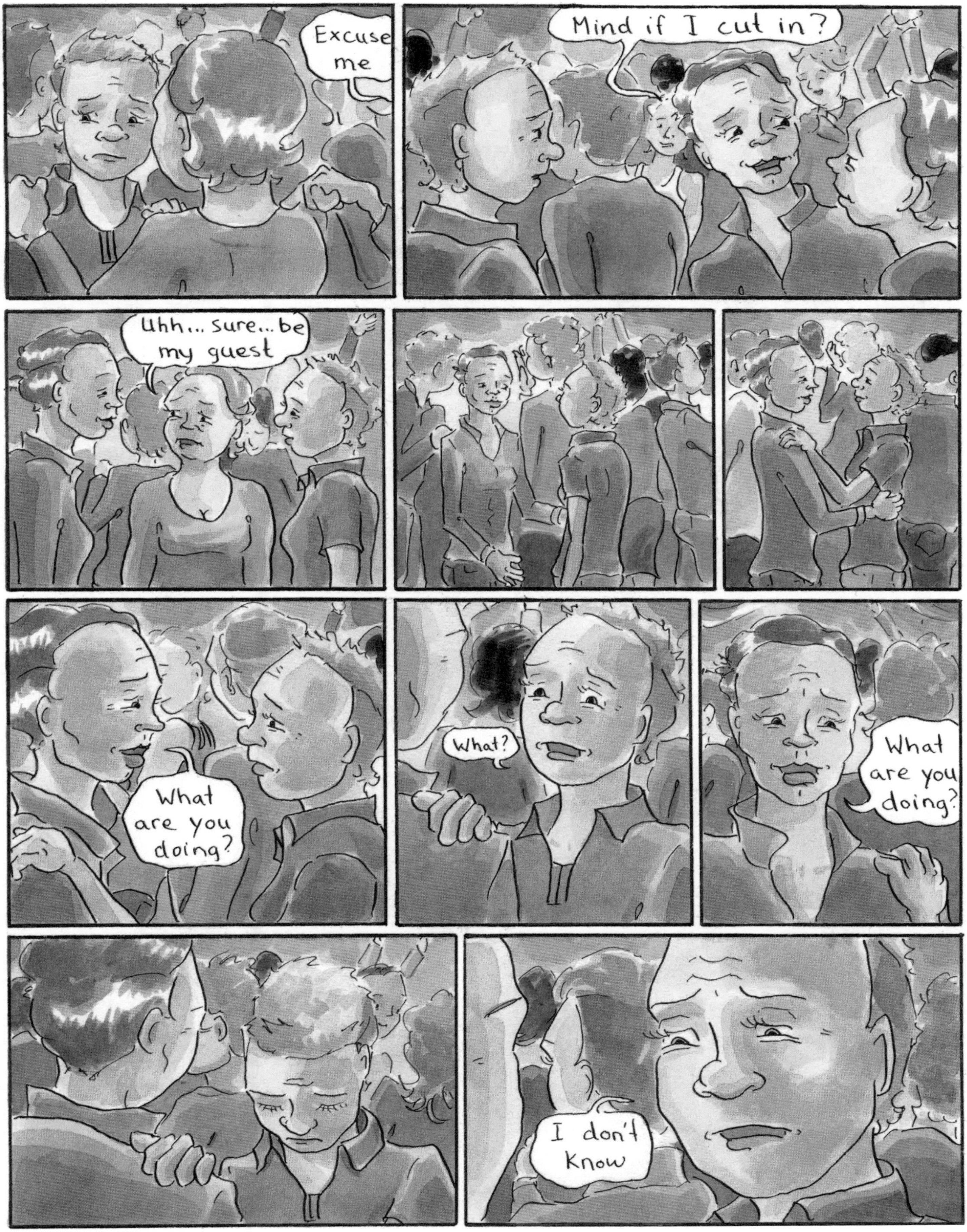
Excuse me
Mind if I cut in?
Uhh... sure... be my guest
What are you doing?
What?
What are you doing?
I don't know

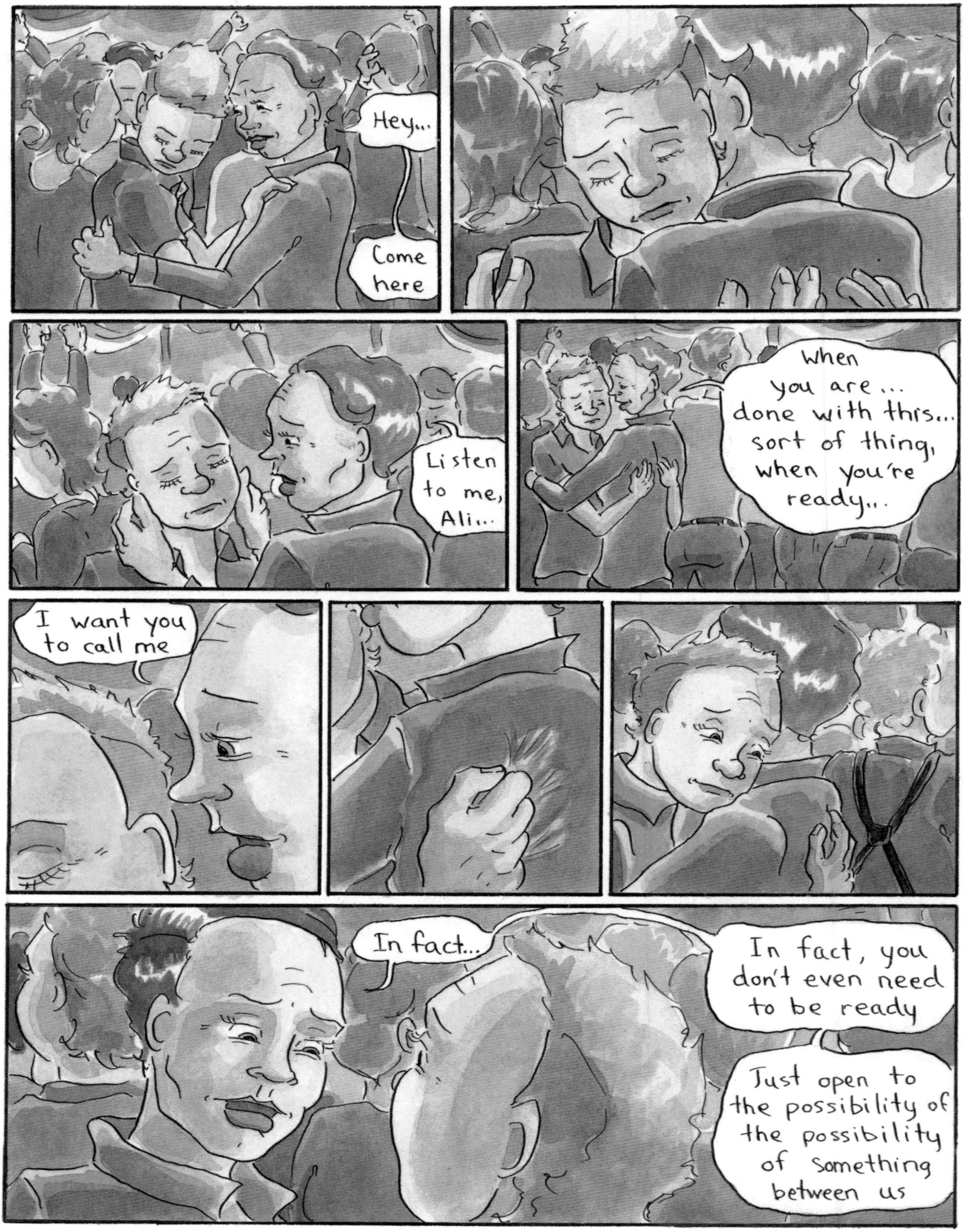
Hey...
Come here
Listen to me, Ali...
When you are... done with this... sort of thing, when you're ready...
I want you to call me
In fact...
In fact, you don't even need to be ready
Just open to the possibility of the possibility of something between us

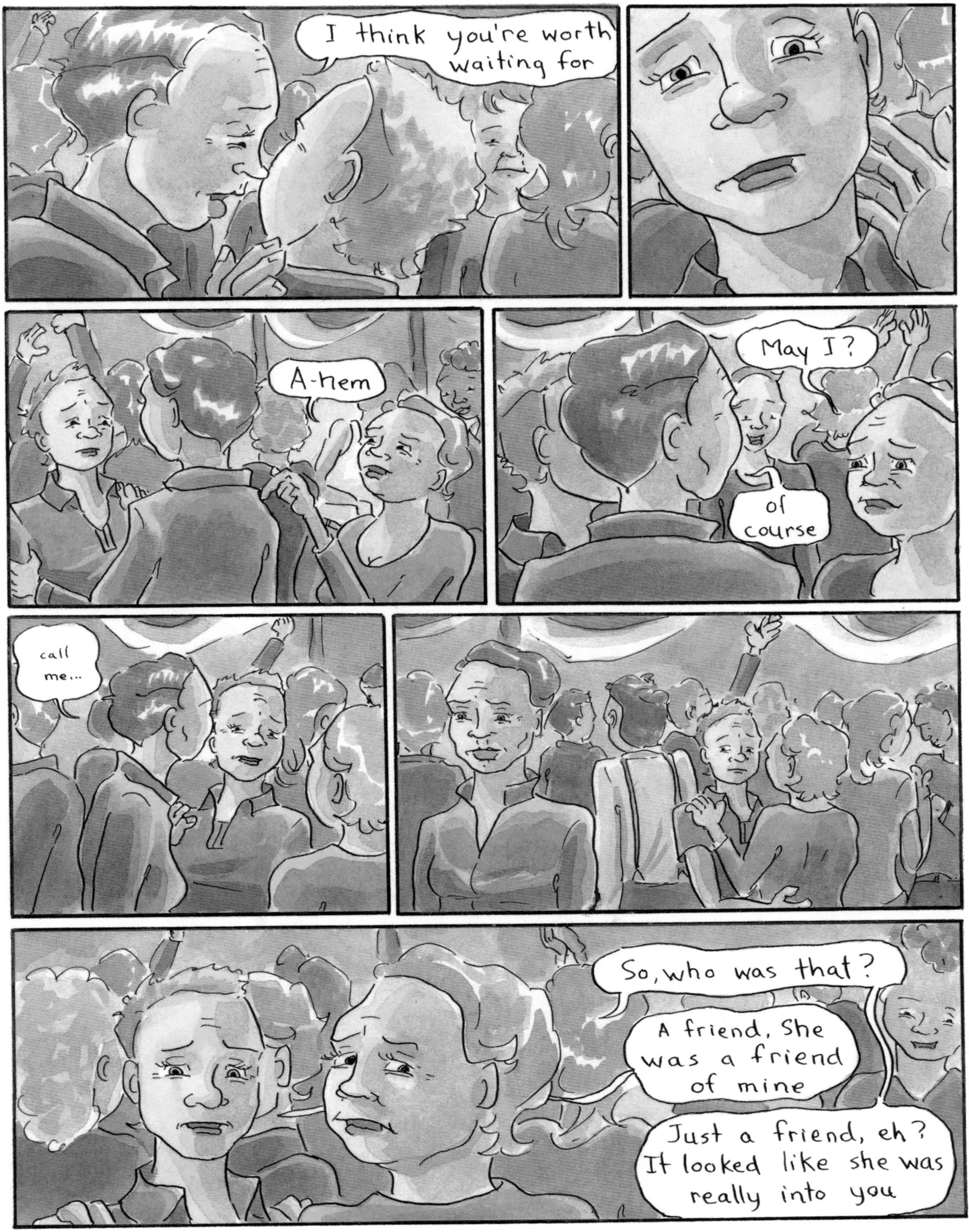
I think you're worth waiting for
A-hem
May I?
of course
call me...
So, who was that?
A friend, She was a friend of mine
Just a friend, eh? It looked like she was really into you

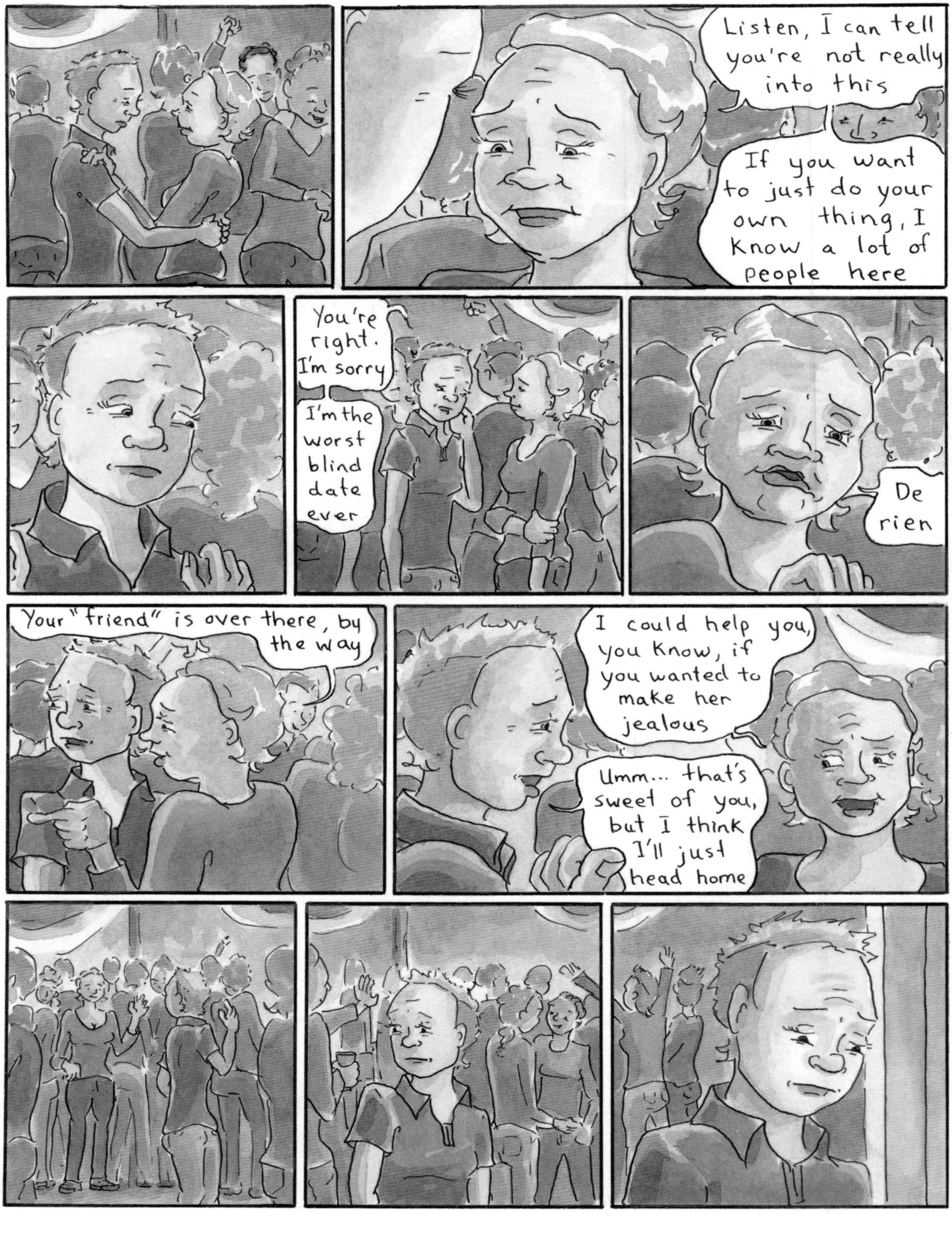
Listen, I can tell you're not really into this
If you want to just do your own thing, I know a lot of people here
You're right. I'm sorry
I'm the worst blind date ever
De rien
Your "friend" is over there, by the way
I could help you, you know, if you wanted to make her jealous
Umm... that's sweet of you, but I think I'll just head home

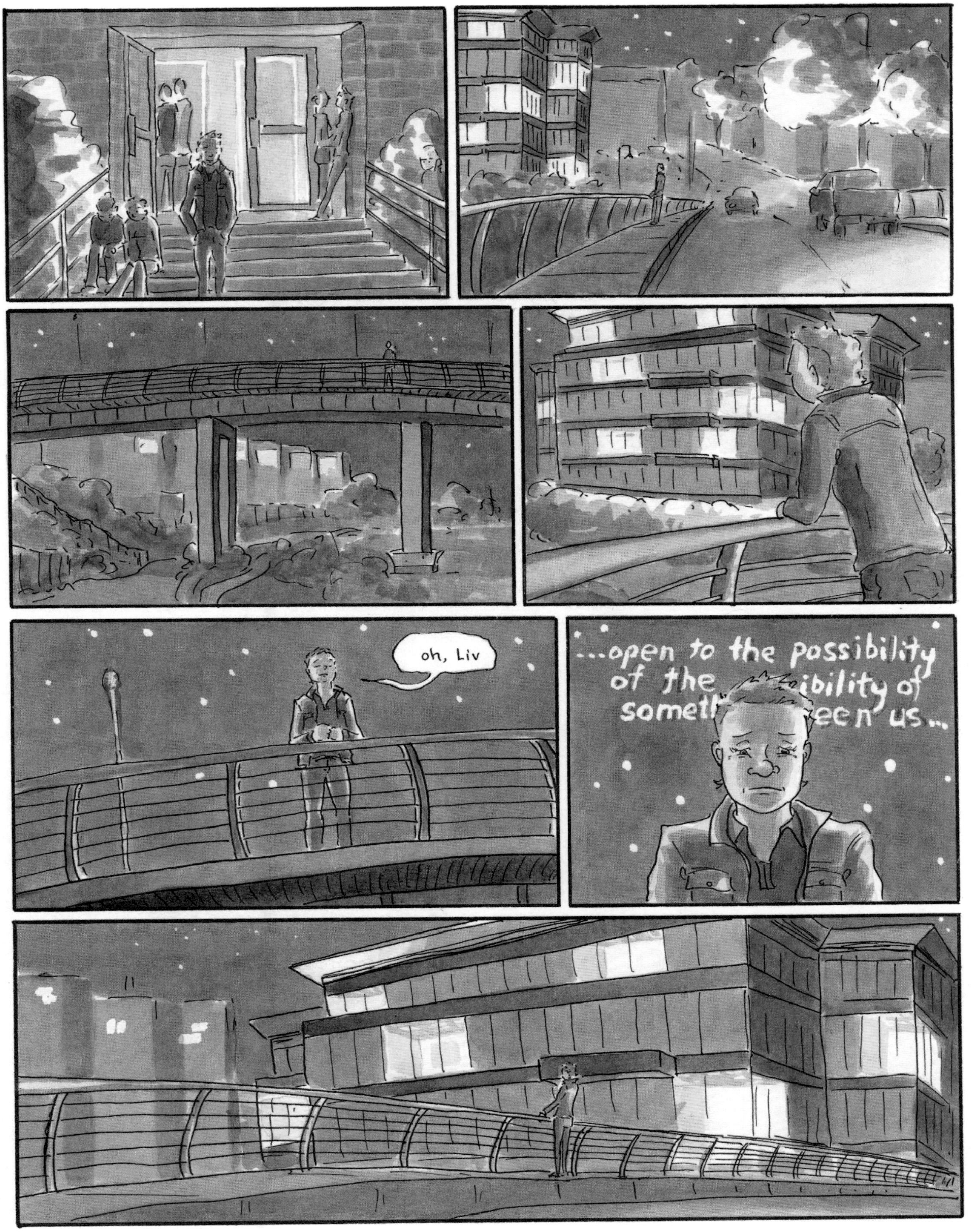
oh, Liv
...open to the possibility
of the ibility of
someth een us...

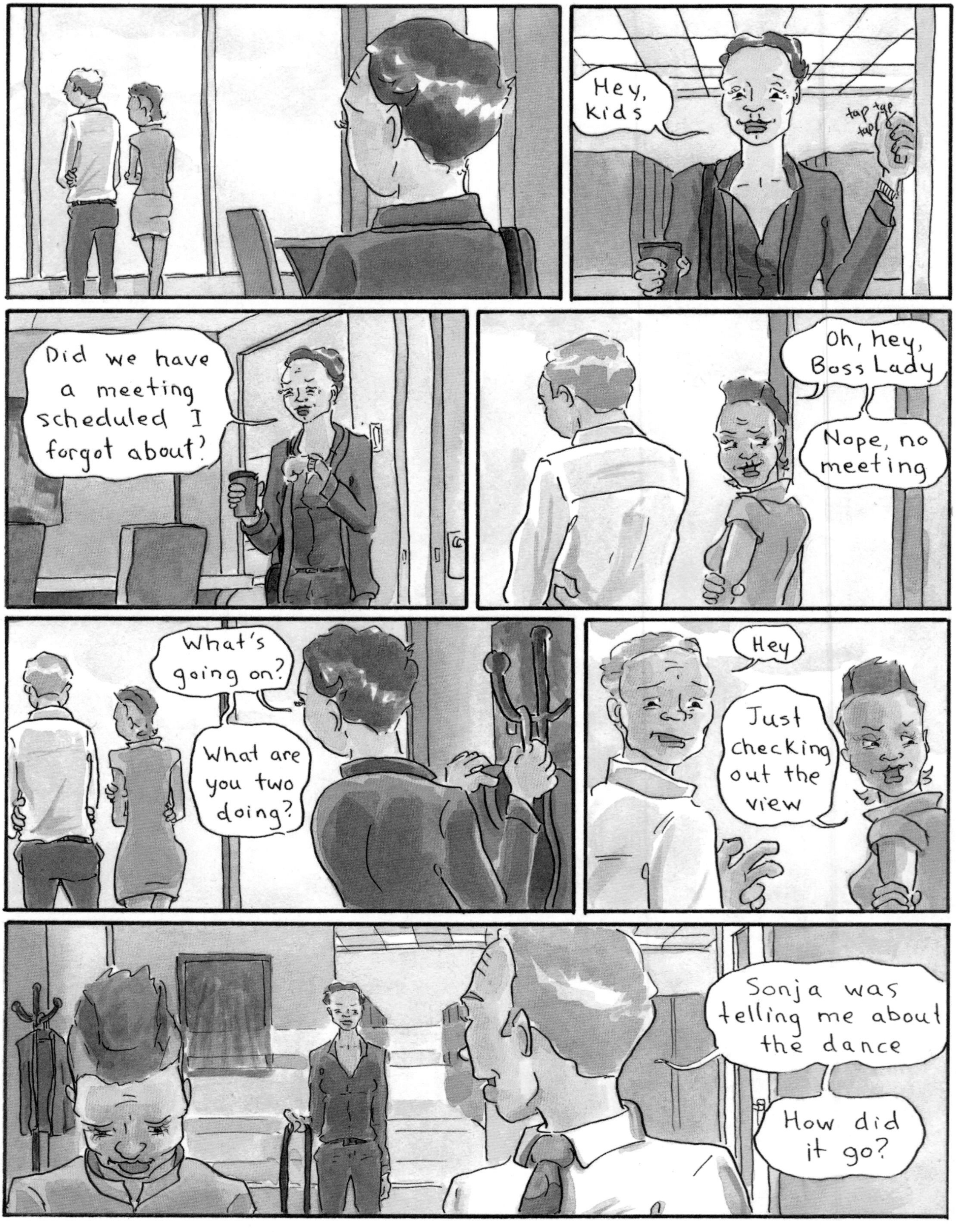
Hey, Kids
tap tap tap
Did we have a meeting scheduled I forgot about?
Oh, hey, Boss Lady
Nope, no meeting
What's going on?
What are you two doing?
Hey
Just checking out the view
Sonja was telling me about the dance
How did it go?

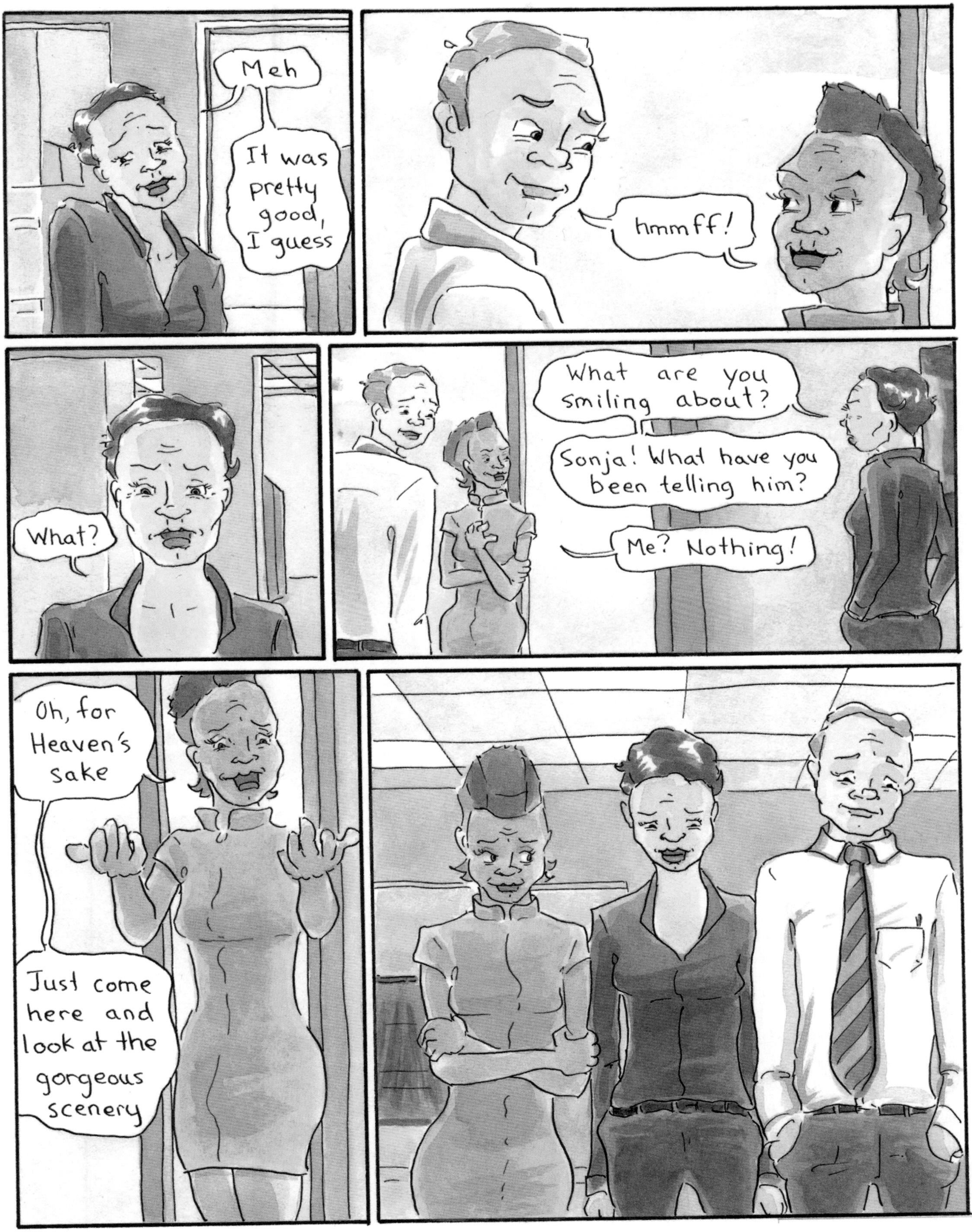
Meh
It was pretty good, I guess
hmmff!
What?
What are you smiling about?
Sonja! What have you been telling him?
Me? Nothing!
Oh, for Heaven's sake
Just come here and look at the gorgeous scenery

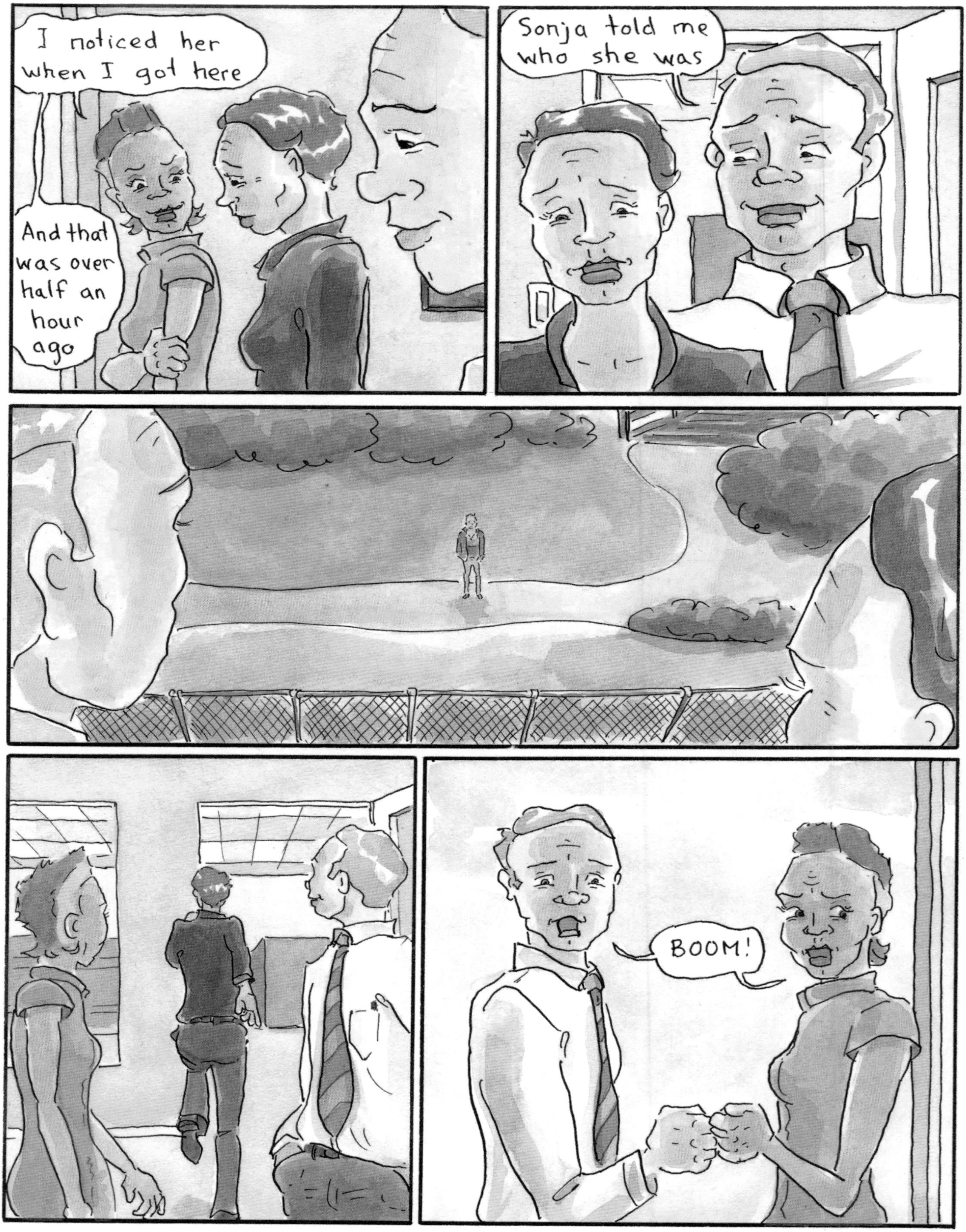
I noticed her when I got here
And that was over half an hour ago
Sonja told me who she was
BOOM!

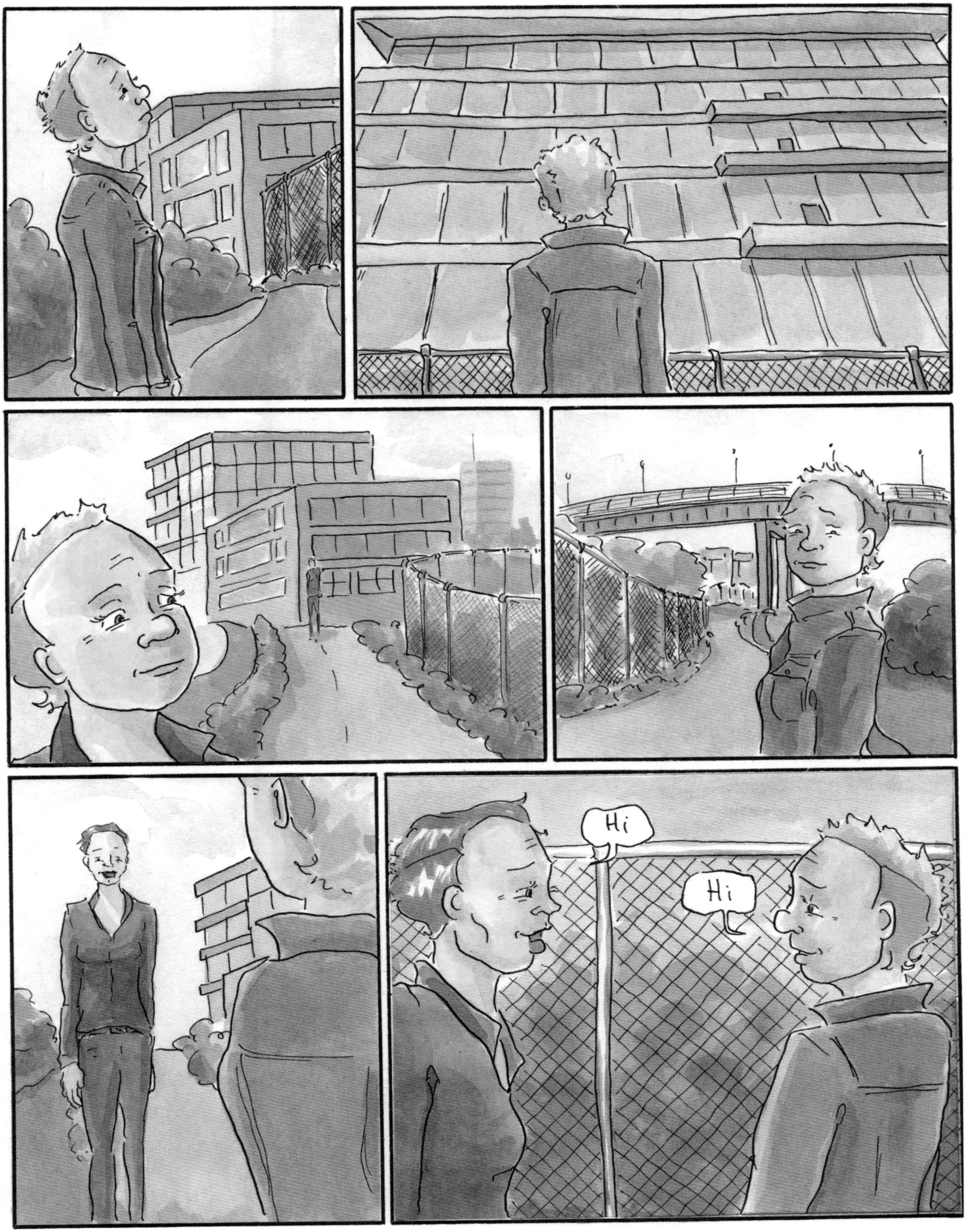
Hi
Hi

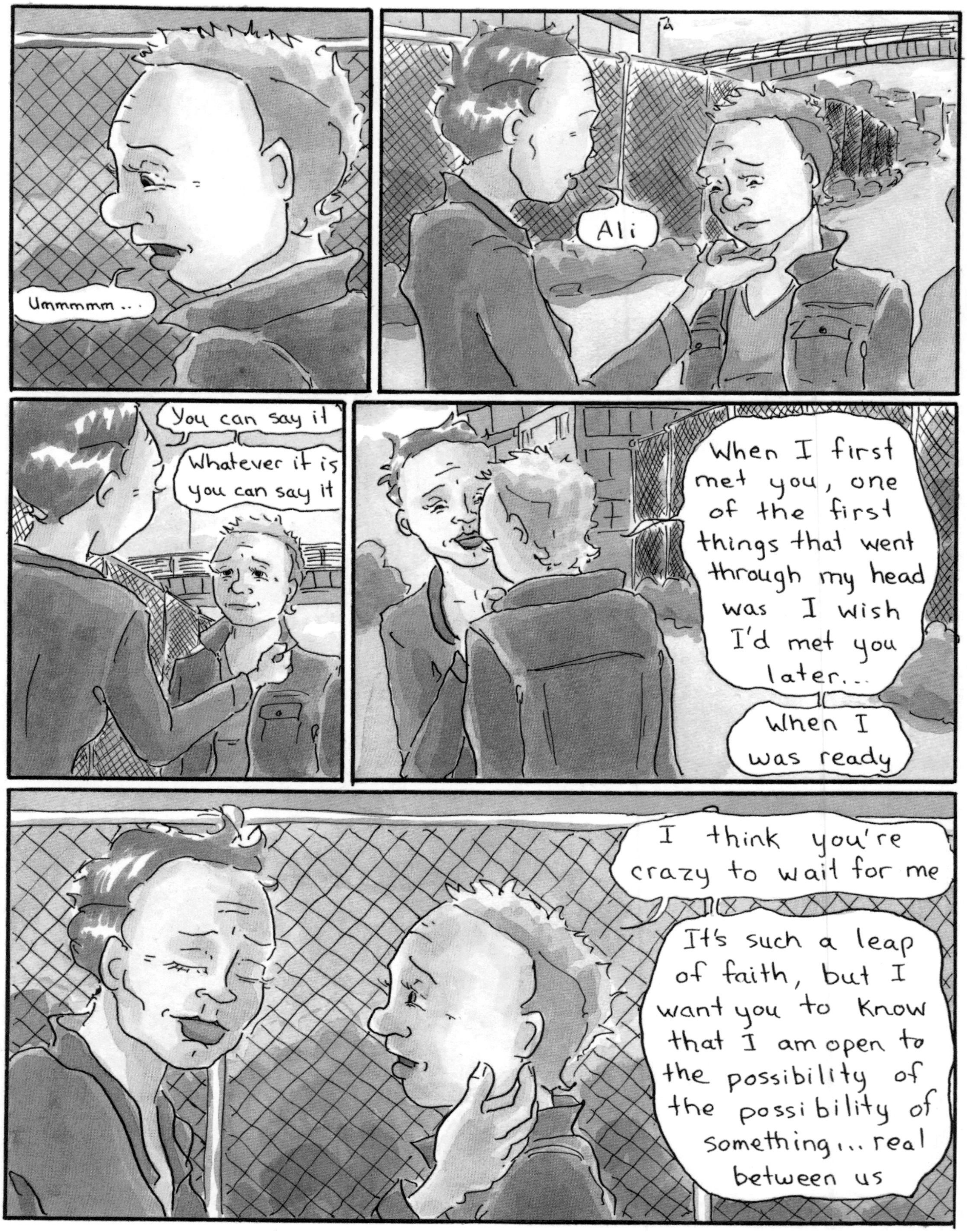
Ummmmm...
Ali
You can say it
Whatever it is you can say it
When I first met you, one of the first things that went through my head was I wish I'd met you later...
When I was ready
I think you're crazy to wait for me
It's such a leap of faith, but I want you to know that I am open to the possibility of the possibility of something... real between us

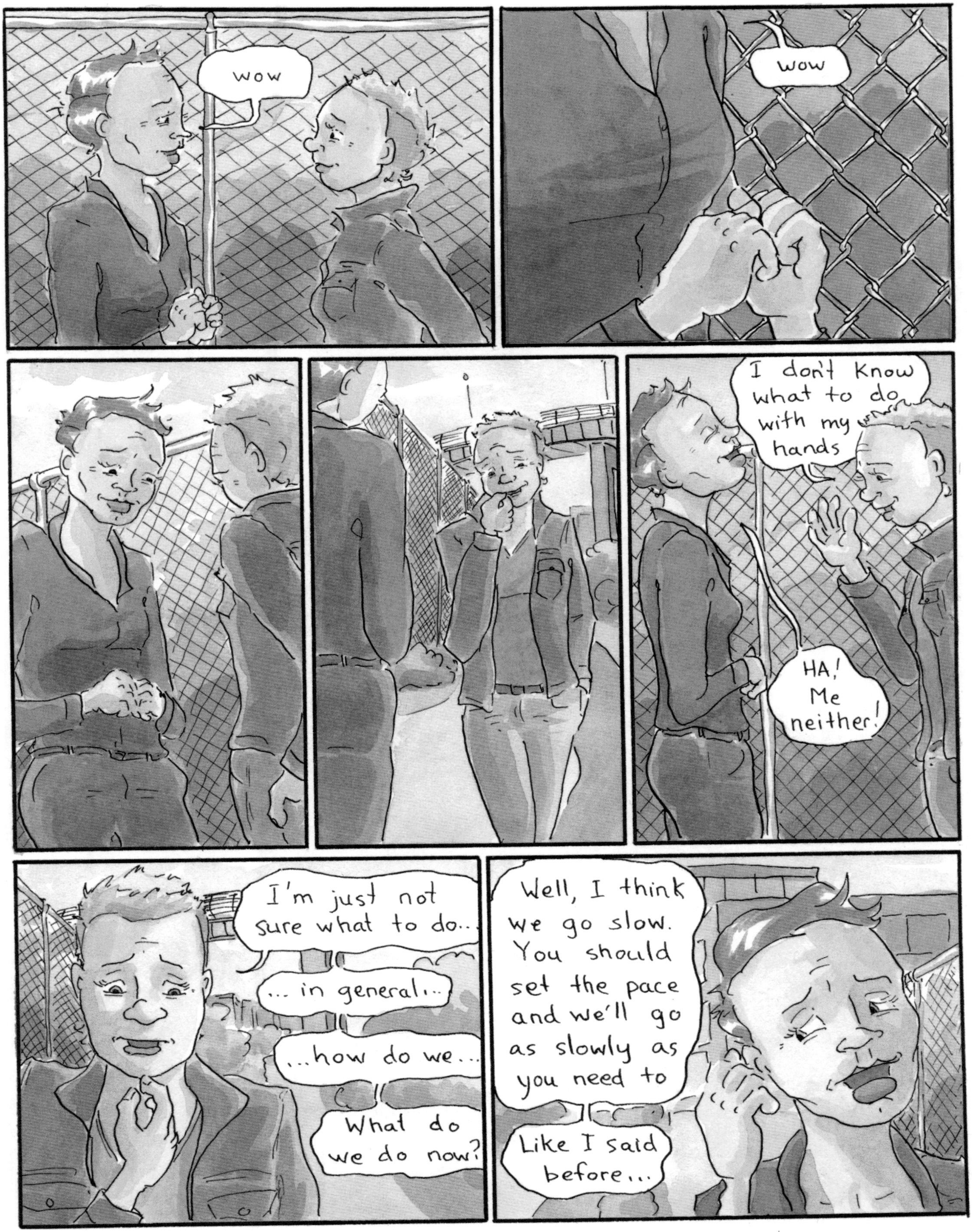
wow
wow
I don't Know what to do with my hands
HA! Me neither!
I'm just not sure what to do...
... in general...
...how do we...
What do we do now?
Well, I think we go slow. You should set the pace and we'll go as slowly as you need to
Like I said before...

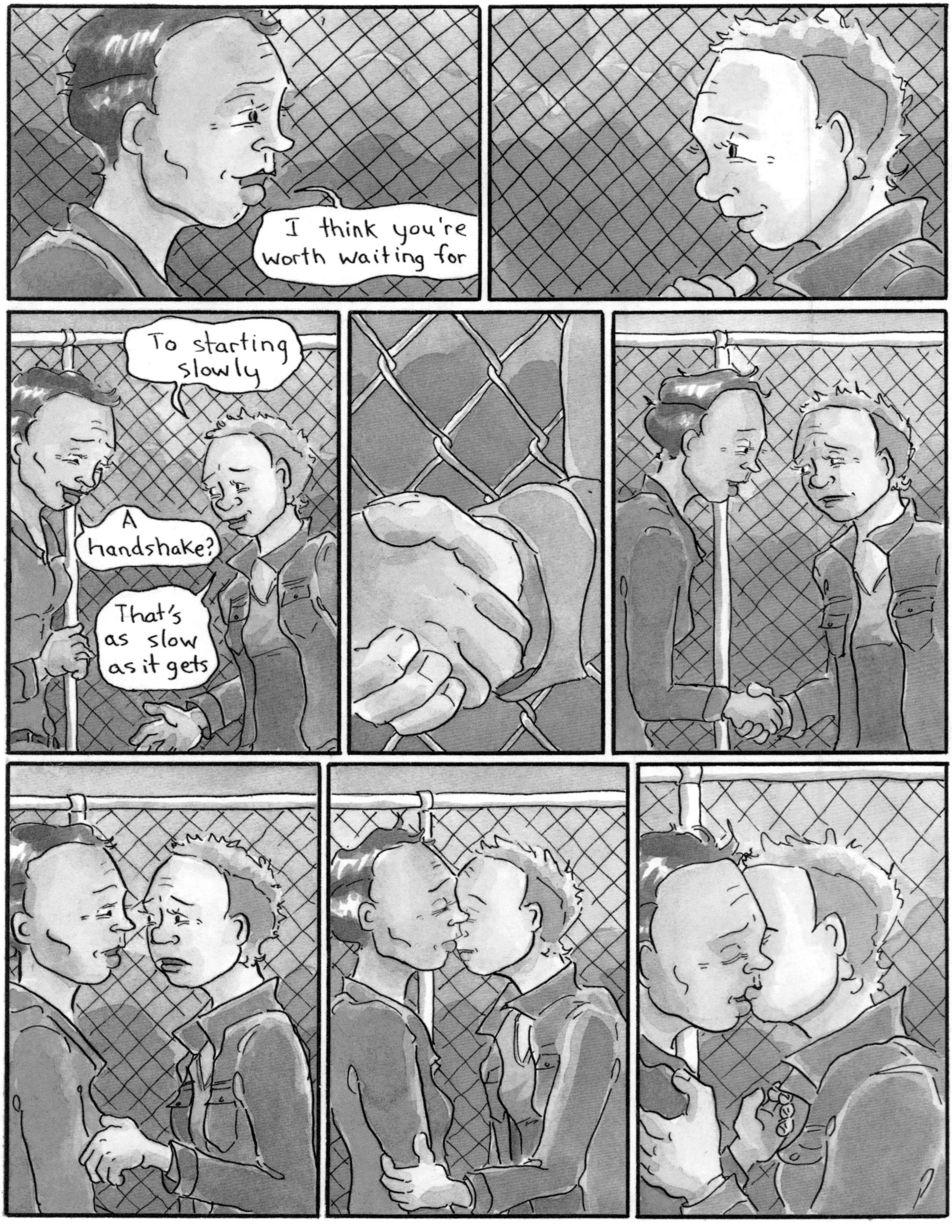
I think you're worth waiting for
To starting slowly
A handshake?
That's as slow as it gets

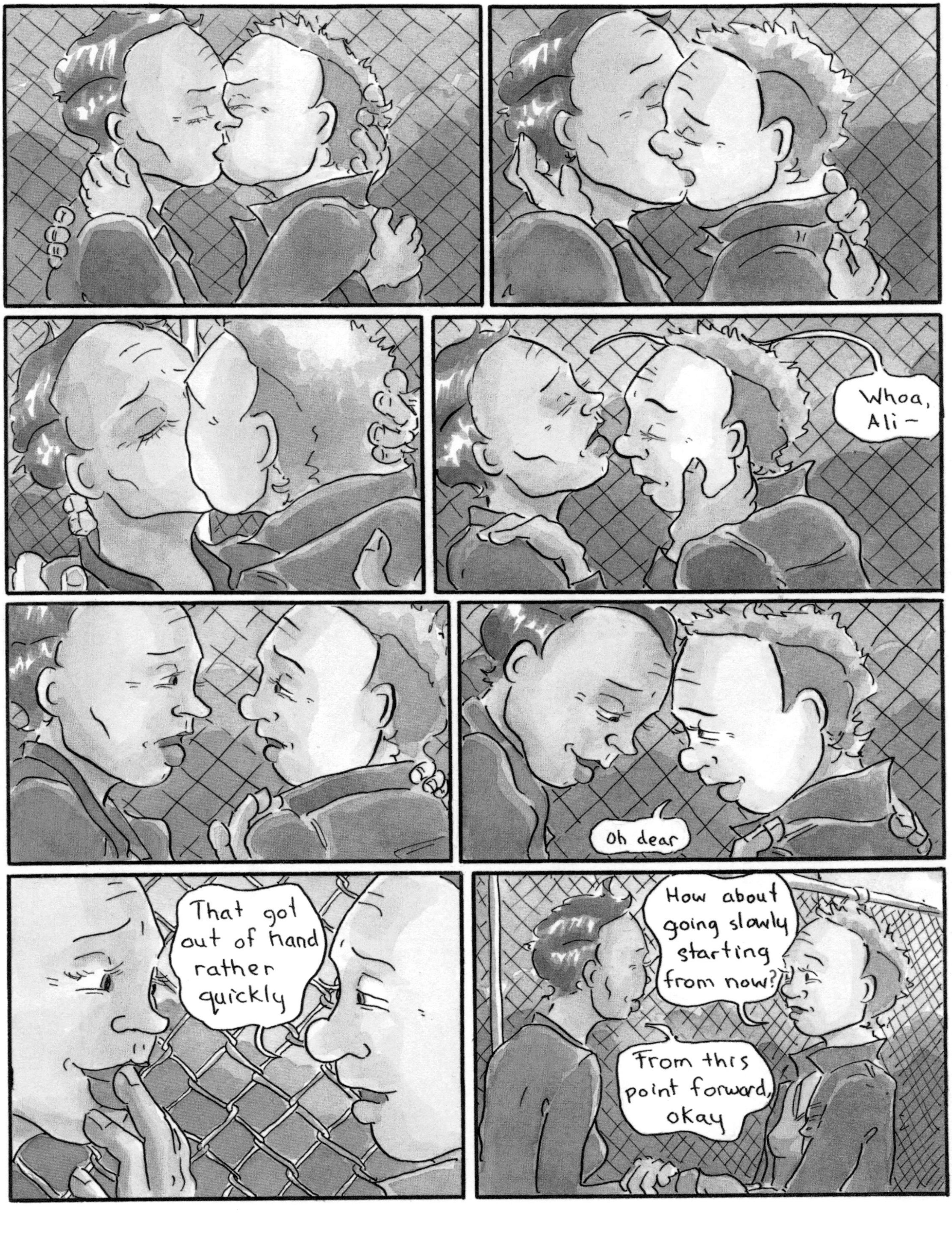
Whoa, Ali-
Oh dear
That got out of hand rather quickly
How about going slowly starting from now?
From this point forward, okay

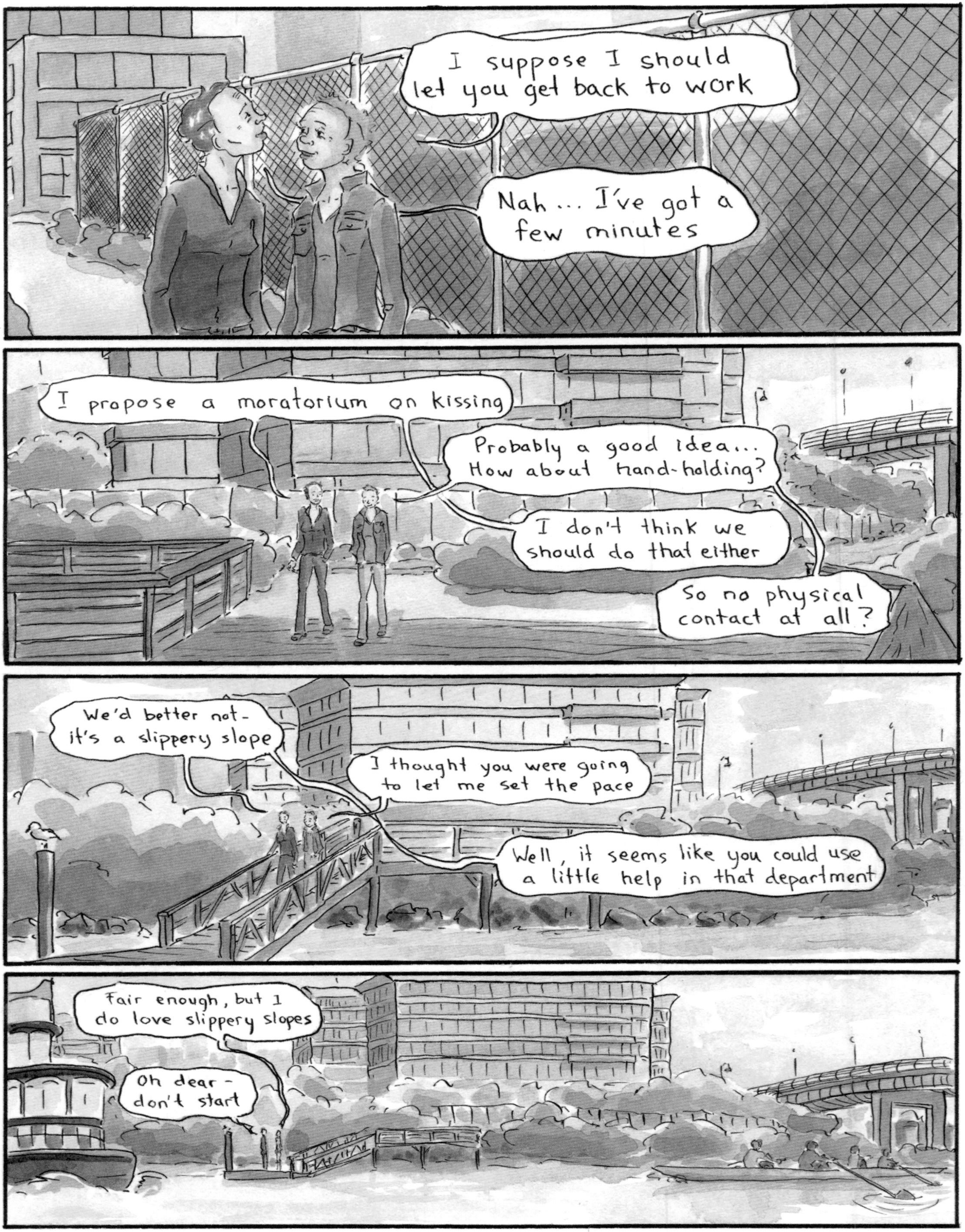
I suppose I should let you get back to work
Nah ... I've got a few minutes
I propose a moratorium on kissing
Probably a good idea... How about hand-holding?
I don't think we should do that either
So no physical contact at all?
We'd better not- it's a slippery slope
I thought you were going to let me set the pace
Well, it seems like you could use a little help in that department
Fair enough, but I do love slippery slopes
Oh dear - don't start

The
End

Photo: Vanessa van de Mortel

Lisa Maas is an artist who began drawing comics as a teenager. She can't remember if taking a night school cartooning class was the cause of this love affair, or if she was already smitten beforehand: a classic "chicken and egg" scenario. *Forward* is her first graphic novel. She lives in Victoria, BC, Canada.